Schooling Passions

Schooling Passions

Nation, History, and Language in Contemporary Western India

Véronique Benei

Stanford University Press
Stanford, California

Stanford University Press
Stanford, California

Printed in the United States of America on acid-free, archival-quality paper

Library of Congress Cataloging-in-Publication Data

Benei, Véronique.
  Schooling passions : nation, history, and language in contemporary western India / Véronique Benei.
      p. cm.
  Includes bibliographical references and index.
  ISBN 978-0-8047-5905-2 (cloth : alk. paper) — ISBN 978-0-8047-5906-9 (pbk. : alk. paper)
  1. Nationalism and education—India. 2. Citizenship—Study and teaching—India. I. Title.
  LC94.I4B44 2008
  379.54—dc22

                         2007045352

Typeset by Bruce Lundquist in 10/14 Minion

To Camille, Ambre, Galane, Anna,
Jade, Clémentine, Eglantine,
Pablo, Rachel, Alice, and Aurion

Le temps était long, l'histoire était brève,
Les mystères éternels réjouissaient les horlogers
Et les enfants énuméraient en chœur
Les règles d'or de la réalité.

Paul Éluard, *Marc Chagall*

Nation-watching would be simple
if it could be like bird-watching.

Eric Hobsbawm, *Nations and Nationalism since 1780*

Contents

Illustrations

Acknowledgments

WHEN I STARTED WORK on this project in the late 1990s, I never imagined feeling compelled one day to write this dreaded phrase. But there I am. "Because this book has been long in the making," it owes debts and thanks to innumerable people, including ghosts. The latter have been duly propitiated, so only the living appear in this section. They still account for a long list. Some are colleagues, some of whom have become friends; no doubt they will recognize themselves. As usual, it is difficult to do justice to all those who gave, offered, and shared over so many years. Apologies are therefore in order to those not explicitly named.

Special thanks are due to the various agencies that funded parts of the research: the Economic and Social Research Council (ESRC) from 1998 to 2001; the Centre National de la Recherche Scientifique (CNRS), especially the Direction des Relations Internationales; and the Franco-British program on globalization run by Jackie Assayag and Chris Fuller. Subsequent research visits were supported by the ESRC, the London School of Economics (LSE), or the CNRS.

In no small measure, my greatest debts of the past decade are owed to the CNRS and the LSE. The former provided me with the material security needed to freely take off to other horizons and embark on an ongoing *passeure*'s journey, back and forth between English- and French-speaking academic worlds. My colleagues first at the Centre for Sociologie, Histoire, Anthropologie et Dynamiques Culturelles, Marseille (SHADYC), then at the Maison Française in Oxford, and now at the Laboratoire d'Anthropologie des Institutions et des Organisations Sociales in Paris (LAIOS) have accompanied me in this trajectory in various ways. I am especially grateful to Marc Abélès, director at LAIOS, for his generous welcome into the center. Special thanks are also due to Jackie Assayag, with whom I shared many of the developments leading to this book and much more; some of his inspiration runs through these pages. Thanks, too, to my colleagues Irène Bellier, Catherine Neveu, Enric Porqueres i Gené, and Sophie Wahnich for sharing various topical interests with me, not least of all that in emotions; and to Gérard Lenclud, then at the Direction des Sciences Humaines et Sociales, for his long unstinting support, as well as Marc Gaborieau, Catherine Clémentin-Ojha, Frédéric Landy, Jacques Pouchepadass, Jean-Luc Racine, Marie-Louise Reiniche, Gilles Tarabout, and Denis Vidal at the Centre d'Etudes de l'Inde et de l'Asie du Sud for their trust and backing in critical times.

The LSE, especially the Department of Anthropology, introduced me to the ways of "Anglo-Saxon academia" many years ago. In particular, Chris Fuller helped me make my first steps and has since expressed sustained encouragement and critical support, reading and commenting on most of my prose over the years; so has Johnny Parry, most recently with incisive comments on a penultimate version of the manuscript. Laura Bear has been a wonderfully stimulating colleague and friend throughout, and an attentive and sensitive reader. I was fortunate to share an office with Stephan Feuchtwang for many years and have benefited from intense discussions and his insightful comments over several portions of drafts. Deborah James, Martha Mundy, and Michael Scott have offered welcome forays into other regions and topics; and Maurice Bloch provided for the Malagasy French connection. Catherine Allerton, Rita Astuti, Fenella Cannell, and Matthew Engelke have been stimulating colleagues. Peter Loizos always graciously supplied bibliographical references, and Henrike Donner, insightful suggestions in addition to her linguistic skills. Charles Stafford made my first steps into U.S. academia unreservedly possible at a time of organizational juggling; Olivia Harris kindly welcomed me back, and Margaret Bothwell and Yan Hinrichsen, and Camilla Griffiths have been great departmental managers and administrator, respectively! John Harriss, then at DESTIN, was a generous partner in discussion and commentator for many years. I am also grateful to Anthony Smith and John Hutchinson, as well as the members of the Association for the Study of Ethnicity and Nationalism (ASEN), for welcoming me into their passionate study group one academic year; thanks, too, to Jude Howell and the Centre for Civil Society, as well as to my colleagues at the Institute of Education in London.

Versions of parts of this book have been presented in lectures, seminars, workshops, and conferences in Britain, France, India, Colombia, Australia, and the United States. Thanks are owed to all those who gave me the benefit of their comments on those occasions. A few "in the West," however, deserve additional mention. They are, in no particular order, Sherry Ortner, then at Columbia University, as well as Nicholas Dirks and Val Daniel; at the University of Michigan at Ann Arbor, Sumathi Ramaswamy for her inspiring encouragement, Barbara Metcalf, Jayati Lal, Nita Kumar, Tom Metcalf, Stewart Gordon, and last but most crucial, Lee Schlesinger, whose relentless questioning forced me to anchor my arguments ever more firmly; I also thank all the other participants in the lively and thorough discussions of the Kitab Mandal; then at the University of Chicago, Sheldon Pollock, and William Mazzarella, John Kelly, Adam Smith, Shreeyash Palshikar; at the University of Edinburgh, Patricia Jeffery, Roger Jeffery, and Jonathan Spencer; at Oxford University, Nandini Gooptu, Barbara Harriss-White, and David Washbrook; and on various occasions Mukulika Banerjee, Filippo Osella, Caroline Osella, and Geert de Neve, as well as Sudipta Kaviraj, Peter Robb, and Sunil Khilnani. Adrian Mayer kindly shared his boundless knowledge and introduced me to the royal family in Kolhapur. To Étienne Balibar I remain indebted for his generosity and some inspiring conversations over several years.

Although writing this book started years ago, it truly began in earnest over my two-year stay in the United States. I am particularly grateful to Princeton University and Yale University for their institutional support and hospitality, for the kind and efficient use of their libraries, and for the experience of teaching in yet another academic community. As a Visiting Research Scholar at the Princeton Institute for International and Regional Studies (PIIRS) and Lecturer in the Department of Anthropology in 2004–2005, I wish to thank Miguel Centeno for his lively directorship, as well as Atul Kohli, Gyan Prakash, Greg Bell, Joyce Slack, Susan F. Binding, and Geraldine Horner; at the Department of Anthropology, Carol Zanca for her amazing efficiency and Mo Lin Yee for her kind diligence, Leo Coleman, Mekhala Natavar for her zest for life, Carol Greenhouse for her supportive enthusiasm, Larry Rosen for his constant generosity and good humor (even when inflicted with an entire intermediary draft a year later), Abdellah Hammoudi for his philosophical warmth and sagacity, Gananath Obeyesekere for a common interest in psychoanalysis, Jim Boon, John Borneman, and most specially Isabelle Clark-Decès and Jim Clark for their generous hospitality. Maria DiBattista and Pat Heslin (then) of Rocky College provided me with a base away from home; and Walter H. Lippincott kindly shared his operatic tastes with me. Ravi Sundaram unwittingly drew my attention to the notion of "sensorium." Archana Joglekar, Marathi friend and beautiful soul, enchanted me with her dance. I also wish to thank Jean Leca for his encouragement as I started work on the manuscript, as well as Fred Appel for reading through an earlier version of what was yet to become this book. My warmest gratitude goes to Thomas Hansen for his unfailing support over the years, especially for making my stay at Yale University possible as a Singh Visiting Lecturer in the MacMillan Center for International Studies while teaching in the Anthropology Department in 2005–2006, as well as for his generous comments on a fledgling version of the manuscript; to Dhooleka Raj for her administrative care and academic wit; to Lauren Leve for jokingly putting me on the lead to queer theory (which I took seriously); to E. Annamalai for graciously surviving an embarrassingly premature version of a chapter; to Durba Chattaraj for sharing her "embodiedness of language" with me. I am also grateful for comments on chapter drafts from Joe Alter and Joe Errington and to the members of the South Asia Reading group and the South Asia seminar at Yale, especially Karuna Mantena, Barney Bate (who also read more of my prose), Mridu Ray, Srirupa Roy, Jayeeta Sharma, Radhika Singha, and Phyllis Granoff. Thanks, too, to Barbara Papacoda, Marie Silvestri, and Karen Phillips for their administrative assistance, and to librarians Emily Horning and Rich Richie. My gratitude goes to Peter van der Veer for reading an earlier version of the manuscript, as did Gyan Pandey, whose support and understanding have been critical in the last stages. In other ways, I am also thankful to Arjun Appadurai for his food for thought.

The research on which this book is based would not have been possible but for the inestimable wealth of support—institutional, intellectual, and personal—received in various parts of India: in Delhi, the Delhi School of Economics, the Nehru Memorial Trust, the University of Delhi, the National Centre for Educational Research and Training, Hari Chopra, Radhika Chopra, Krishna Kumar, Arun Kelkar, and Dipankar Gupta; in Mumbai, the Tata Institute for Social Sciences, Mumbai University, S.N.D.T. University and their libraries, and the Marathi Grantha Sangrahalay, Denzil Saldanha, Sharit Bhowmik, Ramesh Kamble, Y. D. Phadke, Satish Kulkarni, Sulochana, Arun Khopkar, Chandrakant Joshi, Prabhakar Pendharkar, and Arvind Ganachari. In Pune, my gratitude goes to the university, the Fergusson College, and the Ranade Institute as well as the Archives Section in the Department of Education and the Bhartiya Itihas Samshodhak Mandal, Aalochana, the Film and Television Institute, and the National Film Archive of India, and their libraries. Special thanks are also due to the staff of the Maharashtra State Textbook Bureau. The "International Maharashtra connection" welcomed me many years ago, and I learned a great deal from all of them, especially Irina Glushkova, A. R. Kulkarni, Jim Masselos, Anne Feldhaus, Eleanor Zelliot, Meera Kosambi, Rajendra Vora, and Jim Laine. I also owe a great debt to Ram Bapat for his unfailing support and intellectual generosity, only matched by his dizzying erudition and passion for debate; to Sujata Patel, Sharmila Rege, Ashok Kelkar, G. P. Deshpande, Vidhyut Bhagwat, Surendra Jondhale, Gayatri Chatterjee, Vaishali Diwakar, and S. M. Dahiwale, who introduced me to Kolhapur. In Kolhapur, Professor Dhanagare, then Vice-Chancellor of Shivaji University always graciously facilitated my research. The latter greatly benefited from Trupti Karikatti's invaluable help and companionship as a research assistant over these years of fieldwork. I am also indebted to Ashok Chousalkar for his intellectual engagement and constant readiness to share his knowledge with me, Bharti Patil for her helpfulness and her sharp mind, as well as Vilas Sangave, Maya Pandit, B. D. Khane, Kavita G. Patil, M. A. Patil, Tyagraj Pendharkar, Nisha U., and Bhaskar Bolay. Ashok Karamde, who helped in translating shloks and mantras. The Education Department of the municipal corporation of Kolhapur introduced me to some of the institutions where research was conducted. Of all the preliminary schools initially surveyed, those where the bulk of the research was done deserve special mention for letting me share their daily routines so intimately and continuously. I cannot repay what I have received from them; had it not been for the generosity of their respective staffs, pupils, and parents, this book would not exist: the Vidhyapeeth Marathi Shakha, the New High School Marathi Shala, the Pratapsingh Vidhya Mandir, Santa Gadge Maharaj Shala number 7, Urdu-Marathi Shala number 53, and the Warna nagar Sainik School. Very special thanks are also due to Shahu Maharaj and his royal family. To the Pandat family, I am grateful for their trust and friendship, and to Jaydeep and Mrs. Borgaonkar, for their caring and good-hearted hospitality. My lasting gratitude also goes to longtime friends: the D'Mello family in Bombay and for some years now also in Canada and Australia; and in various other parts of Maharashtra, Simrita Gopal Singh and Kedarnath Awati, Siddhartha, Sandhya Mawshi, and Admiral Awati.

Many other long-standing and new friends across several continents must be mentioned at last. Their love, care, and supportive humor enabled me to get this book "out of my system." Nadia Benlakhel, my ever faithful "sister," and her "Belles" have made life in Paris fun; Floortje and Philippe Dollo, and the

"Brooklyn Dolls" provided good mood and wine, especially in the United States; Poonam Srivastava, my favorite reiki master, has remained a true cosmic friend throughout. Konstanze Merkel has methodically helped me grow into my own, and Karen Atkins also taught me to care for my body/mind. Gabriella Romani, my Italian teacher, has become an enduring friend, and Leonor Arfuch offered me a brilliant demonstration of "feminismo rico." Special thanks also to Kate Hayes, and Patrick Arnold, Moley, Richard, and Heidi Hayes for their enduring hospitality and munificent contribution to my ongoing growth into English literacy; and to Eliza Kaczynska-Nay and John Charvet, Vera and Oliver for showering their kindness and generosity upon me. The Randriamaros of all three generations deserve mention for their unconditional friendship of *many* years. James and Yuko Bourlet found my beloved "Molesworth" again within two years of its "disappearance," and David and Val Batterham provided precious support in times of flood. With my brother, Franck, and his family, I shared many memories, in addition to champagne, music, and creative passions. My uncle, Reg Brinded, generously fed my interest in things British and imperial all these years, and my aunt, Minou Brinded, gifted me with her warmth, sparkling intellect, and cheerful liveliness. Finally, my mother, Thessy Benei, deserves all my gratitude for her optimistic faith and visceral anchoring in life, and for teaching me a beautiful lesson.

At Stanford University Press, I wish to thank Kate Wahl for her enthusiastic support of this book from the very beginning, and Joa Suorez for her efficient liaising. The two reviewers also helped me tie up some loose ends. I am especially grateful to Susan Wadley for her strong support. Daniela Berti in Paris and John Smith in Cambridge graciously provided diacritic fonts, and the latter, critical emergency assistance. Last but not least, I am grateful to Cynthia H. Lindlof for her meticulous editing.

The usual caveats apply, and perhaps more so in the present case. Most, if not all the shortcomings in this book are due to what my best-meaning friends and family call my obstinacy. The reader may opt for another term.

Note on Transliteration

ALL WORDS from the Sanskrit, Hindi, Urdu, and Marathi that occur more than once or twice in the text are transliterated with diacritical marks on their first appearance; thereafter, they are printed without diacritics and their spelling is adjusted to the commonest usage: *ch* for *c*, *v* or *w* for *v*, *sh* for *ś* and *ṣ*. Some specific adjustments have been made for the Marathi language: *ru* for *ṛ*, and *dnya* for *gya*; in addition, many words ending with a consonant are not pronounced with the usual *devanāgari* short vowel *a*, which has therefore been omitted. Because plural forms may be unfamiliar, I have added an *s* to create the plural of transliterated words. The titles of songs, chants, poems and prayers, and entire sentences have *not* been transliterated. Terms and names that occur more than once or twice in the text are listed in the Glossary.

The Marathi-speaking region of the Bombay presidency became Bombay state after Indian independence; the state was renamed Maharashtra in 1960. The name of its capital city was changed from Bombay to Mumbai in 1995. Throughout this book, I use the modern names for the state and city, except where the historical context requires "Bombay."

Schooling Passions

Prologue

*Nationality is something sentimental too; it is
body and soul at the same time.*

Ernest Renan, *What Is a Nation?*

HOW DOES ONE BECOME viscerally French, English, Indian, and so on? What is it
that makes one *feel* irrefragably so? What does it take for us to turn into those
embodied, emotional nationals, even as we see ourselves as "so many other
things," and much as we at times love to disown "our own nation"? How does
this incarnation of the nation occur in our souls, minds, and bodies? Conversely, if love of the nation is spontaneous and instant, "in your guts," why
does it need to be constantly reproduced and sustained?

The present entanglement of "the national and the global" has brought renewed salience to these questions. Movements of populations across national
borders have increased in visibility, and discourses about "the global" in vocal-
ity. Yet neither has shooed away the reality and lived experience of nationhood.
Contrary to some wishful thinking, the nation is here to stay. So are the many
visceral expressions and manifestations of national belonging. The issue of civic
entitlement, too, is as fraught as ever, in light not only of recent migrations but
also of the dialectical redefinitions of the so-called local and global. These reflect in competing imaginings *within* nation-states the world over to the point
that different visions of the nation have seen the radicalizing of the "production and reproduction of majorities and minorities," at times leading to violent
confrontation. In India, the confrontation has mainly occurred between Hindu
nationalists and members of the larger minority, that is, Muslims. Attempts
made by extreme Hindu right-wing political parties are aimed at redefining
membership in the national community along ethnic and religious lines; this
entails building an exclusively Hindu raj whence the members of Muslim and

1

other non-Hindu—as well as "improperly Hindu"—communities would be excluded. These exclusivist endeavors have long been accompanied with repeated outbreaks of violence of varying magnitude. They have also generated activist, intellectual, and scholarly engagement.

Studying communal violence was until fifteen years ago largely the preserve of political scientists exploring nationalism and its various predicaments (Vincent 1990: 26). Today, by contrast, these topics have become central for anthropologists interested in the political. Apart from burgeoning work on democracy, much of the literature in India so far has understandably concentrated on riots and their aftermath. Yet such a trend has largely missed out on the "before" of violence, that is, the larger *upstream* processes potentially feeding into aggressive political projects. These are nurtured over many years, even decades. In the "making and continuation of contemporary political arrangements," they have largely contributed to the "production and reproduction of majorities and minorities," which historian Gyanendra Pandey (2006: 1) has called "routine violence." What feeds into exclusivist political projects indeed does not spring ex nihilo; rather, it is constantly reproduced and takes shape in the many folds of everyday life. Senses of belonging, these most seemingly natural and obvious pillars of identity, are not manifested only in forms of extreme violence. Especially in times of political stability, senses of belonging are "naturalized" in the banality of quotidian processes.

This book therefore shifts the focus away from registered sites of extraordinary communal violence onto ones of daily production of "banal nationalism."[1] The phrase refers to the experience of nationalism being so integral to people's lives that it goes unnoticed most of the time. Yet, as we shall see, the banal nationalism thus constructed in the routine of everyday life is an ever incomplete one: it is constantly in the making. The very impossibility of completion, though unnoticed as it may be in the folds of daily life, also makes this process a source of anxiety. The same obtains of many other "banal" nationalisms, and the formulation appropriately denotes the formation of patriotic sentiments in all kinds of nations, whether "established" or younger ones.[2] Similarly, the distinction between "national" and "nationalist" is a tenuous one, more a matter of perspective than of objective science. What is deemed "national only," in the sense of a justifiable and legitimate expression or manifestation of interest in the nation, versus what is condemned as "nationalist," in the sense of supposedly irrational passions of nationhood, is often really the same, depending on the onlooker's perspective. Such notional relativity informs much of this book, and I will use the terms "national" and "nationalist" almost interchangeably. Documenting the making of banal nationalism, then, entails scrutinizing the daily, apparently benign production and reproduction of processes of local, regional, and national identity formation, or rather, identification.

Some brief clarification is in order. I find the notion of "identification," as an analytical tool, more precise and heuristic than that of "identity." It is understood that identities are neither individual nor purely collective but rather provide means for individuals to internalize belonging and for the community to instate or prescribe subjectivities (Balibar 2003). Yet the problem with the term and its usages is that in many analyses, "identities" tend to get "congealed" and "essentialized" in fixed space and time. In contrast, the term "identification" lays stress on the processual agency of social actors. It thus leaves the way open for indeterminacy and the necessarily fragmentary character of all projects of self-formation, be they individual or collective. Furthermore, this is so even if and when the *act* of social actor(s) identifying is consubstantial to the psychological *orientation* of the self in regard to the object of identification, with a resulting feeling of close emotional association; or even when the process is deemed largely unconscious and denotes the modeling by an individual or a group of thoughts, feelings, and actions after those attributed to an object are incorporated as a mental image. These definitions are neither mutually exclusive nor contradictory, and we shall see how a psychoanalytic approach may in part illuminate aspects of national and regional identifications (Chapter 3), both at a collective and an individual level (see Obeyesekere 1981, 1990 for an exemplification of how these two levels articulate in a psychoanalytic anthropology; Borneman 2004 for a psychoanalytic interpretation of the end of political regimes). To a significant extent, this book is precisely concerned with the agency *within* the internalization of socialization. Of interest here is what both becomes *and* begets an "unconscious" process (Hall 1996; Segal 1996). However much solidly grounded, identification remains fleeting and changing; it is better understood as a resource, leaving space for competing modes of action and appropriation. Where the term "identities" appears, then, it will be to particularly emphasize the fixedness resulting from identification processes—a fixedness often resonant with specific political projects that make this crystallization central to discourses and practices of representation for a given social group. But prior to identity and its attendant political repertoire awaiting deployment in myriad forms, there is "identification."

Increasingly in the world of nation-states today, local, regional, and national processes of identification are in part relayed by state institutions penetrating everyday life. Most potent among them is formal education, seen as both a prerequisite for the stability of the state and a powerful means of national integration.[3] Consequently, the socialization of children has become more intricately embedded in a multiplicity of culturally defined norms and rules from an early age (Kumar 2001). This also occurs in the western regional state of Maharashtra, where I conducted fieldwork in primary schools and kindergartens in the locality of Kolhapur in the late 1990s and early 2000s. An analysis of socialization can therefore no longer confine itself to a study of initiation rituals or everyday processes occurring at the levels of family, caste, community, village, neighborhood, and so on, all traditional objects of anthropological inquiry. For an overwhelming majority of urban and rural Maharashtrians today, patterns of authority and models of behavior are jointly produced by family members (whether parents or other elders) *and* teachers. The family, apart from mass media, may still be the primary source of influence about politics. Yet in a regional state where the literacy rate averages 75 percent, the first stages of schooling in particular play a crucial part in providing exposure to political life and symbols of nationality and nationhood, as they do in other nation-states (Connell 1975).

Formal education has become a major arena of dispute on the subcontinent in recent years. In India, in particular, its prominence in the fierce debates pitting partisans of Hindu nationalist (*Hindutva*) forces against secularists has generated anxieties among members of the minorities, social activists, intellectuals, and scholars alike. After a *Hindutva*-led coalition came into power in the 1990s, the population felt the menace of an accrued Hinduization of the core institutions of Indian society. At stake was the potential unraveling of the nation-state's secular constitutional principles. Much public attention focused on the rewriting of history and the redesigning of secondary school curriculum (Menon and Rajalakshmi 1998; Muralidharan and Pande 1998; Sahmat 2002; Sahmat and Sabrang.com 2002; Deb 2003; Habib, Jaiswal, and Mukherjee 2003; Mohammad-Arif 2005). These are definitely crucial indications of the ideological choices made by Hindu right-wing forces with respect to the production of future generations of Indian (or Hindu?) citizens.[4] The emphasis placed on secondary and higher education (in keeping with a predisposition dating back to colonial times) has nevertheless preempted a clear understanding of the very *process* of contemporary nation building. It also raises questions about the relationship of schooling to nation building and underlying theories of learning, suggesting that children of a younger age are alien—or, at best, irrelevant—to political processes, including those of patriotism and nationalism. By contrast, I aim to demonstrate in this book that crucial to the production of local, regional, or national attachments are the educational processes taking place from a much earlier age, right from the beginning of socialization and as early as kindergarten.

Kindergartens and primary schools are unexpectedly fruitful sites for exploring the culturally gendered production of the political in modern nation-states. These spaces mediate home and nation, playing a constitutive role in the daily lives of children who move back and forth between them. Schooling does not only entail modeling of disciplined bodies and "normalized" social and political persons (Foucault 1979, 1981); just as important is social actors' embodied cultural and social (re)production of regional and national senses of belonging and identifications. Central to my demonstration is a notion that these feed on, and into, lived experiences of sensory and emotional bonding developed in the everyday intimacy of home and family.

The heart of my project therefore articulates a political anthropology of the senses with one of embodied passions and emotions. Rather than work along the Geertzian lines of a dichotomy between civil and primordial ties that would run the risk of further naturalizing an arbitrary distinction between "North/West" societies and their "less fortunate South/East" counterparts, I contend that focusing on the *emotional and embodied* production of the political provides a more radical approach in any given context. Such a framework furnishes a way out of binary models as well as intellectual and theoretical biases.[5] It also allows one to register more complex realities so far left largely unexplored. In this book, I show how processes of identity formation are embodied daily and draw upon cultural repertoires of emotionality. Emotionality is produced through, and feeds into, political, cultural, social, economic, and gender negotiations of nationhood and citizenship central to the everyday production of rights and entitlements. In these everyday processes of subject, self-, and national formation, both the state and its representatives, and ordinary citizens—including children—play a crucial part. Just as important, these processes acquire meaning as *embodied experiences involving sensory (re)configurations*.

Whereas the notion of "sense of belonging" has become commonplace in discussions of national sentiments, the emotional and sensory dimension invoked by such a phrase has received scant attention.[6] Here, by taking the "senses" seriously, I seek to illuminate the ways in which emotions and passions, as socially and culturally produced, form an integral part of forming the senses

of national belonging. Documenting the emotional sensory and embodied production entering in the daily manufacturing of nationhood and citizenship implies querying: How do the senses come into play? How are they harnessed in
the everyday project of nation building at the most banal and quotidian level
of experience? How are they actively produced, reshaped, and reinterpreted
by social actors? To address these questions requires a phenomenological approach, which is developed in this book, particularly in Chapters 2 and 3.

A phenomenological approach does not preclude a comparative project. On
the contrary, it calls for one that would jointly pay attention to the complexities
of vernacular realities, not only to rightfully "decenter" Europe (Chakrabarty
2002) but also to illuminate both the contingent nature and the concomitant processes of social and political formations in different parts of the world, whether
in the so-called West or in India. In their explorations of the ritual, cultural, and
linguistic idioms of "other" societies, anthropologists have long demonstrated
the necessity to heed local semantic and vernacular notions. With regard to the
study of the political modernity–related topics of nationalism, civil society, and
citizenship, however, such an idiomatic concern has remained conspicuously
absent. The reason may be that reflection on, and exploration of, these topics
has traditionally been the preserve of political philosophy and political science,
whose theoretical instruments are grounded in a European tradition claiming
universality. Nevertheless, even critical perspectives in relation to the foundational period of the Enlightenment have largely neglected vernacular languages
in their reflection on the modalities of European-originated political concepts
and notions in non-European contexts (for notable exceptions, see Kaviraj 1992;
Burghart 1996; Rajagopal 2001).

Arguably, the neglect of vernacular categories has precluded an understanding of both their attendant social and cultural semantic repertoires and
local negotiations. Yet their unraveling remains indispensable for a thorough
comprehension of the cultural entailments of political processes, forms, and
models, especially of the nation-state. The fact that the modern nation-state is
a "foreign transplant" in India, for instance, should not monopolize the terms
of debate. What requires scrutiny are the historical configurations and the modalities of the development of specific, idiosyncratic, local forms (Gupta 1995;
Fuller and Benei 2001; Hansen and Stepputat 2001; Kaviraj and Khilnani 2001).
Pursuing a quest of essential, irretrievably "emic" differences does not lead one
very far.[7] To dismiss non-European political forms as purely nonviable under
the pretense that they do not conform to either European ones or the original

model, or worse still, that they are associated with repertoires of a kind different from those deemed extant in the West is both unproductive and unfair. As I argued elsewhere (Benei 2005a), comparing Indian empirical facts with European theory has precluded heuristic understanding of both the Indian context and the analogies and similarities that might be drawn between the Euro-American and Indian cases, especially regarding the issue of secularism. The work of Peter van der Veer, for instance (1994, 2001; van der Veer and Lehmann 1999), has highlighted movements back and forth of the concomitant processes of social and political formations in the West and in India. Thus, arresting parallels and embedded developments of secularity, religious reform, and idioms of morality acquire visibility in *both* locations. This, in turn, illuminates the measure of contingency in Europe's or India's "unique" trajectories. It also reinscribes their respective uniqueness in a web of parallels, cross-borrowings, and similarities as part of a worldwide humanity. Such a comparative endeavor, although not occupying center stage, also animates the soul of this book.

Before inviting the reader to pursue further, I wish to share two incidents as a caveat. The first was related to me by one of my colleagues in Britain upon his return from a lecture tour of U.S. universities in 2003, just at the time of the U.S.-led invasion of Iraq. Some students, mainly American and Indian, commented to him on the mistrust of all things patriotic and nationalist they perceived in my writings. Of course, the different genealogies and realities of nationalism in Western Europe, the United States, and India probably accounted in part for their comments. Yet these comments arrested me, because, perhaps somewhat naively, I had until then assumed that being critical of patriotism and nationalism was any anthropologist's job. Don't most of our lives spent as academics revolve around deconstructing naturalized "things," be they common sense, feelings, narratives, practices, or all of these together?[8] The second incident occurred a few months later, in July of that same year. I had been invited to give a lecture at the "Gender Seminar Series" of a well-known Indian university's department of sociology. I had chosen to present the premise of what is now Chapter 3 in this book. The students were mostly female, including only three or four males, one of whom I had met earlier in the corridor. Hearing that I was visiting from an academic institution located in Britain, he quipped: "So you have come funded by the VHP or some other such *Hindutva* organization?" I was rather puzzled and unsure of the question's implications with respect to NRI funding and the general climate of communal violence in Gujarat and elsewhere in India at the time. I did not yet know this student was

Muslim. My attempts at reassuring him of my benign funding sources hardly did anything to dispel the doubtful look on his face. I then gave the talk, followed by a discussion. After a few noncommittal questions came this particular student's turn. He launched into an accusatory diatribe of pro-*Hindutva* sympathies. Apparently, what had irked him was my focusing on *Hindutva*-related practices—and exemplifying a gesture during presentation—occurring during the nationalist ritual marking the beginning of school days in ordinary Marathi schools (Chapter 1). Following some clarification on my part, the exchange continued after the seminar, the student telling me of his and his parents' secularist involvement. To this day, I have remained thankful for his sharing with me, however briefly, his experience of growing up in Bombay/Mumbai in the highly volatile 1990s and early 2000s.

What these two incidents illustrate is the acute sensitivity of the subjects I address in this book. That I, an outsider, could be understood to hold such extreme and antithetical positions on nationalism ultimately confirms the highly contentious and visceral nature of everyday processes of nation building. I have attempted to do as much justice as possible to the complexity of social, cultural, and political life in this part of India. May it provide the reader with enough to cultivate sensitivity toward these delicate issues. This, at any rate, is what I see as the wider purpose of an anthropological contribution.

Introduction

Sensitive Subjects: Producing the Nation at School in Western India

[C]ar dans les siècles démocratiques, ce qu'il y a de plus mouvant, au milieu du mouvement de toutes choses, c'est le cœur de l'homme.
Alexis de Tocqueville, *De la démocratie en Amérique*

IMAGINE YOURSELF in western India in the winter of 1999–2000: Kolhapur, the southernmost town of Maharashtra state and a friendly, industrious provincial district capital. Wherever you walk in the busy streets, people are going about their business as usual. Yet the atmosphere is almost eerie. As days and weeks go by in the ordinary course of life, you can feel an almost relentless fervor around you. Is it a result of the silent, ubiquitous, visual reminders that the nation has recently been at war?

The events took place some hundreds of miles further north in Kashmir a few months earlier. In the first weeks of May, as the snow began receding, the military went on their first reconnaissance patrol in the Kargil heights. Upon discovering Pakistanis trespassing over the Line of Control between the two countries, Indian troops sought to regain the lost territory. After two months of fighting, the Indian military made a successful final assault in mid-July at a height over five thousand meters. The events were assiduously covered by the mass media, from feverish TV news bulletins to fiery press declarations and reiterations of devotion to the Indian nation. That the mass media should have played their part in keeping the citizenry alert to the national issue by relaying and furthering a sense of besieged nationhood in all corners of the national territory was only to be expected. After all, the press alone has often been construed as a fundamental instrument for the production of a sense of nationhood in modern times (Anderson 1983). What was perhaps less foreseeable was the intensity with which ordinary social and political actors in Maharashtra elected this moment for renewing their pledge of allegiance to the "mother country," then and for the following two years. This they did through relentless flag exposure.

9

The flag display around the time of war in Kashmir in the late 1990s was no mere celebration of the habitual, taken-for-granted artifact of the nation, with its horizontal stripes of saffron, white, and green. The patriotic icons reproduced on fabric or paper are usually seen hanging in front of institutional buildings; passersby—adults, children, and even babies—hold them in their hands along parade routes on national public holidays. In such obvious moments of national devotion, the whole population reiterates its pledge of allegiance to the country whose sovereign people became free to govern their own destiny more than sixty years ago. The flags then serve as so many reminders of the solemn engagement of unity in freedom that the Indian people took (or rather, in whose name a handful took) at the time. Children also bring these vouchers of national integrity to school on these extraordinary occasions, while teachers display them in classrooms and headmasters and headmistresses give them pride of place on their desks. However, in the year 2000 in Kolhapur, the extraordinary had become ordinary. In addition to the freshly painted tricolors on some facades and signs of hotels, restaurants, and shops, the streets thronged with an ever-inventive and creative reappropriation of the national icon. You could see women walking about wearing "flag saris": the garments, symbolic of every married woman's status in Maharashtra, were graded from green to saffron via a white band; alternatively, women sported only green and orange shades in a matching duo of sari and blouse.[1] Some of the schoolteachers I had met in primary schools earlier also wore them.[2] So did girls on their birthdays. The visual dimension of this devotional and patriotic inscription in public spaces was also a conspicuously gendered one. Whereas women sartorially carried and protected the nation upon their own bodies, men could be seen proudly riding Hero Honda motorbikes with the tricolor painted across the frame. A rickshaw driver had stitched his own version on his back seat, with three vertical (instead of horizontal) stripes ornamented with two (instead of one) wheels on either side of the seat. His colleagues at night sported tricolor woolly caps. Others hung tricolor plastic bead necklaces from mirrors; so, too, did many car drivers. Toward the end of that year, the Hindu festival of Diwali was also an occasion for families to hang strings of tricolor lanterns in front of their houses.

Thus was a powerful visual semiotics summoned in the daily sharing of the tragedy of the nation. Yet it has to be envisaged in combination with other forms of sensory experiences, auditory ones in particular. Television news-bulletin presenters, politicians across the political spectrum, schoolteachers, children, and other ordinary citizens alike all proffered their acoustic production with regard to the treachery perpetrated by the nation's archrival enemy. Thus, if most of the continuously conspicuous aspects of these everyday performances of national reconnection engaged the sense of sight, it is only the tip perception of the iceberg of sensory national re-creation. As we shall see further, sight is but one of the senses called upon by political modernity, contrary to a commonplace giving it primacy over all others. For the moment, beginning with this nationalist visual semiotics provides an immediate entry point into the social and political processes involved in the production and sustenance of a nation.

Tricolor Semiology and War Culture

> [A] flag represents an ideal. The unfurling of the Union Jack evokes in the English breast sentiments whose strength it is difficult to measure: the Stars and Stripes mean a world to the Americans, the Star and Crescent will call forth the best bravery in Islam. It will be necessary for us Indians—Hindus, Muslims, Christians, Jews, Parsis and others to whom India is their home—to recognize a common flag to live and to die for.
>
> **Mohandas K. Gandhi, Young India**

> [T]he flag is not an object but a relationship.
>
> **Raymond Firth, Symbols Public and Private**

National flags are the most external and immediately visible rallying symbols of nationality and citizenship, serving as metonyms for the nation at large. As such, they are expected to elicit unrestrained allegiance (Firth 1973), an allegiance nurtured in various ways in many nation-states, ranging from daily praise and worship to occasional display and tribute. In the United States, the icon is not only honored in school morning assemblies but also constantly exhibited outside most public buildings as well as individual homes, particularly since the events of September 11, 2001. In Britain, the Union Jack is also very conspicuous, albeit in a more mercantile fashion since the 1960s (Firth 1973). By contrast, in most parts of India, the national flag was never very visible outside particular annual manifestations. Yet, in Maharashtra, the Indian tricolor had become strikingly conspicuous in the wake of the events in Kargil. This sudden change requires further investigation.

Sight, Modernity, Democracy

The production and display of national flags in public spaces are arguably crucial to the visual shaping of "image democracy," to borrow John Tagg's formulation. In his discussion of sight and modernity, Tagg drew on Walter Benjamin's by now reference piece, "The Work of Art in the Age of Mechanical

Reproduction" (1968). Benjamin in this essay discussed the loss of "aura" of the object brought about by photography as a medium of reproduction ad infinitum. Drawing on these insights, Tagg argued that the "real pictorial revolution effected by photography concerned the ease with which individual likeness could be systematically recorded, giving photography a key role in bureaucratic institutions, including the police station, the insane asylum, the school and the prison" (Tagg 1988: 56–59, cited in Przyblyski 1998: 2). Tagg particularly emphasized the withering away of the aura associated with unique works of art in favor of a photographic "democracy of the image." Tagg's argument may be extended and qualified in regard to mass production processes, especially those of nationalist symbols and artifacts.

What remains unacknowledged in Tagg's Benjaminian stance, however, is the crucial part played by ordinary social (and political) actors in an image democracy. The flag displays here represent a means for expressing the actors' tacit participation—both collective and individual—in the intensive celebration and symbolic preservation of the nation's image. In Kolhapur in 1999–2000, this act of political (re)connection was accompanied by an impressive appropriation of mass products whereby people selected iconic items to concoct their own nationalist bricolage. Here was an example of dialogic social agency and mass production defying the habitual, slightly contemptuous vision à la Adorno of ordinary people's passive ingurgitation of mass culture. Whether flag saris were mass produced following a specific demand or whether they triggered the latter is beside the point. The usual mass production of the national synecdoche had been diverted from its ordinary channels as social actors actively transformed these otherwise codified attributes of public patriotism into daily icons of both personal allegiance and market commodity. These insignia of nationalist semiology became integral to the everyday lives of ordinary citizens, transcending creed, caste, age, language, gender, and other barriers. Consequently, the replicated, transposed, and reclaimed reproductions of the national flag were the "mere trifles" that transformed an urban social and cultural landscape into a national one. Such a national landscape was also closely associated with imagined as well as remembered notions of territorial preservation and, consequently, war.

War, National Community, and Social Memory

War has been one of the most powerful motifs shaping the social memory of "imagined communities" the world over (Mosse 1990; Audoin-Rouzeau 1993; Becker 1994; Hinton 2002; Taylor 2002). In India, war since independence has been crucially constitutive of imaginings of citizenship wherein borders and frontiers played an essential part. Just as in European nation-states (Balibar 2004), territory and national frontiers have centrally defined patriotism and historical consciousness, with their physical reality becoming the object of many projections of national identity. Hence the potent symbolism of territorial violation superseded other potentially rallying factors in triggering war together with reiterations of national love. Indeed, the war in Kashmir took place a year after another major event occurred in the life of the Indian nation. Nuclear tests were conducted in the desert of Pokhran in Rajasthan in May 1998, causing great pride and rejoicing among the citizenry.[3] The successful tests proffered a mirror of accomplished modernity reflecting a "shining India" (to borrow the slogan from the Hindu right-wing coalition then in power at the central level). In keeping with the masculinist theme and attendant anxiety that have animated Hindu nationalist ideology since its inception, these tests also elicited boastful claims underpinned by a gendered imagery among some Hindu right-wing activists (Bhatt 2001). The declarations made by the leader of the regional "sons-of-the-soil" Shiv Sena Party were among the most sexually explicit: Hindus, since the nuclear tests, were "no longer Eunuchs." Even more than these nuclear achievements and their gendered symbolic resonance, the subsequent war in Kargil crystallized devotional allegiance to the (feminine) nation. That the "body of India" (Assayag 1997; Ramaswamy 2001) should have been violated acted as a much more potent trigger.[4]

Furthermore, rather than the high-spiritedness and lightheartedness that ensued as a result of the demonstration of nuclear prowess, these later events generated moments of grave recollection and moral indignation that fed into a "war effort," as well as a "war culture." The press, in particular, furthered the imagination of a besieged national community in its attempts at sustaining the population's interest. Indian citizens were invited to support and glorify their soldiers. For over a year until December 2000, newspapers, English and vernacular, regularly published stories of heroic soldiers meeting a tragic death in Kargil. Great care was often taken to pay tribute to their families for having sacrificed their boys in the name of the country. Various good deeds accomplished by "citizens fulfilling their duties toward the nation" were also repeatedly reported in the press at the time. Arguably, the daily reiteration of their sense of moral outrage as well as their appreciation of both the dignified grieving of soldiers' bereaved families and the courageous contributions in cash and kind made by ordinary citizens in Maharashtra opened up a crucial space for discussing the

Kargil events, strengthening connection to the Indian nation anew. Because of the foundational rivalry between the two warring nation-states of India and Pakistan and the sensitive location of Muslim populations in the former, however, this space was more open to some citizens (i.e., Hindus) than others (i.e., Muslims). Furthermore, this aperture enabled the (re)production of an entirely legitimate war culture plunging its roots ever so firmly in the recent past of the postindependence decades as well as in the region's martial tradition.[5]

The memory of the preceding wars with Pakistan (1965) and China (1962), the latter of which had involved defining and contesting territorial frontiers, was reactivated by the discussion of the Kargil events. The media crucially sustained intensive mnemonic social activity around these events, rallying citizens to reminisce and, in the process, define themselves anew, as Indians. This is, of course, not to suggest that media alone played an overdetermining part. As Brian Massumi (2002: 43–44) has insisted, "Media transmissions are breaches of indetermination. For them to have any *specific* effect, they must be determined to have that effect by apparatuses of actualization and implantation that plug into them and transformatively relay what they give rise to (family, church, school . . .)." So the feverish production of media-enforced patriotism intricately interwove into its narrative numerous and repeated references to these earlier wars. By November 2000, recent heroes, as well as veterans of the 1962, 1965, and 1971 wars, were honored in commemorative programs throughout the districts of southern Maharashtra. The press reported these daily, with photos and texts galore. Such a process of collective remembering even went further back in time. The glorification of pre-1947 veterans conjured up memories of the freedom struggle and liberation of the country from the "British yoke." The local press began to observe and report an increasing number of freedom fighters' commemorative events and/or death anniversaries. These events were elevated as exemplars of national dedication for the benefit of future generations. Thus, such mnemic social activity was the incessant product of popular, public, and media interactions feeding into one another. As important, these processes were also relayed and amplified in the space of school.

Primary Schools at War

The performative demonstrations of national preservation and regeneration also occurred in primary schools, where they formed a central part of a dialogic field between pupils and teachers and further constructed school as a space where wider issues within society at large resonated and even crystallized. If devotion to the country does get reshaped and reenacted anew in everyday life (Billig 1995), in these moments of heightened national awareness in the year 2000, devotion had clearly intensified. It gradually came to inform most of the interactions between pupils and teachers. In many instances, teachers explicitly voiced their support of the national tricolor in front of the pupils in an attempt at shaping their senses of civic morality. While encouraging them to discriminate between right and wrong as they grew into Indian citizens, teachers actively nurtured and cultivated the trope of war among the young. This was particularly reflected on the walls of classrooms and school halls, covered in posters prepared by pupils together with their teachers. From photo collages of rockets and explosions to drawings of soldiers on the battlefield in Kashmir, these posters acted as powerful visual reminders that the nation was at war, including on educational premises. In most institutions, the posters were pasted on the main board by the entrance, as if reclaiming the wholeness of the body of India and of its citizens—pupils, parents, and teachers.

In these celebratory displays, the figure of the "soldier" (*jawān*) emerged as a powerful one looming over the entire school space, both material and rhetorical. Whether in corporation-run or private schools, in Marathi- or Urdu-medium institutions, the modern warriors were not represented only on drawings and collages. They were also impersonated by the (male) children themselves on occasion. As we shall see (Chapter 3), even toddler boys in kindergarten (*bālawāḍī*) were taught to march and hold and fire dummy rifles in annual school shows. In addition, teachers in their frequent impromptu references to the defense of "our country" (*āplā deś*) emphasized the duty to support "our soldiers," who were fighting and giving up their lives for the sake of the *desh* and of their own brothers. The soldier thus epitomized the utmost form of sacrifice.[6] His was a superior one offered for the preservation of the whole nation and his fellow citizens, his "national kin," as underlined in the pledge printed on the front page of every schoolbook in India. Praising "our soldiers" consequently signified more than just reminding "ourselves" that the nation was engaged in hostilities; it was tantamount to sharing in the sanctity and celebration of the national sacrifice. This constant rhetoric suffused not only morning assemblies but also many lessons in class; classes in geography, history, and Marathi provided the best opportunities, where the military motif regularly appeared in teachers' routine interjections of opinions.

One should nevertheless understand that children were far from passive recipients of bellicose pedagogy. In their interactions with their teachers and other adults, pupils developed their own negotiated understandings of social and political life. They had grasped very early on that the country was at war and also partook of the patriotic effervescence. Thus, on an October day in a Class 4 (nine-year-olds) at the All India Marathi School,[7] the most progressive school in Kolhapur, I spotted a girl sporting a tricolor *tikkli*. This was the first time I had seen such a forehead decoration replacing the usual burgundy or red round dots, or even the fancy-hued and irregularly shaped figures studded with fake pearls and other trinkets. In the same classroom, another girl had covered her head in a handkerchief with tricolor prints. As the teacher, a stout Dalit woman in her midforties was talking to a colleague at the door of her class, I asked both pupils the meaning of what they were wearing. The first one answered, "[It is] for the country" (Deshasathi), and the second asserted, "Our flag" (Apla jhenda). As she overheard the dialogue, the teacher turned around and nodded approvingly, vigorously flexing her muscles. Wearing a beaming smile on her face, she proudly asserted, "For the country," adding for my benefit, "We need utmost pride for the country, don't we?" (Abhiman pahije, deshaca, 'he na?). On another day in a Class 3 (eight-year-olds) in the same school, a female pupil, Vanita, had colored a map of Maharashtra with the tricolor. Whereas the arts teacher inspired the map, she explained, she had decided on her own to fill it in with the national colors. On other occasions, pupils visibly reproduced the gender-role division extant among teachers. If girls and boys alike peppered their sketchbooks with war motifs and inscriptions of "Victory to the soldiers" (*Jay jawaan*), girls during recess drew colored-powder drawings (*rangoli*) of not only the usual floral patterns and geometric designs but also motifs of soldiers' guns, rifles, and helmets on the ground; they also dressed in matching patriotic saris on their birthdays, whereas boys wore battle dress, drew battle scenes, and played "Kargil war."

That some of these tokens of national allegiance may be part of an endeavor to "please the teacher" is a possibility, although not an exclusive certainty. At any rate, it is significant that pupils of various ages, in the two years that followed the Kargil events and in tune with the general atmosphere prevalent in wider society—including at home—partook in their own ways of the ongoing war effort and of the war culture thus daily reactivated. In these times fraught with patriotic emotionality, this war culture provided them with a most fertile training ground for zealous citizenship and active participation. Furthermore, this national patriotic landscape is also a regional one that calls for further exploration: Maharashtra was apparently the only state in the country where such national fervor ever engulfed the citizenry to such a prominent and visible extent, as several observers testified in other parts of India at the time. As we shall see in Chapter 4, this national war culture drew on the rich and multilayered one that constituted the production of locality. For the moment, however, I delineate the remaining theoretical premises of this exploration.

Sensitive Subjects: Education and Nationalism in Everyday Life

In its "modern" materialization as an institutionalized system of knowledge production and transmission supported by a curriculum and a schooling system, formal education has long been of interest for political scientists, sociologists, economists, and developmental planners (Rudolph and Rudolph 1972; Jeffery and Basu 1996; Jeffery and Jeffery 1996). Sociologists in their studies of schooling have devoted most of their attention to an understanding of social reproduction, whether of the elite or of particular types of discrimination (social, racial, ethnic, and so on). By contrast, anthropology has relegated the field of education to its margins, largely confining it to education departments and colleges. For the most part, the work thus produced (Spindler 1955, 1982, 1987; Heath 1972, 1983; Spindler and Spindler 2000) has had little effect on the long tradition of anthropology in the (former) colonies, occupying itself instead with informal systems of knowledge transmission until recently.

Former generations of anthropologists primarily concerned with nonindustrial societies, where mass educational systems did not exist, were predominantly attracted to traditional areas of cultures—however constructed these were—and focused on informal structures of knowledge transmission and socialization processes, including initiation and life-cycle rituals. Long undergirding anthropologists' primeval concern with the study of pristine cultures and societies was a regime of authenticity in the discipline that prevented envisaging such postcolonial educational projects as truly authentic. Only today, a long time after postcolonial societies began to build a national system of education since their independence, have anthropologists begun turning their gaze to these societies to some effect (Scrase 1993; Levinson, Foley, and Holland 1996; Stambach 2000; Hall 2002; Sarangapani 2003; Kaplan 2006).[8]

This book, then, explores the most banal, ordinary dimensions of embodied and emotional nationalism integral to educational processes in a modern nation-state today. It does so from an anchorage in the western regional state of Maharashtra, namely, the locality of Kolhapur in the late 1990s and early

2000s. The gaze, however, does not limit itself to the state's representatives alone, here, the teachers. Instead, it attaches itself to the idioms through which ordinary actors make meaning of their everyday political world by focusing on issues of identity construction in relation to the locality, the region, and the nation. How urban middle- and lower-class citizens of all faiths negotiate the processes of self-making at individual and collective levels in a thus far "secular state" constituted by an overwhelming Hindu population forms the main background interrogation. The regimentation of bodies crucial to this production in fact pervades the entire space of school as well as the quotidian routine punctuating the lives of many pupils, in India as in most nation-states. For this reason, attention must be paid to all of the minutiae of daily life at school, as well as to all extracurricular activities, ranging from school trips to annual events such as competitions and parents' gatherings. These also form an important part of the regular production of identifications and deep at-tachments through the "cultural artefacts of nationalism" (Anderson 1991: 4) in primary schools in western India. Some clarification regarding the formal educational system is in order.

Educating Citizens in Postindependence India and Maharashtra State

Education in India is a matter of both central and state policy. General guide-lines produced by the National Centre for Education, Research and Train-ing (NCERT) in New Delhi pertain to the aims and objectives of education and to the curricula to be evolved for different stages of schooling.[9] The last guidelines evolved by NCERT came out in 1992 and are still based on the 1988 report. In the 1980s a major change was made to the national goals of educa-tion.[10] Whereas the National Policy of 1968 was first and foremost aimed at promoting "national progress, a sense of common citizenship and culture, and [at] strengthen[ing] national integration," that of 1988 stressed how education should "contribute to national cohesion, a scientific temper and independence of mind and spirit—thus further[ing] the goals of socialism, secularism and democracy enshrined in our Constitution." The last three goals mentioned refer to political modes of governance that have increasingly come under attack since the 1980s, as the Congress government and party started losing ground to Hindu nationalist movements. Officials drawing up national recommenda-tions may therefore have felt it necessary at the time to restate those previously taken-for-granted goals. Subsequent events have proved them right.

From the moment that the pro-*Hindutva* Bharatiya Janata Party (BJP)

came to power in Delhi in 1997 until its defeat in the elections of May 2004, the central government was repeatedly subject to pressures from the Rashtriya Swayamsevak Sangh (RSS) to give its policies an explicitly Hindu slant (Benei 2001b). This included the application of a yoga-cum-Sanskrit-cum-ethical education scheme throughout India (Kesari 1998) with a view to building a "strong nation," proud of its rich Hindu heritage and ready to defend it by physical force. The RSS also demanded that the central government issue guidelines to all academic institutions, making it mandatory to display photographs of "national heroes" who had contributed to the "building of the Indian nation," specifically *Hindutva* ideologues such as V. D. Savarkar (see Savarkar 1999 for a presentation of his political program). Pressures in the educational field proved mostly unsuccessful in the first years, partly because of the renewed opposition of secular parties. The Hindu right, however, made further inroads into higher educational bodies and institutions at the NCERT. After infiltrating the NCERT, the central government started putting into action its plan of revising the entire national curriculum framework for education (Rajalakshmi 2000). It proposed substantive alterations to the existing system, overemphasizing religious (Hindu) education "as opposed to education about religions," together with an "overplay of the importance of indigenous education without giving a coherent critique of the perceived dangers of globalisation, an overdose of national identity bordering on jingoism, and an attempt to highlight the need to redefine the existing understanding of secularism" (92–93).

States, however, do enjoy a right of autonomy in educational matters and may decide whether or not to follow the national recommendations. This right explains why particular kinds of politically or religiously influenced curricula have long existed in some states, such as in the northern Hindi belt over which the RSS has had a strong influence for decades (Kumar 1992). The continual tension existing between central and state policies also reflects the difficulty that a federal state like India has to face with respect to the simultaneous construction of a nation and strong regional states. Arguably, the kind of nation desired by the state determines the kind of education it imparts, not only at the national level but even more so at the regional one. An emphasis on the nation-state nevertheless does not necessarily imply opposition to regionalism, as can be seen from the Maharashtrian case.

The state of Maharashtra was governed by a "saffron-colored" BJP–Shiv Sena coalition from 1995 to 1999.[11] From the time the coalition came to power in March 1995, it carried out various social and economic schemes, accompanied by a hardened "sons-of-the-soil" drive, at times nearly assuming the form of ethnic cleansing primarily targeted at Muslims but also at Indians hailing from other regions (Hansen 2001; Eckert 2003). Most of the official schemes failed, which further strengthened the xenophobic attitude of the saffron coalition and its supporters. In the educational field, however, evaluating the success of BJP–Shiv Sena policy proved more difficult. The government's power regarding educational matters is theoretically circumscribed by that of separate bodies such as the Maharashtra State Centre for Educational Research and Training (MSCERT) and the Maharashtra State Bureau of Textbook Production and Curriculum Research, otherwise known in Marathi as Patthya Pustak Mandal or Bal Bharati, after the name of the building that houses it in Pune.[12] It receives its directives from the MSCERT, whose autonomous status keeps it free from any possible pressure from the state government, unlike educational administrations in some other states, such as Uttar Pradesh, Madhya Pradesh, and Bihar. Government control over these two bodies would therefore be a rather unlikely prerequisite for significant transformation of the school curriculum in Maharashtra.

Yet the changes that occurred at the time seemed more ambiguous. The BJP–Shiv Sena government implemented measures voted in by the previous Congress government, although there is reason to believe that the Statewide Massive and Rigorous Training for Primary Teachers (SMART PT) program conducted in the late 1990s, supposedly according to the last NCERT recommendations (1988), was also given a definite RSS twist (Benei 2001b). The contents of the new textbooks showed a much more nationalist and xenophobic bias. In addition, the pro-*Hindutva* state of Maharashtra was first in promoting the dissemination of yoga classes, before similar pro-*Hindutva* educational attempts later took place at the central level. No less significant, bearing in mind the crucial place ascribed by RSS ideologues to (pseudo-)military training, was the Maharashtra government decision to carry a military schooling project one step further. The project was started in 1996 and invited applications from local educational societies for the creation of "A Military School in Every District" (*Pratyek jilhyat sainiki shala*), as explained in the posters sent to each school throughout the regional state. As we shall see, however, such a project did not appeal solely to the *Hindutva* coalition government (Chapter 6). The projection of a strong, disciplined, fully fledged modern citizen reflected in the mirror of Maharashtrian society at large. The extent to which the institution of school is a meaningful one in Maharashtra now requires specification.

Of Total Institutions and Unclosed Spaces

School today has become a privileged site where ideas and practices about socialization are both produced and transmitted. Even for young children at an early age, patterns of authority and models of behavior are now jointly produced by both family members (whether parents or other elders) and teachers. Consequently, rather than a "total institution" in the Goffmanian sense of closure entailed by the formulation, school here is envisaged as constantly open and in dialogue with other institutions and society at large (see Srivastava 1998 for a similar argument). What takes place within schools both reflects and informs wider conceptions and debates, including those pertaining to the locality, the region, and the nation. At times, school may even amplify some of these debates, as illustrated by the repercussions, in primary schools in Kolhapur, from the Pokhran nuclear tests of May 1998 and the Kargil war of April–July 1999. Upon my return six months after the war, I certainly did not anticipate such a display of patriotism so far away from the scene of conflict. Clearly, a "Kargil syndrome" was lingering. Particularly noteworthy was the consensus in the views and attitudes of teachers and parents. Here was a matter of uncompromising, viscerally anchored national pride. There seemed to be no question among adults—including Muslims—that celebrating the Indian victory in Kargil and the spirit of fighting and war with young children might have been counterproductive to achieving the otherwise professed goal of a peaceful Indian democracy. On the contrary, views concurred on the desirability of building a "strong" nation in the most concrete sense of the word, a view congruent with that shared by many *Hindutva* followers, as is well known. While disrupting commonly dichotomous understandings of secular and religious nationalism (Chapter 1), this congruence of parents', teachers', and children's (to a lesser extent) views with those of Hindu nationalists confirms the need for an articulation of life at school with life in society at large.

Furthermore, school is also a particular kind of space in metaphorical, figurative, and empirical senses. Although its physicality is rarely evoked, the specificity of school reflects in its space being enclosed within gates and grids. Its buildings—frequently made of unappealing square concrete blocks—are often the tallest, largest, or most visible in a neighborhood, to the extent that they are used as landmarks for directions. As such, school is not just a space for learning and official education but one of the most omnipotent manifestations of the state in people's lives and/or surroundings that powerfully inserts itself into the imaginaries of social actors, whether literate and "educated" or not. As an icon of state modernity whose contours are delineated in contrast to the rest of the ordinary everyday, school, then, crucially marks the quotidian reality of social actors. It also forms part of a continuum of spaces between home and more public spaces, as illustrated by the fact that even though enclosed, school is rarely shut off, even physically, from the rest of social space: grids are kept ajar, and gates are often wide open, even during school hours. This material flexibility best illustrates the lability and ambiguity of the space of school as clearly marked off as different, autonomous, endowed with authority and state legitimacy, yet also made, reappropriated, and inhabited by social actors, teachers, children, and to a lesser extent, parents.

In documenting the visions and practices of nationhood and citizenship that ordinary social actors forge and reshape in their daily dealings with state primary schooling, and bearing in mind the importance of culture in processes of state formation and operation (Steinmetz 1999), this book pays due attention to the ways in which schooling as a state apparatus feeds upon and into cultural processes and attachments, drawing upon existing structures of feeling and material constitutive of ordinary social actors' repertoires of public culture and popular knowledge. At the same time, it shows how schooling reshapes these repertoires in a process attuned with dominant ongoing narratives within wider society while crystallizing these narratives. In such a naturalizing process, this crystallized knowledge acquires further authenticity and legitimacy while being reappropriated by social actors. Central to this reappropriation are bodily practices and emotions.

Toward a Phenomenological Anthropology of the Body and Emotions in the Political

If national unity is maintained and produced by a daily routine rather than by a "vague [and] intermittent . . . allegiance to a civil state" (Geertz 1973: 260), this routine implies more than mere bodily disciplining of pupils. It involves the *joint*, intricately imbricated production of cultural and political schemata together with bodily experience. Drawing on Raymond Williams's notion of "structures of feeling," understood as never a given but constantly reshaped—consciously as much as unconsciously—by social actors in the course of ordinary life, I aim to demonstrate how bodily experience is itself constituted by cultural and political schemata.[13]

A large corpus of work on the anthropology of the body has been brought to light over the past decade. Some of it has documented the bodily techniques

and affective dispositions related to "the inscription upon bodily habits of disciplines of self-control and practices of group discipline, often tied up with the
state and its interests" (Appadurai 1996: 148). Yet, rarely have these practices
of citizenship manufacturing (Benei 2005a) been approached phenomenologically, discussing bodies from an anchorage in empirical reality, and least
of all in relation to political imagination (although see Feldman 1991). When
they have entered discussion, bodies mostly served as testamentary bearers of
exactions and atrocities committed upon them. More rarely have they been
envisaged *prior* to the eruption of violence—ethnic or otherwise—as constitutive parts toward the production not solely of social and cultural persons but
also of political, and especially national, ones. The very political socialization
of these bodies right from infancy remains to be documented. In attempting
such documentation, this book seeks to offer an understanding of the "sense of
psychic, and embodied, rage" attendant on the "sentiments of ethnic violence"
whose meaning lies "within large-scale formations of ideology, imagination,
and discipline" (Appadurai 1996: 149) and that are not exhausted by cognition.
To reach such an understanding, I explore the symbolic and affective dimensions of political emotions, drawing on, and departing from, existing work on
the anthropology of bodies, emotions, and language.

In an ambitious article about liberty and political emotions, Reddy (1999)
argued that the social "constructedness" so often highlighted in recent anthropological works did not leave much room for agency and individuality, let
alone liberty. In the case of political emotions, and especially those multiscalar
attachments whose production I seek to document, the issue is further complicated by the fact that we are dealing with endeavors of an explicitly collective sort, that is, national projects and nation building. This entails achieving a
delicate balance of exploring the collective, cultural, and social dimensions of
these emotional political projects while giving voice to individualities and their
variously idiosyncratic understandings of these projects. The most promising
tool for achieving such an equilibristic construction is a phenomenological one.
Recourse to it stems from the recognition of the inadequacy of paradigms used
in sociological research on violence that are largely dominated by a causation
model. An uncritical "scientific hunt for causation" (Whitehead 2004: 55, cited
in Staudigl 2005: 4) has prevented acknowledging the "corporeality, the non-
instrumental expressivity or 'senselessness' of violence as integral parts of this
phenomenon." By contrast, moving away from any causational explanations
and reinstating the phenomenological dimension of lived experience enable

one to register other levels of embodied emotional experience that may—or may not—be harnessed into the production of violence, as well as to delineate its collective, social, and cultural framework (Chapter 2). Hence, in the chapters that follow, the two central notions developed are those of "sensorium" and "embodiment."

Sensorium and Embodiment: Producing Visceral Senses of Belonging

Several years ago I discussed in a preliminary article the public liturgies starting each school day in this part of Maharashtra (Benei 2001b) and ended with a reflection on their "experiential specificity of effects" (Csordas 1994). I pondered whether the children also get transformed in the process of chanting the liturgies and to what extent. What bearing did singing, chanting, and calisthenics have upon both the students' individual bodies and on the collective school body thus produced and incorporated concomitantly with the national one (Chapter 1)? I argued then that through this public worship of the nation, children were simultaneously creating their physical and emotional selves and enacting and embodying "India" into existence. Children, in other words, were phenomenologically taught to "feel" the nation within their own bodies.

This reflexive attempt was met with some skepticism at the time. The question of practice efficiency was often raised in the ensuing discussions: Did these daily ritualized iterations, as well as the constant rhetoric of nationalism that suffused daily life at school, really succeed in ingraining a sentiment of devotion and loyalty to the nation in these kids? What puzzled me were both the formulation and the content of the question. Anthropology, and the other social sciences to varying extents, are disciplines marked by various works that have reinstated the body as a primary medium for socialization, whether in the sense of a disciplining documented by Foucault or along Bourdieu's notions of habitus and bodily *hexis* inspired by Mauss's foundational text on bodily techniques.[14] That socialization does take place largely through social actors' bodies—however these are to be defined and located, socially, culturally, historically, and politically—has now become commonplace. The question of efficiency, therefore, seemed both inappropriate and unproductive. Inappropriate because it smacked of antiquated positivism and functionalism and summarily brushed aside heuristic epistemologies constitutive of the social sciences in the past decades. Unproductive because, if this kind of question were to be asked at all, it may well have been so of any other process of socialization falling within the purview of anthropological inquiry. What of class and gender, for instance?

No scholar today would deny the respective embodied dimensions of either class or gender. So why question so vehemently the embodied dimension of nationalism? I shall return to this in Chapter 2.

Here, I want to draw attention to the "commonsense" notion of personal experiences of schooling that we, as academics, feel entitled to draw upon in our scholarly discussions. These discussions are almost inexorably drawn back to a kind of natural positivism: "Does it work?" is relentlessly asked. So comments of the following type may often be heard: "According to my school experience, it doesn't work: I was made to sing the national anthem every day of my student life, and this has not turned me into a blind and stupid, emotional patriot." Beyond a somewhat naive conception of pragmatics, whereby the "work of culture" (Obeyesekere 1990) and society might only be approached through explicit discourse, it is significant that the same proponents of such bold declarations would often privately confess later on that "each time [they] heard the national anthem, whether [they] liked it or not, it gave [them] the creeps." In some ways, these testimonies inadvertently point to the crucial dimension of the formation of a patriotic attachment as embodied emotions of national belonging nurtured over time. The emotional and corporeal dimensions inherent in the construction of national attachment in Maharashtra form the main focus in this book. In studying the various registers of expression of emotions *and* emotional practices, I document the articulation of the production of political emotions with language ideologies that play a central role in the functioning of particular institutions of power such as schooling (Schieffelin, Woolard, and Kroskrity 1998: vii).

In my attempt to articulate bodies, languages, and emotions, I expand further on the notion of "sensorium," introduced by Walter Benjamin in his *Arcades Project* (1999). As is now well known, Benjamin was fascinated by the technologization and commodification of things characteristic of nineteenth-century European modernity, the former of which, he claimed, generated a new apperception of the urban, industrialized world, a new way of being into this world. What, for instance, characterized the three figures of the flâneur, the gambler, and the collector in nineteenth- and early twentieth-century Paris, Benjamin argued, was their "reception in distraction," that is, the fact that all three are "touched and inspired" by "the world's scatter": "they spend themselves and expand themselves in being dispersed to the current of objects. And their reception in distraction . . . is *not merely visual but tactile and visceral; it involves their whole sensorium*" (Eiland 2005: 11, emphasis added). These three figures, with those of the ragpicker, the sandwich man, the street-corner boy, the dandy, and the prostitute, "embodied new human capacities and reactions to stimuli in the metropolitan street," especially in relation to the "new 'haptic' and 'optic' environment of the big city" (Benjamin, cited in Lloyd 2002). Thus, new subjectivities developed out of the "complex kind of training" to which "technology has subjected the human senses" in the late nineteenth and early twentieth centuries. Although Benjamin at times insisted on the variegated dimensions of this new sensory disposition, at other times he also seemed to place more emphasis on the gaze and the visual aspect of modern apperception. Since then, many scholars of modernity have made passing references to the notion of sensorium without elaborating on it, and they, too, have mostly concentrated on sight.

Sight, as is well known, is considered to have played a pivotal role in the realization of "Western modernity" (Latour 1986; Ong 1991). Singling out the visual sense, however, operates within a sensory stratification and specialization whose counterpoint often is the repression of other perceptual dispositions (Feldman 1994; Seremetakis 1994). It obfuscates the fact that sight is only one of the senses involved in a general apperception of the modern world and the construction of a modern political subject, as shown by the works of historians and anthropologists that reinstated the other senses.[15] While drawing on these approaches, throughout the book I revisit and redeploy the notion of sensorium as entire sensory apparatus, especially by locating and illuminating various historical, social, and cultural sensory configurations and mediations participating in the formation of senses of regional and national belonging.

The notions of sensorium and embodiment are especially deployed in an examination of two powerful resources for the production of incorporated senses of belonging to locality, region, and nation: namely, the sensitive subjects of language and history.[16] Chapter 2 focuses on the production of attachment through language ideology and its incorporation; Chapters 3 and 4 document the gendered production of a continuum between home, school, and nation, as well as that of locality and historiography, respectively. Central here is the notion of embodiment or incorporation, which presupposes that one cannot distinguish the *contents* of the process from the *process* itself, as the two are mutually produced. Incorporation refers to the formation of a habitus that not only has to do with corporeal practices but also conjures up socially and culturally produced emotional, sensory, and cognitive resources enabling interiorization of the self. Thus, the manufacturing of interiority and embodiment cannot be dissociated from that of a collective regional and national self. If the notions of sensorium and embodiment may at first glance appear somewhat far-fetched in the consideration of nationalism, I aim to show that they are in fact central to an understanding of the production of political attachment. By answering the questions of how people come to substantialize and bond with their nation, how they become passionate in its defense or praise and express their senses of belonging, this book sheds light on how passions of belonging come into existence and acquire such central import in people's senses of self.

Of Sociological Parameters, Writing Experiments, and "Historicality"

In more ways than one, this choice of focus is the product of a writing process that spanned several years and that bears elaboration. First, this writing process has theoretical and analytical consequences, highlighting particular dimensions of self-making while leaving others in the shadows. This obtains of a more sociological dimension relegated to the margins, especially a treatment of parental strategies and school choices in relation to economic opportunities and political affiliations and leanings. Such a marginalization was also dictated by empirical fact: at the level of primary instruction and save in the case of minorities (Chapter 5; Benei 2005c), most parents opted for the school closest to their homes. They did so especially if the school had a good, or decent enough, reputation. This disconcertingly crude finding was common among Marathi-speaking parents of children attending corporation schools (although in this case, economic considerations also played an important part) as well as those in privately run schools. Political preferences, much to my disappointment, did not appear as a primary motivator for most parents of children attending Marathi schools (at the time of research, an overwhelming 84 percent of children attended Marathi-medium schools). Of course, such a bare fact neither exhausts the analysis of differential strategies occasionally existing even within the same family nor dispenses one from a sociological analysis in its own right. The same is true of a more thorough discussion of class and caste in relation to the (re)production of social inequalities within schooling, despite some treatment of the issue throughout the book.[17] The military school discussed in Chapter 6, as much as the differential languages of instruction and the very existence of privately run schools, point to the crucial dimension of class in the production of schooled identities.[18] A similar point may be made of caste, also a major object of sociological inquiry in studies of social system and schooling in India, especially in relation to unequal access to schooling facilities (Nambissan 2003; Subrahmanian et al. 2003). It is true that caste today forms an important part in the production of identity markers, including in the most extreme forms of—conscious and unconscious—Hindu-inflected or Hindu-sympathetic behavior. This book nevertheless presents only basic contextualizing data throughout the chapters inasmuch as my project is less concerned with hierarchy than with the production of a "common substance," a shared "essence of belonging." Rather than reiterate the importance of caste in contemporary India, then, this book wants to lay emphasis on shared icons, signs, and substances (Daniel 1984) of nationality. It seeks to document a process that cuts across classes and castes and speaks to each and every individual about both his or her sense of belonging to locality, region, and nation and sense of entitlement to being part of a national community. In regard to the latter, predominant divisions constructed and reshaped within the context of school along the lines of "faith" appear to have acquired much more visibility and disruptive potential.

Second, this book to a certain extent represents an experiment with writing anthropology. As often happens, the project at a given moment seems to take on a life of its own, deviating from its intended course. Remarkably, whereas this aleatory character is generously invoked in the phase of fieldwork—the literature abounds with examples of researchers gone to the field to investigate political parties and who came back with a full study of village rituals, or vice versa—it becomes more suspicious at the time of "writing up the material." The "empirical facts" are now there to be presented, according to a more or less fixed storyboard. Where chance and contingency had received pride of place, they are no longer personae gratae. Anything that may appear too distractive from the initial synopsis is oftentimes ruthlessly put aside, "for later." In some ways, this book falls prey to this predicament. For in the course of writing and regularly browsing through the wealth of material accumulated over the years, I often felt I was not doing justice to the richness and texture, the depth and significance of the lives of all the people met over the length of this research. Furthermore, each time I looked back on the original synopsis, I was also struck by the distance gradually widening between the imagined project and its written materialization, a result of serendipitous readings and encounters that changed the course of thinking and writing.

Though liberating as it was, such a free, open writing process had another unintended consequence. The divide in the book is unequal between teachers—the most prominent—parents, and children, despite the research project revolving around the latter as main targets of educational and other socialization processes, including political.[19] The overall difficult conditions of observation in cramped and overcrowded classrooms called for a predominantly collective form of interaction with the pupils at school. My keen interest in observing the "spontaneous" eruption of national and regional affect in everyday life was also matched by a sheer reticence at artificially provoking such an eruption by engaging in the question-and-answer interview of the type practiced in the few available studies concerned with children's understandings of the political (Percheron 1974; Connell 1975; Coles 1986). Consequently, unless students brought up the discussion in one way or another, I avoided prompting them about my own topics of interest even while with them outside school. If such self-restraint made fieldwork more challenging and uncertain, it also allowed more spontaneous expression and richness of material. At the time of writing, however, I found myself in a predicament as to how to reintroduce children's voices in the chapters' narratives as these had gradually shaped up. To be sure, I could have shifted the projectors' lights onto the pupils within the chapters themselves. This was done to a certain extent: although pupils' agency is not always foregrounded, it operates as a running thread throughout, enhanced by means of writing techniques ranging from dialogues to depictions of classroom observation, to third-person reconstitutions. Yet more was needed in light of the original project. Indeed, I wanted to demonstrate and document how even at a young age, children are already not just "imbibing" knowledge and information, contrary to the many pronouncements of pedagogy still extant in Indian primary schools even today. Rather, children *process* knowledge and information and develop understandings of things political, though fragmentary these may be.

Encouraging evidence in the respective cases of Australian and North American children (Connell 1975; Coles 1986) had demonstrated that children do relate to the political world they live in, even if sketchily, and even at ages early as five and six; some of the details they mention about real politics may be mere scraps, variously woven into narratives about their everyday lives and imaginations. If they do not have a conception of politics as a distinct sphere of activity, children are able to make meaning of political life. What sense, then, did they make of the Kashmir events that gripped the "Maharashtrian nation"? How were they affected? How did they express their interest—or lack thereof—in the topic? We encountered some answers to these questions earlier; other answers were meaningfully provided by drawings, a technique long used by child psychoanalysts, from Melanie Klein to Robert Coles. Drawings, together with the commentaries children offer on them, may serve as windows into their worlds, imaginings, and understandings. Whether drawn upon my request or spontaneously, or even already made in their sketchbooks prior to my visits to the school, pupils' drawings show that children indeed process much more political information than is often acknowledged, which demonstrates their autonomy as agents. Far from furthering a vision of children as passive recipients, this pictorial evidence suggests that they are also very active in, as it were, the manufacturing of nationhood and citizenship. There remained, however, the issue of incorporation of these drawings in the book. Were they to be the object of a separate chapter pontificating on theories of childhood socialization and psychoanalytic interpretations? This ran the risk of once again muting children's own voices through overly academic appropriation. So another experiment appeared necessary. It requires elaboration, and to begin with, a brief foray into the implications of this project as, willy-nilly, a state-related one.

In a critical essay published in 2002, Ranajit Guha, well-known founder of subaltern studies history, engaged with what he called the "statist predicament of South Asian historiography" (74). Such a predicament, he claimed, was characterized by the haunting gaze of the nation-state looming ever so large over historical narratives purportedly describing Indians' everyday lives. The categories of "worker," "citizen," and "woman" used by historians have an unfortunate effect: that of inescapably reinscribing people's lives within the narratives of the state while flattening out the "historicality" of their experiences. By this, taking his cue from Rabindranath Tagore's essay on the same (see Guha's appendix for a translation), Guha meant much more than what the historian can usually grasp in her or his scientific-minded factual accounts: "multiplicity and singularity, complexity and simplicity, regularity and unpredictability of" a human's being in time and being with others (46). Such historicality, as might be expected, is best captured by literature and fiction.[20] Although it is not my purpose to give an account of the richness of Guha's essay, here I want to both engage with his statist stance and vindicate his take on historicality.[21] On the one hand, as justly remarked by Chakrabarty, Guha's critique of the "aspirations of the masses to statehood and to state-centred identities" (2004: 129) relegates to oblivion the fact that the state does play a fundamental part in people's ordinary lives, from delivering ration cards, to supplying postal and other services or organizing chaotic elections, and as important, to providing basic elementary education. On the other hand, any narrative of life in a state institution, precisely because it is located in that particular space, is bound to be caught in the webs of shortcomings entangled in the "statist predicament." The present book is an obvious case in point, even though I have attempted in some of the chapters (especially Chapter 3) to lift the statist veil of people's lives and suggest a much fuller and richer complexity. Still, more was needed in regard to the children being central to this project.

Here is the experimenting. Between chapters written in a more academic style, I have interspersed "interludes." These consist of my own reflections on extracurricular activities (e.g., "On Drawing," "Drawing Gender, Drawing War," "Of Inspirations and Aspirations") and what I have called "moments of suspension" (in an interlude of the same title) as well as, crucially, of vignettes made of children's drawings and narratives. These vignettes are meant to operate as contrapuntal voices, as in a musical score. They provide an avenue for bestowing more visibility on children in the entire project. In addition, they open up a wider space for the expression of their agency in the processing of information, knowledge, and more largely of socialization. Even as some of these voices are narrativized (e.g., "National Anthem and Other Life Stories," "Drawing Gender, Drawing War"), they make heard vocalizations on the pupils' everyday lives in general, and their social, cultural, emotional, and political surroundings in particular. They are expressions of both disillusionment and resignation, and excitement and aspirations. These voices also offer a decentering of adults' regimentation techniques rather than a parroting of them. Moreover, some of the narratives are written in the first person, whereas others borrow from the stream-of-consciousness Joycean technique (although there is much more punctuation here than in Molly Bloom's famous closing chapter in *Ulysses*). The experimenting goes even further inasmuch as these children's voices are fictional. Already in the process of interacting, observing, and transcribing empirical facts and gathering material, subjectivity—even when subdued and muted—is so fundamental to anthropological practice that whatever account we may give is de facto fictional.[22] Furthermore, these voices are fictional in the sense that they do not all emanate from a single, unique individual. Although most of them do, some are the product of collages of "real" voices and moments shared in the course of fieldwork with children in and out of school, within the classroom, at lunchtime, during recess, after school, at home, and so on. These latter voices are "reconstructions," assemblages if you will, of comments and expressions of feelings and sensitivities encountered in my interaction with "real people" made of real flesh, bones, and much else. For instance, the Sunila presented in one of the vignettes is a combination of several female pupils ("Drawing Gender, Drawing War"). I am aware of my own background, a "white"—though mixed—predominantly European one with the privileges and limitations entailed by this location, and the bearing it may have on my attempts to convey what a Sunila sees in a Mohina Bai as a window onto wider horizons; horizons extending beyond the shanty dwellings of a dark, minuscule, damp, and hot single room for a family of seven in a slum in Kolhapur. Yet this endeavor is neither about romantic voyeurism nor about redeeming expiation for an easier material life. What it is about is uncovering the historicality of ordinary life, revealing the vibrant space of human doubts, fears, worries, and uncertainties, as well as enjoyment, aspirations, longings, and desires, through "coaxing up images of the real" (Ortner 1995: 190). It is now time to situate the scene of these emotions and affects in greater depth.

Situating the Context: Maratha Historical Legacy and Social Reform Movements

Set along the western industrial corridor linking the regional state capital of Mumbai to that of Bangalore in Karnataka, the town of Kolhapur today is famous for its recently built industries, ranging from sugarcane to mechanics to engineering, as well as its leather shoes, gold jewelry, and inordinately spicy cuisine. But there is much more to Kolhapur than meets a hurried traveler's eye. Even amid the fumes of buses, trucks, cars, and scooters noisily plying its busy roads and congested center, the town has an unmistakable languor. It is the languor of a friendly provincial town "still human size" (by Indian standards), and of a welcoming Mahalakshmi temple.[23] It is also a somewhat aristocratic languor that attaches itself to the parks, buildings, and former palaces. For Kolhapur was an independent kingdom until 1949, before merging with the then state of Bombay. So the town possesses a rich historical heritage on several counts. It traces its genealogy back to Śivājī Bhonsale, the seventeenth-century hero-warrior and founder of the "Maratha nation" (Chapter 4), and its more recent past of non-Brahmin movements in the nineteenth and early twentieth centuries also has made it a stronghold of social reform in southern Maharashtra (Zelliot 1970; Copland 1973; Omvedt 1976; Mudaliar 1978; Kavlekar 1979; Gore 1989). The former kingdom today is particularly known for its advancement of lower castes and classes and for the promotion of education among the poorest population at the turn of the twentieth century under the aegis of Chhatrapati

Shahu Maharaj (Copland 1973; Kavlekar 1979; Sangave and Khane 1994; Benei 1997). The chhatrapati himself is revered as a great, enlightened ruler who donated much land and money to the building of educational institutions, from schools to hostels and boarding lodges. Such a predominantly Maratha and Maharashtrian non-Brahmin background offered a welcome contrast to that of its rival city, the historically influential Peshwa Brahmin-dominated Pune, stronghold of the Maratha Empire from the late seventeenth to the early nineteenth century. Deemed "educational headquarters" from the days of the Bombay presidency in the nineteenth century, Pune was at the heart of educational innovations and policies under the British. This legacy reflects in the number of colleges and famous Orientalist institutions known the world over, even today. In comparison to the Puneite intellectual heritage, Kolhapuris would often qualify themselves with some embarrassment as "not as refined," especially in their mastery of the Marathi language.[24] Immediately nullifying such a confession, however, would follow a claim to Kolhapuri distinctiveness predicated on a strong "Maratha culture" encompassing all Maratha-allied and lower Hindu castes in Maharashtra. For all these reasons, Kolhapur held the promise of a fascinating location of inquiry where differential notions and practices of education could be hypothesized to exist. If education was to be less Brahminized, more ecumenical, and less Hindu oriented, Kolhapur would be the place. Yet my fieldwork experience revealed otherwise.

To be sure, social welfare policies were inaugurated by Chhatrapati Shahu Maharaj at the turn of the twentieth century. A dense network of privately initiated and run educational institutions also started in the wake of social reform movements that spread across this part of Maharashtra (Benei 1997, 2001b). Nonetheless, even thirty years ago those entering the profession of schoolteacher in Kolhapur overwhelmingly belonged to Brahmin and urban middle-class Maratha literate families of the surrounding region: very few were of the Maratha-allied and Scheduled castes. Only in the last fifteen to twenty years has the voluntarist policy of "universal education" conducted by the regional state over several decades finally yielded significant results in this domain. Many of the young teachers belonging to Maratha-allied and Scheduled castes today are first-generation graduates, with parents and grandparents that are half-literate small farmers or laborers.[25] The local educational fabric in Kolhapur is largely made of urban lower-middle- and middle-class society, of which primary schoolteachers are probably among the most telling representatives.

Both as agents of the state and ordinary citizens, primary schoolteachers occupy a particular position in the participating in and making of ordinary, banal nationhood. In their professional capacity as representatives of the state, teachers do play a prominent role as social actors. In a country where an average of two-thirds of the total population is literate (over 75 percent in Maharashtra and almost 80 percent in Kolhapur, per *Census of India* [2001]), their social, economic, and professional capital endows them with a moral authority that may become instrumental in shaping pupils' and parents' attitudes on various matters, including national. Whether belonging to Brahmin and Maratha-allied castes, non-Hindu or lower castes and classes, teachers at school often played a most vocal part in the patriotic upbringing of children, at times relay-

Map of India showing Kashmir, Maharashtra, and Karnataka.
SOURCE: Courtesy of Tsering Wangyal Shawa, Geographic Information Systems Librarian Head, Digital Map and Geospatial Information Center, Geosciences and Map Library, Princeton University.

ing regional and national messages, at other times publicly voicing their personal opinions. This was so in all five schools where most of the research was conducted: the two old schools located in the heart of town, Varsity Marathi School and Modern Marathi School, famous for their long Hindu orientation and a staff who predominantly belonged to upper and middle castes and classes; the most progressive and ecumenical All India Marathi School; and the two corporation-run institutions (one Marathi, hereafter "Marathi Corporation School," and one Urdu, hereafter "Urdu Corporation School") located in the Sachar Bazar area on the outskirts of town, where a large number of lower-middle- and middle-class and -caste teachers worked.

What was more perplexing to me, however, was how my hypotheses were to be confuted. Brahmins, although distinctly cultivating difference, claimed an intimate share in the local historical, including Maratha, heritage, the term "Maratha" here encompassing all Maharashtrians. The strong sense that Brahmins have of belonging to a superior caste even in Kolhapur seemed at first difficult to reconcile with their claims to being a part of a seemingly contradictory, and perhaps also mutually exclusive, sociohistorical setting. However, what some Brahmins and members of other castes in Kolhapur exemplified was the plurivocality of understandings crucial to studies documenting the production of senses of belonging. I was rather unprepared for the apparently antithetical view of Brahmins embracing the local king's heritage as their own when he had opposed their ancestors in a major controversy over his status and legitimacy as a Kshatriya (Copland 1973; Sangave and Khane 1994; Benei 1999); nor had the literature trained me for encounters with members of Maratha and other allied castes who both stoutly defended social reform and shared so many anti-Muslim views and Hindu political inclinations with their more assertive *Hindutva* counterparts.[26] Consequently, while documenting ordinary people's daily routines, this book also highlights the ambiguities of what it means to be a Maharashtrian Indian citizen, whether Hindu or Muslim, and belonging in a lower-, lower-middle-, and middle-class urban setting today.

On Drawing

ALTHOUGH THE ACTIVITY OF DRAWING was meant to be part of the official curriculum set up for all primary classes by the government of Maharashtra a few years ago, in practice it was rarely given any time in school (except at All India Marathi School). The teachers would often tell pupils to draw at home in their sketchbooks. They could make drawings relating to current events or anything else of their choosing. Among the motifs recurring year after year were the Hindu elephant-headed god Ganesh and a flag-raising ceremony, in relation to the September Ganesh festival, and the January 26 celebrations of Republic Day (date of the Constitution signed in 1950). Some sketchbooks included several pictures of statues of Ganesh and depictions of Indian flags. In the years 1998–99 and 1999–2000 especially, the other dominant motifs were soldiers' helmets atop an Indian flag, as well as fighting soldiers, the latter particularly in boys' sketchbooks. The other most common drawings represented houses, some with people usually identified as siblings and other relatives living with the child; various landscapes; swastikas (the Hindu/Jain cross drawn in reverse by the Nazis in their quest of Aryan origins) made of grains glued onto the page; decorative designs made with painted and glued dried vegetables; pictures of popular Indian cricket players; stickers of the TV serial hero Shaktiman (an Indian variant of Superman, endowed with yet more powers than his Western counterpart, as he was described to me by some of his fans); and pictures of wild and domestic animals. In Class 4, the history curriculum is almost entirely devoted to Shivaji, and pupils' sketchbooks were unsurprisingly replete with pictures of the maharaj (Chapter 4).

Birthday girl wearing a "flag sari" with matching tones of green and saffron. Varsity Marathi School, Kolhapur, February 2000.

Drawing of "India Rocket" with the national tricolor. The rocket assumes the shape of either the Taj Mahal or a mosque (the artist, Sunil K., age nine, declined to comment any further). Varsity Marathi School, Kolhapur, January 2000.

1 Singing the Nation into Existence
Devotion, Patriotism, Secularism

A sentence which has no sense does not commit you to anything.
Ernest Gellner, Interview

THE DAY IS JUST ABOUT TO BEGIN at Varsity Marathi School, one of the oldest and most popular Marathi primary schools set in the bustling heart of Kolhapur. It is January 1999. Just like any other day, the pupils have assembled in the playground under an already scorching sun. They are standing in columns corresponding to their class divisions. Mandabai, a middle-aged teacher who is in charge, presently signals to the peon (someone of low administrative rank, who, in schools, usually works as a gatekeeper or does other menial jobs) to begin playing his large drum (*dhol*). The silenced children are made to stand absolutely still, their arms stretching downward. Latecomers are hurried into their respective columns with a perfunctory slap on their head. All at once, the pupils raise their right hands to the forehead in a military salute and start rocking to and fro to the martial Hindi command of "one-two one-two one, one-two one-two one" (ek-do ek-do ek, ek-do ek-do ek) shouted out by Mandabai. The Brahmin woman's shrill, powerful, energetic voice is being relayed by a microphone. The children now stand still, their arms stretching downward again. Meanwhile, another teacher joins in with the sound of a harmonium (*peti*), the same type notably used in singing sessions of popular forms of devotion (*bhajana*).[1] As Mandabai bellows at the children in Hindi: "Attention! Ready to start the rāṣṭragīta: start!" (Sawdhan, rashtragit shuru karne ka tayar: shuru kar!), the pupils begin to sing the Indian national anthem:

Jana-Gana-Mana-Adhinayaka, Jaya He
Bharata-Bhagya-Vidhata
Punjab-Sindhu-Gujarata-Maratha-

Dravida-Utkala-Banga

Vindhya-Himachala-Yamuna-Ganga

Uchchala-Jaladhi Taranga

Tava Subha Name Jage,

Tava Subha Ashisha Mage

Gahe Tava Jaya Gatha.

Jana-Gana-Mangala Dayaka, Jaya He

Bharata-Bhagya-Vidhata

Jaya He, Jaya He, Jaya He,

Jaya Jaya Jaya, Jaya He.

The other teachers have been singing along. They are standing nearby, up-right and stiff, their arms stretching down either side of their bodies, just like the children. They, too, are singing the nation-state into existence. For this is "moral education" (naitik śikṣaṇ) time, the time to pay tribute and show one's love to the nation, (re-)creating it in the process; the time to build future generations of patriotic Indian citizens in the state of Maharashtra.

THE DAILY CHANTING of the nation into existence provides an apposite entry point for exploring issues of formation of patriotism and nationalism, and of a sensory repertoire that draws upon other experiences of the devotional in everyday life. It also enables one to draw unexpected convergences and similarities between Indian, European, and North American histories and cultural trajectories of secularism and patriotism. Everyday rituals of publicly worshipping the nation extend beyond Maharashtra or India. In England, too, daily assemblies are conducted in some schools, and religion is taught as part of the curriculum. There have been flag-raising rituals in schools in the United States since the 1880s, wherein the nation celebrates itself routinely (Billig 1995: 50). In many ways, these rituals and procedures are reminiscent of liturgical ones extant in Christian celebratory services, whether modeled on the Church of England or brought by the Pilgrims. In this sense, these rituals and procedures partake of a theology of nationalism, a notion common to many nations across the world, however different they are. A "theology of nationalism" may indeed encompass at least three meanings. First, it may refer to the explicit conception of nation building as a theological project, that is, one informed by claims to adhere to an already existing religious doctrine or set of principles.[2] Such are *Hindutva* projects of nation building, where Hindu right-wing parties purport to draw on ancient Hindu scriptures to reinstate the kingdom and rule of the god Ram (*Ramrajya*). Second, the notion of theology of nationalism may also usefully highlight the religious rituals used by ideologues and other nation builders in their construction of a secular nationalism, as was the case after the French Revolution. In their attempts at instating a "secular nation," the oft-cited paragons of hardcore secularism heavily borrowed from popular Catholicism (Ozouf 1988).[3] The French case, although extreme, is by no means exceptional. Rather, it points to a more general, and third understanding of the notion of theology of nationalism, that of the sacral element underlying most projects of nation building. Whether explicitly conceptualized as religious or purportedly secular, the production and sustenance of nations are endowed with an inevitable sacredness. It is not the place here to supplement the reflection on the modalities of this sacredness (see Anderson 1983 for his account of the concomitant fall of the great religions with the rise of nations). Rather, my intention is to draw attention to the usually unseen or unacknowledged similarities existing between European and Indian forms of nationalism. The politically correct and sacrosanct distinction between secularism and religious nationalism, or between secularism and communalism, is but a tenuous one, even in India (Hansen 2001). To begin with, a detailed analysis of the nationalist liturgical procedures starting the school day is required to highlight the specific modalities of nation building in Maharashtra. Explicitly religious and cultural motifs of everyday life are intertwined and embedded in life at school and summoned in the production of a devotional sensorium forming the background to the formation of national(ist) bonding. Those motifs are significantly informed by the categories of *bhakti*, *desh*, and *dharma*, crucial to an understanding of (Hindu) nationalism in this part of India and fraught with delicate implications for a discussion of secularism.

In the next chapters, I explore the daily singing and ritual celebrations taking place throughout an ordinary school day as well as the pedagogical techniques used in the classroom, and the phenomenological experiences of social actors. These are all mediated by particular deployments of bodies, emotions, and languages and the development of semantic repertoires and specific sensory registers. In Chapter 2, in particular, I discuss the emotionality and corporeality produced in this part of India along with language ideologies in the formation of a linguistic sensorium upon which are predicated senses of belonging, regional and national. Here, by contrast, I focus on the *concepts* and *repertoires* involved in the daily production and cultivation of national(ist) sentiment and a devotional sensorium at school.

Everyday Banality, Nationalism, and Patriotism

As one moves away from the extraordinary violence of conflicts and zooms into the particulars of everyday production of nationalism, the notion of "banality" becomes central to understanding processes of nation building. If the formulation of "banal nationalism" echoes that of Hannah Arendt on the "banality of evil" in her famous work on the bureaucratization of violence under the Nazi regime, in Michael Billig's usage (1995), the notion encapsulates the extent to which senses of national belonging, rather than erupting ex nihilo, are nurtured and become so integral to people's everyday lives that they go largely unheeded. "Daily," avers Billig, "the nation is indicated, or 'flagged,' in the lives of the citizenry. Nationalism, far from being an intermittent mood . . . , is the endemic condition" (6). The notion of banal nationalism needs further elaboration in comparative studies. It also entails clarification on the distinction between patriotism and nationalism. Many students of Western nationalism have restricted the category of "nationalist" to the description of "irrational" events, such as outbursts of violence, riots, and civil wars occurring in "other" parts of the world, thereby denying the concept any other reality (for a similar argument, see Chatterjee 1993). For the latter, the term "patriotism" is preferred and, of course, positively valued and appropriated, so that "our good patriotism" eventually stands in opposition to "their evil nationalism" (Billig 1995), or in a more recent version, "their evil fundamentalism." Needless to say, such a dichotomous conception does little to advance our understanding of the formation of national sentiment in any part of the world. Arguably, however, provided they be relieved of a simplistic and bellicose usage, the distinction between the categories of nationalism and patriotism may serve heuristic purposes. In this chapter, I want to dialectically approach them by exploring their local modalities and the articulation thereof. Schools are obvious privileged sites for the production of "the ideological habits which enable . . . nations . . . to be reproduced" (Billig 1995: 6) at the heart of everyday life. The phrase also aptly describes nationalisms in "non-established nations," particularly India. There, as in most other nation-states, the value of *amor patriae* is nurtured together with the love for parents, the family, and elderly people, through the acquisition of basic knowledge.

Educational agendas and their implementation provide a vantage point for a comparative study of Indian and Western nationalisms, including their more totalitarian dimensions. Indeed, the educational program conducted in Maharashtra in much of the 1990s shares many common features with some

organize exercise

nineteenth-century European nationalist programs and their use of singing and calisthenics. Singing and calisthenics belong to a particular type of knowledge deploying the body in ways different from most ordinary teaching. These practices also bear emotional dimensions meaningful for a cultural construction of the self. Collective singing in particular is a powerful way of binding people together, as research on nationalism in Europe, Germany in particular, has shown.[4] Attempts were made in the very first years of the nineteenth century to create singing schools for spreading German language and culture. These attempts were concomitant with educational innovations meant to "regenerate the German nation" in a response to Johann G. Fichte's call in his *Addresses to the German Nation* (*Reden an die deutsche Nation*, 1807).[5] Thus, Friedrich L. Jahn attempted to promote German patriotism by founding physical education societies designed to build young people's character together with their corporeal strength (Thiesse 1999: 60). These societies held meetings during which the young minds would be read the *Nibelungenlied*.[6] The combination of these language deployments, singing, and physical education fed into the development of German nationalism throughout the nineteenth century and were later harnessed into the project of National Socialism in the early decades of the twentieth century, with the result that is now history.

In India, a similar process of nation building occurred slightly later, also drawing on musical repertoires and physical education. Forms of popular culture played an especially important part (Goswami 2004), including in Maharashtra, where, in addition to attempts made at devotionalizing music as part of a (Hindu) national project (Bakhle 2005), nationalists at the turn of the twentieth century began collecting ballads and songs in earnest (Dighe 1961; Deshpande 2006).[7] *Kirtankar*s, too, played a meaningful role in the awakening of a nationalist/regionalist consciousness, harnessing *kīrtan*s, or popular devotional songs that drew heavily on the regional *bhakti* tradition and the poetry associated with it since the thirteenth century (Divekar 1990; Schultz 2002). All these regionalist and nationalist forms of popular expression have, since independence—and especially since the creation of the Maharashtra state in 1960—crucially converged and further fed into the production of regional and national selves. Such a reshaping of regional and national structures of feeling owes to various influences perceptible even today at the most banal, quotidian levels of experience in the space of school.

If the work of contemporary *Kirtankar*s was most influential in reshaping regional structures of nationalist feeling, another powerful line of influence was the relaying through some Brahmin educationists of the Rashtriya Swayam-sevak Sangh (RSS) ideology. The latter drew inspiration from totalitarian movements taking place in Europe in the 1920s, notably German National Socialism. In their most exacerbated form in Maharashtra in the late 1990s and early 2000s, educational practices bore an uncanny resemblance to the earlier German ones. In RSS branches and schools, extracts from the great Hindu epics of the *Ramayana* and *Mahabharata* were read and a rather biased Indian history taught, along with a similar emphasis on bodily discipline (Sarkar 1995; Setalvad 1995). More generally, such bodily emphasis has become an integral part of physical education in schools in Maharashtra today. If it is not associated with deliberately distorted history, physical education is nonetheless put at the service of nation building and fully integrated into the morning liturgy that opened this chapter. The combination of singing and calisthenics is an essential component of daily contemporary school life that requires analysis. However, analyzing the practice of singing in India entails examining its specific and intricate relationship to the notion of *mantra* (ritual formula, chant) and its performative power.[8] It also entails exploring the homology between school and temple particularly evidenced by some of the ritual procedures extant in schools in this part of Maharashtra. (Compare Srivastava [1998], chap 4, on the elite Doon School.)

Of Performative Power, Schools, and Temples: Singing the National Goddess into Existence

> *Thou art the ruler of the minds of all people,*
> *Dispenser of India's destiny.*
> *Thy name rouses the hearts of Punjab, Sind,*
> *Gujarat and Maratha,*
> *Of the Dravida and Orissa and Bengal;*
> *It echoes in the hills of the Vindyas and Himalayas,*
> *mingles in the music of Jamuna and Ganges and is*
> *chanted by the waves of the Indian Sea.*
> *They pray for thy blessings and sing thy praise.*
> *The saving of all people waits in thy hand,*
> *thou dispenser of India's destiny.*
> *Victory, victory, victory to thee.*

India has often been labeled a "society of speech, prayers, and chants," as well as a society of discourse and "of the oratory." Whether this is specific to India is obviously debatable although unimportant here.[9] Important is the way in which speech, prayers, and chants on the one hand, and discourse and oratory

which something effect can to produce
faith + obedience produces which

on the other, combine as resources in the production of a devotional sensorium along with that of nationalist and patriotic sentiments. Crucial here is the belief in word efficacy: efficacy of the word uttered, said, chanted, and sung. It is this belief that presides over much of everyday speech and prayer, from singing and rituals in temples to politicians' endless speeches, as well as the daily reiteration of the national anthem, the pledge (*pratigyā*, hereafter *pratidnya*), and other songs, chants, and prayers in morning liturgies at school. Such efficacy lies in the notion of the word as *mantra*. In the case of the national anthem, the efficacy is unaffected by the latter's genealogical teething troubles. Contest over the narrative of its creation still prevails in Bengal today. Many oppose the version of the anthem first sung (on December 27, 1911, at the Calcutta Session of the Indian National Congress) to welcome King George V, and later in government schools and in scout groups, which fostered loyalty to the British throne.[10] Be that as it may, most parents and teachers in the schools where fieldwork was conducted in Kolhapur have reinterpreted it as a "prayer to God" (see the English translation above): from Brahmins to Marathas to allied and Scheduled castes, including some Dalits, from members of the upper-middle classes to those of the lower classes, the notion that the anthem is a prayer to God as the nation is a widespread one. Regardless of its troubled genealogy, therefore, the performative efficacy of the song as national *mantra* ensures continuity between the time of its writing by Rabindranath Tagore and the present. Moreover, contrary to its rival "Vande Mataram" (see note 10), this *mantra* is acceptable to both Hindus and other "communities" in India. For instance, Muslims, whether secularist or not, can relate to "Jana Gana Mana" as a secular masculine representation of the nation-state while ignoring any religious dimension altogether. As for many Hindu Marathi speakers, there is no contradiction between the masculine wording of the song's deity and their dedication of the anthem to Bhārat Mātā, or Mother-India; this reconfiguration of the imperial salutation for national purposes borrows from early conceptualizations of the Indian nation marked by explicit and traceable forms of Hindu religiosity redefining India as a goddess (Goswami 2004).

Here, rather, it is meaningful that *mantras* are usually considered the most important aspect of daily worship, as well as conceived as "sound aspects of the realities that they designate."[11] The enumeration of the different parts of India in the anthem truly refers to India as a deity: the several territorially named elements (Punjab, Sindh, and so on) function as metaphoric referents for the demographic components of the nation (Punjabis, Sindhis, and so on), con-

Singing the national anthem (*rashtragit*) at morning assembly. Modern Marathi School, Kolhapur, October 2000.

stituting the limbs of the "body of India" (Assayag 2001; Ramaswamy 2001, 2003). Furthermore, foremost in this act of quotidian re-creation of the national deity by means of *mantra* is the importance of proper uttering and pronunciation, according to the official pedagogy promoted in refresher courses at the Teachers' Training College of Kolhapur. In February 2000, during such a refresher course, a former local school principal taught the trainees how to teach the *rashtragit*, particularly emphasizing the importance of prosody. He made proper pronunciation central to the process of explaining the meaning of the words while pointing out on a map the regions mentioned in the anthem. So, too, in schools, did teachers throughout the day lay emphasis on the proper pronunciation of *prāmāṇit bhāṣā*, that is, the "standard" version of the Marathi language deriving its authority from its legitimacy as "superior knowledge."[12] This emphasis on proper pronunciation culminated in the pronunciation of the national anthem, toward which exertions often superseded the search for meaning. Significantly, when asked the meaning of the national song, pupils in Classes 3 and 4 did not know. By contrast, they were all able to pronounce and chant each and every word of it precisely.

Beyond the importance attached to pronunciation, the dominant praxis in schools shares other interesting similarities with religious practice, whether Brahminic or popular. The conditions of performance also bear on temple conceptualizations and procedures within the space of school. This Hindu praxeological dimension pervades the Marathi-speaking educational scene at large in Kolhapur. Here again, it is encountered at the level of both primary schools and district Teachers' Training College. The college regularly organizes one-week refresher courses throughout the year. Among these are singing courses, further testifying to the importance of songs and singing in Maharashtra and their use as a pedagogical resource. When I attended one of these *Git manch* in February 2000, one of the trainees, an experienced teacher in his midforties, elaborated on a comparison between *dev* (god), *prārthanā* (prayer), and *paripāṭha* (the routine at the time of morning assembly): "As one is at the temple, one should be at the time of paripath, collected and silent." A further illustration of this equation of school with temple can be found in one of the mottoes commonly written on classroom boards at the beginning of the school day. Mottoes exist in all types of schools, whether municipal corporation or privately run, including more secular ones run by Antar Bharati, the nationalist and socialist educational society. They are either written in chalk on the board as part of the daily "good thoughts" (*suvicār*) or in calligraphy on posters mounted on the classroom walls. One of these explicitly articulates the connection between temple and school as follows: "School is not a theater but a temple" (*Shalahi rangbhumi nasun te devalay ahe*).

The homology between school and temple requires further exploration. The similarities between the two institutions and the respective associated procedures are not only symbolic and performative but also structural. The space of school is re-created as that of a temple during the morning assembly. Worship (*pūjā*) of other, presiding deities (Ganesh and Saraswati), for example, may be performed in the equivalent of the temple's "inner sanctum" (*garbagruha*), that is, the school's office, just before or during the singing of the national anthem. Alternatively, incense is burned and waved around the office perfunctorily. Even in the most secular schools, Hindu chants will be sung, whether in Sanskrit or in Marathi. The officiating teachers are usually among the senior staff, often Brahmin or Maratha women in their mid- to late fifties. What they actively accomplish at the opening of these assemblies may in some ways be compared to preparing the deity (*alaṇkāra*), together with the crowd of "devotees"—the other teachers and the children—directing their ritual offering of singing (and calisthenics). The term *alankara* encompasses the meanings of "provid[ing], mak[ing] ready and fit for a purpose, prepar[ing]," and so on, as well as "adorning, beautifying, ornamenting." Ornamentation refers both to an object of decoration and a *process* of preparing an image of a deity for worship, of dressing that image with the attributes defining the deity. The notion of membering, giving form and power to an image (Coomaraswamy 1939: 377) is especially relevant to the school setting: the "adorning" of the nation as Bharat Mata is meant to re-create "her" anew and empower "her" daily. The hymns, "with which the deity is said to be 'adorned,' are an affirmation, a confirmation and magnification of divine power to act on the singers' behalf" (377). Associated with the notion of glorification and magnification inherent in the meaning of "adorning" is that of "leading the deity into form" by means of ritual formulas or *mantra* (Davis 1991: 128). The observation made about the Tamil temple of Tiruvanmalai at the time of the *alankara* ritual therefore obtains of the situation in school morning liturgies whereby "the divine in its maximum degree of condensation and in its multiple virtualities—*these include the Devi*—is entirely rendered present *hic et nunc* at the centre at each and every period of time during which the deity's body is constructed and reconstructed in its entirety."[13]

Thus, the performance and power of the word chanted in a temple are replicated in school. During the remaining part of the morning liturgy, the singing of the national anthem and the recitation of the pledge are followed by the utterance of yet more *mantra*s, among which is the school prayer. This can be a prayer to Saraswati, the goddess of learning; to Ganesh, the elephant-headed god, remover of obstacles, whose cult was revived by both Lokmanya Tilak (Cashman 1975) and Maratha leaders (Kaur 2004, 2005) at the turn of the twentieth century; another strophe (*śloka*); or a patriotic song.[14] This can be followed by some more *shlok*s, a moral story, news items, and another collective song (*git manch*), the latter generally secular. Concluding the re-creation of Bharat Mata is the vigorous shouting, in military fashion, of slogans such as "Bharat Mata ki Jay" (Victory to Mother India), "Hindustan zindabad" (Long live India), with right fists raised. The school day also theoretically ends with the

Morning liturgy.

chanting of either the "Pasaydan" or of "Vande Mataram," alternatively thank-
ing the goddess or "putting her to sleep." The "Pasaydan" refers to the last nine
verses of the "Gyāneśwarī" (hereafter "Dnyaneshwari") usually sung to thank
gods at the end of the school day. The morning and evening sequences may be
customized according to the schoolteachers' preferences, but it is understood
that they should always be performed in the same fashion, similar to temple
procedures described by Reiniche and L'Hernault.[15] However, as is well known,
practice often contradicts theory, and some changes do occur that disrupt the
orderly routine. What remains, then, is a sense of authoritative norms and rules
undergirded by the observance of some invariable elements—whether ritual
components or sequential structures.

At first blush, it would seem that the homology between school and temple
goes further, as the orthopraxy of speech, utterance, and pronunciation extant in
temples similarly plays a crucial part in the space of school. So do rote learning
and memorization in the performance of daily liturgies.[16] In fact, memorization
pervades the entire learning process and is in some ways a logical extension
from temple procedures, albeit with a phenomenal sociological difference:
where the temple memorizing is the privilege of an officiating elite, here it is
rendered accessible to—even forced upon—the collective social unit at large. It
must be noted, however, that memorization and rote learning are common to
many educational processes the world over and do not necessarily entail any association with temple or other religious practices. Furthermore, and as important, the homology between school and temple does not exhaust the analysis of
this morning liturgy. In many ways, what is being performed daily is a singular
mix of religious and civic rituals. So, for instance, the fact that the teachers
in charge, in some way acting as officiants and other priestly equivalents, are
women also suggests another legacy, more directly political: that of meetings of
Congress in the twentieth century where women were newly invited to participate in, and officiate, some form of public rituals.[17] Similarly, that the everyday
ritual is also meant to include presentation of news items and culling from the
morning press suggests an act of (re)connection quite comparable to that described by Anderson (1983) in other, so-called secular contexts. News reading
here converges with rote learning and memorization in the production of everyday, banal nationalism. Their use, both as a general pedagogical practice and
as continuation of a more specific value education performed in the classroom
(pāṭhāntara) bears illustration to this (however Hindu-inflected) civic and national ritual. To illustrate this, let us return to Varsity Marathi School.

At the end of the assembly just described, I followed Mandabai, the teacher in charge of the *naitik shikshan*, up to her Class 2 (pupils age seven). Unlike some other classrooms in the same school, this room had bare floors covered in rugs, with no benches or tables. Its walls were decorated with posters illustrating various topics, among them Hindu religion and nationalist leaders. After a *puja* to Saraswati, the lesson started—rather, the value education continued: first with the singing of a Ganapati *stotra* (a hymn to elephant-headed Ganesh), followed by a Maruti *stotra* (to the monkey-god Hanuman). Without pausing, the pupils then struck up a song devoted to the love of, and for, mothers (*Ai majhya guru*), followed by the "Five salutes" (*namaskārs*) (the first three addressing country, parents, and teachers); only then did they recite the lists of the Marathi and English months, respectively, the days of the week, the lunar days (*tithi*s) of the Hindu lunar month, the seasons (in both Marathi and English), the lunar asterisms (*nakshatra*s), numbers (multiplication tables), followed by all the songs and poems thus far learned from the Class 2 standard Marathi-language textbook, all sung in the same breath. All this was performed within ten minutes, rather mechanically, the children rocking their bodies to and fro while enumerating those strings of lists in repetitive tones.[18] Thus was the daily liturgy begun in the playground through singing and gesticulating continued in the classroom.

In such a continuation of the morning liturgy, the re-creation of the national mother-goddess was also mediated by displaying and conjuring more mundane representations of the nation-state. For instance, exhibits of the "body of India" figured prominently in the form of maps attached to the classroom walls.[19] These maps had either been drawn during one of the creative activities (*karyanubhav*) or, for the majority, brought by the pupils themselves. By the same token, the *paripath* ended with the recitation of currency charts. To be sure, the recitation served arithmetic and economic pedagogy. Yet it should also be apprehended in relation to the production of a sense of national belonging. Indeed, if flags and maps are conspicuous emblems of nationhood, so are coins and notes (Billig 1995: 41), and the currency is taught, learned, and remembered daily in primary schools in Maharashtra, from displays on classroom walls to the chanting of equivalences (how many paise in a rupee, etc.). Furthermore, the quotidian enumeration of these iconic manifestations of the Indian nation-form suggested an attempt at celebrating its continuity over time. Pupils chanted the equivalence of not only "new" paise to rupees but also of annas to rupees, a currency discarded since 1957 with the decimalization of Indian currency. Although elderly people—especially in rural areas—still count in annas (twenty-five, fifty, and seventy-five paise represent four, eight, and twelve annas, respectively), counting in annas did not make any sense to most schoolchildren in Kolhapur in the late 1990s and early 2000s. Yet the mere performative reiteration of this "currency chanting" was integral to the daily forging of a collective sense of nationhood, past and present. In sum, far from some "nationalist propaganda" being transmitted to the children, a nationalism totally integral to school life and everyday knowledge was actively produced by both children and teachers, offering a rather persuasive instance of daily banal nationalism (Billig 1995).

A fuller understanding of the specificity of such banal nationalism requires analysis of its associated local forms of patriotism. The definition of citizenship in this part of India is predicated upon that of belonging to Maharashtra as a cultural and political entity. If the singing of the nation into existence provides a means by which all Maharashtrians may imagine themselves as Indian citizens, in these daily school routines, the production of love for India articulates with practices of regional Maratha/Maharashtrian patriotism.[20] As is well known, the idea of an Indian independent nation was born in the time of the British Raj and eventually materialized through regional movements—drawing on what C. A. Bayly (1998) defined as "regional old patriotisms," themselves instrumental in shaping the regions (see also the seminal work of Cohn, particularly 1987b). This is especially so in the almost archetypal instances of Bengal, Maharashtra, and Tamilnadu, where clear cases of "old patriotisms" elaborated over several centuries were used by intellectuals, politicians, and other citizens as resources in the awakening of a national consciousness.[21] Chapter 4 will explore at length how Marathi speakers conceive of their relationship to the Indian nation through a regional prism (see also Benei 2001b). Here, I wish to explore further the conditions of the Marathi speakers' attachment to the nation/region and the anchoring of the attachment in regional forms of devotion. The national liturgy, apart from its unvarying sequential order and essential elements of national anthem and pledge of allegiance, is also a product of local cultural devotional forms subsumed under the notion of "devotion to the land" (*deśbhakti*).

Political Devotion, Embodiment, and Popular Participation

In a recent volume on war and politics in twentieth-century Europe, Christophe Prochasson (2002: 443) observed that to Tocqueville, every political regime was endowed with a particular emotional system. The establishment of popular sovereignty, for instance, was linked to the reign of emotions (*le règne des émotions*). Popular sovereignty entailed good rhetoric of the kind that moved people (448). Although the psychologizing of politics has been a controversial topic, Prochasson arguably draws attention to a heuristic tool. On the one hand, the validity of an argument about emotional differentiation between political regimes does not appear convincing: both authoritarian and democratic regimes have been shown in history to play on the production of similar emotional repertoires, only to varying extents. On the other hand, provided that the disdainful ring and thinly veiled characterization of democracy as demagogy be discarded, and the restrictive vision of plotting politicians rallying "the masses" by means of strategically emotional speeches be abandoned, the notion of political affect is useful for envisaging the emotive dimension inherent in *any* political process. In the next chapter, we shall examine the phenomenological aspect of such a dimension. Here I confine myself to a conceptual exploration of "what moves people" and of the ways in which political discourses and practices of devotion to the nation (*deshbhakti*) play on regional traditions of "devotion to the godhead" (*bhakti*) in Maharashtra.

Devotion to the Nation and Regional Patriotisms

The recent notion of *deshbhakti* encapsulates a "sense of loyalty to the homeland" (Bayly 1998: 27) in which the highly polysemic concept of *desh* designates the region as well as the country, and even smaller units of "patria" defined in terms of villages, clusters of villages, and fiefdoms (Bayly 1998: chap. 1; Benei 2001b; Goswami 2004). In all these senses, the *desh* is conceptualized in relation to a sense of belonging to the soil and according to a physiological-political humoral theory. This humoral notion encompasses physical well-being and social and ecological harmony, together with an ethical mode of governance characteristic of old patriotisms in India (Bayly 1998: 17, chaps. 1, 3). Furthermore, the notion of cosmic moral order entailed by the concept of *desh* is extant in the composite *swadeś*, where the prefix *swa* denotes "one's own, proper." Such a composite is often combined with the other central notions of language and "religion" that in the nineteenth century came to define a sense of belonging to the *desh*, as in the triad *swadesh, swadharma,* and *swabhāṣā* (one's own country, one's own religion, and one's own language, respectively).[22] The nationalist developments occurring in Maharashtra at the time were similar to those in various parts of India known for their strong local patriotism. Thus, the trinity *swadesh, swadharma,* and *swabhasha* was reconstructed during the anticolonial struggle in a process similar to one documented in northern India (Kumar 1992).

Concepts closely imbricated with the notion of *deshbhakti* were forged at this time and functioned as analogous referents to "Western patriotism" (Bayly 1998: 3–4): the respective Marathi and Hindi terms of *swadeshabhiman* and *swadeshhitkari*, referring to love for one's country, were purposely coined from the earlier cognate words *desh* and *deshmukh* within Indian intellectual circles. In Maharashtra, students and teachers at the Poona College played a prominent part in these conceptual redeployments (Bayly 1998: 90), similarly to processes described at length primarily in studies of Western nationalism (Hobsbawm 1992; Thiesse 1999). It is important to note, however, that these inventions were neither elitist nor "artificial." They were predicated on notions of old patriotic bonds, which may account for the root *desh* being chosen in the first place. Although these terms seem to have emerged in the early nineteenth century from "early contact between missionary dictionary-makers and the Indian learned, [they also] predated the emergence of modern nationalism by several generations" (Bayly 1998: 4). In fact, it might even be argued that some of these notions date back to earlier times, possibly as early as the fifteenth century, albeit in association with a somewhat different usage. As Bayly insists, "[The] sentiment of attachment to land and political institutions developed rapidly in some regional Indian homelands between 1400 and 1800. In particular cases, most evidently in Maharashtra, a patriotism underpinned by language, devotional religion and economic integration was energized by an expanding state which promoted themes of war and remembrance" (1998: 36).

The latter themes of war and remembrance are especially important to the official narrative articulating the establishment of self-rule (*swaraj*) in the early twentieth century with the work of *bhakti* inspired by the saints of Maharashtra, as we shall see in Chapter 4. Here, by contrast, I focus on the existence of a dominant form of patriotism that gradually built up in the course of four centuries prior to British colonization and partly drew on devotional songs and prayers. It is noteworthy that these are replete with references to the region as a geographical, if not political, unit of worship. For instance, *bhakti* to Bharat was already inscribed in the thirteenth-century *bhakti* of Maharashtrian saint Dnyaneshwar.[23] Of course, the notion of Bharat was different from that of the postcolonial nation-state of today. But it already entailed conceptualizing a larger unit that encompassed Maharashtra (actually, the hilly western ghats), in which "people could and did imagine yet wider communities" (Bayly 1998: 37).

These imaginings and senses of being part of a wider community are reflected even today in devotional popular forms, especially that of *bhajan* (song or music composition meant for worship or offering prayers to a deity, especially in *bhakti* movements). For example, most *bhajans* begin with the *shlok* "City of Alankar, holy land of religious merits" (Alamkapuri punyabhumi pavitra). This *shlok* is commonly sung in schools in Kolhapur during morning assemblies or later in the classroom, regardless of the type of school considered. The *shlok* is addressed to Saint Dnyaneshwar, native of Alandi, a famous pilgrimage site also known as Alamkapuri, "city of *Alankara*," in explicit reference to the holiness and the re-creation of the deity at the shrine. The *shlok*, which follows in the translated and original versions, was written four centuries after Dnyaneshwar died, possibly by Ramdas or one of his disciples, and is contemporary with Tukaram, a seventeenth-century Marathi poet.[24]

> Alandi, holy land full of merits
> There the holy son is being given a hard time
> Remembering him brings you heaps of great blessings
> I salute my revered guru Dnyaneshwar.

> Let all differences [among people] be ended
> Once again may this thought be espoused by Bharat [this nation]
> Let Arya dharma be a teacher to the world
> Oh god, in the world let universal "religion" prosper
> Glory to Raghuvir Samarth [i.e., Ramdas].

> Alankapuri punyabhumi pavitra
> Tithe nandto Dnyanraja supatra
> Taya athvita mahapunyarashi
> Namaskar majha shrisadguru Dnyaneshwarashi.

> Jao layala matbhed sara
> Punha varo Bharat ya vichara
> Ho-o jagaca guru arya dharma
> Deva jagi vadhwi vishvadharma
> Jay Jay Raghuvir Samartha.

The Alamkapuri shlok may obviously be interpreted differently from the context in which it was composed. Nonetheless, what ensures its contemporary relevance is the particular meaning many of the notions it contains have

acquired in the course of the last two centuries. There is no question of anach-
ronism here. It is a matter of reinterpretation and, perhaps, resonance. All the
concepts (holy land, Arya Dharma, Bharat, and so on) that bore a different
meaning in the context at the time it was written resonate with a situation
today in which social actors, whether mildly Hindu sympathetic or assertively
Hindutva, can find meaning. This is made especially possible by the collective
act of singing, which articulates devotion to the regional homeland with that
to the national homeland. Thus, in this collective expression of "telescoped"
devotion, the use of a kinship vocabulary acquires particular and renewed significance in the context of the modern nation-state.

A closer look at the translation opens windows into the association of forms
of devotion to the homeland with idioms of regional kinship and morality. The
phrase "holy son" here refers to Dnyaneshwar, whom his fellow Brahmins subjected to hardships for translating the Bhagavad Gita from the Sanskrit into
Marathi—or rather, writing a commentary on it that he would not translate
into Sanskrit. The entire *shlok* is remarkably informed by a kinship vocabulary:
suputra (auspicious son), *nandne* (being subjected to the trials of life with in-
laws, ordinarily applicable to a woman's situation), *varne* (to marry—either a
husband or a wife—and by extension, to accept willingly and forever). As noted
previously, this *shlok* is among the most popular ones in Maharashtra and commonly sung during morning assemblies in schools. The vocabulary of kinship
it invokes, also extant in other *bhakti* poems, resonates in interesting ways with
the notion of "kinsman," and by extension "brotherhood" (*bhāūband*), characterizing the national vocabulary—whether in the pledge of allegiance or in
songs—in accordance with kinship terminology usages conveying notions of
national imagined community (Anderson 1983). The idea of Indians as a large,
united family is also explicitly expressed in the pledge, a fundamental *mantra*
immediately following the national anthem as part of an unalterable sequence
in the morning liturgy. Even its solemn performative quality is meant to impart
a sense of common brotherhood: the pupils are first made to stretch out their
arms so as to stand in evenly spaced rows. The teacher in charge then summons them to begin reciting the pledge, in Marathi, while holding their right
arm horizontally as if taking an oath in court. A literal translation in English-
language textbooks reads as follows:

> India is my country [*desh*]. All Indians are my brothers and sisters [*bhauband*].
> I love my country, and I am proud of its rich and varied heritage. I shall always
> strive to be worthy of it. I shall give my parents, teachers, and all elders respect

and treat everyone with courtesy. To my country and my people, I pledge my devotion. In their well-being and prosperity alone lies my happiness.

The pledge is printed on the first page of every schoolbook from Class 2 onward, for all subjects and in all languages used as a medium of instruction. Even kindergarten and Class 1 pupils learn it from older children at the time of naitik shikshan, mumbling it as well as they can.[25] By taking this "mantra pledge" daily, schoolchildren of all ages are performatively re-creating the conditions of possibility of India as a large family of "brothers and sisters."

Fists raised while performing the "Vande Mataram" exchange with the teachers at morning assembly. Varsity Marathi School, Kolhapur, December 1998.

In many ways, *deshbhakti* in the present national sense encompasses various series of developments in the meaning and practice of Brahminic chants as well as more popular forms of *bhakti*. The latter importantly defined local idioms of morality integral to notions of social and cultural personhood, as in Tamilnadu, where long before any notion of Tamil nationalism arose, "being a good *bhakta*" was synonymous with "being a good Tamil" (Prentiss 1999: 9). The intricate entanglement of *bhakti* with the Marathi language in western Maharashtra offers a similar case evidenced in Marathi schools in Kolhapur today. Thus, in February 1999 at the Marathi Corporation School (in Sachar Bazar), when I asked Class 3 pupils what they had sung outside on the ground at the beginning of the school day, they answered, "The national anthem." As in many other instances, they were not confident about the national anthem's meaning although they knew its words perfectly. So as I asked why they sang it, along with the Ganapati *stotra* and the school prayer they performed every day, one girl responded, "Because we are devotees" (Amhi bhakta ahot, mhanun). It is on this tradition of religious patriotism that the formation of a notion of national patriotism was built, in this part of India as in Bengal and Tamilnadu. Therefore, before we explore the implications of the contemporary notion of *deshbhakti* any further, the foundational one of *bhakti* requires elaboration.

Devotion, Embodiment, and Participation

In its common usage, the term *bhakti* emphasizes "the emotional current in religious devotion" (Kakar 1999: 111). In Maharashtra, the *bhakti* tradition and its lived experience have been a powerful one since the thirteenth century, with the Marathi commentary on the Bhagavad Gita by the regional poet and saint Dnyaneshwar.[26] Even today, many sessions of *bhakti* worship, consisting of collective singing of hymns known as *bhajan*s and *kirtan*s draw on this tradition. A substantial number of the hymns and prayers sung in schools are also products of this tradition as well as of the later *bhakti* cult of Rama developed by Namdev in the fourteenth century in the tradition of Ramananda (Ahmad 1999: 151). In contrast to the habitual emphasis placed on the emotional experience of religious devotion inherent in the notion of *bhakti*, Karen Prentiss sought to offer a new perspective. Drawing on the root of the word, which signifies "to actively encourage participation" (1999: 6), Prentiss proposed an understanding of *bhakti* as a "doctrine of embodiment" that urges people toward active engagement in the worship of God. Rather than being confined to established modes of worship, *bhakti* should consequently be made the foundation of human life and activity in the world: "As a theology of embodiment, *bhakti* is embedded in the details of human life" (6).

The difficulty with Prentiss's thesis, however, lies in the fuzziness of her notion of "embodiment." The term at times refers to a personification of *bhakti* itself under the guise of a wandering woman traveling from south to north (Prentiss 1999: 31–34); at other times *bhakti* is localized in regional-language expressions, poetic voice, region, pilgrimage, and saints (40); at yet other times, the term denotes the incarnation of *bhakti* through its saints within a given tradition; and "the accessibility of God to embodied humanity . . . represented precisely in the details, including the names and life stories of special bhakta, the language of the *bhakti* hymns, and the efficacy of certain named regions" (41). It may be that by "embodiment" are meant all these definitional layers at once. Yet some clarification would help unleash the heuristic potential of this notion within the context of school. Such a notion of embodiment indeed appears crucial for an analysis of schooling and social and political devotional personhood. As an alternative theoretical perspective, it is susceptible to a phenomenological approach, for the embodied quality of (*desh*)*bhakti* also pervades life at school. Devotion to the nation is not only crystallized in the morning liturgies but imbues each and every action throughout the school day. A good *deshbhakta* should exemplify (or perhaps "embody") his or her devotion in myriad ways, ranging from the most trivial and unnoticeable to the most visible and explicit, as will be shown in the following chapters.

If the specifically postcolonial national form of *bhakti* draws on repertoires of popular devotion and participation, however, it can nonetheless not be merely equated with regional *bhakti*. Indeed, teachers summon a highly eclectic mix of older forms and traditions with newer ones dating back to the independence period—a time of high patriotic spirit and political fervor—weaving in many other strands of Marathi popular culture. Today, these unprecedentedly include Hindi-language elements.[27] Importantly, no specific orthodoxy seems to govern the selection of *shlok*s and songs other than a concern for patriotic and moral edification. Whereas the notion of *deshbhakti* is explicit in schools and teachers' training colleges, it never operates within the parameters of a purist register. For instance, teachers often seemed surprisingly unconcerned about the period and identity of the composer, or even the language of composition: asked to identify the language of a particular *shlok* (even the national anthem, for that matter), they would often indistinctly and alternately define it as Marathi or

Sanskrit. Nor did teachers lay emphasis on historical accuracy, but rather on the performative power of the words as *mantra* (see previous discussion).

Furthermore, although the national anthem and many recent patriotic songs have been included as staples, they are not restrictive, and the implementation of *deshbhakti* is deliberately left for schoolteachers to concoct. For instance, some—mainly Brahmin teachers—made collages of songs and prayers from famous excerpts in Sanskrit and Marathi *bhajan*s, including extracts from Marathi movies of the past five decades; others—Brahmins, Marathas, but also members of "lower castes"—would select Hindi pieces (especially songs from 1950s movies). In sum, this *deshbhakti* is an ever-evolving one, now encompassing features of popular culture beyond the sole region of Maharashtra, not least those of Hindi cinema. Thus unfolds a vibrant and lively "tradition" of modern *bhakti*, constantly being reshaped by all its participants. This eclecticism and amalgamation suggest a kind of bricolage, although not in the fully Lévi-Straussian sense. If the repertoire is heterogeneous, it is not limited. The Sanskrit and, more often, Marathi forms coexist with secular freedom fighters' songs, Hindi film songs, and other children's songs devoid of specific patriotic meaning. It is precisely this intertwining of ordinary children's songs together with explicitly "patriotically devotional" ones that enables naturalization of banal nationalism. Such banal nationalism is also peculiarly tainted with religion, as we have seen. In this sense, it is as much "banal Hinduism" that is being produced as "banal nationalism." How can we then assess both productions?

Secularism and Patriotism: An Unhappy Combination?

At first glance, the Marathi evidence suggests a religious conception of patriotism in antithetical relation to the apparently secular English one. The discrepancy between received English usage—generally unquestioned in discussions of secularism—and the Marathi term translating as "patriotism" results in a theoretical and semantic abyss. It is so especially in light of the latter's association with another slippery concept, that of *dharma*. The notion of *dharma* is fraught with conceptual and semantic difficulties. Compounding this difficulty is its frequent translation into an equivalent to the Western notion of "religion."[28] To begin with, it must be emphasized that the so-called separation of religion from political power is an ideal, a norm, and an incomplete and unique product of European post-Reformation history (Asad 1993; van der Veer 2001). The universalization of the concept of "religion" as an easily identifiable and watertight set of beliefs and practices enclosed in the "private" realm of individuality is closely related to Europe's exposure to the rest of the world, where it exported its specific version of modernity. Arguably, it is also from the depths of this theoretical and semantic abyss that all kinds of misunderstandings and erroneous conceptualizations may surface and develop. This renders the task of examining the implications of the notion of *dharma* ever so necessary for a discussion of secularism and patriotism, especially in view of the heightened communal tensions that have pervaded Indian society in the recent past.

On the one hand, the term *dharma* can be understood as "religion," in a way similar to the so-called book religions (Judaism, Islam, and Christianity), due both to the religious movements initiated in colonial times leading to the concept of *sanātana dharma* (eternal religion) and to subsequent developments over the past century (Thapar 1985). Notwithstanding this restrictive redefinition, *dharma* has also retained connotations of socioreligious moral order, law, and duty, making it akin to "the right order of life and worship" (Bayly 1998: 27) or, with reference to *Maharashtra dharma*, "Maharashtrian moral order" (23).[29] The notion of *dharma* therefore encompasses the meaning of "appropriate way of life." Therein lies the ambiguity and consequently the difficulty of drawing a line in everyday life between obvious *Hindutva* militancy and a mere Hindu worldview providing an idiom of morality.

In many ways, the Hindu atmosphere pervading the classroom in Marathi schools is but another instance of dominant religious and moral idioms comparable with the Christian ones that earlier generations of schoolchildren in India had to contend with during British rule (Viswanathan 1989). In this sense, *Hindu dharma* in the late 1990s and early 2000s often bore a meaning akin to "culture" among social actors belonging to a broad spectrum of political inclinations and faiths: even Muslim teachers in Marathi schools used the term in reference to a consensual dominant culture that they felt part of to variable extents. Yet some teachers, including Hindu ones, were also critically aware of the political implications of *dharma* as "Hindu religion," even if neither Muslim nor Hindu teachers openly commented on them. As often happens with sensitive issues, only in impromptu situations would this awareness surface. Such was the case in the exchange that I had with Aruna Kothe in December 1998, a few months into fieldwork at the Varsity Marathi School.

Aruna Kothe was an elderly Brahmin teacher whose strong *Hindutva* proclivities had been apparent on a number of occasions. She was also aware of the interdiction made to civil servants in Maharashtra state of being affiliated with the RSS, in stark contrast with the move made by the prime minister in the neighboring state of Gujarat at the time, with the results that are now history. Although Arunabai was close to the female Rashtriya Swayamsevika wing of the Hindu right-wing organization, she took care to specify that she was not officially part of it. One day as she asked about the main difference I perceived between schools in Kolhapur and those "in my country," I candidly offered this response: "We do not teach religion [*dharma*] at school there" (Amhi tithe dharma shikhwat nahi). Arunabai's immediate response was, "Oh, but we don't teach religion here either" (Nahi, amhi pan dharma shikhwatac nahi). What she claimed they taught in schools was "Indian culture" (*Bhārtīya saṃskṛti*). Arunabai's statement much echoes the ongoing debates in some public circles, in which the fine line between overt Hinduism as a political militant project and a culturally dominant system has been displaced from the locus of "religion" to that of "culture," with a similarly blurred result.[30] In the space of school and pedagogical discourse, this fuzziness is further compounded by the use of another, central notion, that of *saṃskār*.

The signification encompassed by the term *samskar* may alternate depending on the contexts at play. From its meaning as a "rite," "ceremony," or "sacrament," the notion also extends to "purification," "improvement," and "refinement." In the last three senses, it composes the root of other words expressing a state of being "cultured," "well reared," and "of refined taste." One of the best examples of the notion in Maharashtra lies in the well-known book written by educationist and freedom fighter Sane Guruji, *Shyam's Mother* (*Shyamci ai*). This book is one of the Marathi favorites among both teachers and children, even today. First published in 1935, it was reprinted in a thirty-fifth edition in 1999 and consists of the author's childhood recollections. Through a series of examples drawn from life experiences, Shyam's mother teaches her son several lessons about respect, generosity, and so on, all qualities contributing to the making of *samskar*. In schools, teachers like Aruna Kothe used this book as well as hymns, prayers, songs, moral stories, and thoughts for the day. They taught them to the children with the explicit purpose of cultivating *samskar*. Such moral edification, the teachers proffered, was crucial to a child learning "how to behave" (*kase wagayce*) so as to grow into a well-rounded, moral person and citizen (*nāgarik*).

How are we to reconcile these vernacular notions with the English ones of "patriotism" and "secularism"? Can these even be reconciled? The answer is not easy to determine. However, an anthropological project should attempt to address this issue, precisely through a comparative approach. What follows, then, is one such attempt. In his introduction to a collective volume on *bhakti* in North India, David Lorenzen (1996) reproached Ashis Nandy with his "anti-secularist" position. Nandy, he claimed after many others, is mistaken in his view of an all-tolerant Hinduism conceived as the cement of Indian society in lieu of a "pseudo-secularist" project lacking sense and reality for the majority of Indian people. Nandy's positions have long been attacked, especially for their utopian vision of political Hinduism. What the ethnography in this chapter suggests, however, is that if his advocacy of middle-class hegemonic Hinduism is untenable (Nandy 1990; Lorenzen 1996: 7–8), Nandy's conception of largely Hindu-inflected social and political fields in India today is certainly more attuned with vernacular praxis and conceptualization of the notion of *deshbhakti* than are those of most of his scholarly contemporaries. Arguably, any discussion of secularism in India, and for that matter any secularist project, must reckon with local empirical and historical realities. Rejecting any notion of popular devotion as "religion" and therefore taboo in the public sphere of political and academic discourse, lest one be branded a supporter of *Hindutva*, is unproductive. It misses out on the constitutive dimension of vernacular idioms of political, social, and moral personhood that have to this day shaped popular understandings of loyalty to the nation, or patriotism. To be sure, that we are dealing with *deshbhakti*, "devotion to the nation" premised on popular forms of devotion, certainly begs the question of how to conceive of a secularist attachment to the nation, or rather, the *patria*. The question here is twofold. First, it is that of the meaning of "secularist" in the Indian context. Second, it is that of the historical contingency of secular forms of political governance, in India as in Europe and elsewhere. Let me first attend to the former.

As is often remarked, secularism in India has come to mean tolerance of all creeds, rather than their relegation or disappearance from public view pure and simple. Yet there seems to be a persistent misunderstanding in the debates about secularism conducted in the English language, because of their seeming obliviousness to the various vernacular understandings of the term. To be sure, the public hue and cry over the celebration of the nation through particular forms of "religious" devotion rightly and poignantly draws attention to the disruptive implications these may have for non-Hindu citizens. And indeed, the pedagogical predication of citizenship on the Hindu moral notion of *samskar* always runs the risk of overinterpretation by extreme right-wing elements of the society consequently rejecting alternative visions and constructions of citizenship, thereby denying the status of fully fledged citizenship to members of "minority communities," that is, non-Hindu ones. Therein lie all the ambiguity and slipperiness of

Indian secularism. For the Hindu majority, the notion of "secular"—in the sense of ecumenical—is manifested in Hindu praxis. Even songs seeking to promote tolerance of all religions are couched in the terms of a Hindu prayer and performed in similar ways in schools. Such is the case of the commonly sung "Unity Song" ("Khara ci ek to dharma" or "Ekatmata git").[31] Yet this should not preclude one from envisaging a peaceful Hinduism, reconciled with other "religions." The forms of *bhakti* centered on the Vithoba shrine at Pandharpur, for instance, brought about "a certain measure of reconciliation with the presence of Islam in India" (Ahmad 1999: 151). Most influential among Marathi saints, Tukaram (b. 1608) shared a similar conception of God as Kabir's and occasionally used Sufi terms in his hymns.[32]

Granted, such reconciliation is tenuous, as suggested by Ahmad, who remarks: "And yet according to Tara Chand 'he was a contemporary of Shivaji and one of the inspirers of the spirit which welded the Marathas into a people'" (1999: 151). To Ahmad, this translates as "another interesting case of Bhakti eclecticism paving the way for anti-Muslim militarism." Whether this view of *bhakti* is fully justified or not may be a matter of debate. The fact nevertheless is that other later religious reform movements did emerge in antagonistic construction against Muslims. Such is the case, for instance, of the Hindu cow movement that spread in northern India in the nineteenth century as part of a communalist and nationalist awakening (Pandey 1990). Maharashtrian revolutionary leaders, who founded the (in)famous RSS in Nagpur in 1925, were also eager to promote the cow protection movement. It is with this history in mind that the educational project of the late 1990s and early 2000s in Maharashtra should be approached, and the potentially deleterious implications of the new textbooks envisaged. A simple example should suffice: that of the 1999 version of the Class 5 *Marathi as a Second Language Textbook*, whose main client minorities in Maharashtra are Muslims. Lesson 17 consists of a poem celebrating the virtues of the cow, ending with "This is how useful the cow is, it [feels, looks] like a second mother!" (Ashi upyogi ahe, gay, waatte jashi ki dusri may!) (35). The injunction clearly resonates with the precepts of Hindu *sanatana dharma* and the cow protection movement. Moreover, given that the prelude to communal riots from the late nineteenth century onward involved the slaying of cows on the Muslim side (and that of pigs on the Hindu side), this exhortation by Marathi-speaking educationists to respect the cow as a mother must be interpreted as an explicit command especially targeting Muslim communities. Such a command owes to the counterprojection against Muslims that was instrumental in the historical and ideological construction of the Marathas into "a people" over the past centuries (Chapter 4). Nevertheless, *bhakti* in its most reconciliatory forms bears potential for the pursuit of a truly secular society. This potential might profitably be acknowledged, celebrated, and nurtured, especially in the renewed climate of communalism in India today.

Furthermore, if such an emphasis on the religious dimension of local forms of patriotism and nationalism may still appear far removed from developments that occurred in the so-called West (van der Veer 1994, 2001), it may not necessarily be so on closer look at the categories of secularism and patriotism. To begin with, the idea that ethics and values can be empirically separated into personal and social categories is a fallacy, even in Europe and the United States. As important, the category of "patriotism" in most European languages entails notions of Christian religion and culture, not only in Britain, which is constitutionally a Christian kingdom, but in other nation-states less explicitly religiously informed. Historically, the notion of patriotism involves the transposition of a notion of "defense of Holy Land" to that of national soil, and vice versa, with the concept of Holy Land developing in association with that of *patria Christi* from the later Middle Ages (thirteenth century) to the twentieth century. The kingdom became *patria* (fatherland), an object of political devotion and semireligious emotion (Kantorowicz 1981). In the early thirteenth century, the only domain where *patria* had retained its full original meaning was in the language of the Church. A Christian was a citizen of a city in another world. The true *patria* was the kingdom of Heaven. A Christian martyr, who had offered himself up for the invisible polity and died for his divine Lord, was the genuine model of civic self-sacrifice. The new territorial concept of *patria* therefore developed as a secularized offshoot of a Christian tradition. Thus, the new patriotism thrived on ethical values transferred from *patria* in heaven to polities on earth. The equation of *patria* with the "holy soil" is especially relevant here: the patriotic notion was endowed with religious, emotional values whereby to defend and protect the soil of one's country came to have "semireligious" connotations relating to the defense and protection of the sacred soil of the Holy Land itself. Consequently, death in Crusaders' wars became interpreted as self-sacrifice for one's *patria* as well as for the Holy Land, and the sacrifice being realized for one's brothers similar to the self-sacrifice Christ had made for humankind. Thus, an emotionally powerful religious connotation of political death in war as the transposition of Christian martyrdom to war victims of secular states has been effected even in the West. To this day, such connotations have retained their evocative force, both symbolic and emotional, as testified to across Europe by the annual memorial services to the Great War (celebrated in church in Britain, as opposed to lay services in France—*laïcité oblige!*); or even, in Britain, the annual "poppy appeal" to contribute to the fund for those killed in war and the aura of sacredness surrounding it. Mention need not even be made of the embeddedness of a Christian idiom in the *doxa* and praxis of internal and external U.S. politics. All these developments across a wide range of temporalities signal a need to reconsider the too often assumed radical difference of the West in matters secular, however the term is to be defined. These same developments must be considered in any balanced understanding of political processes elsewhere in the world of nation-states, especially in India.

Openings

This chapter has described and discussed the daily performance of the nation in India and the various cultural, symbolic, and devotional repertoires it concomitantly draws upon and reshapes. Such a quotidian performance occurs only at school, and in no other modern institution (apart, possibly, from the army), making school a unique site for the ritual creation and embodiment of the nation as well as a space that reflects, resonates with, and amplifies ideological processes at play within larger society. The collective (re)enactment of national devotion and the production of an emotional attachment to the nation are predicated upon an everyday devotional sensorium. Although the latter is largely informed by religious notions of popular Hinduism subsumed by the concept of *bhakti*, the production of emotional attachment is by no means specific to Indian schools. Mass education plays a similarly prominent role in building national love the world over. What is singular are the modalities of nation worship, coterminous with vernacular idioms—ritual and linguistic—rooting patriotism in local forms of devotion. Devotion to the nation here is partly predicated on local popular forms of *bhakti*, commonly translated as "devotionalism," some of which hark back to the thirteenth century. As we have seen, however, these forms of devotion to the region and the nation do not exhaust the cultural repertoire at play.

Furthermore, if the contents of these devotional forms are specific, their conceptual associations share some similarities with other forms of patriotism existing in Europe and North America. In European schools, for instance, it is through the idea of the nation that children are taught legitimate feelings of love, learning paeans and poems in celebration of the nation's grandeur and beauty (Thiesse 1999: 238). The specificity of the institution in a relatively new nation-state such as India, however, is to place emphasis upon the national *integration* of all citizens. Perhaps this integration is nowhere more realizable than in particular locales whose very construction is predicated upon such an integrative vision. That, as suggested by Johnny Parry, in the Nehruvian space par excellence of the Bhilai steel plant, people from all parts of India should be more tolerant of faith, class, regional, and ethnic differences proves the point.[33] As for other places, the local historical configurations at play may jeopardize achievement of such an integrative project. Indeed, there exists an arresting tension between the secular ideal professed by the constitution and the regional implementation of the national project. On the one hand, citizens are invited to view themselves as part of a single imagined community, in spite of their differences. That this is still considered a fundamental prerequisite in Maharashtra, both by the state's successive governments and the teachers, is evidenced not only by the continuous directives given in this respect but also in the choice that teachers make of teaching patriotic songs to the children. On the other hand, as we have seen, the repertoire of these songs is a long-standing Hindu one; even Hindi and Marathi movies dating from the independence period to this day are endowed with such pervasive "Hinduness" (Vasudevan 2000; Benei 2004). Popular and public culture is therefore central to teachers' negotiations of the state goals and objectives, whether in their capacity as its representatives or as ordinary citizens. In this process, ordinary social actors' agency surfaces most prominently. This bears further elaboration.

Due to the nature of the project, a tension will be perceptible throughout the book between a Spinozist framework and one granting some degree of free will and agency to those passion- and emotion-stirred social agents in their processual identification to locality, region, and nation. The project, while concerned with documenting the institutional production of national allegiance and its attendant construction of the state in everyday life, also seeks to make meaning of varyingly coherent fragments of state projects as much as of ordinary actors' lives. It seeks to illuminate how social actors, including children, are not simply passive agents; they negotiate these multifarious processes, singularly and individually. The wide array of possible negotiations ranges from almost unconditional allegiance and wholesome identification to downright rejection, via claims to leeway or autonomy, not always explicit but nevertheless extant, if only in the form of minimal discursive subversion. Examples of such individual negotiations may be found in regular acts of mild insubordination, such as regularly coming in late to school or reluctantly performing devotion and allegiance to Bharat Mata during morning assemblies by mumbling the national anthem or the pledge. Of course, empirical evidence can only be fragmentary, as none of the pupils so explicitly articulated acts and personal views, whether in the space of school or the intimacy of home. It may also be that these acts of negotiation are much easier to acknowledge and articulate several decades later, regardless of the nation-state to which they pertain. And so the seemingly sibylline quote at the beginning of this chapter may now be appositely situated more fully, and justice rendered to Ernest Gellner's account of his summer camp memories in former Czechoslovakia (1991: 63):

> I did regularly go to summer camp, and the ritual of raising the flag was accompanied by an oath of loyalty to the Czechoslovak republic, and I always used to miss out one word. Not because I had any intention of committing high treason against the republic—quite the contrary: the family had basically loyal gratitude for Masarykian liberalism. But I didn't see why I should close my political options so early: I didn't wish to bind myself. It seemed to me slightly premature, and I hadn't figured it all out. So I used to miss out one word of the oath at random. A sentence which has no sense does not commit you to anything. I would not articulate some parts of the sentence in such a way that the whole sentence made no sense as an oath and consequently didn't bind me.

In the following interludes and chapters, we shall encounter other examples of such negotiations while analyzing of the production of national(ist) emotions as processes of embodiment. Articulating with a discussion of a devotional sensorium, discussions of the phenomenological implications of the "affective shaping of nationhood" (Yano 1995: 20) will also lead us to explore negotiations of a linguistically incorporated sensorium: Marathi-language ideology therein provides a potent frame for defining idioms of morality associated with the attempted making of a well-rounded civic person, a true samskara-predicated national bhakta or devotee citizen.

National Anthem
and Other Life Stories

Of Bharat Mata and Sunita's Grandmother

It is *naitik shikshan* time at Modern Marathi School, just outside the bustling heart of the city. This morning, Sunita left home with a heavy heart. Aji's health has been going from bad to worse these days, and Pappa is very worried. Everybody loves Aji in the house because she tells so many great stories of when Pappa was a little boy; she would take him to the market with her, and he would say clever things to the shopkeepers. But Aji is not the same since Baba left them last year. It was one of these cold winter days, and Baba had been lying in bed for a while, with some infection in his chest, eight-year-old Sunita recalls. Baba passed away during the night, leaving Aji alone after so many years spent together raising their children and grandchildren. Sunita could not help her mind wandering away as she stood in her column preparing herself to start singing the national anthem with her fellow pupils. Baba and then Aji—this was so sad. "Sawdhan, rashtragit suru ke liye, teyar! Rashtragit suru kar!" bellowed Mandirabai, the teacher in charge of the morning liturgy while beginning to play the peti. As the sound of the accompanying drumbeat resonated, played by some Class 4 girl, the junior pupil straightened herself and started singing along with the others. Sunita had always enjoyed humming the anthem, especially when attending public functions with her parents on holidays, like that Republic Day she was not so sure what it was about, something to do with the country—that much she was positive about. And "Bhagwan" [means "God"] did she love her country! Pappa and Ai had explained to her how lucky she was to be living in India, a proud and ancient country. In class, too, all her teachers had always emphasized how beautiful and great a country this was, for which they should all have cause for pride. Bharat Mata, their mother to all. So we should try to do everything for her, Kumarsaheb had once explained. Even the rockets shot the year before—whether into space or in the desert—Sunita was not sure why it mattered—but she remembered that people had become so excited at home, in her neighborhood, and generally all the "big people" (grown-ups) she knew around her. This would protect Bharat Mata and them all for sure, especially against Pakistan. Even Mohanbhai, the shopkeeper around the corner from home, who used to be so quiet and shy around his customers, even he had shared in the general rejoicing. And all of this was in "her" honor. So was the national song, and in honor of all Indian mothers. So it made you so jolly to start the day singing it. This had been one of Sunita's favorites since kindergarten, although of course, in those days, she could hardly say the words. But by the end of Class 1, she and all her friends knew them by heart. And so heartily did they sing. Yet that morning, as Sunita found herself singing, tears suddenly began rolling down her cheeks. She could not really tell what was happening to her. The song, the feeling of pride, the sadness of her heavy heart, all of these intense feelings commingled within her. She felt the salty liquid insistently dropping to the corner of her mouth. At last the anthem ended, and she was able to wipe her face and recompose herself, in a few moments of respite adjusting her distance from the pupils around her to take the pledge. With a bit of luck, nobody would have noticed.

Anil and This Thing You Sing in the Beginning

Anil was not late to school today. For once, the soon-to-be nine-year-old even made it in time for the *paripath* at Varsity Marathi School. The *paripath*, that thing you sing in the beginning, with all the others. Even the teachers sing it. And you'd better stand still and pretend, because otherwise they come and slap you on the head. Especially Radhabai—oh, that slap she gave Prakash the other day. Oh well, yes, I know, we are supposed to be standing properly and straight right through all of it, especially the *jana-gana-mana* song. Even if you can't sing, you have too. And so I pretend; I even pretend I know the words. But in fact I don't. Am not quite sure what it is about anyway. Bharat Mata sure enough, but why should this matter so much? I find it so boring to have to go through all this stuff, with the prayers and all. But you are not supposed to say so, so I keep quiet. Even with Prakash and Atul, or Pradeep, we never speak about it. So if you can't tell your best friends, or even your own brother, who can you tell?

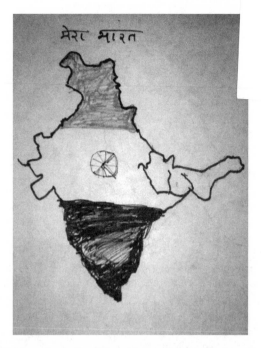

Map of India colored as the national flag. The caption, in Hindi, reads "My India" (Mera Bharat). All India Marathi School, Kolhapur, February 1999.

Surely not any grown-up. They are all so serious about it. Or maybe that foreign bai who comes in ever so often and sits in the classroom with us. *She* does not seem to be so worked up by it. Once she walked in late and did not even stop until the end of the song. Somebody must have told her afterward, because now she looks like she stands straight and still with everybody else, even if she can't sing along, and after all, it is not her country; why should she; she keeps very quiet until all of it is done. Oh, I'd better watch out; Rukminibai is glaring at me. What have I done? And so Anil straightened himself up, just in time to shout "Bharat Mata ki Jay," mechanically raising his fist with his fellow pupils.

2 Producing Good Citizens
Languages, Bodies, Emotions

[A]nd the body is our anchorage in a world.
Maurice Merleau-Ponty, *Phenomenology of Perception*

Political integration has already taken place to some extent, but what I am after is something much deeper than that—an emotional integration of the Indian people so that we might be welded into one, and made into one strong national unit.
Jawaharlal Nehru

Just like you have sucked your mother's milk, you have at the same time imbibed your mother's language.
Shantabai Vankudre, mother of Sushila, Class 3

THE CLASSROOM IS RATHER BARE, with four to five rows of wooden planks aligned on the floor for the pupils to sit on, a few posters of the national and regional leaders (*nete*) stuck onto the dark painted walls, and an uneven board covered in neatly chalked words. These would hardly be legible in the room darkened by the stormy, cloudy skies of a March afternoon were it not for the light filtering in through the half-closed shutters. At times, a slight breeze gently pushes the shutters back and forth, relieving the fanless room's occupants from the humid heat. Behind the small desk to the right of the board is sitting Mr. Pawar. The young Class 3 teacher, in his early thirties, was posted two years before, in 1997, at Marathi Corporation School. The school is one of seventy-two run by the municipality of Kolhapur. Located in the slum area of Sachar Bazar, the institution is also competing with the All India Marathi School, founded and run by the progressive socialist Antar Bharati society, and the Urdu Corporation School that caters to most of the Muslim students of the area. Apart from its small size, however, nothing really distinguishes Marathi Corporation School from its counterparts: the teachers have undergone the same training as their colleagues and are equally paid by the state government. Their schooling years have been similarly shaped by a patriotic education geared toward national "emotional integration." The latter was deemed "easily the most important component element . . . of . . . national integration" in a homonymous *Report* (1962: 1) commissioned by Jawaharlal Nehru in the late 1950s. "Emotional integration" has been a staple of the national curriculum for the past forty years. Even today, the report in which the concept first appeared in many ways prefigures and informs much of the ideology undergirding life in primary schools in Maharashtra. Emotional integration is not only instantiated in textbook contents but also permeates routines and procedures of daily national production, whether during morning liturgies (Chapter 1) or in classrooms like that of Mr. Pawar.

The Marathi lesson has already started. Today, it is devoted to a recapitulation of the vocabulary learned in the course of the past few months. Mr. Pawar has concocted a revision schedule of his own based on the syllabus. His neat and clear handwriting covers the entire board: words in four columns on the left-hand side face whole sentences on the right. Armed with a ruler, he points to each word methodically, column after column, the pupils repeating the words in chorus. At times the teacher interrupts his enumeration to call for a distracted pupil's attention, firing copious chalk bullets at the recalcitrant pupils; at other times he selects several students to repeat words and sentences one after another. And so the repetition goes:

"My school is very nice, my village is beautiful, I like my country very much, I have pride and respect in my country, in my country live people from different jāt,[1] in my country people live happily." [Majhi shala chan ahe, Majhe gaon sundar ahe, Majha desh mala khup avadto, Majhya deshaca mala abhiman ahe, Majhya deshat vividh jatice lok rahtat, Majhya deshatil lok anandane rahtat.]

Mr. Pawar's choice of words and sentences is nothing exceptional in this part of India. Rather, his examples are integral to the daily iterations of devotion to the Indian nation in the Marathi language. Although the lexical selection here is clearly informed by the official textbook in use in every Class 3 across the regional state, it also partly stems from Mr. Pawar's own inspiration. For there exists no stipulation of procedures for vocabulary revisions along such explicitly national lines. Asked why he chose these examples in the first place, Mr. Pawar seemed somewhat puzzled. He had not really given it much thought. Wasn't it obvious that children had to be taught how to love their country (deshvar prem thevayce) and become good citizens (cangle nagarik huvayce)? Was it not the

it because natural through repetition constant reiteration

same where I came from? This, then, is an illustration of Maharashtrian and Indian nationalism at its most banal level of quotidian experience.

How does the nation become this natural object of devotion, and what are the modalities of this "affective shaping of nationhood" (Yano 1995: 20)? How are political emotions constructed? In the previous chapter we conducted a conceptual and ethnographic exploration of "what moves people" and of the ways in which political discourses and practices of *deshbhakti* play upon regional traditions of devotionalism in the production of a national devotional sensorium. This exploration brought home the usefulness of the notion of political emotion for envisaging the emotive dimension inherent in political and social processes. I now turn to the phenomenological entailments of such a notion by addressing the issue of the intertwined production of ideals of love of nation and good citizenship feeding into the construction of national citizens. This requires identifying the kind of labor that goes into the naturalizing objectification of the nation, and through what mediations. This chapter explores the mediation of language, both as ideology and incorporated practice. Rather than confining my analysis to the level of linguistic performance, I also examine the embodiedness of discourse on language. My reflection is situated at the crossroads of three main anthropological trends: an anthropology of emotions, of bodies, and of language ideology. Anthropology, and the other social sciences to varying extents, has been marked by various genealogies of works reinstating the body as a primary medium for socialization. That socialization does take place largely through social actors' bodies—however these are to be defined and located, socially, culturally, historically, and politically—has by now become a commonplace. Similarly, it has been firmly established that language and emotion are social, cultural, and political practices. Yet little work has sought to explore the intersections of the production of language ideologies and emotions with any notion of embodiment in the formation of national attachment. In this chapter, I seek to illuminate the crucial dimension of *embodied* linguistic emotions of national belonging nurtured through schooling.

Elsewhere (Benei 2001b) I showed how children through morning liturgies create their physical selves while enacting and embodying the nation into existence. I want to pursue this approach here and explore the ways in which the body is not only one of the main sites of inscription of a national project of citizenship through the disciplining procedures extant in everyday life at school but, as crucially, a phenomenological site of feeling and experiencing the construction of the nation. In other words, the body is not solely acted upon and acting in a subjected rapport to discipline and inscription of the law; it is a *felt and feeling* body. Arguably, much of the production of national bonds in the early years of socialization, especially schooling, involves teaching and learning how to "feel" the nation. Here I aim to unravel the joint modalities of embodied self-formation and instantiation of the nation, and its articulation with idioms of citizenship. As I will also suggest, the plasticity of the body is, however, not exhausted by either this national emotional sensorium or its associated project of collective and individual self-formation.

First, I want to take you out of Mr. Pawar's classroom on the periphery of Kolhapur and drive you fast-forward in time, to another, more popular school situated in the bustling heart of town. It is a year later, at the Varsity Marathi School, one of the oldest privately run Marathi primary schools. It is Saturday noon, and the school day has just ended. We are in the teachers' room. The new Congress government in the regional state has just announced its decision to introduce compulsory English from Class 1 onward. Ms. Kirari, the school headmistress, who, like many of her colleagues, has always voiced her pride in her "Indian culture," is strongly opposed to such a measure. She is vehemently discussing the government's intention with her staff. I have known Kirari Bai well for over two years. She is a strong-willed and generous lady in her early fifties and is often rather outspoken. Never have I seen her behave so passionately. Her face is red with anger, her hair flying loose as she gestures forcefully in the course of her diatribe against the new government's "populist policy."

A few days later, when we meet again, Kirari Bai takes up the topic afresh on her own initiative. Although she has cooled down by now, she makes no mystery of how dear to her heart the issue of language is, shaking her head in negation: "No, it is definitely not good, one should not do it." "Why not?" I prompt her. Her answer is pat:

> "Before, we had the Moghuls, in the times of the Muslims, and we had to learn the Persian [*Farsi*] language. Then with the advent of Shivaji the Marathi language was successfully imposed. But then, later on, the English came and forced their English language on us. Then we got our independence, and our Marathi, our own language [*swabhasha*] back again. Now, what is the point of imposing the firangi [English] language on us again? Besides, learning in a foreign tongue is just so unnatural [*aswābhāvik*]. Learning in a foreign language is not right [*barobar nāhī*]; it hinders the child's development. It is more natural [*swābhāvik*] to learn in one's mother tongue [*mātr bhāṣā*]."

Throughout this chapter I will use Kirari Bai's visceral linguistic performance as a guiding thread and tease out its underlying understandings, assumptions, and implications. But first, let me delineate the contours of my theoretical positioning at the crossroads of an anthropology of emotions, bodies, and language ideologies.

Public Emotions or Private Feelings?
Toward Phenomenological Reconciliations

My purpose here is not to offer one of many possible genealogies of the wealth of works on emotions in anthropology. Rather, it is to highlight some important developments and emphasize avenues yet to be fully explored in light of a phenomenological approach. Hildred Geertz long ago suggested in her work on Java that outside/inside feelings and emotions are mutually constructed by adjustments and approximations (1974: 261). It is in the process of social interaction that people can form both their own personal and more or less collectively adjusted understandings of the specific repertoires of culturally legitimated emotions at their disposal. Geertz's insight, however, remained rather isolated in the following decades. Only in the past twenty years has emerged a critical engagement with the theories of emotion that had remained prevalent in the social sciences. These theories propounded particular ideologies of self, gender, and social relations that reinforced the notion of higher forms of rationality characterized as technical, nonemotional, and nonmoral, in opposition to the "private realm of home, family, and love" as the site of individual expression of real, authentic selves. In the United States, Joe Errington was among the first to criticize such a dichotomous vision of emotion and reason. He was soon echoed by Michelle Rosaldo (1984), whose article on self and feeling sought to approach emotion as intricately and complexly interwoven with systems of cultural meaning and social interaction. Lila Abu-Lughod and Catherine Lutz—both separately and in a collective volume (Abu-Lughod 1986; Lutz 1988; Abu-Lughod and Lutz 1990)—further engaged with these "tropes of interiority" supposedly defining the proper realm of emotions in association with the natural body. By virtue of their location in the natural body, emotions were then deemed as the most innate and irrational, hence least lending themselves to sociocultural analysis. Turning this position and its attendant *doxa* on its head, Abu-Lughod and Lutz sought to understand emotional discourses as "pragmatic acts and communicative performances" (1990: 11), placing an emphasis on the fundamental constructedness of emotions.

This furthered an understanding of the social and cultural dimensions of emotions, highlighting their negotiated nature as cultural constructs, in a dialectic between universality of feelings and the culturally specific range of their definitions, productions, and experiences. At the same time, the understandable distrust in Western theorizing of emotions led to an overemphasis on cultural relativity and distinctiveness at the expense of both theoretical and experiential convergences. Furthermore, the anthropological discourse of emotion became predominantly concerned with verbal productions, whether everyday conversation (including songs, poems, etc.) or more formal, elaborate, or artistic. Although acknowledged in these explorations, the bodily discourse on emotion was relegated to the margins of analysis.[2] In other words, emphasizing the sociality of emotions often entailed glossing over their individuated bodily production, depriving anthropology of the possibility of reflecting upon the phenomenological experience of their joint formation with that of social and individual bodies. However, all emotions are expressed and displayed by means of *bodily* performance, whether collectively or individually. As Margaret Lyon has insisted, social relationships are "necessarily bodily: social processes are not just given being through ideas, rules, and customs" (1995: 254). Lyon's further comment more than a decade ago that "[i]t is through the study of emotion that anthropology may best be fully 're-embodied'" (256) has powerful resonance even today, despite recent theoretical attention paid to the phenomenological dimension of emotion.[3] It is also an invitation to further our understanding of emotion by giving recognition to the body not only in relation to the mind but also as integral to the conception of emotion per se (256).[4]

Bodies, as is by now established, are as much the principal medium for most socialization processes as they are social and cultural constructions. Bourdieu's notion of "bodily hexis" as a "set of body techniques and postures that are learned habits or deeply ingrained dispositions that both reflect and reproduce the social relations that surround and constitute them" (as summarized by Abu-Lughod and Lutz 1990: 12) has become received wisdom in the social sciences. Other works have made much of Foucault's insights into disciplinary processes (1979) and the notion of individuals', agents', subjects', actors' bodies as the site of the "inscription of the law."[5] Arguably, heeding the embodied dimension of socialization also illuminates the processes at play in the quotidian production of national imaginings and senses of belonging. Among other things, an emotional, embodied discourse of the nation is produced in the morning rituals as much as in the ordinary school day routine in Kolhapur. It does not consist only of words, verbal utterances, and gestures, through which emotion, however defined, is expressed at every level of language, from intonation to inflection, grammar—especially syntax—and vocabulary (Ochs and Schieffelin 1989; Besnier 1990; Irvine 1990; Errington 1998a, 1998b). It is also concrete, physical, embodied. For this reason, it is as much a collective discourse as an individuated one (or whatever finer continuum of experientiality between these two arbitrary extremes is available as a cultural resource), without any necessary implication of primacy or authenticity of one over the other.

Bodies, Emotions, Nations

> [O]ur mental life is knit up with our corporeal frame, in the strictest sense of the term.
>
> **William James, "What Is an Emotion?"**

As intimated earlier, Michelle Rosaldo's article inspired a large part of the intellectual approach to be found in later work on emotion. However, such inspiration has been partial, for Rosaldo was genuinely interested in the notion of embodiment. She explicitly referred to "flushes, pulses, 'movements' of our livers, minds, hearts, stomachs, skin" as "*embodied* thoughts, thoughts seeped with the apprehension that 'I am involved'" (1984: 143). Such a phenomenological awareness seems to have been lost in much subsequent work.[6] I want to pause on Rosaldo's comment of "I am involved," which resonates with the approach developed by Maurice Merleau-Ponty in his *Phenomenology of Perception* (1989). Drawing upon earlier conceptions that emerged in the late nineteenth century (especially Husserl's notion of "I-can"), Merleau-Ponty expanded on the notion of the body as the medium of involvement in the world. Rather than the objective body, he saw the "phenomenal body," that which has a representation/consciousness/image of itself, as our medium for relating to the world: "The body is the vehicle of being in the world, and having a body is, for a living creature, to be intervolved in a definite environment, to identify oneself with certain projects and be continually committed to them" (1989: 82). This conceptualization of human beings anchored in the world through their bodies parted with a dualistic—and still prevalent—assumption of disjunction between organism and psyche (88).[7] Here I want to take this insight into an exploration of the ways in which bodies are, through what might at first sight appear "mere" disciplining, also made to feel the nation in the space of school.

Even in schools where the morning assembly would regularly take no more than ten minutes, the body always operated as a fundamental vehicle for producing a national attachment, with different drills being practiced at each stage. In the process, the idea of the body of the nation (Assayag 1997) was enacted by the pupils, congruently with the idea advanced more than a century ago by the historian of religions Ernest Renan (Prologue). In all the schools visited, pupils would sing the national anthem while standing, keeping their bodies upright and stiff, arms alongside. This would be followed by the recitation of the pledge (*pratidnya*) in Marathi, with the children holding their right arm horizontally as if taking a pledge in court. After the *pratidnya* would ensue the school prayer, other *shlok*s, and more contemporary songs, promoting various topics ranging from national unity to girls' schooling. All these sung items were often interspersed with simple calisthenics, involving arm raising, repeatedly putting the legs apart and together, sideways movements of the arms, and so on. Orchestrating the session, the teacher in charge—often a middle-aged Brahmin or Maratha woman—would lead the children into gymnastic movements while singing along with them. In many schools, this was accompanied by continuous drumming performed by an office boy, a teacher, or a pupil while the other teachers stood by their divisions and joined in the singing, their bodies stiff and their facial expressions grave, adding to the martial physicality of the ceremony. What we have here is an exemplification of incorporation of a "spontaneous" national sentiment, also acknowledged—yet hardly documented—in Europe (Thiesse 1999: 14). This incorporation is integral to the child's everyday life, blending patriotic sentiment with other, ordinary matters (Chapter 3).

Moreover, the idea of this national physical integration is made very explicit in the official textbooks produced by the Maharashtra State Bureau and in some of the supplementary ones used for physical education prepared for each class by private educational publishers. Thus, the textbook *Vocal and Physical Education* (*Sangit ani Sharirik shikshan*) designed for Class 4 and published by Vikas (literally, "progress") starts with the *pratidnya* and the *rashtragit*. It includes the song "Jay Bharta," inspired by the national anthem and additionally glorifying Hindu gods and all the various revolutionaries and builders of modern and independent India.[8] The song also appears as the first lesson in the official Class 3 Marathi-language book, together with explicit instructions as to how it should be practiced and repeated individually and collectively, accompanied by, or interspersed with, calisthenics.

This disciplining of bodies, both at the time of the morning liturgy and later on in the classroom, is regulated by the concept of *sista*. Commonly translated as "discipline," the term also refers to the controlled immobility and stiffness that pupils are expected to adopt, whether during phenomenological experiences of daily assembly in alternating drills and physical training (PT) movements with rigid, standing postures or in classroom situations. A teacher calling for pupils' silence or attention, for instance, will often shout: "Shistit basayce; gap basayce" (Sit properly; shut up [literally, "sit quiet"]). As important, the notion of *shista* encompasses the meaning of moral rectitude and is explicitly enacted as such in everyday school life as well as in the official pedagogy. To give an example, the Class 3 Marathi book mentioned contains another instance of incorporation of the nation: the very first story in the language manual emphasizes the bodily and moral rectitude to be observed while singing the *rashtragit*. It is a masterpiece of the nationalist pedagogical genre and a wonderful Bourdieusian illustration of how "obedience is belief and belief is what the body grants even when the mind says no."[9] The story is narrated by a schoolteacher and is about untrained schoolchildren on their first school day. The narrative adroitly weaves another story into the plot, that of a retired army officer (*subhedar*) walking past the school with a water jug in hand. As he hears the shouting of the call to attention (*sāwadhān*, the call marking the beginning of both military and nationalist school drills, as well as ending the first ritual in wedding ceremonies; see Benei 1996), the retired officer "instinctively" straightens himself up to adopt the *shista* position and drops his jug to the ground. The last words of the story provide an excellent illustration of the intricate relationship between the teaching of the nation and the disciplining of bodies:

> Like [that of] the *subhedhar*, the body of each schoolchild should become proper, fit . . . . While singing the *rashtragit*, correctness should be displayed. Whenever and wherever our country's *rashtragit* is started playing, we must stop and stand in the *sawdhan* position; we must show respect to our *rashtragit*! (*Marathi Bal Bharati* 1998: 11)

This intricate interplay of bodily and moral rectitude undergirds the attempted production of a social body of future generations of Indian citizens: a social body that should ideally be unconditionally devoted to loving and serving the nation. These last two aims of unity of and love for the nation are made explicit in the pledge, as we saw in the previous chapter. In many ways, this example of schooling projects draws attention to the embodied kind of morality integral to the formation of personhood and citizenship, and to which language socialization practices crucially contribute while shaping notions of ethnicity and cultural identity (Garrett and Baquedano-Lopez 2002: 350). I now turn to these language socialization practices.

Language Ideologies, Standardization, and Nationalism

Language invites people to unite, but it does not force them to do so.
Ernest Renan, *Qu'est-ce qu'une nation?*

Language acquisition obviously entails more than a child simply learning to produce "well-formed referential utterances" (Garrett and Baquedano-Lopez 2002: 342).[10] It involves the child's developing skills in order to use language in socially appropriate ways and make meaning of culturally relevant contexts and activities. These are determined by language ideologies, that is, "self-evident ideas and objectives a group holds concerning roles of language in the social experiences of members as they contribute to the expression of the group" (Heath 1989: 53, quoted in Woolard 1998: 4). In other words, ideologies of language articulate historical constructions with the developmental process of language acquisition, as well as with local notions of cultural and group identity, nationhood, personhood, and childhood (Garrett and Baquedano-Lopez 2002: 353–64). Working with the notion of language ideology has rendered possible a "debunking" of the claims to pristine purity and authenticity inherent in most nationalist language ideologies. In particular, it has highlighted the contingency and arbitrariness of language as a referent and mediation for the imagination of the nation. Despite Ernest Renan's comment of over a century ago upon the arbitrary equation of language and nation, fetishization of language as a referential system for a national community of speakers has been the consequence of Lockean and Herderian ideologies (although distinct as language philosophies) and their profound impact on the modern theories of linguistic nationalism prevalent since the nineteenth century in Europe and elsewhere (Kroskrity 2000: 11). Many studies of nationalism across the world stressed the prominent part linguistic factors have since played in the cultural formation of the nation—whether at a national or a regional level (Anderson 1983; Gellner 1983; Hobsbawm 1992; Hastings 1997). Linguistic movements in the formation of ethno-nationalisms have also been documented in the subcontinent (King 1996; Rahman 1996, 2004; King 1998). In India, regional nationalisms have been intricately associated with regional languages, particularly in Bengal, Tamilnadu, and Maharashtra (see Phadke 1979; Cohn 1987b; Ramaswamy 1997). The case of Maharashtrian nationalism and Marathi language offers a particularly rich historical instance of a linguistic and cultural regionalism mediating national sentiment.

The very issue of how languages come to be naturalized in locutors' representations requires further probing. Why are conceptions of languages as "discrete, distinctive entities . . . emblematic of self and community" so universally prominent (Fishman 1989, quoted in Woolard 1998: 18)? Here I seek to reach an understanding of such emblematization through Marathi discourses of belonging. The mediatory role of linguistic ideologies in relation to language and emotion (Wilce 2004: 11) also calls for a phenomenological exploration of language ideologies and their physicality as indigenous discursive practices as well as lived, embodied experiences. In Maharashtra, as we shall see, social actors both possess and share a language ideology of Marathi and have a linguistic discourse on the physicality of emotion. The first step of the demonstration, however, requires probing into the idea of an imagined, homogeneous language for national purposes.

At first glance, there may appear a contradiction between Marathi linguistic belonging and Indian nationalism. Yet, as shall be seen in Chapter 4, the two are intricately related: the notion of a Marathi/Maratha nation stands in Maharashtrian conceptualizations as *the* precondition for the possibility of the Indian nation. Marathi-predicated Maharashtrian nationalism owes much to the processes of homogenization that have accompanied the development of the language into a nationalist/regionalist ideology. Indeed, Marathi nationalism clearly instantiates the notion that if language alone suggests—mostly in the form of poetry and songs—"a kind of contemporaneous community" (Anderson 1991: 145), "homogeneous language is as much imagined as is community" (Irvine and Gal 2000: 76).[11] Marathi's normalization and homogenization were enabled by the philological efforts of British linguists and educationists working closely with local Sanskrit pundits in the mid-nineteenth century (McDonald 1968a, 1968b; Nemade 1990; Benei 2001b; Naregal 2002). In the process, the Marathi spoken by Pune Brahmins emerged as *the* sanctioned legitimate standard. The colonial concern for codifying and standardizing Marathi and its (written) usages later proved indigenously instrumental in its development into a medium of communication for Marathi speakers whose "dialectal" varieties had heretofore made it difficult for them to communicate with one another.[12] Consequently, official Marathi today is to some extent a modern creation, and the underlying standardization process

was at the core of the birth of a vernacular print literature providing recon-
ceptualization of social and political space on the basis of a unified "imagined community": through this literature were produced common ideas about
Maharashtra as a region celebrating a glorious martial past and *bhakti* tradition. The (re)definition of a modern Marathi and Maharashtrian identity thus
participated in the emergence of a regionalist consciousness in the last decades of the nineteenth century. This regional consciousness was also largely
nationalist.

Marathi provided the medium for celebrating at length the "idea of India."
Indeed, despite full recognition within the regional state of the role Hindi
played as a linguistic and national unifier, the notion of "Marathi language"
(*Marathi bhasha*) operated as a powerful, rallying trope and a crucial mediation for the production, assertion, and defense of a sense of both regional and
national belonging.[13] Evidence of this in the space of school lies in the contents
of the language textbooks designed by the regional state's production bureau
for Classes 1 to 5, and in the wealth of poems and songs pupils learned and
were made to recite, sing, and mime. The primary Marathi language manuals
are replete with poems, stories, and songs glorifying India. Even the Class 1
Marathi textbook has its fair share of devotional national contents. In addition
to reproducing the words of the national anthem on the last page of the book
under the title "Our National Song" (Aple rashtragit), it has a twelve-line poem
entitled "This Is My Country of India" (Ha majha Bharat desh). These are the
poem's first and last lines:

This is my country of India	Ha majha Bharat desh
Superb, superb is my country	Chhan chhan majha desh
. . .	. . .
My country is superb	Majha desh chhan ahe
India is my country.	Bharat majha desh ahe.

This kind of poetic declaration is reiterated throughout the day, whether by
rote learning of the textbook contents and recitation at the time of the paripath
(Chapter 1); by teachers selecting examples "at random" for the purpose of illustrating a point, grammatical, geographical, historical, or otherwise; or, as we
saw in Mr. Pawar's class, merely practicing acquired vocabulary. Among the
examples selected, the stories of independence heroes and nationalist fighters,
especially Mahatma Gandhi and Subhas Chandra Bose, figure prominently. Telling these stories provides occasions for teachers to proffer side commentaries,

often ending with an exhortation for the pupils to emulate these edifying models. These moments are clear instances of affect being linguistically mediated, permeating talk and "infusing words with emotional orientations" (Garrett and Baquedano-Lopez 2002: 352; see also Ochs and Schieffelin 1989; Besnier 1990), and in which the very celebration of the nation occurs in the intricate folds of a linguistic intimacy with the region.

Such an intimacy is further undergirded by the concept of "one's own language" (*swabhasha*). The notion may have already existed prior to the colonial encounter; yet it was reinscribed as a political and nationalist one in the throes of redefining and strengthening a sense of *communitas* predicated upon a sense of belonging to the soil as *swadesh* (one's own country) and sharing *swadharma* (one's own religion; although see Chapter 1 for the ambiguities of such a definition) in the late nineteenth and early twentieth centuries.[14] In Maharashtra today, this trinitarian conceptualization meaningfully informs the reworking and reproduction of emotional structures of feeling. In Kolhapur, in the late 1990s and early 2000s, Marathi-speaking parents of both English- and Marathi-educated children often expressed their attachment to Maharashtra as a whole in those very terms. This connection between language and the (re)production of a sense of belonging (to both a community of speakers and people living on the same soil) is also poignantly revealed in the wording of Kirari Bai's impassioned diatribe and emotional expression, verbal and bodily. Furthermore, in using the notion of *swabhasha* as standing in opposition to other languages (especially English), Kirari Bai was reproducing a pattern common among Marathi speakers today. Many parents and teachers similarly expressed their contrasted attachment to the Marathi language, resorting to the popular expression of *swataci bhasha*—as in "Amci bhasha 'he, swataci" (This is our language, our own). Often, they would utter these words while scanning them, with an emphasis on each syllable; the physicality of the utterance would also be completed with a gesture of the hand (palm flat, or fist) tapping on the chest or heart. Of all the embodied aspects of such a testimony, this gesture, common in many other contexts of claiming, confessing, and pledging faithfulness, best signals emotional involvement.

This emotional involvement vividly resonates with discursive practice where even the pronoun used in discussions of ownership of the Marathi language crucially encapsulates and furthers a sense of cohesiveness of the thus-constituted Marathi-speaking *communitas* in opposition to the linguistic outside. Like most Indian languages, Marathi has two pronouns for the first-person plural pronoun *we* used in English: one is the exclusive *āmhī* (*āmce, -ā, -ī* for neutral, masculine, and feminine possessive forms respectively), which demarcates the speaker from her or his audience. In contexts where the audience is meant to be included in the speaker's reference group, the pronoun used is the inclusive *āpaṇ* (*āple, -ā, -ī* in possessive forms). Hence, there is always a notion of clear demarcation in ordinary and daily speech and interaction between those who do belong to one's group of elocution and those who do not. Of course, such demarcation is highly fluid, variable, and context specific.[15] When used in discussions of belonging, however, such a lexical marker powerfully contributes to emphasize—and thus reinforces—a collective sentiment of cohesion. Therefore, when, as in political discourses, teachers address their audience referring to "our country" using the phrase *apla desh*, they are clearly calling out to the children as part of the same united, exclusive group. The potentialities of such a deictic marker are obviously vast and need to be borne in mind in a reflection on identity, citizenship, and belonging (see also Billig 1995 on the notion of deictic marker). They have special import given the close association of *swabhasha* with *swadesh*, especially with respect to conceptualizations of members of non-Marathi-speaking, non-Hindu communities in Maharashtra (Chapter 5). For the moment, I want to concentrate on the predication of Marathi language ideology upon notions of naturalness mediated and legitimized by the concept of "mother tongue." I wish to illuminate the ways in which schools are sites of language naturalization and homogenization, thereby creating a conscious notion of the mother tongue "already there" as an object and a medium of love and attachment. This "already there," however, is by no means a natural given. Rather, it is itself the product of early childhood socialization processes occurring in the intimacy of home (Chapter 3). Schools, therefore, draw upon, amplify, and crystallize senses of linguistic belonging while making the latter's ideology explicit and further anchoring it in lived and experienced bodies.

Mother Tongue, Naturalness, and Philological Explorations

What accounts for the meaningfulness of language ideology as both social practice and pedagogical tool is its experiential association with the concept of "mother tongue." Language ideology crystallizes, almost reifies, Marathi-as-*swabhasha* as the naturalized object of motherly love experienced in the infancy of social and family life. Notwithstanding the cultural specificity of its conceptual formulation, however, this crystallization of mother tongue and its lived experience is not unique to the Indian case. Rather, it is congruent with the many processes of national formation that took place from the late nineteenth century onward and wherein language played a constitutive part. Today, as Woolard noted, with the equation of one language to one people "has come an insistence on authenticity and moral significance of 'mother tongue' as one first and therefore *real* language of a speaker, transparent to the true self" (1998: 18).[16] By the same token, the emergence of a Marathi-speaking national (e.g., pan-Indian) consciousness was coextensive with a conception of a true, authentic yet new and modern Marathi-speaking self. This requires qualification.

Dating the concept of mother tongue among Indian vernacular speakers prior to the advent of European philological influences in the nineteenth century has generated some debate. On the one hand, evidence has been proffered of earlier notions linking regional language with mother tongue (Bayly 1998; also see Ramanujan, quoted in Prentiss 1999; Chapter 1). Lending further credence to this thesis is the concomitant movement of written vernacularization following "the old cosmopolitan epoch" observed in southern Asia and western Europe in the first half of the "*vernacular millennium*" (1000–1500) wherein "vernacular literary cultures were initiated by the conscious decisions of writers to reshape the boundaries of their cultural universe by renouncing the larger world for the smaller place" (Pollock 2000: 592, emphasis in original). In Europe, the historical construct of the mother tongue took shape at the time of written vernacularization (Haugen 1991: esp. 79–80, for Germany in particular). On the other hand, as Sheldon Pollock remarks, "The expression 'mother tongue' was current in no Indian lexicon before European expansion" (2006: 319). The concept of mother tongue in India only emerged in the latter half of the nineteenth century under European philological influences (Ramaswamy 1997: 15–17). It may be that the concept was largely alien to Indian vernacular speakers in southern India prior to the advent of standardization in the nineteenth century. At any rate, the concept today is a powerful vector of regional and national identification. As in Tamilnadu, the mother tongue can be seen as both bonding its speakers in a "net of unity . . . as firmly and surely as the love of their mother(s)" and potentially transforming its speakers into patriots and citizens (Ramaswamy 1997: 53, 57, 140). This is particularly so when the state assumes its promotion in various arenas of everyday life, especially schooling.

The felt authenticity of the idea and lived experience of the Marathi language as mother tongue has in many ways been relayed by schooling, not only at an official level with explicit discourses promoting a Marathi-predicated Maharashtrian identity but also, and most important on the ground of everyday practices, intricately linking it to an idiom of motherhood. Thus, the large number of prayers and poems in Marathi addressed to both mother and motherland and officially part of the syllabus are supplemented by primary schoolteachers' own daily pronouncements on the topic (Chapter 3).

The deployment of the trope of motherhood in imaginings of the nation since the nineteenth century has received renewed attention in the last decade. Gender-conscious scholars have devoted their efforts to exploring the gendered dimension of nationalism and nationalist sentiment, showing "how (middle-class) women came to be sanctified as reproductive beings through valorisations of the ideology of motherly love" (Ramaswamy 1998: 83; see also McClintock 1993; Sarkar 1995; Gupta 2001; T. Sarkar 2002). In a suggestive article on the somatics of nationalism in Tamilnadu, Ramaswamy documented the tropes of motherly intimacy and the somatic imagery of the mother's body parts and substances (milk, tears, womb) that Tamil nationalist discourses associate with the notion of mother tongue. Using "body language" as a conceptual grid, Ramaswamy mapped the ideological work to which various parts and substances of the female body are subjected in nationalist discourses serving the project of incorporating citizens into the emergent body politic. In the end, Ramaswamy argues, nation and citizen-patriot in Tamil India relate to each other politically, materially, and emotionally, as well as somatically: "the nation is a somatic formation . . . because it exists, literally, *in the guts* . . . of its female embodiment, *and of her citizen-subjects*" (1998: 79–80). The tropes of the mother tongue are "part of a routine repertoire deployed strategically . . . guaranteeing effectiveness of somatic imagery in nationalist discourses" (84).

The modalities either of this strategic deployment or of this somatization, however, remain unspecified. Here, rather than suggest or endorse a principled effectiveness (in the sense of producing a decided, decisive, or desired effect) of the political use of this somatic imagery by skilled politicians, I want to concentrate on the deployment of the mother trope in ordinary people's everyday life experiences and explore the modalities of its instantiation. Taking Ramaswamy's proposition of the embodied mother tongue literally, I aim to document the cognitive and phenomenological deployment of this trope. In particular, I seek to understand the articulation between the level of somatic imagery and its transposition to "the guts" of its ordinary citizen-subjects. Documenting such a transposition requires that we recognize it as *not* metaphorical (Strathern

1993). In the next chapter, I document how the mother trope operates at various levels in the construction of emotional bonding and attachment both to family and national values. Here, I want to emphasize the *physicality* of the mother-tongue ideology for its speakers. This physicality is evidenced in the analogy often drawn between mother language and biological mother. Thus, Mr. Joshi, an art teacher running a cultural center for schoolchildren, explained in the summer of 2003:

> Before traveling abroad, it is important that we should first see our gaon, Maharashtra, our desh, etc. Today, everybody wants to go to America; people are all forgetting their mother tongue. . . . Yet your mother tongue is like your mother's womb: you cannot forget it. Moreover, it is unique. Just like you only have one mother, so you only have one mother tongue. It cannot be changed.

Mr. Joshi's statement echoes those frequently made by both female and male parents and teachers, who identified other bodily parts and substances, the mother's milk in particular. Thus, Shantabai, Maratha mother of Sushila, a Class 3 student at Modern Marathi School quoted earlier, states, "Just like you have sucked your mother's milk, you have at the same time imbibed your mother's language."

Both Mr. Joshi's and Shantabai's words are strikingly reminiscent of the views of the eighteenth-century linguist, poet, and philologist Johann Gottfried von Herder, famous for his influential theology of cultural nation building premised on linguistic revelation through one's people (*Volk*). At the core of Herder's vision of national forms lies an organic connection between human language and natural and historical forces that the most enlightened people would realize. The "true character" of a nation, its soul, spirit, and genius, would be reflected in, expressed through, and further strengthened by the uniqueness of its language conceived, produced, and transmitted as mother tongue. Especially noteworthy in the present case is that, if language is more than a mere cognitive tool, it is also associated with motherly substances *and* operates as a material object: it is the very *substance* of one's cultural and national being.[17] Thus, by going away, by leaving one's homeland, one loses one's own culture and, more precisely, the nurturing substance of motherly milk and idiom. In some ways, it is as if the humoral theory of old *patriae* analyzed by C. A. Bayly (1998) had been transposed and transmuted into that of the mother tongue in a triadic association with soil and faith. We need to go one step further and examine how the notion and ideology of mother tongue are embedded in a process that concomitantly naturalizes language. The apparent "obviousness" and "naturalness"—and their emotional implications—of the Marathi language need further attention, especially because they are crucial elements in ordinary Marathi speakers' discursive iterations. Furthermore, paying heed to local understandings of "naturalness" also illuminates the moral dimension associated with somatic and emotional notions of language.

Linguistic ideologies characteristically operate a kind of neutralization or naturalization of language value through semiotic processes erasing both the historical contingency of languages and the relations of power and interest underlying them (Spitulnik 1998: 163). This begs the question of how ordinary social actors produce, posit, and understand such naturalness. Drawing on discursive constructions of language as well as observations and descriptions of speech acts and performances, I contend that the construction of "naturalness" is premised on an understanding of language as incorporation, both as discourse and practice. We have just encountered Mr. Joshi's views on the substantialization of language and the fear and anxiety attached to the idea of identity loss generated by distance and forgetting. Although such fears and anxieties culminate in comments from expatriate Maharashtrians, they are generally pervasive in discussions "back home," especially of the medium of instruction for schoolchildren, as suggested by Kirari Bai's passionate defense of Marathi over English at the opening of this chapter.

Yet if Kirari Bai's statement was clearly one of the best articulated ever encountered in the course of research, it was in no way exceptional. Many Marathi-speaking parents shared the same fears of potential identity loss associated with the teaching of, and in, the English language. Moreover, the discursive (and pragmatic) favoring of instruction in Marathi was by no means specific to *Hindutva*-sympathetic teachers or parents. In addition, such a preference recurred both among parents of children schooled in the Marathi language and among those whose children attended English-language institutions. In both cases, the discursive preference was primarily couched in an idiom of naturalness associated with the notion of mother tongue: "Learning in one's mother tongue is so much more natural [*swabhavik*]" was a leitmotif among parents who would cite evidence of children having gone through the primary phase of instruction in their native language as being more scholarly grounded than others.[18] Here, the Marathi word used for "natural" crucially illuminates the breadth of the semantic repertoire of emotionality characterizing Marathi language ideology. Naturalness is conceptualized as both an emotional *and* embodied state.

natural/native

what is natural is emotion

The word *swabhavik* (from the root *bhāv*) encompasses many layers of meaning, including that of a natural state of being, innate property, disposition, nature, but also, as important, sentiment or passion, emotion or feeling, a class of affections, *as well as* the actions, gestures, or postures constituting corporeal expression thereof. When Marathi native speakers elaborate on the naturalness of their language, therefore, they are often—whether consciously or not—playing into an embodied experientiality of linguistic emotion.

Perhaps the best exemplification of such embodied experientiality lies in the expression *trās yene*, as in the phrase "Tras yeto, English maddhe shikayla." Such a statement was often encountered among parents voicing their concern about the difficulty caused by the unnaturalness of learning in any language other than one's mother tongue. Loosely translated, the sentence means "It creates problems, to learn in English." The semantic register is however much wider: *tras* in Marathi may refer as much to emotional as physical issues. Consider, for instance, the common expression *kunala tras dene* (to give a hard time to someone). In the idiom of domesticity, and especially among married women, the expression is used with reference to kin relations within the conjugal family, whose epitome lies in the figure of the mother-in-law. Narratives pertaining to daughters-in-law—young brides in particular—suffering at the hands of their mothers-in-law would often be couched in these terms. In this context as in others, *tras* could be psychological, emotional, and physical. To return to the context of learning, the physical connotation of *tras* must be taken seriously, rather than hastily dismissed as merely metaphorical. As Andrew Strathern argued, the notion of metaphor should not be considered as a heuristic device for the "unfamiliar or the strange." In contrast, Strathern proposed, we should favor an "against metaphor" perspective and take discourses about bodily emotions literally: "A stress on metaphor goes with a textual emphasis, but 'reading the body' may require us to alter our categories more radically" (1993: 6). Here, it must be emphasized that the expression *tras yene* is also used in association with the disruption of the ordinary course of bodily functions, especially that of the digestive system. Important to note is that the verb "to digest" (*pacavne*) itself conveys connotations of harmony, and its use in the negative sense is common to refer to disruption of social and political order and the resulting degradation of moral order. Thus, if a battle is lost, the shame incurred in defeat goes "undigested" (*apacavleli*).[19] When parents or teachers voice their concern about the naturalness of learning in one's mother tongue (and the converse *tras* generated by learning in any other idiom), therefore, they are not just demonstrating the appropriateness of such a conceptual vocabulary in the South Asian context today, despite its historical genealogy of vernacular language ideology rooted in the West (Nemade 1990; Pollock 2006: 318–19). They are also explicitly referring to a phenomenological understanding of language. Both vocabulary and understanding also entail a moral dimension, which requires elaboration.

Anxious Emotions, Idioms of Morality, and Family Tropes of the Nation

Language does not only encode embodied emotions; it also forms the basis for the socialization of morality, that is, the social sanctioning or rejection of actions (one's own and others'). As participants in everyday routines internalize and express emotion, they also learn to make sense of the moral order they are actively constructing through interaction with others. Notions of morality are thus negotiated through linguistically (and corporeally) mediated understandings of daily life and events, providing bearings for one's place in the world, both as an individual and as part of a collective (Abu-Lughod and Lutz 1990: 13). Producing a sense of national belonging, whether through morning school assemblies or throughout the day—during language and history lessons in particular—was mediated by a Marathi vocabulary of kinship. This vocabulary furnishes a moral trope for articulating belonging to the family community of the nation identified by Anderson (1983). Here, in addition to the mother trope analyzed previously, the kinship one of "brothers and sisters" (*bhauband*) informs the pledge daily recited in Marathi. The pledge is taken almost verbatim from the *Report of the Committee on Emotional Integration* commissioned by Nehru in the early 1960s. The national leader envisaged such emotional integration as central to his project of nation building and explicitly resorted to metaphors and rhetoric of kinship: the nation was understood as a mother, whether implicitly or explicitly, and her children, the citizens of India, were to be *bhauband*. The term possesses many layers of meaning in Maharashtra: predicated on *bhāū* (literally, "brother"), *bhauband* defines a kinsman, or in some contexts, all agnatic kinsmen. By extension, it can apply to all the men of a village. In all these senses, the term often conveys a strong sense of emotional and practical commitment, sharing, and friendliness, implying some form of cohesion and loyalty. As suggested earlier, such notions of cohesion and loyalty are integral to the Marathi language ideology, with the result that any move away from the language is conceived by Marathi speakers as a form of betrayal; a betrayal not only of language and its incorporation but also of *desh* and *dharma* (associated with *bhasha*, as discussed earlier) and of the community of the (Marathi-speaking) nation. Thus, parents' affective bodily displays accompanied assertive vocalizations about the necessity to teach in Marathi as against the *firangi* language. This moral imperative was also voiced by social actors who did not abide by this rule, as will be seen shortly. But such are the entailments of Marathi ideology that the moral and embodied emotionality associated with the notion of the language remains a powerful one. This bears elaboration.

In a recent article about the linguistic choices and dilemmas obtaining among Marathi speakers in the face of a so-called English-mediated globalization, I discussed the complex tensions between the educational and professional choices linked to middle-class aspirations and expectations on the one hand, and local and regional linguistic attachments on the other (Benei 2005c). I showed how the notion of morality tied up with the Marathi language ideology is reflected in the contrapuntal conception of "foreign" languages held by many Marathi speakers. English occupies a particular place in this linguistic moral economy. Kirari Bai's virulent statement about British rule indicates the lingering malaise associated with the "colonial language" in this part of India.[20] In many ways, such a malaise has moral resonances dating back to British educationists' attempts at disciplining and moralizing the Marathi language in the course of their standardizing endeavors (Benei 2001a). Today, this malaise is compounded by the perceived lack of morality associated with American English. Many Marathi-speaking middle-class people in Kolhapur can boast about a—however distant—family connection currently living, studying, or working in America; however, the underlying fascination for the new world's promise of a potential site for better economic opportunities, prosperity, and happiness is also matched by ambivalent imaginings of a land of high rate of divorce, loose morality, and loss of parental and filial values. In these representations, America often emerged as the place of all moral and familial perdition, in a sense, an archetypal site of Kaliyuga. Remarkably, the tensions documented here were as salient in cases of successful exposure to English-language instruction. The decision parents made to have their children learn in a language other than Marathi often gave rise to anxieties of cultural loss similarly couched in an idiom of morality. An example is that of Baba Pankat, the head of a Bhangi (ex-Untouchable) family.

At the beginning of my research, the family was composed of sixteen members spread across three generations living together. Two of the sons ran the prosperous spare-part workshops started by their father decades earlier. Baba, in his mid-seventies at the time of research, recalled the early days when he had to do his caste's calling (scavenging) and had to struggle hard through the educational system, paying for his studies by working as a mechanic. His educational beginnings were harsh and besmirched by the stigma attached to his "caste untouchability." Baba remembered not being allowed to sit within the classroom at the primary school and having to follow the lessons from the threshold. Against all odds, he managed to study up to Class 7 in Marathi at Kolhapur New High School before switching to English Class 5. He left after finishing Class 6. In the following two generations, those of his children and grandchildren who, regardless of gender, could handle studying in English were sent to English-language institutions, and the less academically able ones went into Marathi instruction. Some of the English-educated children pursued higher education and later secured mid-ranking jobs in a company and the local administration, respectively. Even so, Baba, for whom (particularly English) education was a precious asset representing a means of escaping the socioeconomic status ascribed to him by his caste, sometimes expressed a sense of unresolved tension between the desirability of learning in one's mother tongue and that of acquiring the linguistic proficiency necessary to rise above the condition of one's caste. Over the years that I got to know him, Baba, who had consciously pushed the ablest among his offspring into English-language instruction, would increasingly confide that he "had made a mistake" (majhe cukle), "now felt bad" (atta wait watle) because "one should definitely learn in one's mother tongue" (matru bhashemadhyec shiklec pahije).[21]

Like comments by many Marathi parents and teachers, Baba's were not just an elaboration on the naturalness of learning in one's mother tongue. His formulation also suggested moral self-condemnation, as in English: *cukṇe* in Marathi bears the dual meaning of "making a mistake or a blunder" and of "being morally wrong, unjust," "straying or wandering," "deviating from a righteous path," or even "falling short of one's duty." By the same token, the concept of "wrong" (*wāiṭ*) also has moral connotations: *wait* can be approximated as "bad," as in "I feel bad," but it can also mean "foul" or "evil." If it was not "wrong" strategically for Baba to have pushed his offspring away from education in their mother tongue, it was so morally, even though the aim of socioeconomic upward mobility had in his eyes been a legitimate one. So Baba concurred in the statement proffered by Kirari Bai at the beginning of this chapter, contrasting the notion of *wait* with that of *barobar*, or "right, correct, good": "It is not right to learn in another language but one's mother tongue." The moral condemnation implicit in these judgments suggests a sense of anguish and betrayal generated by the neglect of the Marathi language. It is in fact in similar discussions that anxieties and fears about loss of linguistic and cultural substance become explicitly formulated. For, as C. Wright Mills had already written in 1940: "[M]en live in immediate acts of experience and their attentions are directed outside themselves until acts are in some way frustrated. It is then that awareness of self and motive occur" (905). In Kolhapur and elsewhere in western Maharashtra, such anxieties were rarely manifest until parents and teachers made linguistic and educational choices that elicited questions about their implications.[22]

Finally, drawing on Mills's proposition that "typal vocabularies of motives for different situations are significant determinants of conduct" (908), it may be argued that these anxieties are also caused by the tension between *moral* vocabularies of motives associated with Marathi language ideology and strategic choices that run counter to them. There is, as Mills suggests, a sense of self-fulfilling realization in the process of motive enunciation (907), a kind of performative iteration: the act of describing one's motive is not related exclusively to experienced social action. Rather, it is about "influencing others and [one's] self." Mills's argument resonates with the concept of "emotive" inspired by Austin's notion of "performative" and developed by William Reddy in his history of emotions: its heuristic value is to point to the performative (in addition to embodied) character of discursive iteration of emotional attachment (Austin 1962; Reddy 2001, cited in Wilce 2004: 14). In sum, it is as if by reiterating one's emotional attachment to language and nation, one has experienced it more fully. This has yet wider ramifications touching the core of local notions of patriotism associating the *patria* (Bayly 1998: 26) with *dharma*. As Baba and many Marathi speakers of his and younger generations would often proudly assert, "It is our language, our own" (Amci bhasha ahe, swataci). In some ways, then, neglecting "one's own mother tongue" amounted to an act of moral and political deviance, and of potential regional and national treachery. This is so also because of the notion that the correct mastery of the Marathi language, vocabulary, and grammar is fundamental to the training of proper, fit social and political persons, as I now wish to illustrate by taking you back to Mr. Pawar's classroom, where we began this chapter.

Producing Moral Citizens: Language and Righteousness

We are again in Mr. Pawar's classroom on that hot, humid afternoon, picking up the thread of the vocabulary repetition where we left it earlier. We have just reached the last proposition: "I have pride in and respect for my country"

(Majhya deshaca mala abhimaan ahe), which Mr. Pawar suddenly interrupts, barking to a boy pupil: "Sunil, shut up; sit properly; now it's your turn!" Sunil, who had been whispering conspiratorially with his classmate, instinctively straightens up and, with somewhat startled eyes gazing at the board, begins, painfully stuttering upon the next group of words:

> "Ma-jh, majh, majhya da."
> "Deshat, hurry up, Sunil!" bellows Mr. Pawar impatiently.
> "De-shat, vi-vidh ja-tic."
> "Vi-vi-dha ja-ti-ce lo-ka raha-tat," the teacher pounds in, accentuating each syllable. "Jatice, Sunil, say it again; say it properly. The pronunciation [*uccār*] must be good. Isn't it so?"

Mr. Pawar now turns to the class.

> "Yes!" (Ho!), some children chorus back.
> "This is what correct language [*pramanit bhasha*] is about. What does correct language mean? It means proper pronunciation, and to speak nicely. The way we sometimes speak at home, isn't it; well, this is speaking language [*bolī bhāṣā*], but it is not correct [*barobar*]. It is not good [*cāngale*]. How can you grow into good people [*cangle lok*], good citizens [*cangle nagarik*], if you don't pronounce correctly?!"

Silence fills the classroom, while some pupils nod and gesture in vigorous approval, and others seemingly remain noncommitted. The enumeration, led again by the teacher, continues:

> "In my country live people from different jat. In my country people live happily." [Majhya deshat vividh jatice lok rahtat. Majhya deshatil lok anandane rahtat.]

Inasmuch as morality, justice, and rectitude are characteristic of the Marathi language ideology, they are also inherent in the project of producing a good, schooled citizen. This is particularly evidenced in the emphasis teachers, like Mr. Pawar, often lay upon the notion of *pramanit bhasha*, in opposition to *boli bhasha*. The distinction between *pramanit* and *boli bhasha* is a recurring one in many Marathi classrooms. At a general level, *pramanit bhasha* represents the "standard" version of the Marathi language officially taught in schools in Maharashtra. It is a version deriving its authority from its legitimacy as "superior knowledge" and, as intimated earlier, is the negotiated product of linguistic encounters between British educational officers and Marathi pundits in the mid-nineteenth century. At a more specific level, *pramanit* (from the Sanskrit *pramān*, "proof, evidence, authority") is used in Marathi to denote a measuring standard, in the sense of what is true, just, right, and authoritative. The phrase *pramanit bhasha* thus translates as "the correct, authoritative language" in contradistinction with *boli bhasha* as the "oral language" spoken at home or more generally in everyday life, without much concern for hard-and-fast rules, whether of pronunciation and grammar, let alone punctuation.

Furthermore, the notion of *pramanit bhasha* encompasses proper pronunciation and utterance, to which meaning becomes secondary. Teachers throughout the day lay emphasis on the proper pronunciation of this standard version of the Marathi language, as Mr. Pawar did. As we saw in Chapter 1, this emphasis culminated in learning the pronunciation of the national anthem, which often superseded a search for meaning. Proper pronunciation and the register of *pramanit bhasha* are also intricately associated with notions of good personhood, more generally predicated upon the notion of *samskar*. Teachers in Marathi primary schools often considered the hymns, prayers, songs, moral stories, and thoughts for the day as fulfilling the purpose of cultivating *samskar*. Such moral edification was deemed crucial to a child learning "how to behave" (*kase wagayce*), thus growing into a well-rounded, moral person and citizen (*nagarik*). Marathi language ideology, then, is predicated on idioms of morality that play a potent part in shaping the attempts at producing civic persons, as true *samskara*-predicated national citizens. Implicit in the project of schooling is therefore the understanding of school as a space where students, as future proper citizens, should internalize *pramanit bhasha* naturalizing it as their own *boli bhasha*.[23] Whether this is ever really successful, in Indian schools or in those of other nation-states, is of course debatable. A stark opposition exists between this attempted naturalization and the resilience of everyday speech, especially among students of lower-caste or non-Hindu backgrounds, whose spoken idioms are generally the furthest removed from the version acknowledged as "proper and standard" Marathi.

Notes for a Provisional Conclusion

Central to this chapter is the notion that language and the passion it elicits are truly somatic instantiations. They are so not only in a descriptive, deictic sense but in a more profound, embodied one. It is not language that structures a human being but a relationship to body and emotion that is mediated by language as ideology. And because language—and its ideology—is incorporated in everyday bodily experience of the world as well as relayed in schools to acute levels of emotional figuration, it acquires this emotional and passionate quality for its speakers, regardless of the strategic choices they may make for their children's education. Inasmuch as emotions are socially and culturally constructed, then, we should pay closer attention to what local discourses of emotion have to say about their concrete location. Furthermore, such discourses do not necessarily espouse the unhelpful dichotomy of public (emotions) versus private (feelings). Eventually, the extent to which they are conceived as "personal" and "interior" and culturally constructed is almost impossible to assess. Arguably, the imprecision remains precisely because it is so difficult, nay, impossible, to disentangle personal feelings from public emotions, as both are mutually constituted. This, if anything, should already alert us to the illusionary character of the "public/private" dichotomy (to be discussed later). A phenomenological approach to emotions thus provides a way of reconciling what at first glance appear radically, irreconcilable categories acknowledging social actors' perceptions of them as "embodied." Put differently, the notion of embodiment dissolves the conceptual boundary between public and private. This has far-reaching implications, which I want to begin to unravel here.

In what has come to be considered a foundational text, Jean-François Lyotard argued that the end of meta-narratives such as nationalism was the distinctive mark of postmodernity. Lyotard's comment was undoubtedly generated by the observation at the time of the development of discourses counter to those of nationalism, at the levels of regional, international, and transnational movements. Although his voice was a rather specific one, his observation was shared by many scholars who, whether explicitly engaging with his argument or pursuing other lines of inquiry, joined in agreement until the 1990s in tolling the bell of the national formation. Since then, history has, cruelly and often poignantly, disproved these willful yet un-self-fulfilling prophecies. More nations saw the light of day in the last quarter of the twentieth century, often through bloody and traumatic births amid vivid longings and ethnic violence. If anything, these painful engenderings have brought home the notion that, perhaps more than ever before, the nation form is alive and kicking. Despite these ontological realizations, the category has in many scholarly circles acquired a slightly antiquated ring of passé-ness, overridden by more flashy, trendy notions of "globalization" and "global civil society," whether pragmatic or phantasmic. I suggest that, if the notion of the national formation, despite its dramatic enactments and practical translations in the lives of an increasing number of ordinary social actors the world over, has become taken for granted, it is precisely because it has been *naturalized* to an unprecedented extent. The idea, of course, is not new. Part of the theoretical canvas Benedict Anderson developed was aimed at furnishing the premises for an understanding of how nations become culturally formed, that is, how they come to be produced as cultural, natural units of belonging. Michael Billig later drew attention to the banalization of the nation in people's daily lives, especially through the performative iterations of the nation in the mass media. Yet I want to formulate a different kind of argument and suggest that more than sharing a commonality of nationhood with newspaper readers or "banally flagging" the nation, the naturalization of the idea and experience of the nation entails its "incorporation." It is because of the nation's deep incorporation into who we are as bodied social persons, subjects, and citizens that we can somehow entertain a sense of national belonging, much as this sense may at times be fleetingly vague, and despite a professed lack of patriotic appetence. Remember Bourdieu's pronouncement: "what the body grants even when the mind says no" (1990: 167).

Of course, I do not mean to suggest that this somatization of national emotionality is either ever present or exhausts the potentialities of the body/mind. Such production of an "emotionationality" requires daily labor, as we have seen, and does not determine all social action. Rather, this production allows for the "something recalcitrant in the body" to remain and possibly surface at any time. Embodied emotionationality can never fully exhaust the pliability and resourcefulness of social and cultural agency, whether individual or collective. However absolutist the prevalent ideological structure, any exploration of ideology, both as structure of belief and "interpellative subject positioning," has to allow for some measure of "openness onto heterogeneous realities" (Massumi 2002: 263). Therefore, despite the potency of Marathi native-speaking social actors' emotional social and individual constructions and lived experiences of the Marathi language ideology, a space must be left open for the "conceptual enablement," not necessarily of "resistance" but at least for alternative negotiations "in connection with the real" (263). Thus, for instance, despite teachers' obstinate attempts at impressing a military-like atmosphere during the morning liturgies, much of the school day was characterized more by unruliness than discipline: such unruliness started soon after the classes left the ground of the morning liturgy, as pupils would walk to their classrooms in a sort of stampede. Similarly in overcrowded classrooms, some teachers had relinquished their authority, abandoning any notion of an entirely quiet and disciplined class, and would only mildly, though regularly, "tsa tsa" in vain efforts to impose total silence. Often when teachers under some pretense interrupted their class and momentarily left the room to attend to some more pressing business, general bedlam would ensue. Pupils greatly relished these moments that, in addition to the recesses that punctuated the school day, provided welcome outlets for their energy and vigor. Arguably, these formed as important a part in the production of future Maharashtrian (and Indian) citizens.[24]

The workings of Marathi language ideology therefore have to be understood as both official implementation processes and social actors' agency. Here is the double bind of all processes of language socialization, whether national or otherwise: in the same movement of ideologically shaping, naturalizing, and incorporating language ideologies in the constitution of social and cultural units, language ideologies fail to grasp the totality of agency, unwittingly allowing for interstices and cracks in these processes. On the one hand, even cases of diglossia leave room for negotiating the production of national emotional attachment. In the social production of a schooled self, a readjustment between the language spoken at home and the standardized version taught in school may concomitantly be effected. In particular, variations existing between the official standardized version of the Marathi written in official textbooks and the local brand spoken at home may become erased, especially in the common referent to the notions of "mother" and "motherhood" (Chapter 3). The mother language might thus be envisaged as uniting her dialectal (school)children in her lap. On the other hand, such union is arguably best realized in cases of convergence of family and school idioms. These generally pertain to upper-caste and upper-class Hindu children. Even in these cases, there may always remain unconquered space and unpredictable agency. Ultimately, because even the mother tongue, for all its instrumentality in negotiating internal divisions between different local varieties of a language, is never totally realized, never fully complete, this linguistic incorporation of the nation generates accrued anxieties and fears of loss of substance and morality. These anxieties and fears are inherent in the pursuit of any project of linguistically premised national (or regional) formation, if only because such projects are de facto predicated upon processes of self-definition athwart other idioms, whether these be local, vernacular "dialects" or "foreign-born" ones. So social actors, while beholden to an emotional attachment to a linguistic nation, are deeply—although rarely explicitly—aware of the fragility of projects of language-predicated nationalisms. As the nation (or the region) is working toward its linguistic realization, it is constantly battling with the possibility of its self-perdition.

What implications does this have for the naturalization of a sense of belonging? What kind of community is thus created, and what room is there for an "other," speaking a different language, in the participation in the life of the polis? The issue is obviously further complicated by the fact that this Marathi-speaking Indian citizen is by default a Hindu-inflected one. I hope to have brought to light in this chapter how the project of Marathi self-formation is potentially always an exclusivist one that seeks to exclude other, improper Marathi- or non-Marathi-speaking locutors. Despite an overtly integrational approach, it is clear that those children deemed less capable of becoming good Indian citizens in this part of Maharashtra are those standing the furthest apart from (standardized) Marathi. Later, I explore the ideology of Urdu language among Maharashtrian Muslims and suggest that the room left for non-standard-Marathi speakers is very exiguous. Especially so that the incorporation of a linguistic sense of "self" is an emotional process occurring within early processes of socialization.[25] In the following chapter, we take up again the issue of early processes of socialization and explore their articulation between the space of home and family and that of school. Looking at conceptions of motherhood, pedagogy, and motherland, we show how embodied emotions of national belonging nurtured through schooling draw upon, and feed into, attachments developed in the intimacy of home.

Of Discipline and Teaching

Shanta: Will Beating Us Harder Make Us Learn Better?

Shanta is too tired this morning. Bapu came home late last night, and he would not stop drinking and abusing the whole family, or rather, what is left of it since Ai died last year in a factory accident. Bapu was so mad that even Aji could not reason with him; she, too had to back off from his slapping hands. Fortunately, at least, Ramesh did not wake up; he is so small and so easily scared for a five-year-old; how would he take this from his beloved father? Shanta, just turned ten, sometimes wishes she could still retreat to the younger and happier times when their mother was alive. Then, Bapu was never so angry. Grudgingly, Shanta stretches herself and staves off a tardy mosquito from her cheek. Red moist spot on her skin. No escape for this one. Shanta then reluctantly gets up and opens the one-room shack door to let the fresh morning air come in.

"Bharat Mata" sticker from the Rashtriya Swayamsevak Sangh (RSS) campaign of 2000.

Meanwhile, Ramesh still lays wrapped up in a blanket on the floor, battling in a dream. What will the teacher say? They must not arrive late. What will the teacher do? This new one here at Marathi Corporation School is horrible; his class is hell on earth, the worst you could ever imagine. He does not just beat you up; he strikes and strikes you so hard with whatever comes his way, stick, ruler, chalk, you name it, he strikes you so hard that you almost faint in pain. And this even when you've only made a minor mistake. Just like the other day,

Republic Day (January 26) celebrations. Representation of Bharat Mata with flag and scepter in hand, surrounded by *sants* and policemen. Prathamik Shikshan Mandal, Kolhapur, 2000.

Drawing of a smiling schoolgirl holding a tricolor flag in hand while standing beneath a tall flagpole. The caption reads "Vande Mataram," from the name of the poem, song, and salutation to "The Mother." Sushila M., age seven, Modern Marathi School, Kolhapur, March 1999.

when Anil got his recitation wrong. Or that time, when he pinched Pratima's ear so hard at *paripath*, we thought he would tear it off. And this only because she had forgotten to wash her hands before coming in to school! He looks like he is relishing every bit of it. I agree we need some kind of beating now and again, because it is true that we need to get disciplined at times. Everybody says so. Really, there are times when we get a little too excited and cannot concentrate properly, as Leelabai says, but just a slap with the ruler, as she and all the other teachers do, surely, this should be enough. Will beating us harder make us learn better?

3 Producing Mother-India at School

Passions of Intimacy and National Love

> [T]he public and the private worlds are inseparably
> connected; . . . the tyrannies and servilities of the one
> are the tyrannies and servilities of the other.
>
> **Virginia Woolf,** *Three Guineas*

IT IS GETTING SLIGHTLY CHILLY tonight in Kolhapur, despite the hubbub and effervescence prevalent in the municipal stadium on this Republic Day of January 26, 2000. The Shahu Maidan, as it is locally known, is thronging with parents. As they do every year, they have come to attend their children's performances in the primary schools' competition organized by the municipal corporation. Most of the schools in town have gathered for the event, regardless of their status and characteristics in the local hierarchy—public, privately run, semi-private, elitist, long-standing, progressive, Hindu right-wing—they are here to participate in the yearly patriotic celebration. As the show is proceeding with one school after another, some teachers can be seen busying themselves, proceeding to final checks and rehearsals on the side, applying ultimate touches of makeup on the performers' cheeks, making last recommendations. Children from each school, in turn, present their skits on the stage, with the sound of music of their own choice playing in the background.

One school has just finished its presentation: amid the final beats of the music, the participants are now bowing as the audience claps. As the stage is being vacated, another school prepares to make its entry among hushing noises behind the scenes. Like many schools that evening, this one will start with a welcome song (*swagatam song*), followed by fishermen's dances (*kohli natak*). Like many others, the actors will set their skits in the gracing presence of Bharat Mata, "Mother-India," often with the song "Mere watan ke logon" playing in the background. The song, sung by generations across India on patriotic occasions, has been largely popularized by singer Lata Mangeshkar. Her rendition is such that it is said to have brought tears to Jawaharlal Nehru's eyes upon her first performance. As the music begins, a young girl draped in a pink sari with gold brocade majestically enters the stage from the right. She is young, grave, and beautiful. From either side of her golden diadem are hanging two long, neat plaits of black hair. The audience has become silent and watches her intently as she slides across the platform. She is carrying a tricolor Indian flag in her right hand, holding a trishul scepter in her left. Meanwhile, a polystyrene map of India has been brought to the rear. The national mother-goddess incarnate now stands still in the center of the stage as the last notes of the patriotic song recede. Her figure superimposes itself on the map behind her in a perfect conflation of national territory, divinity, femaleness, and Hinduness. Many men's and women's faces among the watching crowd carry an enraptured look; glowing eyes, intense stares, and longing smiles, heads nodding approvingly sideways, all these bodily gestures suggest an act of (re)connection on the part of much of the local audience whose child is occupying the stage; it is a reconnection with both an imagined and an instantiated ideal of the nation.

In these moments suspended away from everyday life, the young schoolgirl is no longer just an ordinary Kolhapuri maiden, nor is she merely impersonating Bharat Mata. From anonymous maiden, she has *become* the (national) deity incarnate and an object of intense worship reminiscent of Satyajit Ray's filmic *Devi*. The comparison stops here, however. For tomorrow, "Miss Bharat Mata" will return to her ordinary life as a schoolgirl, donning her daily uniform as all her friends do. Yet in many ways this performance is not totally disconnected from everyday life, for the re-creation of Mother-India is also integral to daily (Marathi) school routine, as we saw in Chapter 1. The morning liturgy starting the school day consists of the re-creation of the national deity through praising, singing, and discursive as well as embodied practices. This yearly incarnation of Bharat Mata therefore represents more than a suspended moment in the school calendar: it is a culmination of national imaginings and longings, a crystallization of hopes and dreams, a tangible condensation of the making of Indian "mother-goddess-nation." What are the modalities of her production outside of these liturgical moments? What is it that makes them so potently meaningful in the emotional and symbolic economy of so many Maharashtrians? How is this emotional and symbolic economy daily produced, and how can we tease out the combined aspects of gender and national production in these socialization processes largely occurring at school "where sexual and other identities are developed, practised and actively produced" (Epstein and Johnson 1998: 2)? In this chapter, I pursue the demonstration that cultural and social productions of regional and national identifications within the context of formal education are not only central to the making of the disciplinary institution of schooling, of modeled and disciplined bodies, and of "normalized" persons (Foucault 1979, 1981) but are also cosubstantial to the production of *gender discursivity* and *corporeality*. Deploying yet again the notion of sensorium in a different direction, that of the constitution of spheres of "attachment" (or "bonding") and of "emotional bubbles" developed in the intimacy of home and family, I attempt to reconcile the phenomenological approach already developed in Chapter 2 with a pragmatic and psychoanalytic one. This entails registering and describing what Husserl called "Evidenz"—that is, the matter itself as disclosed in a clear and distinct way by social actors—and redeploying psychoanalytic concepts around its interpretation. Crucial here again is the notion of incorporation, which, as noted earlier, presupposes that one cannot distinguish the contents of the process from the process itself: the two are mutually produced. Thus, the manufacturing of gendered interiority and embodiment is indissociable from that of collective regional and national selves. Furthermore, if such constructions feed upon the articulation of the mother figure at the levels of family, school, and national space, they conversely feed *into* the daily reproduction of Mother-India as a gendered political project.

The mother trope lends itself well to an exploration of categories of gender and national sentiment. Over the last forty years, figures of women have frequently embodied the nation the world over. In India, even in the 1950s and 1960s the promotion of a national development agenda during the so-called Nehru years saw the deployment of the female form.[1] The values of auspiciousness and plenty culminated in the mother figure, alternately nurturing and fiercely protective. These multiple and contradictory aspects of Indian society have played an important part not only in popular culture but also in national constructions and pedagogical projects in which the motif of the mother has become crucially emblematic of the construction and self-projection of the nation (Assayag 2001; Gupta 2001). That education may serve the (re)production of motherhood in India (Kumar 2000) is by now a commonplace. What remains to be analyzed is how the category of "mother" as a hegemonic marker of femaleness and nationhood in social and cultural discourse pervades the pedagogical environment—especially that of primary schooling. To be sure, this "motherly pervasiveness" is not specific to India and has been documented elsewhere. In the United Kingdom, for instance, primary school today is a female national space par excellence (Woodward 2003: 46). Yet in India, it represents much more: the category of "mother" looms large over the production of persons (Trawick 1989), but also of citizens (Ramaswamy 1998) and institutions.

Mother Love, Bonding, and Attachment: Producing a Continuing Sensorium

In many ways, life at school draws upon, and extends, a sensorium constituted in the intimacy of family. It does so both metaphorically and pragmatically, primarily through the mediation of the nurturing figure of the idealized "good mother" and its transposition to that of the female teacher. This is most suggestively captured by one of the favorite stories heard in schools and during a week-long refresher course held at the Teachers' Training College (DIET) of Kolhapur. The story is that of the "female teacher and the little boy." It starts on the very first day of school. After lunch, a little boy walks up to his female teacher and wipes his dirty hands clean on her sari. The teacher, rather nonplussed, scolds the boy. The next day, however, the same pupil reiterates his performance. The teacher tells him off again. At the end of three days of spoiled saris and with irritation mounting, the teacher finally decides to confront the boy's mother. The mother explains her son's behavior: "Just as I am his mummy at home, you are his mummy at school, he trusts you, you take care of him, you are a mother to him, this is why." Although I heard the story in several versions, what always came forcefully across from all the narrations was the transposition of intimacy, security, and trust from the familial environment onto the semipublic one of the school. These two qualities, care and trust, are precisely those that child psychoanalysts Melanie Klein and Donald Winnicott, followed by Erik Erikson and Sudhir Kakar—the latter two with special reference to India—have emphasized as fundamental to the development of the infant or child and the constitution of his or her "emotional bubble." Obviously, what are projected in the sanitized space of the training college and the Marathi primary school are idealized visions of motherhood, mother-child relations, and teacher-pupil relations. In these visions, very little room is left for alternative, harsher realities where the mother would be unavailable, unable, or even unwilling to fulfill these revered duties, or the teacher a regular absentee. Nevertheless, these visions suggest an interesting convergence of popular understandings with scholarly ones about the modalities of the constitution of an emotional and sensory environment at home and at school through the mediation of the "good mother," which need unpacking.

Interestingly, the notion of "the good mother" so prominently expounded by teachers in Marathi schools is congruent with that elaborated by Melanie Klein in a series of pathbreaking conferences in the 1930s. Klein accorded great importance to bodily functions and hypothesized that unconscious fantasy—which she claimed also exists within a child—was always based upon them. Bodily functions also played a crucial role in both the growth of a young child and the child's future development into an adult: "Because our mother first satisfied all our self-preservative needs and sensual desires and gave us security, the part she plays in our minds is a lasting one, although the various ways in which this influence is effected and the forms it takes may not be at all obvious in later life" (1964: 59). Most important, the notion of the "good mother," or "the good breast," has become foundational to modern psychoanalysis. Heavily influenced by Klein's work, Donald Winnicott developed the concepts of "handling" and "caring." Put simply, these lay emphasis on the building of a safe, trustworthy, sensory maternal environment. Expanding the analysis in another direction, Indian psychoanalyst Sudhir Kakar elaborated on the notion of "good mother" by developing the concept of mother's *sensory presence* (emphasis in original) and its vital importance for the infant's earliest developmental experiences and awakenings (1999: 54). An important caveat applies to Kakar's analyses, however: they tend toward reifying the "Indian" in Indian society, essentializing Hinduness, and centering on notions such as "the Hindu psyche" or "the Hindu mind"; these notions are problematic not least because of their engaging a political equation of "Indian" with "Hindu." If we bear these limitations in mind, Kakar's insights are helpful toward developing a notion of sensorium. Unlike Klein, Kakar does not confine the mother's sensory presence to "the good breast" but extends it to actions such as caressing, touch, speech, singing, and so on—in other words, to the constitution of a "primary sensorium." Moreover, in contradistinction to this phase of development being habitually identified with infants in European society, Kakar extends it among Indian children to the age of three to five on the basis of his own observations pertaining to differential experiences of separation and constraints. The extended scope of this period for the production of a primary sensorium significantly suggests the possibility of an even deeper experiential continuum between life at home and life at school; for the experiences of earlier nurturing are largely invoked in Marathi classrooms, where teachers frequently resort to positive associations and normalized memories of "mother-at-home."

Indeed, reference to mother fills the school day continuously. Pupils are constantly reminded of their home and family during lessons wherein female and male teachers regularly take mothers as examples for purposes of explaining or clarifying a point. The material drawn upon here also ranges from distinctly regional stories about seventeenth-century hero-warrior Shivaji and his close relationship with his own mother (Chapter 4), to moral stories popular across many parts of the world. Examples abound, from "One should listen to mummy's advice" (Aice aikayce), narrating the trouble caused for a child who disobeys his mother; to autobiographical accounts, notably by freedom fighter and educationist Sane Guruji (*Shyam's Mother*; see Chapter 1). In addition, the mother's ideal nurturing quality is conjured up and discursively reproduced through various mediations, particularly that of food. In this respect, it is no coincidence that the story of the little boy should take place during lunchtime. In the many references to family life and domestic routine that teachers make, mummy's cooking (*aica svaipak*), to which she is expected to lovingly devote hours for the benefit of her offspring, occupies a prominent place.[2] Even math lessons can provide an impromptu occasion for such culinary evocation; for instance, Ms. Pratima B. at Varsity Marathi School borrows a chapati from a pupil's lunchbox for the purpose of teaching division to her Class 3 and tears the chapati into several identical parts. Arguably, these everyday school experiences crucially reinforce and (re)produce "precursors" constituted in the early phases of an infant's life.

Food as an intimate, tactile, sensual object most often mediates bonding between a mother and her child. In Maharashtra, mothers (and elder females) feed their children from their own hands until the children reach the age of four or five, and this is often accompanied with some playfulness on either part. Following Klein, Erikson contends that these "seemingly small and playful bits in the earliest ritualized behaviour in life" are especially important, for they operate as "precursors to lifelong behaviours of great emotional and adaptive significance, all the way to ritual ceremony" (2002: 18). I shall return to this shortly. For the moment, I want to emphasize that this "maternalization" of the pedagogical space is also congruent with official teachings. For instance, the mother ideology is reflected in the textual and pictorial presence suffusing the official curriculum.

The textbooks produced by the regional bureau are replete with illustrations of the normalization of the mother trope. The latter informs even the pupils' first official encounter with the written word in Class 1. The Marathi textbook (*Marathi Bal Bharati* 1998: 15) presents children with two small pictures of "house or home" (*ghar*) and "mother or mummy" (*āī*), the latter being depicted in a loving embrace with a small child. These drawings are set below a larger one covering the full width of the page, representing a school scene with pupils leaving for home and, prominently displayed, a mother picking up her daughter while carrying an infant on her hip. The words and corresponding phonemes are repeated on three different lines occupying the bottom third of the page. In addition, the figure of the mother recurs in many subsequent lessons, where she is pictured engaging in diverse activities with her children, from going to the market (18), to choosing fruit (20), to having a glass of fresh sugarcane juice (*usaca ras*; 21), and so on. Similar references also appear in the textbooks meant for the next three classes of the primary curriculum.

Mothers do not only metaphorically pervade the public yet secluded space of school. As illustrated by the sari story, the family space itself is re-created at school and inhabited by other mothers, that is, female teachers. In this context, the sari importantly functions as both a corporeal envelope for the female protagonist and a comfort blanket for the child, that is, as a mediation for maternal bonding first constructed in the warmth of home.[3] The sari here may be compared to what French psychoanalyst Didier Anzieu (1989) called the "moi-peau," or "ego-skin," thereby defining a transitional and protective space between the child's bodily envelope and her or his environment. The "ego-skin sari" illustrates the fundamental relation between a motherly teacher and a child-pupil, a relation explicitly articulated by female teachers themselves, even the most severe and awe-inspiring ones. Teachers would often conflate the notions of wifehood and motherhood with the bodily discipline of sari wearing. The wearing of a sari in Maharashtra is emblematic of a woman's married status and, by extension, of motherhood. Congruently, teachers often made comments such as these: "In order to teach, a woman must be married; a teacher is a mother." Or "It is our culture; we must be like mothers at school." Through such statements, these female teachers enacted discursive and bodily incorporation of a norm extant in Marathi-speaking schools, namely, that no female teacher is allowed to wear anything but a sari.[4] This norm is officially enforced from the beginning of teacher training: teachers' training colleges alone have in Maharashtra established the sari as compulsory uniform for female students, thereby explicitly conflating normative patterns of pedagogical behavior with wifehood and motherhood.[5]

It should also be noted that it is not *any* sari that is made compulsory, but the "six-yard sari" (*sawari sari*). This by now "classic" icon of female modernity has come to replace the more traditional Maharashtrian "nine yards" (*nawari*)

Marathi Language Textbook, Class 1, **1998. One of the first lessons Marathi-speaking children learn, on "home" and "mother."**

SOURCE: *Marathi Language Textbook, Class 1*, Pune, Maharashtra State Bureau of Textbook Production and Curriculum Research, 1998, p. 15.

both in urban and rural settings, especially among the younger generations. In rural areas, women married in the past fifteen to twenty years and whose own mothers wore cotton *nawari saris*, have begun wearing polyester *sawaris*. When asked the reason for this choice, they would often declare: "We feel ashamed, when/if we wear a nawari sari" (Amhala laj watte, nawari sari nesli ki). The latter garment in fact embraces and reveals the female form rather conspicuously, as the cloth is passed in between the legs and tied up at the back, leaving the calves exposed. Although it is much more practical than its more recent counterpart for an "active modern life," in that it allows greater freedom of movement for cycling, riding a scooter, or boarding a bus, it makes the female body more open to public gaze. By contrast, the *sawari sari* attempts to conceal much more, as it wraps up the entire lower body. Furthermore, especially in urban settings and in the workplace, women tend to pin the border (*padar*) to the tonal matching blouse, in an ultimate gesture toward keeping modern modesty in its place. At play here is an interesting convergence of idioms of modernity and Victorian-like morality in the production of respectable motherhood and "teacherhood," similar to that documented in earlier projects of national construction (Gupta 2001).

The conflation between "mothers-at-home" and "mothers-at-school" is both made manifest and naturalized through poems and songs. Mothers in Maharashtra have at least since the seventeenth century been associated with the notion of life gurus, even though the majority of them would not have been trained in any formal way. Thus, the famous poem "Guru Brahma guru Vishnu" written by Marathi poet Ramdas exemplifies this equation of mother with guru in its second part:

> My mother is my guru; she is the *kalpataru* [wish-fulfilling tree] to me.
> She is the ocean of happiness; she is the *maher* [a girl's natal family residence] of love.
> She is the stream of *amrut* [water of life or immortality]; my mother is the essence of good.

This song has been sung in Kolhapur for the past fifteen to twenty years in some Marathi schools—including the two most Hindu-sympathetic schools wherein fieldwork was conducted—and more recently in others. The poem is chanted daily, usually during the morning assemblies, whether in the hall or within each classroom. Interestingly, it is through the mediation of the concept of guru that the association (in the psychoanalytic sense) of mothers and teachers seems to come rather "naturally" to children and adults. Thus, when the teacher of a Class 2 of girls at Modern Marathi School attempted to explain the meaning of two chants about mother and country, she asked, "Who is a guru?" Two pupils immediately answered: "God" (dev) and then "Mother" (ai). The teacher then asked the children, "Why? Why is mother a guru?" After much perplexed silence in the classroom, she herself volunteered an explanation: "Because she gives life. Mother, Madam [Bai, used as a term of address for female teachers], they both give life. Mother teaches at home, she feeds you, and Madam continues the job at school and teaches you well." This explicit articulation of divinity and motherhood is of special import with regard to the gendered notion of the Indian nation, Bharat Mata.

Domestic Space, National Space: Producing Mother-India

The conflated idea of mother and country pervades all Marathi-language schools, from the most secular to the most *Hindutva*-leaning ones, where it may take on an exacerbated character. Moreover, the conflated conceptualization of motherhood, devotion, and pedagogy is resonant with Erikson's elaboration of Klein's argument that "capacity for identification with another person [or a deity] is a most important element in human relationships in general, and is also a condition for real and strong feelings of love" (1964: 66). For Erikson, the central element of the ritualization of infancy—which he calls the "numinous"—remains closely associated with the devotional ritual, whether in institutionalized religion or in other belief systems (2002: 19). This is important in light of motherhood providing a common thematic as well as symbolic resource for ideologies ranging from totalitarian to liberal (see Koonz 1987 for the Nazi regime). In these ideologies, motherhood is conceived of as the fundamental constitutive and emblematic expression of the family to be put at the service of the nation. In India, as we have seen, this emblem is especially powerful among the majority Hindu society, for the country is both a mother figure and a (Hindu) goddess. India is indeed Mother-India, Bharat Mata.

Bharat Mata is the product of colonial negotiations from other parts of India, Bengal in particular. Exemplifying the crucial equation of "mother-deity-country" from the very inception of the modern Indian nation is the song "Vande Mataram" ("Mother, I Bow to Thee"), which first appeared in Bankim Chandra Chatterji's late nineteenth-century novel *Ananda Math* (The Monastery of Bliss) (1882), famous for its strongly anti-Muslim overtones.[6] The song is an address to India in the form of a (Hindu) mother-goddess. Importantly, this mother in the novel is devastated and violated, in dire need of protection, and the address is performed by "her sons," that is, men (mainly combatant monks) who have taken up arms to right the wrong done to her. Chatterji's narrative crucially needs to be situated within the production of the Indian nation, where the category of "Bharat" progressively became naturalized as a concrete geohistorical unit involving a gendered territorial mapping: producing the nation came to entail both "naturalizing" an abstraction and endowing it with corpo-reality, not least of all that of a mother (Goswami 2004: 199).[7] Particularly noteworthy in this production is that the modern trope of Bharat Mata came to work as a highly gendered "matrix of nationalist identification and desire" (199). Unfortunately, even with reference to popular nationalism, the repertoire so far discussed in the literature has been of exclusively upper-caste, north Indian Hindu devotional practices. This leaves unattended the advent of such a gendering (apart from a first appearance mentioned in a Hindi play in 1876 [199]), as well as the other repertoires of popular practices feeding into such a construction. Arguably, the conditions of production of such an incarnation require attention, if only because the notion of Bharat Mata has been a political object of contention between Hindus and Muslims since the latter part of the nineteenth century and well into the early decades of the twentieth. More recently in the postindependence decades, the motherly notion has further crystallized nationalist desire among Hindu middle and lower-middle classes.

Similarly to the reconfiguration of space as nation/mother in the colonial period, postindependence Bharat Mata draws on the "constitutive slippage in mother-child relations and that between devotee and godhead in popular Hindu devotional practices" (Goswami 2004: 202). This slippage is exemplified by the singing of "Vande Mataram" in Maharashtra as well. The song is sung on special occasions of national commemoration, although it has long been opposed by Muslim and secular groups. More recently, it has become prominent in the daily marking of school time in an increasing number of Marathi primary institutions in Kolhapur. As elsewhere in the regional state (including Mumbai), pupils and teachers used to end the day with the chanting of the "Pasaydan." This extract from the epic poem "Dnyaneshwari" takes its name from its author, the popular thirteenth-century regional saint and poet Dnyaneshwar (Chapter 1). Despite the poem's long-standing popularity, it is now being replaced with the singing of "Vande Mataram." I first heard the latter sung at a private school in Kolhapur in August 1998. By the end of 1999, it had spread widely throughout the schooling network and was sung in many other (private as well as corporation) schools, either during collective assemblies (rare) or separately in each classroom. The controversial song's accrued resonance in schools may be a product of refresher courses systematically organized for primary school teachers throughout Maharashtra in the mid- to late 1990s under the BJP–Shiv Sena coalition government (see Introduction). Nonetheless, many teachers and parents in Kolhapur claimed to have sung it regularly as schoolchildren, too. Whatever the case may be, it is noteworthy that (Hindu) devotion to the national motherland today appears to have superseded regional devotion.

This pedagogical conflation of domestic, devotional, and national female figures is both meaningful to a sizable number of social actors in this part of Maharashtra and congruent with official expectations at the district level where it is taught, as testified by the proceedings of an afternoon session held in February 2000 at the DIET College during a week-long "singing refresher course." The main instructor was a Mr. Biradarkar, a former headmaster from Kolhapur, who also was a former member of the local RSS branch. After teaching the trainees children's mimes and animal songs, he continued with a "moral story" (*boddh katha*) about two children left to their own devices. One of them did not listen to his parents' advice and consequently ran into trouble, while the other, virtuous child was praised as a paragon to be emulated by the listeners. The instructor concluded the story by emphasizing the morals the trainee-teachers should thoroughly teach the young ones in their care, stating: "To the children, you must tell them these morals, that they must love their mothers [*aivar prem (thevayce)*]." After much persistent exhortation, Mr. Biradarkar added, "So, just in the same way, [they must love] Mother-India; they must learn to love her" (Mag tasec, Bharat Matevar prem, shikayce). And, lest the identification of mother and nation and the compelling nature of the love they were both supposed to elicit were not explicit enough, the instructor burst into an emphatic and feverish demonstration of morning liturgy: after a *shlok* meant to be sung every day, "My Mother Is My Guru" (Ai majhya guru; see Chapter 1), he continued with the national anthem, whose meaning and teaching he explained in elaborate detail. Then he proceeded to recite the pledge, with due emphasis on each word. Next came a series of Marathi and Hindi nationalist songs, the first of which was "Victory to Mother-India" (Bharat Mata ki Jay) and the last, "Mother-India" (Bharat Mã).[8] Here is the literal translation of the refrain: "Say: Mother-India's Victory" (repeated three times) (Bolo Bharat Mata ki Jay).[9] Judging by the body language of most of the trainees, Mr. Biradarkar clearly succeeded. To be sure, not all teachers in the district may have been as interested in this patriotic singing as the majority of their fellow trainees. Even among these, some were more blatantly enthusiastic than others, regardless of gender. However, when it came to punctuating the songs with the above slogans, whether automatically or on their own volition, all of them partook of the collective energetic outburst of these emotional iterations.

Such iterations form an important part of the incorporation process I seek to document and require further elaboration. Incorporation indeed involves the developing of uttering, iterative capacity: songs are important items in the constitution of this primary sensorium, but so are shouts and screams, especially what, in psychotherapeutic parlance and since the work of Arthur Janov (1970), is referred to as "primal scream." Remarkably, in ordinary Marathi schools, iterations of devotion to the nation most conspicuously take place at the time of chanting and praying Mother-India into existence, as well as, congruently with Hindu mythology, invoking the mother-goddess's side as a fierce warrior. It is in this capacity that she protects the country and receives praise from her children, of all ages. In Kolhapur's schools, after singing "Vande Mataram," the teacher would often command the pupils, "Say: Mother-India's?" (Bola: Bharat Mata ki?). The pupils would respond, "Victory!" (Jay!) As the children shouted, they would "automatically" clench their fists promptly as taught to do in the daily morning sessions. The teacher might finally order them once more, "Vande?" "Mataram!" would chorus the children again.[10] Furthermore, the importance of this primal scream is such that in some classrooms, particularly among the junior classes, "Bharat Mata ki Jay!" was the only regular iteration punctuating the end of the school day. This iteration needs to be further qualified, in light of the very notion of "primal scream." In his foundational book, Janov discussed the central issue of psychospiritual, often hidden, suffering. Janov distinguished three levels at which traumatic experiences occur, the second and third ones being related to teenage years and adulthood, respectively. The first-level experiences, which have been the most controversial and debated of Janov's theory, are associated with early childhood deprivation and, as crucially, both the traumas of the birthing process and various experiences of intrauterine distress.

Although Janov's work is still considered a precursor today, it can be situated in a genealogy dating back to the work of Otto Rank, an early disciple of Freud. Freud himself never gave much weight to Rank's insights. Yet the disciple was undeterred in his conviction of the reality of birth trauma and devoted himself unconditionally to the creation of a form of psychoanalysis that worked directly with birth.[11] Rank's work, however, was to remain at the periphery of mainstream psychoanalysis. It was still so at the time when Janov wrote, almost half a century later. Taking his cue from Rank's work and elaborating on the trauma of birth, Janov made central to his theoretical focus the need to be loved and the psychic torments resulting from the unfulfillment of that need. He subsequently devised the famous "scream therapy" that has since known many variants. Although I do not know of any experimentation of this therapy in India, the trauma of birth is not specific to Euro-American countries and linked to their birthing practices alone. Especially among the Indian middle classes, increasing medicalization practices have compounded the probability of traumatic birth (Henrike Donner, pers. comm. 2006; also Parry 1994 about the travails of embryonic life). The point of this clarification is to shed light on the "matrix of nationalist identification and desire" (Goswami 2004) that has known many vicissitudes since its reconfiguration in the latter nineteenth century, especially in the mid-twentieth century in the years of Partition. Arguably, the slogans and other iterations daily regurgitated by children and adults alike in the school space of national reconstruction may be read as unconscious attempts at healing the entangled traumas of their own births together with that of the nation. Inasmuch as the nation is daily produced within their own bodies (Chapter 2), screaming in unison allows conjuring of their own pain, suffering, and anxiety of birth, together with that of the birthing nation. More than just inscribing the nation in their own bodies, then, pupils and—even more so—teachers are in effect transacting its pain and suffering with love and desire for it. Such an interpretation is also congruent with the notion Gananath Obeyesekere (1981, 1990) developed in his work on Hindu and Buddhist myth and ritual that anxieties and deep motivations of the group, by being externalized, enable the individual to share her or his anxiety and achieve "elation or consolation" (1990: 27).

To be sure, the notion of a loving and nurturing mother used for purposes of nationalist constructions is a modern, idealized one whose psychoanalytic and mythological counterpart lies in the figure of the horrific mother (Doniger 1980). Yet the latter precludes neither the foregrounding of the former in contemporary times nor its operating as an all-encompassing, potentially exhaustive figure. On the contrary, it reinforces the thesis of a split—two contrasted, incomplete images. The possible existence and experience of an alternative negative figure may produce and further strengthen anxieties about the ever unrealizable ideal of "the good mother" so dominantly reproduced in the ideological space of school. It might even be argued in light of Juliet Mitchell's (2003) recent study of sibling rivalry in her reappraisal of Melanie Klein's work that these anxieties may render transference at the level of Mother-India a process ever more fraught with potential sectarian violence.[12]

Mother, Country, and Children:
The Performative Power of Tautology

Reconciling a phenomenological approach with a pragmatic and psychoanalytic one also entails addressing the issue of meaning and meaningfulness to the children of what they chant, recite, and sing. Because many of the songs and prayers chanted by the pupils in an average Marathi school refer to Bharat Mata, one may also ponder the meaning the children endow on these songs and prayers. How do they understand this Bharat Mata; how do they relate to "her"? The issue is especially relevant that *mata* in Marathi is only used for goddesses, unlike in Hindi, where the term also signifies "mother" (as in the phrase *mata-pita*). This exclusive meaning raises the issue whether the pupils are able to establish a connection between "India" and "mother" in ordinary life. Evidence from Classes 1 to 4 reveals that most of the pupils had at least a vague idea of this connection. Moreover, if their notions of "motherland" were not yet very articulated, their teachers were often willing to help them make it explicit. In the process, verbal allegiance to both the family and the country in the guise of an unconditional love of the mother and of the motherland reunited, were informally "reenacted" and further nurtured. Bearing witness to this is a session that took place at the Modern Marathi School. The exchange occurred in the class of Ms. Sonya M., a warmhearted woman in her early forties of the Sutar caste (carpenters), according to the following pattern: I put my questions out in Marathi (Class 2, all girls), and then the teacher repeated the questions, at times clarifying and/or illustrating them for the pupils.[13] For instance, when I began by refreshing the children's memories about the start of their school day, with the singing of the national anthem, Sonyabai repeated my words in several different ways. During the entire intercourse, she also encouraged the pupils upon each utterance on their part, by repeating their answers approvingly. Next, I ("VB" in the dialogue) asked:

> "After you have sung the national anthem, what do you say?"
>
> The teacher repeated, breaking up the words and emphasizing thus: "You have sung the national anthem, haven't you? 'Jana Gana Mana,' haven't you? Then after this, what do you actually say?"

Several pupils in a single voice: "The pledge."

VB: "No, before that, just when you finish singing the national anthem."

[*What I had in mind were the slogans performed immediately after the song, in praise of and swearing allegiance to Bharat Mata. Meanwhile, Sonyabai repeated my question, hammering out the words distinctly and loudly several times. A group of children started singing the national anthem, promptly interrupted by the teacher, who repeated the question yet again, helping them to the point of almost giving out the answer.*]

Several pupils suddenly burst out all at once: "Mother-India's Victory!" [Bharat Mata ki Jay!] [*Some of the girls automatically raised their fists as they had been used to doing in the morning assembly.*]

VB: "What does it mean?

The teacher repeats: "What does 'Bharat Mata ki Jay' mean?"

One pupil: "It is in Marathi." [*The slogan, as many others, is actually in Hindi but is also used by Marathi speakers.*][14]

Another pupil: "Bharat Mata is our country."

VB: "What about 'Jay'? What is it?"

The teacher repeats: "Bharat Mata is our country, but what does 'Jay' mean? Whose 'jay'?"

One girl, Purnima R.: "'Jay' is our tricolor [*tiranga*]," referring to the national flag.

[*By that time, Sonyabai has started losing patience. Intent on clarifying meanings for the pupils, she begins pacing up and down the classroom as she speaks with a clear, loud, energetic voice, summoning their attention. Her entire body language reflects her tension and concentration. The children, who were getting slightly fidgety, are quiet again.*]

Teacher: "Our country is Bharat Mata, isn't it?"

The children duly chorus: "Yes!" [Ho!]

Teacher: "We call our country 'mother,' don't we?"

The children chorus again with the same diligence: "Yes!"

Teacher: "Well, we celebrate our mother, don't we?" [Jayjaykar karto, aila?]

The term *jay* (or its reduplicated form) encompasses the meanings of "conquest, victory, and triumph." It is significantly used primarily for deities (as in "Jay Vithoba") and with reference to heroes, warriors, and soldiers, from seventeenth-century Shivaji to the soldiers fighting in Kargil in the late 1990s. By extension, the phrase jayjaykar karne means "celebrating the praises [of a deity, of a hero, an important person, and so on], extolling with acclamations and shouts." The use of such a phrase in the present context vividly illustrates the intricate association of motherhood, divinity, and war. Here again, the children duly chorus: "Yes!" Next, Sonyabai goes on to explain that the chants "Vande Mataram" and "Pahila Namaskar" (which contains separate references to mother and country) are about the "same thing: 'mother' and 'country.'"[15] As no pupil appears to know the meaning of either prayer/chant, the teacher apologetically tells me in an aside that she did not know it either when she was little, in spite of chanting the prayers every day. After her explanations, I pursue the interaction on the meaning of deshbhakti (patriotism; Chapter 1). In order to exemplify the question, the teacher asks the pupils: "Why do we sing a song about the country?" At this point, a pupil named Purnima promptly raises her finger and, in a perfectly logical association with the preceding exchange, proffers: "For our mothers."

Whether Purnima and her fellow students really conceptualized Bharat Mata as a mother at all is obviously difficult to assess from this and other anecdotes. At no point in the course of research did a pupil or a child offer such an explicit verbalization of transference from mother/teacher to mother-as-nation. Yet, the fact that at least an association of "their own mothers" with the country somehow, and however confusingly, did at times surface is enough of a convergence with the bodily processes at play in the crucial early years of schooling and socialization. Indeed, it does not matter whether children understand in the cognitive sense what they are doing. Rather, what does matter is the re-creation of a primary sensorium in everyday life at school. This is accompanied by bodily incorporation of powerful and emotionally resonant songs, music, martial rhythms, beating of drums, and so on. That children may not fully understand or be able to explain (which indicates a higher level of conceptualization) the songs they are taught is irrelevant. It is so both with respect to the phenomenological argument I am making here and to teacher's pragmatics. For, according to the teachers, children should first and foremost *feel* these chants and prayers, imbibe them, all of this contributing toward making them good Hindus/Indians. Other teachers similarly confided that they also did not understand the meaning of the songs and prayers they used to sing at the same age. Parents, too, commented that they were only much later able to make meaning of the prayers and songs they had been made to commit to memory and sing daily as children. What nonetheless made these actions very powerful, according to the Hindu teachers among them (Brahmins as well as Marathas and allied castes), was their being sung as prayers (*prarthana*), imbuing them with a "sacred" (*pavitra*) character. This much, they claimed, was understood by all the children, for it was similar to what would be done at home by the gods' shrine. Such a comment obviously leaves unattended the implications of this pedagogy for Muslim teachers and pupils in Marathi schools (Chapter 5). As we will see, it more generally points to the limitations of emotional incorporation of the nation.

Furthermore, the notion of "feeling the song, chant, or prayer" emphasized by some teachers brings home the utmost import of accessing the songs' melody and musicality, the latter becoming a powerful emotional and sensory reservoir in the daily performance of the re-creation of Mother-India. It is through the constitution of this sensory resource that transference from mother-teacher to mother-nation is actually enacted. Later on or in adult life, the meaning of what was then sung may become more explicit; then, even impromptu situations may trigger some behavior drawing on this emotional and sensory reservoir. This may be the case, for instance, when teachers draw upon their early childhood experiences of singing patriotic songs during refresher courses at the training college. In these circumstances, the adult trainees often appeared strikingly infantilized by their instructors and conformed to a disciplinary pattern internalized from school days, the very same pattern they reproduced in their daily professional life with their own pupils.[16] Other impromptu situations may be more dramatic, especially those triggering anxiety over the threat of the mother-nation's bodily integrity and calling for her protection. The long-standing issue of Kashmir bears testimony to this: it is viscerally impossible for many Indians to conceive parting with "the head of the body of India," whether for the realization of an independent state or, "worse still," for a merger with Pakistan.[17] The issue of the nation's integrity has been emotionally charged since the birth of the independent nation-state. It is in this context that the potent register of war engaged by the "mother" motif at the levels of family, school, and nation must be situated.

War, Gender, and Nation

If Mother-India instantiates the nation, it is also in her name that the frontiers with the archrival enemy of Pakistan must be preserved and war be fought. In the two years that followed the Kargil war in the summer of 1999, this martial quality was redeployed in myriad ways, further reinforcing the gender and warrior ideologies incorporated from an early age. Thus, in the show that took place in the kindergarten section of the Varsity Marathi School in February 1999, the concluding skit pictured "soldiers of Kargil." Fifteen four-year-old boys dressed as soldiers in fatigues marched onstage to the air of "Vande Mataram," cutting imaginary enemies' heads off and killing them in various other ways. The skit ended with the following short exchange between the teachers and the boys, who answered each time while raising their fists:

Teachers: "Say: Mother-India's,"	"Bola Bharat Mata ki,"
Pupils: "Victory!"	"Jay!"
. . .	. . .
Teachers: "Beloved beloved,"	"Pyara pyara,"
Pupils: "Hindustan!"	"Hindustan!"
. . .	. . .
Teachers: "Hindustan."	"Hindustan."
Pupils: "Long live!"	"Jindabad!"

Thus is attempted incorporation of gender together with national sentiment. It is also in this light that we can read the story encountered earlier of the little boy and the teacher's sari. This story is not only suggestive of the imagined conflation of mother and teacher; in addition, it speaks of an especially nurtured, emotional relation between a *female* parent and a *male* child. Such a relation is congruent with the historical construct of Bharat Mata and the dominant patriarchal norms in popular culture where maternal love is supposed to focus on—or be exhausted in—little boys. (The epitome of such a relationship is the mythological one of baby Krishna with his mother, Yashoda, often represented as absolutely wrapped up in her beloved prodigy's pranks.) As such, it is also a vivid illustration of the first phase of gendered national bonding: that of the nurturing mother taking care of her son, until the latter becomes old enough to protect her. This particular relationship is exemplified in various other ways, thus further contributing to the informal production of gender in the pedagogical space. It was especially so in the two years that followed the 1999 war in Kashmir. The events revealed the soldierly heroism of Bharat Mata's sons at the level of the nation. In schools, too, the events gave rise to lessons in masculine heroism. These were noticeably and actively taught by female teachers of all castes and classes. Moreover, in teaching war to male pupils, the female teachers reproduced gendered metaphors of motherhood and war: mothers giving away their sons for the protection of the country.

By way of example, let me take you to the rehearsals and preparations for the annual show of the kindergarten section that took place in January 2000 at

All India Marathi School, the most progressive primary school in the city, run by an educational society founded by a socialist freedom fighter. The teachers, all females from Maratha, Nav Boddh, and Mali castes, are feverishly setting the stage, aligning the children for the last skit and making final recommendations to them.

The show consists of four mimed and danced performances. The first three are ordinary, circular children's dances, including a fishermen's dance (a "must" in all school shows). The last and crowning skit, however, is nowhere near as ordinary. At least, so I think at the time, shortly upon my return to Kolhapur that year. As I will discover in the following weeks, it has actually become part of the ordinary in Marathi schools. Put simply, this skit reenacts "war in Kargil." Six boys aged from three to five are made to lie down while holding a large piece of wood meant to represent a gun. The teachers are now busying themselves in earnest, teaching the boys how to mime rifling and gunning from the ground. Whereas some of the toddlers appear uninterested in the proceedings, others seem more receptive to the martial teachings. All along, a four-year-old girl is dancing hesitantly in the forefront with arabesques gesturing toward the sky, in a shy yet smiling attempt at miming her love of, and delight for, the country. Indicating the centrality of this skit is the eagerness displayed by the teachers to get it exactly right, as well as the amount of time spent comparatively on rehearsing it. As teacher Kamla B. vehemently asserts at the end of the rehearsal: "This is to do as in Kargil; you know, Kargil, there is war over there, they [signaling to the children] must learn."

Female Negotiations

Obviously, such a gendered production and incorporation of the nation at school jointly entails models of "proper feminine" behavior in accordance with patriarchal rules of female subservience. These models are constantly redeployed in daily life. Although the principle of gender equality is conveniently paid lip service—namely, by teaching the basics of the Constitution at the Class 4 level—every single aspect of the school day often reinforces the contrary message, that is, that girls come second. This is exemplified in subtle ways ranging from proxemics to sexuality and hygiene wherein boys are given precedence: for instance, in the seating arrangements in coed classes; while coming out of the classroom at break time, going to the bathroom, getting off the bus during the annual school trip, visiting a public place on the trip; or even when special arrangements are made for boys' proper concrete bathrooms but girls are still expected to go and hide behind a makeshift screen (such was still the case in 2000 at Varsity Marathi School, one of the most popular primary schools in Kolhapur and famously known for its founding by Brahmins).[7]

Because they are exemplified by an overwhelming majority of female teachers, these behavior patterns may also acquire particular significance or legitimacy in view of the conflation of "good wifehood, good motherhood, and good patriotism." Yet enacting these ideals and model behaviors does not preclude a liberating role reversal in which women, by virtue of their positions as teachers, are also able to indirectly convey injunctive messages to male parents while posing as the guarantors of national order. In this sense, this role reversal also effects a pragmatic realization of the transference from "mother at home" to "mother at school." Such transference further enables that from "mother-teacher" to "Mother-India." Through taking their roles as mothers into the national domain, female primary school mistresses effected a link—symbolic, discursive, and pragmatic—between the space of home and school and that of the wider nation. Teachers would often assert, "We are in fact better mothers than these children's mothers, because we know better how to teach them how to behave, how to become clean and proper, how to become good citizens." This they demonstrated in various ways and deeds.[18] Even a Marathi lesson in Class 3 about the invention and introduction of television would provide the schoolmistresses with an impromptu avenue for lecturing on civic and patriotic duties. Thus, at the end of the lesson on that morning in October 1999 at the All India Marathi School, Sherifabai, a sharp and lively Muslim teacher then in her late thirties, proceeded to admonish the pupils to both limit their daily TV consumption and tell their parents to watch the news bulletins. As she bitterly complained that parents tend to turn off their sets as soon as the film has ended and just before the news, a boy exclaimed: "This is just what Daddy does!" Sherifabai promptly answered: "Well, from now on, you must tell your daddy to watch the news. Yes, you must tell your daddy to watch the news so you all get to know what is happening in the country, what is going on in our country [apla desh], what is going on in any other country." She paused, then started again more vehemently, referring to the military (sainik) in Kargil: "While we are sitting here at home watching, they are waging war for our country; they are giving their lives for us. Therefore, we must watch the news."

Furthermore, analyzing instances of dominant role models in the school context begs the question of the processes and margin of negotiation that women may make available for themselves. Much as social institutions are sites of gender role production, they should not be misconstrued as either total or final or as preempting negotiation. Important to note is that the dichotomized understandings of male and female categories in Indian society—and many other societies, for that matter—today are the contingent products of colonial encounters with Victorian notions (Connell 1995b). However, this should arguably not exhaust the field of possibilities for thinking about gender in India. The same comment obtains with respect to the supposed homogeneity of the realities encompassed by the categories of male and female in psychoanalysis. As shown by the work of Nancy Chodorow (1994, 1999), the categories used in psychoanalytic discourse, not least of all Freudian and Lacanian, have largely operated within normative formations tying heterosexuality to male dominance and sexuality to gender.[19] It is with this awareness that we should approach the production of gendered knowledge, bodies, disciplined persons, citizens, and institutions along with norms and values. These processes, no more than early socialization does, imply systematicity or exhaustiveness. In other words, the gendered construction of citizens and nations, even as it occurs through incorporative processes and successive deployments of variously constituted sensoriums, is always an incomplete one. If daily labor is required to perpetuate appearances of habitus-based dispositions, the habitus itself allows for failures and also interstices, from which social actors, as they evolve their socially interiorized selves, can develop "arts de faire" (de Certeau) involving as much accommodation as cunning negotiation. Consequently, whether in the domain of health and hygiene or in that of education, the state's relaying institutions cannot irrefragably impose their will upon social agents. Rather, institutions are made of and by social actors in a series of adjustment processes (Fuller and Benei 2000). Testifying to this is the implementation at the grassroots level of the program in ethical education introduced by the BJP–Shiv Sena coalition in power from 1995 to 1998 in Maharashtra state, wherein teachers negotiated state instructions in their daily work (Benei 2001b).

This raises a more general question of how female social actors generally accommodate the social constraints imposed upon them, and of the interstices within the social fabric in which they can knit their own narratives. What resources do they have at their disposal outside the more traditional settings of rural life and popular songs (Grodzins Gold and Goodwin Raheja 1994; Bagwe 1995; Goodwin Raheja 2003) within the school precincts? Possible forms of negotiation with respect to dominant patriarchal expectations of patriotic and pedagogical motherhood abound. They may range from sheer diplomacy to overt resistance. Faced with significant pressure to conform to patterns of gender domination prevalent in Indian society, female teachers at times actively and subtly engage with them even when they seem fairly submissive to, and instrumental in, furthering them. The dress code provides a telling illustration.

We saw earlier that the "modern sari" dress code strongly prevailed for married women in this part of Maharashtra. Female teachers conformed to such a dress code in their work environment and were often rather vocal about it, sometimes expressing pride in it. Thus, in all the Marathi schools (even the most progressive ones) where research was carried out, the following comment was often heard from the female staff: "It is our Maharashtrian culture, our Indian culture, after marriage, women should wear nothing but a sari" (Amci Maharashtratli sanskruti ahe, amci Bhartiya sanskruti, lagna jhale ki striyala saric nesayci). Female teachers were also prompt to publicly stigmatize any "deviant" form of clothing, whether worn by their colleagues or any other women, including foreigners (such as the anthropologist). Such deviant forms of clothing included Punjabi suits (also worn by the anthropologist), of the type in fashion in Maharashtra at the time, not only among unmarried young girls but also among the urban upper classes priding themselves on a touch of "modernism" and "cosmopolitanism." Yet I encountered two instances where the hard-and-fast rule about wearing saris was regularly broken without any sanction: the arts teacher, Kavita R., and one of the regular class teachers (out of a total sixteen female staff), Pushpa S., both young and unmarried, regularly wore Punjabi suits. Although they were sometimes the butt of jokes from some elder colleagues, they were never much ostracized by the rest of the teaching community, nor were they made to change their dressing habits by the successive headmasters. It was also very clear, at least in Pushpa's case, that her rejection of the expected dress code was an expression of her resistance toward peer and family pressure as well as an open statement of autonomy and independence from patriarchal models of femininity. Pushpa hardly ever wore jewelry or even a light touch of talcum powder, unlike most of her same-age colleagues, and incidentally expressed her lack of enthusiasm about marriage.

If Pushpa's stance lay at the extreme of a negotiation continuum, it nevertheless confirms the more general point that women's displayed conforming to socially and culturally sanctioned patterns of behavior—especially in their capacity as teachers—does not characterize their social action as a whole, whether within or outside of school. To be sure, the discursive emphasis women expressed about "Maharashtrian culture" (*maharashtratli sanskruti*), "Indian customs" (*bhartiya paddhati*), and so on in the course of public conversations may conjure up a vision of extreme rigidity in their observance of patterns of behavior. Such a vision is contradicted by behavior away from professional surroundings, as I observed at a later stage of research. As I began visiting the teachers in their homes, I found their attitudes in the domestic space far more relaxed than in that of school, even among the staunch defenders of patriarchy. In a sizable number of cases, female teachers even behaved at great variance with the norms they professed at work. One of the most senior schoolmistresses belonging to the old Hindu guard, Ms. Pratima Bhaviskar of Varsity Marathi School, was considerably more lenient than her many pronouncements on "Maharashtrian tradition" might lead one to assume: Ms. Bhaviskar was a staunch advocate of married women wearing saris, tying their hair tight, and abstaining from wearing makeup. She had invited me over several times before I was at last able to pay her a visit during the Diwali holidays of 2000. That day in October she introduced me to her two married daughters, both of whom regularly spent most of their entire days in the natal home while their husbands were at work. One of the daughters ran a small beauty parlor in her mother's house and was markedly made up. Both sisters wore Punjabi suits in and out of the house and sported loose hair, as "cosmopolitan" upper-middle-class Maharashtrian women would do. As I gently pointed this out to Pratima Bai, she responded with a slightly embarrassed laugh, "Today, it is 'fashion' [*sic*] to sport 'loose' [*sic*] hair and wear Punjabi suits; this is not a problem." The senior teacher even attempted to persuade me that despite the strict institutional etiquette, I, too, could indulge in wearing my hair loose at school. Pratima Bai was not an exception. Often, female teachers would wear Punjabi suits at home and on family outings and in many instances acknowledged in private their preference for a more comfortable and airy garment.

This is but one of many examples in which the women most assertively observant of cultural norms and rules at school were found circumventing them once far removed from professional gaze. The dress code may have been among the most trivial and oft-recurring instances of negotiation; there were many others, sometimes even involving life-cycle events such as marriages, with arrangements falling outside the purview of ordinary, acceptable possibilities. In all cases, such instances of negotiation confirmed the fundamental importance of situating the school environment within the larger social and cultural context.

As importantly, the unraveling of the multiple, varied, and colorful threads of teachers' personal lives away from work suggests the incompleteness of socialization and normalization processes.

Conclusions   *kinsmen*

Schooling in this part of India articulates a specific production of regional/ national sentiment with a conspicuously gendered one of fictive kin through notions of *bhauband* and "mother." Rather than schools "privatizing" the individual and the family, consequently eroding identifications with kin groups as a basis for resistance to the state, as done in Egypt (Abu-Lughod 1990), here, the very motif of the family, and of the mother in particular, is redeployed as mediation between family, school, and nation. A school sensorium is further produced articulating and reconfiguring early childhood experiences with ones of schooling, from kindergarten onward. This sensorium is at the heart of the production of national (and regional) schooled selves. Thus, as in Japan, the national (and regional) performance of singing actively builds on the "most physically intimate of relationships—that of mother and child" in an attempt to "establish a sensual link between all national citizens as children," not only of their mothers but, as crucially, of the "mother nation" (Yano 1995: 458–59). Unlike the situation in Japan, however, the production of this sensual link in the Maharashtrian case is dual: the very nation needs to be conceived as a mother in order for this connection between all citizens to happen. Conversely, the notion of mother tongue (*matru bhasha*) operates a selection upon the inhabitants of the regional state, marking those deemed more worthy of sharing the *bhauband* community (community of brothers; see Chapter 1) and associate with a regional Maratha heritage (Chapter 2). Thus, an emotional and sensory definition of national and regional identity is created through the trope of the mother.

Here as in many other instances of nationalism, the trope of the mother importantly articulates with a notion of longing. Analyzing the relationship of Indian television and Hindu nationalism, Arvind Rajagopal (2001) built an argument around the notion of desire: the national serial broadcast of the Hindu epic *Ramayana* crystallized a desire and longing for an authentic nation steeped in a golden age. Now, articulating Rajagopal's argument with Kakar's psychoanalytic notion of desire primarily centered on the mother, it can be argued that school itself purports to function as the womb of the nation where, as the goddess of India is daily reproduced, it also produces its children, its future desiring patriots. Such a conceptualization clearly fails to integrate non-Marathi (and nonstandard) Marathi speakers into the regional/national fold, regardless of all the lip service paid to "religious" tolerance and national integration. Even the less *Hindutva*-sympathetic teachers, while explaining conceptualizations of the mother-deity-nation, articulated them in implicit Hindu terms (also often in congruence with the notion of *samskar*; see Chapter 1). Rarely did a Hindu teacher (Brahmin, Maratha, or even lower caste) express a sense of inclusive awareness of non-Hindu pupils. It is not that the most progressive among them entertained similarly exclusive views of citizenship as those of their RSS-, BJP- or Shiv Sena–inclined counterparts. To some well-meaning, even ecumenical teachers, this formulation in Hindu terms was due to the dominance of Hindu culture as an implicit definer of national culture across India. Yet, arguably, such was the powerfulness of phenomenological school experience primarily premised on Hindu notions that it went unnoticed, or rather, that its political implications did not often surface.

In rethinking gender production in nationalist discourses and practices within the space of school, this chapter also offers a reconsideration of the dichotomous notions of "private/public space." Much has been written about postmodernity and the "decentering of the self." Crucial in this repositioning of the interiority of the subject has been a legitimate critique of the Enlightenment notion of a consistent, unified self operating within a rational Habermasian "bourgeois public sphere" (Habermas 1989). By contrast, postmodernist scholarship placed an emphasis on the notion of a fragmented self, as well as on the plurality of discordant and conflicting voices that surfaced upon lifting the illusory veil of consensual rationality (Lyotard 1984). It may be that tolling the bell for meta-narratives such as the "rational, bourgeois public sphere"— and its oft-attendant nationalism—was unduly optimistic. Yet the critique articulated by some of the thinkers of postmodernism had heuristic potential (Lyotard 1993), in particular in the recognition that "modern" societies, too, rely on "grand narratives." Even Habermas's discussion of the Enlightenment is another attempt at authoritative explanation, itself calling for deconstruction. In an important collective volume, Craig Calhoun (1997) and others (especially Nancy Fraser) pointed to the largely sexist, class-determined, and idealistic bias of the Habermasian concept. However, most, if not all of this critique has been couched in terms of *qualifying* and *redefining* such a public sphere, maintaining the same terms in operation within the derived set of oppositions that have organized Euro-American modern epistemological understanding of the sexual since the beginning of the twentieth century.[20] A similar situation obtains in subalternist and postcolonial scholarship.

There appears to be a paradox in the subalternist and postcolonial scholarship's embrace of postmodern deconstruction. Prominent in, and constitutive of, the intellectual enterprise of the subaltern studies has been the cultivation of vocal plurality. The reinscription of the "voiceless" yet agentic masses within meaningful historical narratives has been accompanied by a need felt to radicalize a critique of the Enlightenment. Whereas subaltern studies have voiced the necessity to decenter both the colonial meta-narrative of capitalism and the body of knowledge it had constituted, they have not gone as far as putting in question the "omniscient and ordering categories" (Arfuch 2002: 18–19) prevalent in the Enlightenment paradigm. Indeed, subalternist scholars have largely continued to work within the same categories used in the construction of a rational, bourgeois discourse congruently with the emergence of nationalisms. And thus the overarching notions of "public" and "private" spheres have remained largely unchallenged in many debates in South Asian and, more generally, postcolonial studies.

Yet these spaces of the public and the private remain arbitrarily defined, standing in an intricate relationship. Works illuminating the debates of the nineteenth and early twentieth centuries about the social conditions of women (widow remarriage, dowry practice, marriage age, and so on) demonstrated the important role women played as fully fledged social actors both in the private sphere and in the construction of public (Hindu) Indian national identity and imagery, thus implicitly shadowing the lines of a public/private dichotomy (Kumar 1993; Sangari 1999; Gupta 2001; T. Sarkar 2002).[21] Despite these breakthroughs, however, the inadequacy of the respective notions of public and private spheres remains to be fully discussed.[22] My purpose is not to expand unduly on this question here. Rather, it is to point to the need for such a discussion to take into account the concomitantly constitutive dimension of gender as discursive, material, and embodied production. Arguably, documenting the production of gender and nation together with spaces in the making of institutions and persons provides an alternative way for thinking beyond these respective dichotomized understandings.

Moreover, the notion of a (school) sensorium predicated upon the primary sensorium formed in the early years of infancy confirms that if the categories of "public" and "private" spheres were good to think through in the first place, and especially to describe the constitution of a national, media space and attending

processes in the nineteenth century, today these categories h
often taken for granted as empirical realities endowed with
reified concreteness, thus functioning as a "crystallization o
in every circumstance" (Arfuch 2002: 75). By contrast, the
developed here helps puncture "the antagonism between the intimate ٍ,
and the public/social one," which "is nothing else but a discourse effect: rules,
constraints, power devices, impulses and emotions" (74). Finally, the tyrannies
and servilities of the public and private worlds that Virginia Woolf bemoaned
no longer appear distinct; rather, they are the product of an arbitrary distinction that dissolves into the world of everyday life today. Arfuch adds that the
political transformations of the last decades as well as the incessant deployment
of new technologies have definitively done away with the classic sense of public
and private, to the point of turning the distinction to be tenuous and "ineffable"
(76). I would like to suggest that this is so in light not only of these political and
technological transformations but, perhaps more fundamentally, of processes
of construction of the self that occurred with generalized schooling. In the following chapter, we pursue this discussion further with the (re)production of
history and masculinity.

Drawing Gender, Drawing War

IF TEACHERS WOULD LEAVE some leeway for the pupils to include various motifs in their sketchbooks, parents, especially of middle-class children, would often take an interest in the drawings and consequently inform their young ones' choices to a certain extent. Despite parents' contributions in the selection and production of a picture, however, pupils were the prime actors. The differences observed between girls' and boys' books, therefore, generally correspond to socially and culturally constructed representations of gender roles in society at large, to which children are exposed from an early age. Thus, although girls' sketchbooks had multiple references to Kargil and the war, those of the boys were by far the most replete with them. Thus, one boy's drawing book at Varsity Marathi School contained a picture of a rocket. Sunil, its artist, laconically commented upon it: "Pakistan." I responded: "Yes?" Sunil went on nodding silently. His fellow pupil and friend Pradeep proffered an interpretation for me: "It is like the battlefields in Kargil; this is what our soldiers use, rockets, they use." The telescoping of two moments close in time (see Introduction) is particularly noteworthy here: the nuclear tests done in the Pokhran desert of Rajasthan in 1998, together with the Kargil war in Kashmir that followed a year later.

In the same class, another boy, Mukesh, had pictured the national Indian flag with a gun and a helmet on its edge displayed across the flag. He had added a caption, which he read for me with much enthusiasm and shiny eyes: "hero" (*vīr*). Such motifs were popular in other classrooms and schools, too. So were newspaper collages, such as the one another boy had made on a full page captioned "India" (*Bharat*), consisting of photographs of soldiers in action as well

Drawing of soldiers fighting in various positions on the Kargil heights. In the background can be seen the national icons of helmet with rifle, symbolizing national valor and bravery, and the Indian flag. Varsity Marathi School, Kolhapur, December 1998.

as featuring in celebrations in their honor upon returning from Kashmir. Other sketchbooks also included some of the collectable items published in the newspapers (see Introduction).

Sunila (age nine) and her Muslim Teacher

I like Mohina Bai. Well, she is a Muslim all right, but who cares? I know what Ai says about them, but Mohina Bai is different. She cares about each one of us here at All India Marathi School like nobody ever has, not even Shantatai, the teacher who lives around the corner from us in the Bazar. Shanta's been so good and supportive; it really is thanks to her that little brother Sunil has not dropped out of school. He hated it so much to start with. He was terrified, would cry all the time, no stopping him; the minute Ai would leave the gate, he would try to run away back home with her. So Shantatai took him in her class, and this was how he got used to school. But Mohina Bai, she knows what life is about. She has seen many places. She has been all over India. And each time she comes back from one of her wonderful trips, she tells us all about it. And when I grow up, I want to be a teacher like Mohina Bai; I want to travel all over

Drawing of Indo-Pakistan war in Kargil. Two soldiers in combat. The one standing on the right is wearing the colors of Pakistan; the one on the left, those of India. The caption reads "Kargil." Ashok L., age eight, Varsity Marathi School, Kolhapur, December 1998.

India, too, but I also want to go abroad and study hard so I, too, like Mohina Bai always says, I, too, can live up to my dreams of getting a good job and earning good money. Anything is possible with some willpower, she says. Even if we wanted to, she told us in class, we, too, could become cosmonauts, like the boy in the poem in our [Marathi] textbook who wants to travel up to the moon. Even we girls, she says. I wonder about this, actually, because people say only boys do that sort of thing. But then, when we did the skits in class, each time, we were one boy and one girl traveling together across space. So maybe Mohina Bai is right; even we girls can do it. If boys can, why not girls? But for this, you need to study very hard, especially science. It is difficult, but I like it. And, as Mohina Bai says, science is most important in your life; if you understand it well, it helps you live better; with science, you can shed these prejudices and superstitions that uneducated people have.

4 Historiography, Masculinity, Locality

Passions of Regional Belonging

Andrea: "Unhappy the land that has no heroes!"
Galileo: "No. Unhappy the land that needs a hero."
Bertolt Brecht, *The Life of Galileo*

[T]he force of sound in alarming the passions is prodigious.
Charles Avison, "An Essay on Musical Expression"

IT WAS LATE IN THE AFTERNOON as the bus entered Satara, a city once the seat of Maratha power. On that hot and dusty April day, the atmosphere aboard was one of tranquil torpor. As the bus made its entry into town amid general indifference and drowsy passengers, a three-year-old suddenly sprang to her feet, shouting: "Shivaji Maharaj! Shivaji Maharaj!" Drawn out of some aimless reverie, I turned around to discover the girl's radiant face a few seats away from mine. "Shivaji Maharaj! Shivaji Maharaj, look, look!" Neelima kept shouting excitedly. Her finger, pressed against the window, pointed at the majestic bronze statue standing outside. The seventeenth-century hero-warrior was mounted on a horse, impervious to the traffic and horns of modern times. The bus drove around the monument. The little girl by now stood on her bench seat with great trepidation. A few other passengers turned their heads to watch the child in amusement. Seated next to her, her parents smiled proudly at their daughter's precocious achievements. The family was from the well-off middle classes of Kolhapur, on their way to some relative's wedding a few miles further. Nodding in approval, the parents praised their daughter: "Yes, Shivaji Maharaj, our Shivaji Maharaj, that's right. Well done, Neelu!"

This brief encounter several years ago on an intercity bus in the south of Maharashtra changed the course of my research. At the time, I was working on a sociological project looking at higher secondary educational facilities and industrialization (Benei 1997). I had envisaged studying regionalism and nationalism in an educational setting, focusing on university- and college-level

students as a kind of follow-up population. In a matter of a few seconds, Neelima brilliantly shattered this plan, bringing home to me the need for studying
regional attachments along with *early* socialization processes occurring in the
making of a social, cultural, and, should we add, political person. In the previous
chapters, we encountered some of these processes at work in the construction
of an attachment to the nation and the production of gender. We pondered the
importance of the Marathi language ideology in relation to modes of emotional
production of citizenship (Chapter 2), especially premised on the development
of a motherly bond and an early childhood sensorium (Chapter 3). Here I want
to shift the focus to the production of both locality and regional attachments
by means of historiographical resources. In so doing I want to redeploy and
extend the notion of sensorium; from the preverbal, affective primary sensorium developed in the early years of social life to an emotional linguistic one
that includes singing, the sensorium developed throughout school years and
into adulthood is one gradually involving verbal resources as well as cognitive
ones. Yet these cognitive resources are not devoid of emotionality at all; they
are constantly and dialectically colored by affects. I focus in this chapter on a
particular type of resource at play in reasoning and narrativization, namely, historiography. Arguably, this cognitive resource is a major site for the production
of gendered senses of regional belonging.

In the case of Maharashtra, historiography has also been instrumental in
producing a hegemonic notion of regional masculinity. Such a notion needs
further explanation in light of the increasing body of work that has renewed
perspectives on gender since the mid-1990s (Butler 1990; Connell 1993, 1995a,
1995b; Mosse 1996; Ortner 1996; Goodwin Raheja 2003; Chopra, Osella, and
Osella 2004; Srivastava 2004). These works have stressed the importance of envisaging the concept and practice of gender as relational: both the production
of the men/women difference and the notions of femininity and masculinity
should be envisaged as plural. Rather than a singular concept, masculinity, for
instance, is best approached as a set of hierarchically positioned constructions
of manhood. These positionings may vary in time and across different sections
of the population. They may also generate alternating dominant—or even hegemonic—conceptions of the entailments of "masculinity." These, in Maharashtra
as in many other parts of the world (Connell 1995b), are linked to issues of political and social power and representation. In this chapter, I focus on a crucial
emblem of both Maharashtrian masculinity and political power and representation: the figure and history of Shivaji Maharaj. The regional seventeenth-

century king today is not simply revered as the maker of self-rule (*swaraj*) and
founder of the Maratha nation through defeating the Mughal power in Delhi
and the Deccan sultanates then ruling over Maharashtra. As Thomas Hansen
once remarked, "The Shivaji mythology is a nodal point, the historical fiction at
the heart of state practices, political rhetoric and historical imagination in this
part of India" (2001: 21). Several decades after the creation of the Maharashtra state in 1960, the iconic figure of "Maharashtrianness" today graces public
spaces with a unique sensorial omnipresence, ranging from institutional sites
renamed after him to the "proliferation of visual cues," especially in the form of
statues in parks and other important places.[1]

Shivaji Maharaj therefore provides an apposite entry point into the complex entanglement of idioms of regional masculinity and attachments. These *primeval*
regional attachments combine ties of language, history, ethnicity, and religion
that are often subsumed by the category of "primordial ties." In contrast to this
category, I explore the theoretical alternative possibilities offered by the notion
of sensorium, here primarily understood as a historical sensory reconfiguration. Finally, I seek to illuminate how the production of the region and of the locality articulates with that of the nation. Against the grain of the oft-heard and
facile argument of the nation imposing itself on the locality, the Maharashtrian
example invites one to envisage the *joint* production of locality and nation.[2]

IN HIS CRITICAL REVIEW of theories of primordialism, Arjun Appadurai remarked:
"[T]he creation of primordial sentiments, far from being an obstacle to the modernizing state, is close to the centre of the project of the modern nation-state."
Indeed, the nation-state itself draws on "culturalist mobilization" in its attempts
at creating a culturally homogeneous citizen (1996: 146). Appadurai was careful
to emphasize that such projects may also trespass borders; hence, movements
in exile making claims to nationhood also play on a culturalist logic whereby
identities take cultural differences as "their *conscious* object" (147). Conversely,
even for locally situated social and political actors, local events acquire meaning through a close imbrication of various scales—from local to regional to
national, transnational, global, and so on. Most of the literature discussing the
contemporary institutional production of ethnicity and violence nevertheless
lays much emphasis on the bioproduction of identities at the nation-state and
transnational levels at the expense of other, more local ones. Yet transnational
and national projects more often than not have to contend with processes occurring at the levels of region, locality, and so on. Regional states in India are

a case in point, and the Maharashtra state offers a fascinating illustration of attempts at producing a homogeneous citizen. Whether run by a long-standing dynasty in the Congress or by an extreme right-wing populist coalition, the state has since its inception sought to build Maharashtrian citizenship upon notions of Hinduness, Marathaness, Marathi language, and a historical heritage anchored in the figure of Shivaji Maharaj. Furthermore, the relation of the region to the nation is an intricate one in this part of India, and the notion of Maharashtrian citizenship predetermines and encompasses that of Indian citizenship, as we shall see. For the moment, I wish to focus on the production of a regional sense of belonging and the part played by history therein.

In South Asia, as elsewhere, history may, as much as language (Chapter 2), operate as a powerful vehicle for producing and transmitting senses of belonging (Lelyveld 1978; Hobsbawm 1992; Kumar 1992; Amin 1995; Hastings 1997; Pandey 2001; Deshpande 2006). It is not the purpose here to enter postcolonial debates on historicity and the definition and dating of a sense of history in non-European contexts. Suffice it to say that in the Indian case, these debates have partly revolved around the issue of whether Indians had a sense of time and history prior to British colonialism, and partly around the colonial ne-gotiated modalities of modern historical practice (Kaviraj 1995; Thapar 1996; Sarkar 1997; Rao, Shulman, and Subrahmanyam 2003; and more specifically on Maharashtra, Deshpande 2006, 2007). As importantly, a concern for identifying alternative historiographical sources for "challenging the state's construction of history" has been powerfully voiced by the subaltern studies (Pandey 1991: 571). Although I share Gyan Pandey's concern for "recover[ing] 'marginal' voices and memories, forgotten dreams and signs of resistance" for purposes of writing a history that would not be beholden to "victorious concepts and powers like the nation-state, [and] bureaucratic rationalism" (1994: 214), I contend that we must also reckon with the *effects* of modern state apparatuses on the production of history, and on an unprecedented scale. As the colonial education system pro-vided avenues for a job and a middle-class status for an ever-increasing num-ber of aspirants, it transformed the significance of, and expanded the access to, history, the latter now leaving the confined dwellings of scribes employed by notables (Deshpande 2006) and providing the means for expressing collective identities defined in various ways (Cohn 1996; Sarkar 1997). But only with the advent of a generalized system of mass education in postcolonial India—and even more so since the creation of the regional state in Maharashtra—did his-tory, and institutionalized knowledge generally, acquire such prominence in actors' and citizens' imaginaries. Arguably, schooling has further strengthened a sense of history in the "modern sense" among members of the public.[3]

At the level of grand meta-narratives of the nation, this sense of history has been supported by usages of historiography deriving their legitimacy from scholarly authentication, as illustrated by the recent and still ongoing historiographical debates in India pitting leftist historians against Hindu right-wing ideologues. Some of these debates have an uncanny resonance with earlier colonial ones that saw British historians and educationists, from Mills to Macaulay and other administrators of the presidencies at that time, bent on "extirpating obscurantism, superstition, and fanciful mythologies, from the Indian psyche" (Trautmann 1997; Prakash 1999). In the current debates, lack of scientific spirit has appeared as a recurrent motif in judgments passed against textbooks that tend to blend mythological stories with factual histories of, say, national leaders. That myth and history could thus find themselves amalgamated in official contemporary manuals purported to enlighten the Indian masses is interpreted as a blatant sign of misplaced religiosity flouting itself in the face of constitutional and rightful secularism. It is deemed unacceptable by both secular elites and scholars. How one can take such amalgamating as serious scholarship has been the relentless question asked on many sides of the secularist debate. Two points require elaboration.

First, it must be noted that such a juxtaposition of the mythical and the historical does not characterize only recent endeavors undertaken at the national level (NCERT) under the Hindu-right wing coalition in power until May 2004. It has also long been extant at the regional level, not so much in official manuals and textbooks as in primary schoolteachers' pedagogical discursive practices.[4] In Maharashtra, for instance, the teaching of history as a separate subject officially starts in Class 3. In the preceding years is taught "environmental science" (*parisar vidnyan*). To this end, and contrary to the rest of the syllabus, teachers have no textbook to follow and are thus left with a significant measure of freedom for introducing the young pupils to the specificities of their local surroundings. When asked to orally list the topics they encompass in these teachings, schoolteachers often offered a list of names ranging from stories about Ganesh and a nearby Ganesh temple, Maruti, Mahalakshmi temple (famous in and outside Kolhapur), as well as Shahu Maharaj and Shahu Palace (the Old Palace that houses a museum of the former local king's memorabilia; discussed later), types of grains and trees, the nearby industrial and commercially successful town of Pratinagar (name changed, Chapter 6), and invariably, Shivaji

Maharaj. Marathi teachers and other adults regularly referred to these characters by using the category of *deivat.*

Second, this practice confirms the necessity of heeding the vernacular categories that ordinary people use in their daily lives, providing another perspective on some English-dominated discussions (see Chapter 1). Lying in between the historical and the mythical, the category of *deivat* might indeed be called devotional by many standards. The term can be used for both deities and humans of high stature, including religious and historical characters, parents, and teachers. In all these cases, the character thus labeled is held in an affectionate relationship with the locutor. Arguably, this popular category invites a reconsideration of the oft-bemoaned blurring of the categories of "mythical" and "historical." I will return to this later. For the moment, I concentrate on a particular example of *deivat*: that of Shivaji Maharaj, hero-warrior incarnation of the Maratha nation.

This heroic figure offers a privileged entry point into the production of locality and masculinity. It also presents an interesting parallel with models of national heroes in Europe. In a pioneering volume on the comparative making of national heroes, Pierre Centlivres, Daniel Fabre, and Françoise Zonabend (1999: 5) noted that the figure of the "ploughman-soldier" has often been an archetypal model that best represents legitimate attachment to a nourishing soil and mother earth. The character of Shivaji appositely fits that model inasmuch as he is often portrayed—even in competing versions—as the chief of the Marathas, a caste cluster known as warriors and tillers of the land (on the Maratha-Kunbi complex, see O'Hanlon 1985). Particular among these are the Mawlas (from the Mawal country in the Konkan), appearing by Shivaji's side at all important moments, from childhood play to his taking an oath to build an independent kingdom (*swarajya*) and throughout his heroic struggle to achieve his ends. This friendship with the loyal sons of the soil is one of the recurring motifs in both the Marathi cinematographic production about Shivaji until the 1980s (Benei 2004) and the school curriculum. Although children are likely to have come across his august figure in many public places across urban Maharashtra, this year is their first, and long, official encounter with the near-legendary hero: the Class 4 history textbook is almost entirely devoted to the narration of his legendary deeds. This year-long curricular focus on the character of Shivaji is remarkably reminiscent of, and congruent with, the didactic uses of history propounded by nationalist educationists such as V. K. Chiplunkar in the late nineteenth century: biographies of great men, to

Chiplunkar, represented among the best historical resources for imparting the "teaching of morality and the importance of certain kinds of behaviour and actions in life" (*nitibodh*; Deshpande 2006: 15). It is to the official narrative in the syllabus as well as to its enactment in primary schools that I now turn. Rather than debunking the myth and drawing attention to the "cracks" in the narrative of the hero's deeds (see Laine 2003 for a masterful and no less consequential demonstration), my aim is to document its contemporary institutionalization through daily school production.

Popular Culture, Institutionalized Knowledge, and Social Agency

The institutionalization of Shivaji's history is a complex issue for several reasons. First, Shivaji has long been a popular figure, resuscitated by various leaders, such as social reformer Mahatma Phule and freedom fighter and nationalist Bal Gangadhar Tilak in the late nineteenth century (Cashman 1975; O'Hanlon 1985). Throughout the twentieth century, Shivaji was the stake of many other, oftentimes conflicting, reappropriations (see Hansen 2001 for a discussion of a more recent one, that of the sons-of-the-soil Hindu right-wing party Shiv Sena since the 1960s). This suggests an interesting paradox. The reappropriation of the hero's character, narrative, and purpose by social actors of all persuasions shatters the notion of an omnipotent state imposing its designs on its citizens. However, an overwhelming majority of these social actors today have been educated in the Marathi primary school system in the last forty years, learning from the same, unique, Class 4 Shivaji textbook. This simple fact has a number of consequences and implications, especially in terms of class and gender, which require sociological elaboration.

My contention is that, contrary to an oft-found argument predicated upon a reference to *powada*s and other popular ballads and legends, knowledge about, and celebration of, Shivaji at a *widespread popular* level is a rather recent phenomenon in Maharashtra. This phenomenon not only owes much to anticolonial reappropriation by Bal Gangadhar Tilak but is also largely linked to the growth of literacy across the regional state. This phenomenon is also gendered, given that literacy initially spread among male Maharashtrians. Even today, those most left out of the literacy process in Maharashtra, that is, elderly illiterate women living in rural areas or in urban slums, may not be able to even identify a picture of the great hero-warrior. They are also the ones least likely to have seen movies of Shivaji at the time of their release because of limited access to outside sources of entertainment. As an illustration, let me take you to the slum of Sachar Bazar where I conducted part of the present research.

The year was 1999, a time of hot public debate about the date to be adopted for the annual celebration of Shivaji's birthday, Shivaji Jayanti. The debate hovered around comparative calendrical issues and historical details, and its inconclusiveness resulted in the adoption of a *second* date for the celebration. Shivaji Jayanti thus became celebrated twice in the year according to both calendars.[5] One might therefore have expected any Marathi speaker in Maharashtra to at least have an inkling of who Shivaji was. That afternoon in late March 1999, my encounter with Sunita's grandmother proved me wrong. Sunita was in Class 4 at the only Marathi corporation school in the vicinity.[6] That day I had gone home with her after school. Her brother and sister were sitting with me on the floor in the one-room shack that they shared with their father (the mother had tragically died two years before) and his mother, Rukminibai, well into her sixties. As we were chatting away, Rukminibai came back from her work as a domestic servant. Soon, I could sense the grandmother's uneasiness faced with what she probably perceived as educational authority: her granddaughter had introduced me as "a teacher from France doing some work in Indian schools." The fact that Sunita seemed to know where France was ("a faraway country, it takes ten hours to get there, by plane, oh no, you can't go by car, nor even by bus or boat; you have to sit on a plane to get you there") and that I had regularly spent time in her school seemed to confer some measure of prestige on her. It also had the unfortunate effect of awing her grandmother, hindering the normal flow of conversation. So I tried to shift from school topics to more mundane matters. We began talking about the posters and images attached to the walls in the room. Rukminibai seemed to relax somewhat and offered comment and information on the various family pictures and representations of deities, regional and local. As we went through one picture after another in the room, we hit upon a smaller one of Shivaji's stuck in a corner, at which the grandmother went blank. I asked who this was. Rukminibai helplessly confessed that she had heard about him in other people's homes, but she did not really know who he was. She had not placed the poster; her grandchildren had. But it was to no avail that they shouted the answer to her in disdainful support; Rukminibai had not been schooled, ever, and "what [did she] know, [she could] not read or write, [she was] poor and uneducated, so how [could she] know?" was her mortified answer. This was one of those awkward moments in fieldwork when the fieldworker wishes for the situation not to have been allowed to happen; I, too, felt mortified, for unwittingly subjecting Rukminibai to what seemed a humiliating confession of ignorance. I was also struck by how Shivaji was apparently part of a domain out of her reach, a public and popular domain to which she saw herself as having no access.

It may be that Rukminibai's answer was largely informed by her perception of my "educational persona." Yet this encounter also suggests the generational and gendered dimension of learning about the Maharashtrian nation's founder, so-oft portrayed as pervasively popular. Rukminibai's was not the only case I encountered in the course of research; rather, hers is an illustration of a wider empirical fact and sociological argument about a supposedly public culture, in fact largely informed by institutionalized knowledge. This argument runs surprisingly deep, as similar findings show with reference to knowledge of Shahu Maharaj, the local king who, at the turn of the twentieth century, led a non-Brahmin social reform movement and donated much land and money toward building educational institutions (as well as toward accomplishing industrialization). Apart from those families with a direct connection with the royal house through a history of service, most adult Kolhapuris I spoke to had acquired knowledge about the benefactor at least as much in the space of school as through the yearly public celebrations of his birth held in July (Shahu Jayanti; see Benei 1999). Teachers told pupils about the enlightened ruler when their parents did not, and the most dedicated took them to the museum to see the mounted specimens of the famously adroit hunter. Yet what most of these adults in Kolhapur often reminisced about the king appeared blatantly vindicated by the narrative of his achievements as told in the earlier official syllabus in use from the 1960s through the late 1990s. The 1982 Class 3 Marathi textbook was used until inception of the current one in 1998 and featured the history of Shahu Maharaj as one of the most prominent lessons, consisting of several pages placed near the beginning of the book (16–19).[7] Of course, I do not mean to suggest that schooling alone accomplishes this. As has already been demonstrated in the previous chapters, schooling draws upon existing and evolving structures of feeling and material constitutive of ordinary social actors' repertoires of public culture and popular knowledge. Arguably, however, schooling operates a crystallization of these repertoires while reshaping them in a process attuned with dominant ongoing narratives operating within wider society. In such a process, these crystallized bodies of knowledge become naturalized, authentic, and legitimate while concomitantly reappropriated by social actors.

Furthermore, Rukminibai's reaction and position lie at the end of a continuum, at the other end of which stand young Marathi-educated Maharashtrian males. Some of them have attracted scholarly attention and generated important work, especially in their association with extreme right-wing movements like that of the Shiv Sena (Hansen 2001). Nonetheless, largely ignored is the fact that these young men have all been schooled in the Marathi system. Now, as we have begun to see, Maharashtrian schooling is shot through with a recurring tension between a Nehruvian ideal of integration of all citizens and a more exclusivist construction of a Marathi/Hindu Indian nation. Consequently, the slippage toward chauvinistic regionalism/nationalism is always a potentiality, as will be shown in this chapter. There is something missing in the sociology of *Hindutva* militantism. When the education level of these youths is taken into consideration, it is generally so within an argument correlating higher education and unemployment, turning them into frustrated and dissatisfied agents of violence, hence perfect recruits for Hindu right-wing organizations. The phenomenological and ideological implications of even the basic stages of their schooling, however, have remained unexplored. In what follows, I document how the local/regional historical character of Shivaji Maharaj becomes an object of competing emotional attachment on the part of social actors positioned in the middle of the above-mentioned continuum. I also explore local reinterpretations of this history. Instead of focusing on the space of school, here I want to start with an exploration of the shared archive available to people in this part of Maharashtra.

"Modern" Pilgrimage and Historical Reappropriation: A Visit to Panhala

Among the many topics of wide currency in studies of the subcontinent, the domain of religion and local notions of the sacred has been one of the most covered, from studies of temples to deities, *darśana*, and pilgrimage (*yātrā*) (Fuller 1984; Gold 1988; Eck 1998). The Hindu right-wing's reappropriation since the 1980s of the *yatra* form for strictly political purposes has also received due attention. Yet in the past fifteen to twenty years, another form of *yatra* has developed throughout India, especially among well-off families, urban and rural: these are *yatra* done on a holiday to historical sites and other "places of interest" (in Marathi, *pahanyasarkhi*, literally, "worthy of seeing"). If the creation of the British railway system in the nineteenth century made for increasing pace and movement among Indians, so has the more recent development

of good tarmac roads, highways, and transport industries. Such a development
has particularly facilitated and increased visits by predominantly middle-class
families to natural areas, temples, and other nearby sites of leisure. Whereas attention has been paid to the (at times competing) occupation of public parks in
cities (Kaviraj 1997), an entire body of work awaits constitution on these other
forms of collective and individual self-formation. Arguably, these outings are
occasions for entire families to both actively produce and reenact their senses
of belonging to their locality, region, and nation outside official school visits, as
well as to articulate their own personal and familial histories to the larger one of
Maharashtra and, by extension, India. During these one-day visits, whose regularity and frequency in a year may be highly variable, social actors (re)connect
themselves to, and make meaning of, both natural and historical scapes. In fact,
even the "naturalness" of these scapes is concomitantly produced. It is *from* the
carefully crafted and valorized sites of historical legacy that the natural scenery
around can be enjoyed. The historical loci here function as not just bearings
but also producers of meaning, for collective, familial, and individual memory.
They are so because their historicity is constantly produced by their being used
as such, in a dialectical production of social (and historical) actors. By way of
illustration, let me take you on one of these picnics to nearby Panhala.

Situated at about twenty kilometers northwest of Kolhapur and rising four
hundred meters above sea level, Panhala is one of the many sites of Shivaji's most
well-known heroic deeds. Today, it is known to the lay tourist as a "hill station"
visited for its magnificent views of the Sahyadri mountain range and surrounding landscapes. To any Marathi-speaking Maharashtrian, Panhala means much
more: it is, as a Web page says, "redolent with memories of Shivaji."[8] Panhala is
a Maratha heritage site, where some of the most famous episodes of Maratha
(as well as Mughal and British) history took place. Its geographical proximity to
Kolhapur endows it with a distinctive potential for both familial and collective
reappropriation. Political meetings of all sorts take place there, as if the glory
of the Maratha hero would illuminate the speakers and the audience, gracing
the meetings with an ineffable, magical, cosmic dimension. Moreover, the famous national(ist) singer Lata Mangeshkar is said to originate from Panhala
and has a house there, which adds a more immediate and mundane prestige
to the place. Yet, despite the discursive traces of their existence weaving into
the tapestry of visitors' social memory, neither the meetings nor the popular
singer interests me directly. Rather, families from Kolhapur coming to the site
on Sunday visits do.

To many a family on one of these picnics, Panhala represents a locus for the production of historicity—as well as masculinity. During the relaxed consumption of food, comfortably seated on blankets set in the shade of well-kept lawns in the "family park"—endowed with a children's playground—families commented on the importance of Panhala in the regional (and national) history. I once accompanied the grown-up children of a school headmistress and their friends. The headmistress, Mrs. Herabaikar, had told me how she and her husband, some thirty years earlier, used to take their four children on picnics to Panhala "ever so often" on Sundays.[9] In those days, they owned neither cars nor scooters, and the whole family would go by bus. Upon reminiscing on these outings, Mrs. Herabaikar explained that she would clarify some parts of Shivaji's history to her children on these occasions. On the day I accompanied the now grown-up children, she reiterated the point that these picnics signified both a fun, relaxing time for the entire family and a most vivid and enjoyable way "for the children to learn and remember something about Shivaji's history." As Mrs. Herabaikar put it, these visits provided an avenue for them to make sense of their local history, to relate to it in a more immediate, tangible, and concrete way than through lengthy classroom expositions.

Interestingly, such active transmission and production of knowledge concomitantly reappropriate filmic, popular, and official history, blending them together. In addition, a number of factors suggest that the knowledge appropriated today is still a predominantly bookish—or at the very least, standardized—one. As mentioned previously, the textbook in use has presented the same history to generations of schoolchildren since the 1960s. The narrative it proffers of Panhala's history refers exclusively to the time of Shivaji's heroic and successful fight to recapture the fort, glossing over its much longer history that began in the twelfth century with the Shilahara dynasty.[10] In congruence with this official version, as you overtake middle-class families leisurely strolling along the paths leading around the fort, you will hear comments pertaining just to the history of Shivaji; in particular, comments on how one of his generals, Baji Prabhu, led a fierce battle against "the Muslims" and, in his loyalty to Shivaji, prepared himself to die only after hearing the sound of gunfire signaling his chief's successfully reaching Vishalgad.[11] What one hears then, is a rather faithful rendition of the Class 4 textbook passage. Similarly, my friends playfully struck theatrical poses as we walked along the path of scenes resonating with the primary school curriculum. These scenes have somehow carved themselves a dominant niche in individual, familial, and social memories. By enabling Kolhapuris to articulate these different levels of memories into meaningful and concrete lived experiences of belonging, sites like Panhala serve as a special locus for the production of locality, masculinity, and region.

Such a production is also integrated within the larger network of other local resources of cultural and religious historicity and sociality. Indeed, rather than being isolated, these visits to Panhala are often part of a pilgrimage itinerary that first takes Kolhapuris to Jyotiba temple, seventeen kilometers northwest of Kolhapur on the way to Panhala.[12] In the following section, I elaborate further on ordinary literate people's reappropriation of Shivaji's narrative and its predication upon the official version peddled by the state textbook bureau.

Textbook, History, and Secularism in the Vernacular

Important to note is that the production of primary school textbooks in the state of Maharashtra is entrusted to an independent—though public—organization, the Maharashtra State Bureau of Textbook Production and Curriculum Research. Consequently, the manuals are relatively unaffected by changes in the politics of the regional government. The textbooks to a large extent are the outcome of a consensus among Marathi-language educationists of all walks of life. Although some dissent may occur, the Marathi manuals thus arrived at may be envisaged as useful illustrations of dominant norms and values extant in Maharashtrian society at large.[13] These norms and values have been partly shaped by the reconfiguration of historical and historiographical traditions over the past century. For instance, the Class 4 textbook, almost entirely devoted to the history of Shivaji, draws on some shared historical accounts from early twentieth-century historians (such as Justice M. G. Ranade's) that have fed into Maharashtrian popular culture, including that of Marathi cinema propounded by filmmaker Bhalji Pendharkar.[14] According to Satish Kulkarni, Mumbai-based Marathi producer and film director, schools, at least in urban areas, were important sites for spreading knowledge of "Shivaji cinema" prior to the advent of television and new technologies.[15] Bhalji Pendharkar's films were shown for several decades until the 1980s in schools all over Maharashtra on 16 mm projectors with sound, the equipment provided by the state government's Information Ministry. It is against such a cinematographic background of historiographical narratives that the history textbook for Class 4 was prepared in the 1960s. It was to become the only available version for the following decades. To this day, any attempt to amend it has been met with violent opposition by some sectors of the population, for various reasons.[16]

Lost in Translation: Writing Communal Tensions

In the preceding chapters, we saw that if textbooks provide a window onto the worldview of those who make them and the society where they originate, their analysis can form but one part of the study of syllabi and curricula. However much they partake in the production of a schooled, educated self, they account for only a standardized, almost ossified version. Of immense bearing are the ebb and flow of daily interaction among teachers and children at school, between children, and with their parents and society at large. This calls for an exploration of the articulation between pedagogical tools and daily praxis. What teachers and children do in the classroom (and outside it) becomes of paramount importance for studying the production of senses of belonging, at the local, regional, and national levels. The remainder of this section therefore documents both the contents of the history manual for Class 4 and its usage in the classroom, shedding light on teachers' and children's—as well as parents' in absentia—negotiations. If social actors' interpretations of the official narrative are intricately tied to the textbook's, we shall see that the latter leaves room for great diversity in these matters, including potentially violent reappropriation.

Here again must be taken seriously Sudipta Kaviraj's (1992) advocacy to pay heed to the vernacular phrasings of political notions such as "secularism," "religion," "civil society," and so on used in Indian society. The need to do so is nowhere more apparent than in the comparison of the two versions, English and Marathi, of the Class 4 history textbook in Maharashtra. As noted earlier, the textbook was prepared in the late 1960s, a period of heightened conflict with Pakistan, with repercussions on communal tensions across India. Yet these were also post-Nehruvian times, during which the spirit of the great national socialist and secularist leader still loomed large. The preparation of the textbook reflected these politically conflictual and conceptually eclectic times (as confirmed by a retired educational officer then working at the textbook bureau). A conscious, deliberate attempt was made to produce the textbook within a secularist and ecumenical framework, avoiding any explicit discussion of religion, to the extent that *jat*, rather than *dharma*, was systematically used to also refer to members of other, non-Hindu (principally Muslim) communities.

Despite these conscious efforts to promote an inclusive framework purportedly conducive to social harmony, many secularist critics encountered in Maharashtra commented on what they perceived as a condemnable invitation to violence stemming from the official Class 4 textbook.[17] In their views, the official manuals should lay more emphasis on Shivaji's skills as an administrator rather than tirelessly detail the hero's warfare and acts of aggression, even in the name of self-rule. Of the nineteen lessons devoted to the history of Shivaji's making of *swaraj*, they remarked, thirteen deal with war, conquest, battle, spilling of blood, heroism, bravery, and so on, while a meager three are devoted to Shivaji's skills as an efficient administrator (lesson 15), a people's king (lesson 18), and a "living source of inspiration" (lesson 19). Even if these narratives are written in an ecumenical fashion, the critics argue, they cannot but generate communal mistrust and hatred because of their antagonistic—and often religious—formulation, whether explicit or implicit. Indeed, despite many corrective attempts throughout the book, a dominant narrative pitting Maratha (de facto Hindu) and Muslim communities against one another emerges. This is largely due to the systematically differential portrayal of the protagonists as Hindus and Muslims, turning religion into the main determinant for social action on either side. Thus, the very first lesson, referring to the two kings ruling Maharashtra at the time of Shivaji's birth, Nizamshah of Ahmednagar and Adilshah of Bijapur, describes their "narrow outlook" and how they "oppressed the people over whom they ruled," preventing the people from "celebrat[ing] their festivals or worship[ing] their gods openly and freely" (1996: 1). The tone is set, and religion appears one of the main reasons why Shivaji will resolve to set up his own *swaraj*, encapsulated by the motto "*Swadesh, swadharma, swabhasha*" (Chapters 1 and 2). Other instances abound (lesson 2) that tie Shivaji's mission to the work of saints of Maharashtra, the latter who "instill[ed] in [people] the desire to protect their religion, . . . preached the ideal of brotherhood . . . and gave them the message of equality [as well as] lessons in good thought and good conduct" (3–8). The social awakening these saints brought through their *bhakti* movements is thus put at the service of a foundational political narrative of the making of *swaraj*.[18] Thus, by both implicitly and explicitly framing the entire account in Hindu terms, the textbook makers have unwittingly given it a communal slant. These criticisms appear justified, since some of the textbook's wording was deemed fit enough to be reproduced almost verbatim by a *Hindutva* Web site, and judging by the latent antagonism existing between Hindus and Muslims in Maharashtra today, which both national and international events of the past decade have contributed to reinforce.[19] In many ways, however, the issue of communalism is also one of shifting interpretation and translation. This bears elaboration.

The history textbook was first written in Marathi and subsequently translated into English and the other five languages recognized for instruction in the regional state. Although the Marathi and English versions are at first blush very similar, they contain a number of divergences that bear potentially deleterious significance in the loaded and sensitive context of communalism in India today. As we will see, the English version creates a more contained, dispassionate reading in two ways: where the Marathi text uses graphic depictions and vivid, direct passages meant to convey the liveliness of the story and arouse the pupils' sustained interest, the English one opts for a distancing effect achieved by a more sober phrasing and use of indirect style. In addition, it reformulates some passages in a more "secular-conscious" garb, even introducing the language of liberalism in its interpolations. For instance, in the English version, the concluding sentence to the lesson on Shivaji as an administrator contains the added phrase "good government": "In this way Shivaji established good government and gave a clean administration to his subjects" (62). Similarly, where the Marathi version maintains an "othering" implying Hindu and Muslim communal distinction, the English translation adapts the Marathi version to the ideal of a secular nation commonly propounded in the English-language print and other media. The English version privileges an egalitarian treatment of Shivaji's subjects even in averred cases of disloyalty: "Such [disloyal] persons were severely punished *irrespective of* their caste or religion" (62, emphasis added). By contrast, the Marathi original introduces subtle distinctions of belonging: "To the traitors he administered severe punishment. Whether he be from his own [stock] or foreign."[20]

The issue of Muslim loyalty is a crucial thread running through the entire manual's narrative. Thus, in contradistinction to the emphasis on faithfulness of Mawlas and Maratha sardars, Muslim officers in Shivaji's armies are referred to in cautious terms whose initial integrative purpose is defused, at least in the original version. Here again, the Marathi and English texts differ significantly, if only by one word. The English translation reads: "His army consisted of Hetkaris, Marathas, and Muslims. One of his naval commanders, Daulatkhan Siddi Mistri and one of his Vakils, Kazi Haidar, were both Muslims. They were all loyal servants of Swaraj" (72). The Marathi original can be translated as follows: "In his armies there were officers such as Daulatkhan Siddi Mistri and similarly his Vakil, Kazi Haidar; they were Muslim. *But* they were all faithful servants of Swaraj" (72, emphasis added).[21] A whole world of understated mistrust lies in this *But*. This very wording generated considerable ambiguity in classrooms, especially in discussions of the notion of *swaraj*, qualified as *Hindavī*.

or rule

The phrase *Hindavī swarājya* itself lies at the center of the tentative secularist promotion of a consensual Shivaji narrative. The official version of the concept proffered in the textbook is that of a secular—Indian style—model of religious tolerance and acceptance within the political community. Thus, in lesson 19, the "dream" of the chhatrapati, *Hindavi swaraj*, is explained as follows: "Anyone who lived in Hindustan, no matter to what community or religion he belonged, was a *Hindavi*" (76). This echoes the very first lesson where *Hindavi swaraj* is said to be "based on justice, fair play and equal treatment to people of all castes and religions" (2). However, the term *Hindavi* is never defined more precisely. Despite the textbook bureau's professed concern for secularism, such lack of clarity leaves the door open for misinterpretation and distortion, even in the classrooms of well-meaning teachers, as will now be illustrated.

Classroom Negotiations: Open Narratives, Ambiguous Interpretations

We are at Varsity Marathi School, one of the oldest Marathi primary schools in Kolhapur. The school is famous for its Hindu leanings and formerly predominantly Brahmin staff, although of late its composition has significantly broadened. It is February 1999, and we are in Mrs. Dalave's Class 4. Mrs. Dalave is a Maratha woman in her early thirties from Nagpur. The decorations are common to most other Class 4 classrooms, with artifacts pertaining to the syllabus (as well as the dominant culture) adorning the walls, from posters of Nehru to Ganesh-as-child; to various pictures of vegetables and grains; a map of Kolhapur district; a poster of famous religious places in Maharashtra; an English chart entitled "Our Great Leaders of India"; posters of Swami Vivekananda, Mahatma Phule, the Trimurti, Subhas Chandra Bose; and a few other pictures. Here, as in other classrooms, most of the children are able to correctly identify the protagonists of each image except that of Mahatma Phule.[22] Crowning all these characters' representations are those of Shivaji.

Mrs. Dalave begins the history period. Today is devoted to lesson 19, entitled "A Living Source of Inspiration." This is the last lesson; it recapitulates the entire syllabus of Shivaji's history. Mrs. Dalave has pupils stand in turn to read a paragraph as the others follow along in their own texts, pointing to each line with their fingers. The teacher sums up each paragraph and explains its meaning, then asks questions to ascertain the children's understanding. Although the method is rather straightforward and lackluster, the pupils answer rather vivaciously. We have just reached the third paragraph, about Shivaji's respect for all saints and religious places, temples, mosques, and churches alike. Mrs. Dalave conscientiously emphasizes this point, reiterating that all kinds of people and "*jat*, including Musalmans" lived in Shivaji's *swaraj*. Now putting her book down, she proceeds to explain, in a pseudo-dialogue form:

"The Muslim armies were more numerous; Hindu people were less. Even then, did Shivaji get scared?"[Musalman phauj jast hote, Hindu lok kami hote, tari Shivarayani ghabarle ka?] [*engaging with the pupils*]

[*The pupils shake their heads no, eyes glittering, their bodies tense, leaning forward on their seats in a posture of intense listening. Rare are the students displaying a total lack of concern about what is presently going on in the room, unlike on many other occasions.*]

The teacher continues: "No! He didn't. He fought for his own dharma, his own language, and his own country" [*swadharma, swabhasha, ani swadesh*]. "He fought for Hindavi swaraj. Jijamata, Shivaji's mother, no?" [*seeking the pupils' assent before continuing*]

"Jijamata, she saw in her dream Shivaji would create swaraj. Who saw Shivaji would create swaraj? Jijamata did, Shivaji Maharaj's mother."

[*The pupils nod in agreement with the by now familiar history. Mrs. Dalave moves on without a pause.*]

"Who was the enemy?" [Shatrun kon hote?]

"Adilshah!" several students shout.

Mrs. Dalave nods approvingly, then adds: "He was a Muslim king. The enemy, who was he?" [Musalman Raje hote. Kon hote, shatru?]

"A Muslim king!" [Musalman Raje!] the pupils chorus.

Later, Mrs. Dalave invites me to test the children's knowledge of Shivaji's history. I am curious to find out what they have understood of it all. Compared with the history of humankind they learned the year before, this one seems more appealing to most of the pupils, especially because it is written "in a story format" (goshtirupat mhanun). Some names have also stuck in their minds more than others. Among them is that of Netaji Palkar, one of Shivaji's lieutenants with a complex story (more of which will be discussed later). Asked about their favorite episodes, many pupils refer to the loyalty and heroic deeds of Shivaji's captains and army. Some girls refer to the king's coronation, which contains one of the most emotional scenes with Shivaji's mother, Jijabai. Here, unlike many other classrooms in this school and elsewhere, no one mentions the graphically violent episodes of Afzal Khan and Shahiste Khan. To boys and girls alike, Shivaji's greatest achievement is without a doubt that of "having fought all his life to bring about swaraj" (janmabhar swaraj nirman karnyasathi ladhat rahile) and "having destroyed the enemy" (shatrunna nash kela), as well as having "founded Hindavi swaraj" (Hindavi swaraj sthapan keli). Upon their mentioning Hindavi swaraj, I ask the pupils to explain the phrase's meaning:

> "Hindavi swaraj means those who live in Hindusthan in free swaraj" [Hindavi swaraj mhanje swatantra swaraj Hindusthanat rahnare], offers Sharmila.
>
> The teacher reiterates: "They can be of any religion, any religion, they can be: Hindu, Muslim, Christian, anything."
>
> [*Then I ask the pupils if they talk about their school day at home. Most of them answer yes. Do they talk about their lessons? Yes. Do they talk about their history lessons, about Shivaji's history?*]
>
> "Yes, at least with mummy."
>
> "What does mummy say, then?"
>
> "Shivaji fought for our swaraj. Had he not established our swaraj, we would all be living in a Muslim raj by now," replies Sharmila.
>
> "He was a great king; he set up a kingdom with rules," Hussain asserts.

I will return to Muslim children's understandings and the space of school in the construction of shifting allegiances and identifications in the following chapter. For the moment, I want to unravel the many other strands of argumentation and reflection offered by this exploration of a history lesson on an ordinary day in a Marathi classroom. I have chosen this particular vignette because, unlike some other examples of clear antagonism toward Muslims—through their systematic conflation with Mughal political power—this one is rich in ambivalence and ambiguity. This ambivalence and ambiguity, both in the teachers', the parents', and the children's cognitive utterances, need attention, if only because these may let the phenomenological balance tilt either way in case of heightened communal tension.

The notion of *Hindavi swaraj* thus formulated is problematic not only because of the ambiguity inherent in it but also because of its performative reiteration. By emphasizing throughout how "Shivaji made no distinction between Hindus and Muslims" (2), and no difference between the holy books of the Hindus and the Muslims (lesson 19), it is clearly a modernist and postcolonial version that is being reshaped here; one of monolithic Hinduism and Islam, and in which difference, on grounds of being negated as a potential cause for (unjust or unfair) action, is discursively reinforced as difference. In the process, the separateness and distinctiveness of both Hindus and Muslims are further strengthened. Consequently, groups and social actors with distinct agendas, including those with Hindu right-wing leanings, may interpret Shivaji's tolerance differently. In the latter version, *Hindavi swaraj* is one of tolerance toward Muslims with the implicit understanding that they are, precisely, merely *tolerated* in Maharashtra. This is the version that Shiv Sena leader Bal Thackeray has repeatedly voiced in his fiery speeches of the past three decades (Hansen 1996, 1999). It also gloomily echoes the speeches and presentations of the Hindu right more generally, whether in the threatening declarations of the chief minister of Gujarat at the time of the anti-Muslim riots in Ahmedabad in March 2002, or those of many *Hindutva* politicians over the past twenty years. The presence of Muslims in India has increasingly been made conditional, that is, conditioned to a majoritarian political principle. Muslims, as part of the minority, should just conform to the majority's rule (including a Uniform Civil Code premised on reconstructed Hindu patriarchal notions; Hasan 1994; Kapur and Cossman 1996; Sunder Rajan 2003). In this version, therefore, religious difference is emphasized only to be negated at the expense of the conception and representation of minorities. Of course, the same official textbook narrative lends itself to other, more generous interpretations. Shivaji's tolerance toward minorities, and Muslims in particular, may also justify reappropriation by members of the Muslim minority (Chapter 5). Yet the Marathi version remains one of systematized communal distinctiveness, wherein the issue of loyalty always seems to loom large. This latter issue is also a powerful motif in accounts of Maharashtrian masculinity against a fantasized "Muslim other."

Producing Gender: Mirrors of Masculinity, Anxieties of Conversion, and Historical Narratives

Although Hindu right-wing groups and parties have reappropriated Shivaji as the epitome of strong and virile, heroic and triumphant Hindu masculinity (Hansen 2001; Jasper 2002), his is a far more ambiguous kind of masculinity. In most of its popular depictions and mass-produced graphic representations, it is neither muscular nor aggressive but rather stakes claims to imperial grandeur and rightful glory.[23] The chhatrapati's coronation lends itself to one of the most popular depictions of such grandeur, and posters of the scene set within opulent, gilded decor and colorful brocades can be seen in many public spaces (shops, restaurants, hotels, bus stands, school classrooms, and so on) in Kolhapur and across western Maharashtra. The poster represents Shivaji as a grand and luxurious lord, although not as an overly muscled fighter.

It is noteworthy that in contrast to current right-wing representations, physical prowess and force are never praised in the school textbook; nor were they by teachers in Kolhapuri schools, for that matter. Rather, they were made despicable and ridiculed in many accounts. Physical strength was on the side of the enemy, whether Mughal or Muslim; it could only be countered with wit and cunning, similar to the Greek *metis*. Indeed, compensating for lack of physical force are Shivaji's mental resources of shrewdness and adroitness. The Maratha warrior-as-strategizer defeated his enemies in taking them by surprise; he was where they did not expect him. He knew where and when to alternately strike and hide along the mountainous ghats of Maharashtra; his was a knowledge of the soil, his warfare that of a "son of the soil." *This* is the true object of praise in the dominant narratives. Time and again, teachers in the classroom would explain and pay tribute to Shivaji's military qualities and especially his warfare strategy, subsumed by the term *ganimi kawa*. This notion literally signifies "cunning, craft, subtlety, wiliness" toward "the public foe" and was rendered in the English textbook as "guerrilla tactics," which it is in effect (lesson 17) (1996: 67–68). The qualities of cunning and deceit in the face of a stronger enemy were thus repeatedly emphasized in textbooks as well as in classrooms.

Remarkably, what was praised as cunning and skill on the part of Shivaji was condemned as treachery on the part of the Mughals and other "Muslim foes." For example, lesson 12 starts with the following words: "Putting his trust in Jaising, Shivaji left for Agra to visit the emperor [Aurangzeb]" (50). But Shivaji's expectations, so the narrative continues, are dashed because the emperor insults him by not giving him the honors due his rank of "king of the sovereign State of Maharashtra."[24] More generally, depictions of Muslims present them as cruel, unjust, and, not least of all, stupid and cowardly. Thus set in such dichotomous terms are the respective encounters with Afzal Khan and Shahiste Khan, among the most popular episodes in Shivaji's narratives. The textbook depiction opposes praise of Shivaji's cunning and skill to condemnation of the Mughals' treacherous wrongdoings (*dagalbaji*). Afzal Khan appears as a "giant of a man" (32) with "unbelievable physical prowess and strength." He is also "full of pride and confident of success" and "full of stratagem" (that is, a treacherous character, 33) whose word cannot be trusted (34). In contrast, Shivaji is valiant ("he did not lose courage," 34), operating upon "strategic moves" and "tactics" (33), all testifying to his cleverness: "Shivaji proved too clever for [the Khan]" (34). Their respective sizes are emphasized, as if to further highlight Shivaji's valor in defeating his unnaturally huge opponent: as the khan takes

Shivaji in his embrace, "[b]efore the giant khan Shivaji looked like a pigmy. He reached only as far as the khan's chest" (36).

The episode of the meeting of Shivaji and Afzal Khan was such a favorite among students and teachers that the latter sometimes capitalized on their portrayal of the "tiny and cunning" Shivaji and the "huge and stupid" Afzal Khan to reacquire pupils' attention during lessons. Kamlatai, an experienced Brahmin teacher at Modern Marathi School, relished in miming the scene, impersonating both characters with much gusto, to the pupils' great delight. One recurrent motif in teachers' and children's narratives was that of the "tiger's claws" (*bichwa*) with which Shivaji killed Afzal Khan. Teachers and pupils alike would mention the Maratha leader's tearing apart the khan's stomach with the claws, per the gory details in the official text. Here again, the Marathi original is written in a somewhat more alert, vivid, and engaging, and also noticeably more graphic, style than its English rendering. A literal translation from the Marathi goes as follows: "With extraordinary agility, [Shivaji] thrust his *bichwa* into the khan's belly, 'swoosh.' The khan's entrails fell out. The khan collapsed."[25] Compare this with the (somewhat) more contained English textbook version: "Shivaji . . . drove his *bichwa* into the khan's stomach and tore apart his guts. The wounded khan fell down."

In this and other accounts emerges a Maratha masculinity counterprojected against a fantasized Muslim other. Such a mirroring production of masculinity also frames another favorite episode among teachers and pupils in Marathi schools: that of the encounter with Shahiste Khan. Compared with the motif of treachery dominating the narrative of Afzal Khan, this one is of cowardice, retreat, and retaliation. In both situations, however, the crudeness of Shivaji's action (hiding a weapon beneath his shirt and ripping his opponent's guts apart, and cutting off his fingers, respectively) is legitimated by initial wrongdoing on the enemy's part: treachery in the first instance and usurpation in the second. As Shahiste Khan has been occupying Shivaji's Lal Mahal residence in Pune, raiding the territory and bringing about misery on the surrounding countryside and people, destroying the crops and taking away the cattle (44), Shivaji determines to kill him. The hero enters the palace at night and, once in the khan's room, takes out his sword. The khan runs away, and as he is escaping through a window, Shivaji cuts off three of his fingers (45).

There is an interesting parallel here with the fate met by Afzal Khan. In both cases, their physical integrity is attacked and successfully undermined. Psychoanalytic interpretations seeing in both treatments forms of symbolic rape and emasculation, respectively, seem quite justified here. The Marathi wording of Shivaji's attack on the khan might be interpreted as symbolic forced penetration, thereby playing on a common analogy in *Hindutva* rhetoric of male and female Muslims as enemies to be emasculated and raped, respectively, in a role reversal of retributive justice against their alleged behavior toward Hindu women. Similarly, cutting off fingers is suggestive of emasculation, with reference to the oft-found association of this body part with the Marathi verb *shirkane*," implying "obstruction or opposition, or effort and vehemence": the phrase *bot* [finger] *shirkane* literally translates as "to penetrate, pierce through or into with one's finger." Furthermore, in addition to strangely rhyming with each other in Marathi, both body parts—*pot* (belly) and *bot* (finger)—may be associated with symbolic and/or political functions. Thus, *pot* represents the stomach, abdomen, or belly; the uterus or womb; the mind or the heart; and the seat of understanding and affections. To rip somebody's *pot* apart therefore amounts to annihilating that person in the most visceral sense of the term: negating the person's right to live *and* to produce offspring,[26] and by extension, the legitimacy to reproduce socially and politically. Meanwhile, *bot* is used to denote power and influence, as in the expression *botavar nacvine*, meaning "to have perfect ascendancy over." Cutting one's opponent's fingers off therefore amounts to destroying the person's sexual and political power. This contrapuntal depiction of degraded Muslim masculinity and virtuous Maratha valor is posited in a communal, antagonistic framework that seems ever so inescapable as we get toward the end of the book, despite the numerous ecumenical attempts peppering it. Such an antagonistic framework also crystallizes and reinforces anxieties around the issue of conversion to Islam, consequently implying a loss of manhood.[27]

The anxieties surrounding the idea of conversion to Islam are also manifest in the manual, wherein attendant narratives abound—followed by successful reconversion to the Hindu fold. Thus, the last lesson emphasizing Shivaji's "large-heartedness" and "religious tolerance" is followed by a long exposition of such instances.[28] It is noteworthy that the protagonists of these moments of conversion and reconversion are among those whom the children remembered most in their recapitulation: For instance, the famous story of Netaji Palkar, which was the subject of an entire film. Netaji Palkar is said to have been "one of the bravest of Shivaji's captains," "a second Shivaji." After being captured by Aurangzeb's troops, he was sent to Agra and "forced to become a Muslim. . . . Ten years later he accompanied Dilerkhan to the South against Shivaji. Netaji, though now a Muslim, had not forgotten Shivaji or Maharashtra. He remembered the past. He was deeply moved. His love for his own country [*swaraj*] and religion [*swadharma*] returned" (73).

Thereupon Netaji begged permission from Shivaji to return to the Hindu fold, which the latter immediately accepted. So "Netaji became a Hindu again and served Swaraj for many years afterward" (74). Here, the conflation between *swadharma* and *swaraj* cannot be better expressed; and with it all the ambiguity regarding Muslims. For even if there were Muslims in Shivaji's armies who "still" were loyal to him, the fact is that the exclusive equation between *swaraj* and Hindu *dharma* is irrefragably strengthened with this last example, almost crowning the entire narrative of Shivaji's making of *swaraj*. This is again made most explicit in the following and last lesson: "He established Swaraj. He did this so that everyone would live in peace and follow his religion without any outside interference, so that the Marathi language, and the Hindu religion [*swadharma*] would acquire their due place of honor. He toiled all his life for the prosperity of his language, his religion, and his country and succeeded in the end" (76).

Seen in this light, the ambiguity witnessed in statements by teachers and pupils (and parents), as in Mrs. Dalave's classroom, is rather unsurprising. What may at first blush appear so is the predilection for Shivaji's history shared by women and girls, given that boys were specific targets in the production of a love for Mother-India and that the contemporary figure of the soldier was particularly valorized and glorified (Chapter 3). Yet it should be emphasized that such a valorization does not exclusively concern young boys. Young girls also partook of such a celebratory mode; they, too, were encouraged to honor this heroism, even if from the distance of spectator and "cheerleader." For, in this part of India, the trope of war pervaded and informed gender hierarchies.

Producing Gender: Masculinity, Femininity, and Empowerment

That masculinity is a relational concept is also true, of course, of femininity. As mentioned above, more recent work has stressed how both masculinity and femininity have to be examined concurrently. The two notions are actively constructed, disputed, and reinterpreted in relation to one another. In the present case, what children are invited to acquire or strengthen in their fourth year of primary schooling is love and devotion toward the foundational hero of Maharashtra. Both boys and girls learn gender. More important perhaps, what both boys and girls learn in school are the *differential roles* expected of them as "good citizens." Chapter 3 discussed how the mother trope operates in the production of senses of belonging to the nation at large, building on an attachment produced in the intimacy of the family and the home, and how it served as a model and an ideal for young girls to emulate. It might appear at first blush, then, that Shivaji does for young boys what Bharat Mata does for young girls. To a certain extent this is a correct assumption. As we have seen, however, boys *and* girls in Maharashtra are the object of martial expectations. Girls, too, partake of the warrior ethos in that part of India. Most boys interviewed in Class 4 stated their preference for the history of Shivaji over that of humankind studied the year before; however, girls, too, vowed their enthusiasm for the chhatrapati's persona and narrative. This leads us to examine another crucial character in the official version of the great Maratha nation's founder, that of Shivaji's mother, who provides an active role model for young girls to emulate.

If Shivaji is the epitome of valor, fortitude, bravery, and cunning, his mother, Jijabai or Jijamata, represents his enlightening force. She is a guiding thread throughout, despite not occupying center stage in most of the textbook. Lesson 4 sets the tone with Shivaji's childhood, in which formative years Jijabai appears as the principal figure, instilling in him admiration for bravery and piety (14). Jijabai is also a teacher, a counselor, and "a source of inspiration" in time of need. As Shivaji turns into a young man and starts traveling around Mawal, meeting with its "loyal, hardworking, and quick-footed" inhabitants "tired of the Sultan's harassing rule," he opens his heart to his mother. Appealing to his divine lineage from both Rama and Krishna as a guarantee of victory, she exhorts him to "destroy the wicked and make [his] subjects happy" (17). Jijabai is also the first to learn about her son's resolve to build *Hindavi swaraj*. She reappears in absentia in lesson 8 before the meeting between Shivaji and Afzal Khan and has an indirect hand in the conduct of political affairs. It is as an overjoyed mother that she reenters the stage in person toward the end of lesson 12, to welcome Shivaji back from Aurangzeb's clutches (52). Lesson 13, devoted to the recapture of the Kondana fort, again makes clear that Shivaji's mother is the one goading him into the building of an independent kingdom (53). Similarly, after *swaraj* has been established and the coronation of Shivaji has taken place in lesson 14, the newly anointed king first pays homage to his mother. As noted previously, girls especially favored this last scene. Suggesting the overarching importance of the deep bond uniting mother and son, even the

English version remarkably retains a highly emotional tone for each of these passages, capturing the poignancy of the Marathi text:

> [Shivaji] bowed before Jijamata and touched her feet. Jijamata held him in a close embrace. Her eyes were filled with tears of joy. Her thirty years' efforts had at last borne fruit. The dream she had nursed even before Shivaji's birth had at last come true. The tears in her eyes were tears of joy and fulfillment. Shivaji Maharaj was also deeply moved. Glory be to both of them. (58)

The last mention of Jijabai appears in lesson 19, where her son is said to have "always obeyed his mother [and] fulfilled her every wish," in a thinly veiled exhortation for pupils to emulate the Maratha hero (76).

Jijabai is thus represented as a powerful mother whose secret ambition and aspiration has been fulfilled by her son. Such a representation is not especially original and reproduces the well-documented gender-role division laying emphasis on women as mothers, in particular, bearers of sons for the reproduction of the nation (see, e.g., Gupta 2001; T. Sarkar 2002; Butalia 2004; Menon 2004). This reading, however, is insufficient. It does not do justice to the active and valorized role of Jijabai as the guiding inspiration behind her son's great deeds. Her example is also a typical one, not just of furthering a free nation through the production of male heirs but, more interestingly, of actively molding her child into the brave, fearless, devoted hero that her son becomes. Jijabai, in other words, is the archetypal mother (Kakar 1999). She is the mother that nurtures and supports, and makes demands on, her son, as she entertains great hopes and ambitions for him in the pursuit of her highest dream, that of political power. As such, Jijabai is a classic illustration of psychoanalytic conceptions of motherhood, the devouring and castrating yet energizing and propelling type that all great political leaders are supposed to have had (see Forcey 1987 for a refreshing discussion of this model). It is thus a reading that empowers (and constrains) young girls as the future producers of sons, in accordance with dominant patriarchal values in Maharashtrian and, more largely, Indian society. These, it should be noted, are the very same ones upon which female units of Hindu right-wing parties and organizations have also actively built in recent years.[29]

Categorical Treachery, Primary Identities, and National Telos

What are we to make of these largely antagonistic narratives in the construction of the nation and of attendant senses of belonging? What part do, again, the senses play therein? More generally, what can a sensory approach contribute to an understanding of issues of identity formation? What other heuristic vocabulary can it help deploy as an alternative to that used in political philosophy and science to analyze political and communal violence? Reflecting on the production and eruption of such violence, Appadurai argued that it is a sense of "deep categorical treachery" and betrayal of intimacy experienced by aggressors that is responsible for the rage they feel, allowing them to become murderers (1996: 154). This sense of betrayal is linked to "a world in which large-scale identities forcibly enter the local imagination and become dominant voice-overs for the traffic of ordinary life" (154–55). The argument might well apply to Maratha, and more largely to Maharashtrian, conceptions of the archetypal other, that is, of Muslims. Indeed, local communalized conceptions build on local and regional history, however much the latter is reshaped and rewritten in the process. In addition, the progressive communalist reshaping of a long history of interaction within the South Asian subcontinent has more recently been compounded by international events in which Muslims have increasingly become demonized. Yet Appadurai's explanation of ethnic violence does not address the measure of viscerality that comes with the "sense of treachery," a viscerality so powerful that it prompts the most benign and innocuous social agent into acts of savage brutality. As the author convincingly demonstrates in the preceding pages, a primordialist conception of nationalism is untenable: of little use is a conception whereby religious or ethnic particularities and ties would be so profoundly anchored in collective and individual imaginations and experiences that they could never be superseded by the construction of an attachment to a larger entity, that, for instance, of the nation. But what is it, then, in the discovery that one's neighbor is "more Muslim than Serb" (154–55) that triggers such emotionally disproportionate reactions? Granted, what may be at issue is that faith in a secular state where religion is kept out of the definition of citizenship might supersede allegiance to the nation. But why and how this issue generates such a powerfully visceral sense of betrayed belonging in the first place requires probing. The dialectic between the two kinds of identities at play remains to be further explored. And here in fact, we may even want to question these categories of "primary" and "secondary" ties in relation to educational projects. This bears some elaboration.

Discussing the notions of primary and secondary identities, Étienne Balibar explained that the task of education "is principally to relativize primary identities, thus calling into question any essentialist adherence to the notion or feeling . . . that by moving away or distancing oneself from them one must necessarily *ipso facto* become 'de-natured' and radically alienated" (2005: 40). Balibar's comment is useful to consider the extent to which the construction of identities—whether primary or secondary—is always a fragile, volatile, and uncertain process, despite educationists' attempts. Further, Balibar specifies that this relativization of primary identities does not amount to "ruling out any conscious, voluntary and implicitly conditional election of such a primary identity as expressive of a significant element of one's own nature" (40). Pushing the argument further, I propose that in the case of dominant ideologies, primary and secondary identities are *concomitantly* produced and in fact indiscernible from each other.[30] As shown in Chapter 3, in Maharashtra the experiences of belonging to one's family, and especially the experience of motherly bonding, feed into the production of a national sensorium together with a primary sensorium, in turn reinforcing the ideological strength of the notion of family ties and motherhood in the service of the nation. Consequently, even the terms of "primary" and "secondary" identities are misnomers. Arguably, one way of getting out of the loop of primordialism is to develop alternative modes of analysis that reinstate the primacy of lived sensory experience. Here I want to further work through the notion of sensorium by focusing on the social and cultural development of particular sensoriums shaping experiences of group affinity and antagonism. In order to do this, I wish to draw you slightly backward in time.

Marathas, Muslims, and the Production of Sensory Identities

> *The full presence of the ethnographer's body in the field also demands a fuller sensual awareness of the smells, tastes, sounds and textures of life among the others. It demands . . . that ethnographers open themselves to others and absorb their worlds. Such is the meaning of embodiment, the realization that . . . we too are consumed by the sensual world, that ethnographic things capture us through our bodies.*
>
> **Paul Stoller, *Sensuous Scholarship***

For a long time during my first fieldwork in a Maharashtrian village, I was intrigued by the seeming aloofness of most Muslim families in relation to their fellow villagers. This was in the northeast of Pune district, a drought-prone area, in 1990–91. I then lived in the *Teli galli*, so named by virtue of the predominance of members of the Teli (oil-presser) caste settled in the alley, where all the houses but one belonged to them. The only non-Teli house was a large three-story building that stood at one end of the alley, just across from my little partitioned one-room abode. It belonged to a Momin joint family. During the day, from dawn to dusk, all its members would go about their business in a way similar to those around them, the women fetching water from the nearby collective tap at 5 or 6 a.m.; then, crouching by the side of their house, they would assiduously scratch pots and pans clean from the previous night's meal while the men stood or sat on the platform (*wata*) brushing their teeth in full public view. Such a conspicuous performance of quotidian tasks was in keeping with the implicit rules of village life that form part of social surveillance mechanisms in rural India. In thus abiding by its tacit norms, the Muslim family reenacted its participation in the daily forging of a common bond of "villageness." Throughout the day, they kept their doors open following village practice, except during lunch hours and afternoon naps in the hot hours of summer, just as their neighbors did. Yet, come dusk and my Momin neighbors would retreat into a specificity of their own. At the socially charged early hours of night when visiting or news exchange would take place from one house to the other in the entire alley (including with the Brahmin family's and my house), with the children often acting as diligent messengers, all of the Momin household would retire into the privacy of their home behind locked doors. Their public performance was over for the day.

I was always struck by what I perceived as an almost schizophrenic way of living on the part of the Momin family because, at first glance, nothing much differentiated them from their fellow villagers. True, the women wore a different marriage necklace (*mangalsutra*), and the men sported regular Muslim caps (as well as beards for the elders among them). Yet the married women wore saris as any married woman in the village did (though they tied them differently), and the unmarried girls wore Punjabi suits as any unmarried girl did. The children attended the local Marathi school, and their educational level was comparable to that of their Teli neighbors, with whom they spoke Marathi, although among themselves they would use a Marathized form of Hindi. At first, then, nothing really singled them out. Yet it was always clear to everyone, including themselves, that they were somewhat different from everybody else. To some, the reason was their dietary habits: Momins regularly ate meat and eggs at a time when a large number of families of Maratha and allied castes— especially the women—had adopted vegetarianism (Benei 1996). To others, the reason was simply that "they were Muslims: they did not go to any temple, but to the mosque; they did not have the same festivals; theirs were different." Although the Momins and their neighbors in the *galli* would invite each other to their homes on special festive occasions, it was always with some ostentation, as if to show some deliberate goodwill on either part. After I no longer lived in the *galli* and following my return from Europe in 1992, I often sensed some slight embarrassment, uneasiness, or at times downright sardonic smiles from villagers living in other quarters when I was invited to participate in a ritual taking place at the Momins' home.

These were the early 1990s, a time when *Hindutva* politicians made regular headlines in news bulletins; these bulletins appeared regularly enough for most villagers to take notice and sometimes talk about both the *yatras* undertaken by the BJP throughout the country and the mounting effervescence around the "Ramjanmabhoomi temple–Babri masjid issue" in Ayodhya. Whether this had had a definite impact on village life and especially Hindu-Muslim relations is difficult to say, as there was no known communal record in the area. Moreover, people were on the whole rather unclear as to the meaning of "all this": to be sure, India had been a Hindu land for many centuries, as the famous TV serial *Mahabharat*, broadcast every Sunday morning, reiterated so successfully at the time (Rajagopal 2001). During these broadcasts the entire village looked like a deserted zone, haunted by the sounds of the few TV sets available echoing from within a few privileged homes, and around which would congregate dozens of less fortunate villagers who commented on the program. What did it mean to roam around the country parading as fake *saddhu*s like this "Advani guy"? Besides, the Muslims had been defeated long ago; so what was all this about? And were we not supposed to live with one another? Yes, but did they have a right to build this mosque in the first place? Most villagers were unsure what the answers to these questions were. Yet it is possible that this faraway, national(ist) issue, just by being increasingly discussed and bestowed visibility in the media in the year of 1992 had acquired some performative reality in a region long engaged in rewriting its past as one of glorious Maratha—and increasingly Hindu—martial heritage. This entanglement of national and regional issues may well have been caught in the daily web of relationships of life in a small village in western Maharashtra, where local economic competition and what seemed to be a recent race toward acquisition of consumer goods were as active as anywhere else.[31] The fact is that Momins were rather well-off by local standards: they owned some land, clothes shops, and large solid-brick houses, and were among the first ones to possess a TV set as well as a supreme item of luxury in those days, a videocassette recorder. As such, the Momins' socioeconomic position was comparable to that of the better off in the village, especially the Jains (Gujarati and Marwari), which may have caused some competition and, possibly, resentment. At any rate, Momin families, and the one I knew best in the *Teli galli* in particular, seemed to somehow be living as "guests" in the village, even when they had been there for several generations.

By contrast, the other Muslim caste in the village was of a much lower ranking: they were called Mulanis and considered on a par—and actually lived—with the (former) Untouchables. However, they were much better integrated into ritual village life. Many Mulanis worked others' land, although they were butchers by calling. As such, they performed ritual functions for the village as a whole, especially at the time of the annual festival in honor of Yemai Devi, when they killed the goats to be offered to the goddess. Mulanis also danced and played music (*shenai* and small tambourines) with musicians of other lower castes at weddings and on other ritual occasions, including Hindu festivals. As important, they were part of the "traditional" system of *balutedar*s and in that capacity performed their part in the village tutelary deity's palanquin (*palkhi*) procession of her two masks (*mukhawte*) at each full moon. Compared with Mulanis' active involvement in village ritual life, the barely hidden reluctance of Momins to take part in the monthly procession was unmistakable. The younger men of the family would sometimes stand outside the house as the *palkhi* went through the *Teli galli* at night; much more rarely would the women of the house acknowledge its passage.

The one thing Momin families could not prevent their children from attending, however, was the daytime "Maratha" drumming that took place during some wedding processions, at the time of the annual village goddess festival (*Yemaici yatra*), and on the national celebrations of Republic Day (January 26) or Independence Day (August 15). Then, the powerful sound of war drumming would resonate throughout the alleys while the dancing mesmerized the crowd, young and old. Young men from the Maratha and allied castes would perform dances, accompanying their movements with small percussive metallic instruments (*lejhim*) to the rhythm of *dhol* and *dholki* drums. These dances offered most suggestive sensory symbols—visual, auditory, but also haptic because of the vibration of the drumming—of "Maratha power." This was a power that spoke of *swaraj*, congruent with the Class 4 textbook narrative proffered in a subheading entitled "The Drums of *Swaraj* Begin to Sound" (1996: 26). Although I was not cognizant of the teachings of the primary school syllabus then, I was always struck by the force and power that seemed to suddenly emerge from these public performances, together with the unparalleled frenzy of movement, sound, and rhythm erupting and piercing through the fragile, yet on the surface quiet, tranquillity of village life. Especially striking was that these were in fact *not* haphazard moments but carefully crafted ones whose success lay in a savvy and masterful progressive dosage of speed, intensity, and volume. Accompanying the musicians (*shenai, dhol,* and *dholki*), a group of young and middle-aged men in either village dress and Gandhi caps, or pants and shirts, would gather in a circle, *lejhim* in hand. As the music started playing slowly to the beat of the drums, the men would begin to dance according to precise choreographed steps, balancing their bodies to and fro in diagonally symmetrical movements of torso and feet, while accompanying themselves with the rhythmic shaking of their *lejhim*. While gathering speed, the dancers raised their *lejhim* higher and higher, some of them throwing them up in the air and catching them again in rhythm. Gradually, as the metallic sound of the *lejhim* increased together with the volume and speed of the music, so would that of the dancers' bodily movements, becoming more and more intense and jerky while their arms stretched ever so energetically in both directions. Some among the ablest dancers even touched the ground with their hands on either side before rising again forcefully up and bending down sideways. As the music and the dancing got faster and faster, the rhythmic beating dominated the scene to the point of finally merging into a continuous loud and sustained, powerful and intense sound, the dancers by then sweating profusely and gesticulating as in a trance. Suddenly, a few slower yet more powerful beats of the drum would signal the end of a phase, with the dancers almost coming to a standstill before gradually building up speed again in the same fashion. The dancing could go on thus for over an hour, especially during processions throughout the entire village.

These were, truly, reenactments and celebrations of masculinity at war: cultivated displays of strength, of tense bodies reenacting assertion of territorial and historical legitimacy, as the procession would cover the main streets of the village once ruled by a raja whose dynasty had long disappeared. It did not matter that most of the performers were actually rather frail and short. At that moment, their shirts and faces besmeared with the colored powders thrown on them by the crowd in the course of their performance, both dancers and crowd partook of an ecstatic essence of Maratha power unleashed by the deployment of a unique martial sensorium building upon what Marcel Mauss termed "montages physio-psycho-sociologiques de séries d'actes" (assemblages of series of physio-psycho-sociological acts; 1950). To be sure, these may well have pertained to a relatively recent or reconstructed "tradition." Yet if there is one thing that may have endured in the urban sensorium of Maharashtra today amid the sounds and fumes of modern vehicles, blasting Bollywood tunes, and *bhajan* music, it is this reshaped form of martial display that speaks of an age long gone by; an age when, to present-day performers and spectators alike, the Maratha nation showed the rest of the country the way to freedom and to nationhood under the leadership of its founder, Shivaji Maharaj. That this historical course may have later been thwarted, first in the times of the subsequent Peshwa rule at the third battle of Panipat (1761) against the Afghan forces of Ahmad Shah, then in the final defeat by the British in a third battle (1818), added yet more historical and emotional resonance to this type of contemporary performance. So did the ultimate loss of status for the Marathas from that of "martial races" in the decades following the events of 1857 (known as the "Sepoy revolt," "Mutiny," and "First Indian War of Independence" in competing narratives), when the men from Oudh (close to Maratha territories and seen as allied to them) were declassified and replaced by the Punjabis to form a new "martial race" (Enloe 1980: 36–37; Cohen 2002). To this day, each one of these events has borne its mark on Maratha social memory. The battle of Panipat, especially, has become a trope of utmost disaster and is the object of regular, though incidental, reference in the vernacular press. What we are dealing with here, then, is an "embodied cultural memory" (Stoller 1997)—as well as an embodied *colonial* memory—that summons all the senses (Howes 1991) into the production of a politics of gender and identity. Much of this aching social memory today is encapsulated within this auditory and bodily sensory reconfiguration and celebration of virility.[32] It is through the dance and music performance that an idealized manhood is realized. Such a "poetics of manhood" (Herzfeld 1985) is also given to experience in urban parts of Maharashtra, although today predominantly in national celebrations as well as in schools, in a suggestive illustration of Adorno's thesis on music.

Even in its most hermetical form, Adorno once professed, music is social. Yet, he added, it is "threatened by irrelevance as soon as all connecting ties with the listener are severed" (cited in Seubold 2001). Although the philosopher and critical theorist here referred to the nefarious gap between the so-called low and high arts, such a comment appositely brings to light the fundamental condition for the sustenance of music's social meaning. The argument might well extend to other performative activities, such as the dancing accompanying the music. The performative and musical tropes of war, grandeur, and loss under discussion are also importantly and regularly activated within society at large, and at school in particular. The military Maratha *dhol* played during the morning liturgy in schools resonate with the ones used during public performances, whether those described previously or those celebrations of Shivaji's life, *Ranata Raja* shows (Jasper 2002), or even on national public celebrations and politico-religious processions occurring at the time of Shivaji Jayanti or Ganesh Chaturthi (Cashman 1975; Kaur 2004, 2005). Although the sensorium of which they form a part has also been enlarged with the harmonium (accompanying not just public musical performances but also school liturgies; Chapter 1), the drumming makes them irrevocably identifiable as military, martial, warlike, and Maratha. Arguably, it is by growing up in such a sensory environment that both boys and girls also learn to experience what it means to be Maharashtrian. Such a sensorium is reinforced in schools with singing songs such as "Amhi Marathe khare" (We Are True Marathas). As I saw the latter song being taught one fine day in February 2000, I was so overwhelmed by the intensity of the performance and the feverish enthusiasm it elicited among both male and female students that I wrote in my diary: "Future will tell if the power of the word sung is greater than that of the word merely uttered. But, judging by Nazi songs, it seems the past has already demonstrated it."

Toward an Anthropology of State Heroes and Sensorium

The expressive formation of masculinity documented here is not only a dominant, regional hegemonic one—however much open to interpretation and reappropriation by various groups—through which both male and female roles are redefined, reshaped, and legitimized. It is also a pervasive one in the regional processes of manufacturing nationhood and citizenship; the Maharashtrian subject-citizens thus envisaged and produced are *Indian* ones, too. Indeed, if conceptualizations of the Maharashtrian regional state and the nation-state are both partly predicated upon shared ideals of Hindu masculinity and femininity, these nonetheless do not hold comparable status. The relationship of the Maharashtra state to the Indian one is a peculiar, genealogical one that requires attention. That, at a legislative level, the regional state is encompassed within the nation-state does not exhaust its definition; rather, the latter stands in contrast with the ideological conception dominant in western Maharashtra whereby the notion of a Maratha nation is *the* precondition for the possibility of the Indian nation. In other words, the Maratha nation is the prototype of the Indian one. Because Shivaji stands as the founder of the Maratha nation and the guarantor of *swarajya*, *swadharma*, and *swabhasha*, he is also the pioneer of the Indian nation at large.

I heard this comment from many locutors of all walks of life and of varying educational backgrounds in western Maharashtra: "After all, does not 'Maharashtra' mean 'the great nation' [*rashtra*]?" Evidence of this ideological and genealogical claim is proffered in the Class 4 textbook's depiction of Shivaji's skills as an efficient administrator, detailing the eight departments into which he divided his administration (administration, revenue and accounts, defense, religious matters, justice, government orders, correspondence, and foreign relations; lesson 15, 59). Ultimately buttressing this claim is the positioning at the end of the history textbook of the first introduction to civics in the entire school curriculum: the last four lessons are devoted to "*Zilla parishad* and *Panchayat samiti*," "our national objectives," "the rights and duties of citizens," and "our national symbols," respectively. Shivaji thus appears as having paved the way for efficient administration, thereby ushering in the premises of good governance in an independent (postcolonial) state. In these late twentieth- and early twenty-first-century teleological narratives, he is the archetype of the good administrator who invented secularism *à l'indienne* before its time.

Yet, rather than a "tangible reality," the hero-warrior is a "model of military masculinity" (Woodward 2000: 644). The hero model provides a crucial reference point functioning as a fundamental icon in the production of discourses of masculinity. What is actually produced is a *desire* for a masculine, virile individual as much as collective self in which women, too, play a part. Such a self may never be fully achieved because of the exacting nature of the relationship between Shivaji as ever a son to his demanding mother, Jijabai, and this unrealizable desire consequently targets the constitutive "Muslim other."[33] This "impossibility of [masculine] identities" (Hansen 1999: 60–65) also accounts for the potential appeal of Shiv Sena and other right-wing extremist outlets that provide reassuringly aggressive masculine narratives and deployments of the self (Hansen 1996, 2001), in which, as it were, the category of the hero *deivat* becomes powerfully all encompassing.

It should also be stressed that the category of *deivat* as one articulating dimension of the sacred—along with the mythical and the historical—in popular imaginaries is not an anachronistic oddity, contrary to what some historians might want to think. On the contrary, it is perhaps best understood as the reinvestment of enchantment amid rigid procedures of disciplinary history, as Sumathi Ramaswamy (2004: chap. 5 in particular) has perceptively argued with respect to the fabulous cartographies of the lost continent of Lemuria. Furthermore, the use of such a category with reference to heroes is not unique to the Maharashtrian—or Indian, for that matter—context. In a previously mentioned volume on the making of heroes, Claudie Voisenat drew attention to the perceptible link between politics and religion in Europe where Christianity largely contributed to legitimate political powers: the national hero, sometimes himself a saint, would ultimately be placed at the core of a state religion, thus acquiring a legendary and mythical aura.[34] Even in Europe, therefore, the relationship between heroism, sacredness, myth, and history was always a tenuous one, blending a secularized image and a religious representation of the national community. This further punctures the unhelpful yet persistent constructions of radical difference between a "religious, spiritual East" and a "material West" and draws attention to the important ways in which parallel constructions have been relayed by state institutions, schooling in particular.

This also calls for further reflection on the notion of sensorium in relation to this particular state institution's effects. Many scholars of nationalism (Anderson 1983; Gellner 1983; Hobsbawm 1992) have noted that education is one of the most crucial constituents for producing a nationalist sentiment. Most of their assertions, however, were predicated on a unique top-down institutional process, persistently overlooking the sensory dimension at play in the affective production of national senses of belonging. However, these cannot be produced through a vertical process. They have to draw upon already existing sensory structures of feeling and their transformative capacity. Nation-states (as well as regional ones) attempt to harness the potential of these sensory configurations in order to serve their own purposes. The regional state of Maharashtra effects a preemptive take on the population's sensory world, thus putting at its service the sensorium developed from a recomposed musical tradition fusing devotional *abhangas* and martial rhythms. Such a recomposed tradition conversely both emblematizes and undergirds the regional state. Thus, the distinction between individual and collective sensorium that a dominant, dichotomous notion of "public/private spaces" would support (Chapter 3) here again collapses as the sensorium developed in the intimacy of home is shot through with sensory elements pertaining to "public culture," and is also reworked in the space of school in accordance with larger social and political, as well as economic and industrial, processes taking place in wider society. In Maharashtra today, many of these processes pertain to the sensory revolution brought about by new technologies and industrialization: commingled are the sounds and fumes of trucks and tractors, the music belching out from loudspeakers outside temples and houses, and visual redeployments of local patriotism and nationalism (Introduction). It is the recomposition of this sensorium that the state is attempting to capture and that also makes it so "modern" (Benjamin's discussion in Thompson 2000).

It should, however, be emphasized that much of what comes into the daily production of senses of belonging is not necessarily part of a specific political agenda, as much of scholarly analysis would have it. To be sure, some teachers were more politically aware and articulate than others. Yet even in cases of blatant historical distortion on the part of teachers and parents, what surfaces is, rather than an explicit political project, the complex, fuzzy, and fragmentary nature of social actors' understandings and representations of their history and historiography. Such distortion may itself be the product of long-standing cultural and historical schemata, for instance, anti-Muslim feeling in Maharashtra. But these are always reshaped and rebuilt in the process of knowledge production and transmission, as well as in light of contemporary developments taking place on larger scales. Any given situation may therefore give rise to the resurfacing—and attendant reshaping—of a plurality of meanings and feelings. These may appear contradictory to the lay and distant "reader" of a "cultural script," but only to such a reader who would fail to see that these are not scripts that social actors perform and play consistently, even in the rather prescriptive space of school. Teachers relay the state's project with a measure of appropriation, in productive tension with the higher forces of social and political order that have been inscribed onto their bodies and senses (as they were tentatively disciplined into studious students decades before), as shown by what goes on within a teacher's classroom. In the following chapter, we pursue this exploration in a contrapuntal context, that of Urdu education among Muslims.

Moments of Suspension
Drawing, Mapping, Singing

THERE WERE MOMENTS OF REPRIEVE within classrooms, even in those of the sternest teachers. Thus Mr. Patil, newly arrived at Marathi Corporation School, was busy on that day of February 2000 preparing a handful of Class 4 pupils (three boys and two girls) soon to appear for scholarship examinations. Meanwhile, the other pupils (aged nine and ten) have lost complete interest in the Marathi grammar lesson. The girls are busy crafting *bindi*. Mr. Patil, for once, does not seem bothered by this lack of attention and goes on to an exercise on sensory properties of daily items (sugar—sweet, etc.), followed with another one on verbal constructions. As I am sitting on a wooden plank at the rear with the girls, one of them offers me a (used) *tikkli*. I accept the mark of friendship, feeling honored though somewhat inadequate to be included in their group; apart from the pen I am writing with and my tape recorder, I have not brought any other commodity suitable for exchange. After recess, the teacher takes up ordinary lessons again, with a poem on the syllabus. He first reads it with all the pupils, then asks the "nonscholarship students" to write it down while he continues with a geometry lesson with the privileged few. Needless to say, most pupils disengage themselves from the assigned task. What follows are, as in ordinary disorganized life, free-flowing moments of unchanneled attention, almost as in a stream-of-consciousness thought process, except that here, rather than thought process alone, these moments also consist of actions, seemingly random and purposeless if one attempts to reframe them within a great scheme of things. No "Ideology" here, no "Nationalism," "Patriotism," or any of those grand projects. Rather, moments of suspension, fragments that let surface free associations in the pupils' understandings, otherwise difficult to capture.

It is during these moments of suspension, of gratuitous exchange and conversation, that I am able to have the most interesting and informal interaction with the pupils in school, away from the teacher's gaze. These moments are part of an undetermined zone where things learned during lessons blend with life learning from outside the alternately protective and constraining space of school: to some of these children, and those living in Sachar Bazar and attending the Marathi Corporation School in particular, the school may appear as an ambiguous space where one is faced with external, authoritarian rules; yet it may also be one where the daily hardships of a difficult family life are somewhat put at a distance. An alcoholic abusive father, an absent mother, or a weak grandmother who may also be physically incapacitated are common fare in the neighborhood; even if most children will not comment on this other than by an embarrassed laugh and a dismissive gesture when prompted by one of their fellow students, this is part of their everyday lives. What these moments of suspension between the realities of home and the authority of the teacher allow to emerge are unique testimonies on how the stuff of these young social actors' daily lives gets intricately intertwined with that of big words and grown-ups' projects; how the teaching of the nation, of the regional hero, and of India as a secular or Hindu country somehow merge or conflict with one another, elicit questions, interrogations, or reappropriation, at times in rather indirect and unexpected ways.

That afternoon, the forsaken female pupils are inclined to drawing. Most students in the school by then know of my sustained interest in their drawings. The year before, I asked them to draw for me "whatever they wanted in relation to Kolhapur, Maharashtra, or India." So Sarita kindly hands me stencil drawings that she made earlier in the week: on one side is a picture of Shivaji; on the other, one of Lokmanya Tilak, the "resuscitator" of Shivaji at the turn of the twentieth century (Cashman 1975). Maps also occupy pride of place, and Pratima is rather eager to show me the one she has drawn on her own initiative: it is a penciled India with the names of each state inked in. She has drawn it from a textbook showing the national map on one side, with the pledge on the other. Another girl promptly hands me a similar drawing. The map of India is among the most popular with pupils, yet it may also give rise to interesting conflated processes. Thus, Kavita's is entitled "Maharashtra."

I ask her: "Where is Maharashtra? What is this?" [*indicating the map*]
"India." [*hesitant voice*]
"So the whole map is not Maharashtra, then, is it?"
"Oh!" [*hand covering mouth in light embarrassment*]

I am unsure what to draw from this exchange. It again suggests an overdetermination of the region over and above the nation, despite the latter's daily building upon a motherly sensorium, although these children's experiences of motherly love may not correspond to the normative ideals professed by the teachers (Chapter 3). This is the only school where I came across such representations of India, including minuscule ones compared with larger maps of Maharashtra.

It is also interesting that such a moment of suspension is followed by an unexpected question. It concerns my "ethnic origin" and is couched in notably essentializing terms. Regularly in all these years of fieldwork in Maharashtra, I have been asked whether I was a Konkanasta Brahmin, or sometimes a Punjabi: my fair skin, light-colored eyes, rather longish face, and height somehow created a doubt, introduced a possibility in my interlocutors' minds. Yet, never before have I been asked whether I am a Muslim. That day, at Marathi Corporation School, Vandana asks me precisely that. I answer, rather surprised: "Why? Who told you I was a Muslim?" Nirmala, her friend, answers: "Well, because you look like, I mean, your face looks similar to Rubina's."

Rubina, who is Muslim, happens to be sitting nearby, next to Vandana. I cannot tell whether her apparent shyness stems from being singled out for her fea-

Drawing of Shivaji Chhatrapati and Vyankoji. Class 4, All India Marathi School, Kolhapur, March 2000.

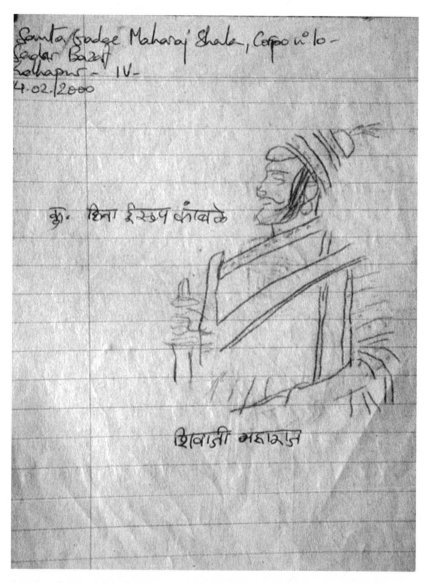

Drawing of Shivaji Chhatrapati. Class 4, Marathi Corporation School, Kolhapur, February 2000.

tures as a supposedly representative member of her "community" or from being made the object of public attention. The question, as well as the answer to my own question, has been exchanged without any trace of animosity or mockery; rather, it shows intense curiosity. This is another instance revealing how children genuinely attempt to make sense of their surroundings (Sachar Bazar houses

Shivaji Jayanti festival. Children usually make these small effigies of Shivaji Maharaj out of clay or plaster and then paint them. Here, children are parading the effigies in improvised "chariots" around the neighborhood. Kolhapur, February 2000.

a large Muslim population) through drawing logical analogies, some of them premised on physical or morphological features.

Meanwhile, Pratima comes up and requests me to now draw a map of India for them. I respond that I do not know how to draw it; will she show me? Disinclined to engage in a role reversal, Pratima shakes off her head in an embarrassed laugh and asks a new question: "So, a drawing of Shivaji Maharaj, then?" The obvious national/regional conflation manifested through mention of the figure of the Maratha hero is soon further confirmed by the offer three other pupils make at that very moment of singing for me one of the most popular patriotic songs across India, "Mere watan ke logon" (Chapter 3).

5 From Becoming to Being Muslim

Urdu Education, Affects of Belonging,
and the Indian Nation

> I wish for you the knowledge of what it feels like to be a minority. . . .
> On one hand, the adventure of having more than one culture to call
> mine. . . . And the pain of wishing that . . . I didn't have to explain my
> actions in my own country. And worse, feeling guilty for feeling this pain.
>
> **Shahnaz Habib,** *The Hindu*

> I am proud of being an Indian. I am part of the indivisible unity that is Indian
> nationality. I am indispensable to this noble edifice and without me this
> splendid structure of India is incomplete. I am an essential element which has
> gone to build India. I can never surrender this claim.
>
> **Abul Kalam Azad, quoted in Mushirul Hasan,** *Islam and Indian Nationalism*

UPON MY RETURN to Kolhapur in February 1999, municipal corporation officials
of the education bureau invited me on a one-day primary school tour in and
around town. The opportunity was not to be missed. My hosts' luxurious mode
of transport (car) seemed a welcome respite from my ordinary peregrinations
on foot, rickshaw, or scooter under an already scorching sun. Moreover, this
tour would supplement my explorations of the local educational scene, as I had
not yet ventured out of town in my visits to private, semiprivate, and municipal
schools. So we set off one fine morning to the outskirts of the city where owners
of sugarcane factories had started schools for their employees' children. On the
way back in midafternoon, we halted in Sachar Bazar, a neighborhood already
encountered in the preceding chapters. The slum area was familiar to me at the
time since I had visited one Marathi school there.

The Urdu-language school of the area, however, had totally escaped my notice. And for good reason: it was tucked away from the main road, hidden behind a mosque, with no other access than by either bluntly walking in through
the mosque—strongly objected to by local devotees—or winding one's way
down through the next *galli* into the inside of the block of narrow and densely
connected alleys (*mohalla*). Thus, apart from parents, teachers, and regular

Muslim devotees "spying" on daily schooling activities, no one ever ventured into this school without a purpose. In more ways than one, its spatial location epitomized the regional cultural aloofness in which pupils and, to a lesser extent, their families lived. Like any Urdu school in Maharashtra, this one catered exclusively to Muslim students.[1] As we entered the Urdu-Marathi Municipal Corporation School on that hot afternoon, little did I know this would become one of my main comparative sites of research. At the very least, the first encounter did not suggest such.

Briskly walking across the mosque, the corporation officials then burst into the deserted school precincts, only to find the head's office empty. Followed a prompt summoning of the four teachers out of their classrooms, who were ordered to find the headmistress wherever she was. As everybody anxiously waited for her to materialize (she was either on an errand or at home; nobody really knew), the tension grew ever so palpable. At last, Leela Sheikh Madam appeared. The senior education official, Pawar Bai—the highest representative of state authority in the situation—took charge of the meeting.

Pawar Bai was also the only female among the inspection staff. A stout and devout Maratha woman then in her late forties, her thundering voice would often resonate as she issued orders to peons, junior officials, or drivers indiscriminately. Her determination was compounded by the piercing glances she would cast about through her gold-rimmed spectacles. Her will was her entourage's command. Earlier that day, she had insisted on making a detour via her house in order to impress her anthropologist guest with her newly built spacious temple room. Now, her pride and enthusiasm were mere memories. She was clearly unimpressed by the headmistress's lack of professional commitment within normal school hours. The headmistress and other schoolteachers were blatantly embarrassed and uneasy as they nervously scrutinized the officials' every change in behavior. Here was a rather unpleasant intrusion by Marathi officials upon the tranquillity of daily school life in an Urdu-language school. What certainly made it worse was the smug arrogance of the said officials, strutting around with the self-important airs of "VIPs" as they addressed the teachers rather abruptly. What I had so far only sensed more than explicitly witnessed in the infancy of this research was suddenly and crudely revealed before my eyes. To be sure, this encounter could be read as one between representatives of higher state authority (corporation officials) descending upon subaltern state servants (the teachers) without notice. To a certain extent, it was. Yet, my experience of other visits to Marathi-speaking schools in similar circumstances told me that the stake of the encounter was only cosubstantially one of state authority and power. It was also *more than* one of Urdu versus Marathi medium of instruction. More important, the choice of these languages had social, economic, cultural, religious, political, and ideological implications that require exploration.

identities are nurtures.

IN HIS VOLUME *Questions of Cultural Identity*, Stuart Hall insisted that "actually, identities are about questions of using the resources of history, language and culture in the process of becoming rather than being; not 'who we are' or 'where we come from,' so much as what we might become, how we have been represented and how that bears on how we might represent ourselves" (1997: 4). The notion of identity thus framed aptly suggests and evokes its close associate, that of "community." By emphasizing the "we" in his formulation, Hall brings into relief the fact that identities, individual or collective, are always constituted in relation to a group, real or imagined. In this chapter, I explore how a community and a sense of belonging thereto are produced, or at least reinforced, through schooling. Such an exploration is especially relevant in modern nation-states today, as the notion of community lies at the heart of conceptions of pluralist political representation. The latter, as is well known, has—albeit controversially—increasingly been envisaged as a trait of "modern societies" and often as a condition for the viability of democracy (Taylor 1994; Kymlicka 1995). Yet in these conceptions, the traits associated with the notion of community are fixed ones, especially so cultural ones. Culturally or ethnically defined communities are seen as "givens." In the debates they generate, they are envisaged as social groups whose fixed sets of characteristics are to be unquestioningly respected and preserved. No sense of the relativity or, at least, fluidity of the notion of community is generally perceptible there; any potentiality of "becoming" is overshadowed by the determinants of "being." In keeping with the theoretical and empirical neglect of such potentialities, little research has so far been conducted on the conditions under which the notion of "community" becomes a crucial category for the imaginary production of social and political groups bounded by a commonality of shared features. Such an imaginary production obviously yields real effects inasmuch as entire groups of individuals may come to view themselves as belonging to the community thus imagined.[2] How, then, do individuals and groups, the majority of whom did not necessarily view themselves as sharing in a group identity become aware of such commonality? How do social actors reshape and make meaning of it in light of social,

What is the binding force.

economic, political, and religious events? The question has special relevance in relation not only to the production of national communities (Anderson 1983) but also to the notions of "dominant" and "minority" communities, and the significance these have acquired in many political contexts across nation-states today (Taylor 1994; Kymlicka 1995; Pandey 2001; Hinton 2002; Taylor 2002; Pandey and Geschiere 2003). It is not the purpose here to critique the problematic character of these notions as they have increasingly been used in academic and political circles. Rather, I want to focus on the following issue: What kind of effects does schooling have on the production of a "minority community," often defined *against* a "majority," and how do members of either group experience the sociological reality thus produced?

The case of Muslims in western India provides a crucial vantage point for exploring these issues: Muslims, as we saw in the previous chapter, represent the "other" against which a common sense of Maharashtrianness has been constructed, not least through schooling. In addition, the position of political power enjoyed by successive Mughal dynasties and Indo-Muslim sultanates from the eighth through to the nineteenth centuries stands in stark contrast to the conversely marginal political position occupied by the "Muslim community" today. The latter is, however, a demographically significant one of "*majority* minority community."[3] The legitimacy of Muslim Indians' participation in the political life of the country has been jeopardized by ongoing attempts made by Hindu right-wing parties to define citizenship along the lines of a monolithically reinvented Hinduism. This has caused great concern among observers over minorities' status becoming that of second-class citizens.

To be sure, referring to "Muslims" as a category in this context is problematic, as this is part of the question at issue: the phrasing "Muslims" runs the risk of freezing and objectifying culture as heritage (van der Veer 1994) by suggesting a clear-cut, well-defined, homogeneous social group whose reality is more statistical and electoral than sociological. Whether social actors of Muslim faith in the past considered themselves as "members of a single Muslim community," even as recently as in the nineteenth century, is still a moot question.[4] Whatever the case may be, ordinary Muslims, as Hasan has insisted, were not "members of a monolithic community sitting sullenly apart, but were active participants in regional cultures whose perspective they shared" (1998: 16). Moreover, even today the meaning of being Muslim in India is highly variable, also depending on factors such as class, caste, regional configuration, and so on, as well as on personal circumstances (Piscatori 1983, 1986). Notwithstanding these definitional difficulties and their methodological and theoretical implications, however, it is also true that the notion of "Muslim community" has acquired an unprecedented reality to which schooling has contributed. This I hope to show in what follows.

In this chapter, then, are explored the differential ways in which Muslim adults and children educated in the Urdu language construct local, national, and pan-regional senses of belonging in Kolhapur. As mentioned in Chapter 2, the complex issue of language(s) in India generated much passion among both ordinary social actors and specialists, with some of the related educational debates rippling from the nineteenth century through to postindependence times. Important for our present purpose is that the carving out of regional states along linguistic divisions after independence further strengthened the crucial dimension of language as a social and political practice in regard to state policies as well as to the construction of communal identities. Here I want to pursue the explorations begun in the previous chapters of the intricate relationship between language and history as markers and definers of cultural and religious identification on the one hand and state schooling on the other.

How, through an expanding state apparatus, may both these subjects become powerful means for further anchoring differential senses of belonging and allegiance while reshaping their attendant narratives? Even though Urdu was the language of the elite in northern India until the turn of the twentieth century, Urdu-language mass education is relatively recent, especially in western India. In Kolhapur, the high school started at the turn of the twentieth century under the auspices of the then-ruler Shahu Maharaj was for a long time the only one available in the district. In keeping with the regional state government's implementation, thirty years ago, of an educational policy allowing any child to study in his or her mother tongue in primary school, Urdu-language facilities were created throughout Maharashtra. In Kolhapur, the municipal corporation opened primary schools under the pressure of some Urdu Muslim residents.[5] Today, the town is host to six Urdu primary schools catering to about two thousand pupils (out of a general total of sixty-one thousand in 1998). Although the school in Sachar Bazar dates from 1963, it consisted of four derelict, dark rooms housing very small numbers of students until recently. As we will see, these numbers have risen steadily for a number of reasons.

How schooling in differential media of instruction may produce heightened polarization of identifications is a crucial issue. To be sure, what gets taught at school is not de facto taken in by passive recipients, and schooling alone does not determine and create senses of belonging and allegiance. As is by now clear from the preceding chapters, children, teachers, parents, and other educational officials play an influential part in life at school, as they negotiate and shape state injunctions, relating them to ongoing political events, both within and outside the country. All these negotiated productions may crucially contribute to the social and political construction of persons and citizens, especially when they feed upon existing structures of feeling within society. Yet, as previously noted, the (re)production of these structures of feeling is also relayed and drawn upon by state institutions, not least of all schooling. How the latter informs or reshapes these is therefore of prime import, especially in the context of recent access to public instruction by a majority of people in Maharashtra. When earlier generations of Maharashtrians did have but a modicum of education at best, schooling played only a marginal role in the everyday (re)production of symbolic bonds and imaginings of identity, ethnic, religious, or linguistic. By contrast, in the past twenty years of generalized access to public instruction, the site of school has come to acquire greater visibility and prominence in ordinary people's lives, operating as a site of identity crystallization. The issue of language and identity in Maharashtra today has to be envisaged in this light. Despite its claims to producing a homogeneous patriotic citizen, schooling has also provided an avenue for sharper differentiation of identifications, especially linguistic ones, endowing them with further meaning. The fact, for instance, that primary instruction is permitted in the regional state in seven languages (Marathi, Urdu, Hindi, English, Gujarati, Sindhi, and Kannada) has enabled distinct linguistic groups to maintain and reproduce themselves; it has also created them and reinforced a sense of unity that did not necessarily exist in such explicit terms in the collective imaginings of members of that so-called group. Whereas language was primarily an indicator of difference that could often be superseded by other characteristics shared with the rest of the regional population, it has become a marker of unredeemable otherness, both in the space of school and within regional society at large. To this extent, it now represents a crucial mediation for claims of belonging to a particular group other than the dominant one, demonstrated in the case of Urdu-educated Muslims in western Maharashtra today.

In Kolhapur, most families sending their children to Urdu school did not themselves speak a "pure Urdu," as noted somewhat disparagingly by some teachers. Rather, they commonly used Hindi, or more often than not, a version accommodated to local variations and dubbed "Mussalmani." Furthermore, both parents and most teachers were overwhelmingly first-generation literates: their own parents were either totally illiterate or had acquired only rudiments of education. In a large number of cases, they had often studied in Marathi, because few alternative facilities existed in the region until recently.[6] By the 1990s, however, Urdu to them represented "their language," "the Muslim language," one that the girls, in particular, were expected to master so as to perform their future roles of family pillars. *They* would pass on this knowledge to their children; *they* would teach them the Quranic inscriptions. As Sheila Bepari, mother of Mobina, then in her teens, explained: "We need the girls to know Urdu so they can read the Quran." To this end, and although several Urdu translations of the Quran have been circulating in India since the late nineteenth century (Robinson 1983: 199), some families in Sachar Bazar supplemented public Urdu instruction with private Arabic lessons from a local Maulana.

Furthermore, rather than the construction of persons and citizens being predicated on the production of regional bonds as in Marathi schools, here it was hardly mediated by any comparable notion of regional attachment—at least, not in the sense nurtured through the official regional history concocted by the educational department of Maharashtra. Such a contrasted construction was particularly apparent in the relationship that Urdu-educated Maharashtrians (all Muslims) entertained with regional history.

Shunning Regional Narratives

One of the greatest differences between Urdu- and Marathi-language education lay in the contrast between the respective modalities of teaching the history of Shivaji Maharaj. As we saw in Chapter 4, Shivaji epitomizes two overlapping conceptions of the "nation": one regional, Maratha, which is the prototype for the other, national one, Indian. In a nutshell, Marathi-educated Maharashtrians conceived of their relation to the Indian nation through the regional prism of the "Maratha nation," of which Shivaji is said to be the founder. The history of Shivaji has been taught to Class 4 children in all Marathi schools across the state of Maharashtra since the latter's inception in 1960. Throughout the year, pupils learn about the cunning deeds of the legendary warrior and his enlightened administrative skills. When asked about this history in Marathi schools, most children would respond with much enthusiasm, often shouting for attention to speak first. In Urdu schools, by contrast, and although the curriculum was identical in all subjects (save for language instruction), Shivaji was not celebrated as the praised hero and glorified founder of the Maratha nation, nor even of the Indian nation. This was dramatically illustrated by the ensuing incidents at the time of my first visit to the Urdu Corporation School.

After the embarrassed headmistress had greeted us, she showed us to the classrooms. Each consisted of a small, dark, stuffy room with a hot corrugated tin roof. None of them had either windows or any ventilation device other than the door and a minuscule opening in the back wall (the fans had long broken down, and no one from the corporation had ever bothered to repair them). To make matters worse, electricity was cut off in the slum that afternoon. The officials purposefully stopped in Class 4. As in the other rooms, the whitewashed walls were bare for the most part, in stark contrast with classrooms in Marathi schools, where posters of Shivaji or related heroes and heroines adorned the classroom walls. As we entered the room, the pupils—mostly girls—stood up to greet us with "Salaam o alaikum," to which the ordinary answer is "Wa Alaikum alsalaam." In the present case, however, the greeting was only grudgingly acknowledged by the officials with a fulminating nod: not only were the pupils obviously not abiding by the new Maharashtrian regulations (given to all primary schoolteachers in Maharashtra during special training programs in the summers of 1997, 1998, and 1999; these regulations included new forms of greeting). To add insult to injury, the pupils did not even attempt to speak the regional language! As the atmosphere grew tenser and the corporation officials made loud sneering comments, the pupils entrenched themselves in unrelenting muteness, further enraging the officials. Feeling increasingly ill at ease, I was suddenly "invited" to question the children on the syllabus and their knowledge of Marathi. The only way I could find to mitigate the command was to comply in Hindi, the "official" national language. Despite its history of nationalized Sanskritization since the nineteenth century and its clear association with Hindu speakers in the northern "Hindi belt" (Lelyveld 1978, 1993; Kumar 1992; King 1996), Hindi in Maharashtra carries overtones of national integration, to the extent that those Muslims studying in the Marathi language and better integrated within regional society would often claim to speak Hindi rather than Mussalmani or Urdu.[7] And so I reluctantly started:

> "Do you speak Marathi?"
>
> "Yes." [*shy smiles, almost inaudible voices*]
>
> "What subjects do you study?"
>
> "Urdu, maths, science, geography, history."
>
> "What history?" interjected one of the corporation officials.

[margin handwritten note: forced nationalism.]

Before I could move on to another question, Pawar Bai, the corporation senior official, lost her temper and, glaring at the pupils, barked in Marathi: "Aren't you studying Shivaji's history?!" [Tumhi Shivaji Maharajancya itihasaca abhyas karta, na?!] [*reluctant nods from the pupils*]

"Well, say so, then!" [Mag, sanga ki!]

[*Then, Pawar Bai prompted the schoolmaster to ask them questions. These, in contrast to those often put to pupils in Class 4 Marathi schools, were of the most basic kind. The teacher asked them very noncommittally; the pupils answered in the same way.*]

"What is Shivaji's name? What is Shivaji's father's name? What is that of his mother?"

Here was a situation far removed from those in Marathi schools where I had witnessed sheer exultation and enthusiasm at the mere mention of the hero's name. At this point, my uneasiness had turned into utter discomfort, and I declined to pursue the question-answer experiment further, much to the education officials' disappointment. We then left the classroom and made for the office. As we sat there waiting for tea, one of the corporation officials remarked in an aside to the senior official: "These people are not teaching Shivaji's history because it is a problem to them." Pawar Bai, for her part, looked profoundly dejected by the blatant neglect of the regional/national hero's history just witnessed. Later on, back in the car, I asked the officials what the issue was about teaching Shivaji's history. The one who had made the earlier comment referred to the "doubt [in English] Muslim people have about teaching it." The official, in turn, explained the reason for their not teaching it was that Shivaji had defeated the Mughal rule over three centuries earlier. In the same breath, she established a connection with her consequent distrust toward unpatriotic Muslims and the need for them to be kept in check by the Shiv Sena Party.

Dominant Regional Narratives and Experiences of "Muslimness"

This incident captures both non-Muslim officials' perceptions of Urdu-schooled Muslims' unwillingness to embrace regional history as their own, and the real reluctance among many Maharashtrian Muslims of different generations toward the teaching of this official history. The Urdu teachers in the course of research later confirmed such reluctance, which was also shared in the other three Urdu schools that I visited in Kolhapur. What may have contributed to it was the awareness among some teachers of the way Muslims are portrayed in the official historical narratives. This was especially the case for those who had been partly educated in Marathi schools. There, as seen in the previous chapter, Shivaji's foes were regularly, although improperly, named "Musalmans" instead of "Mughals" or "Indo-Muslims" (the latter term is commonly used by historians to refer to Persian dynasties in southern India, such as that of Bijapur). Granted, these rulers were Muslims, but such a phrasing creates a sense of antagonism premised on faith rather than on political power. The slippage then becomes easy from a narrative of regional history dominated by Mughal/Muslim rulers—who, it should be noted, were served by Maratha Hindu chiefs, or sardars—to general representations of Muslims as hereditary enemies encapsulated by the label "Muslim enemy" (*Musalman shatrun*), as teachers would often be heard saying in classrooms. These comments were made not just in the classrooms of blatantly pro-Hindu, old-guard teachers working at Varsity Marathi School, but also in most ordinary classrooms, including those of corporation schools, as we saw in Chapter 4.

Such a commonality of views shared by many non-Muslim Maharashtrians in this part of Maharashtra is noteworthy. For, whether implicitly or explicitly, regional history is framed in anti-Muslim terms. We saw in Chapter 1 how older forms of *bhakti* have been harnessed in the contemporary construction of a sense of belonging to both the region and the nation in Maharashtra. These political and religious forms of Hindu piety have also been instrumental in furthering an anchorage of anti-Muslim feeling since the seventeenth century (Bayly 1998: 24–25). Consequently, the issue of whether teachers purposefully transmitted these anti-Muslim views is irrelevant. Teachers' worldviews largely determined and filtered the knowledge they passed on to their pupils, regardless of any conscious or deliberate "hidden agenda." The emphasis they placed in many classrooms on the physical mutilation and annihilation of some of Shivaji's most famous enemies (the cutting off of Shahiste Khan's fingers, the ripping apart of Afzal Khan's entrails), together with their regular ridiculing of these same enemies, was not part of any programmatic ingraining. Rather, they pertained to forms of popular culture commonly found in Maharashtra over the past decades, either in the forms of piety or in reenactments and displays of Shivaji's grandeur in which Marathi cinema played a crucial part, especially in the work of Bhalji Pendharkar (Benei 2004). What kind of effect such formal and informal messages may have had on Muslim students studying in non-Urdu schools is a serious question.

At issue here is not so much that Muslim children in non-Urdu schools are studying in the Marathi language but that they are studying in "Hindu-dominant schools" and, more generally, within an increasingly Hinduized curriculum despite the autonomy of the textbook bureau in the state of Maharashtra. Indeed, compared with the previous series of textbooks dating back to the early 1980s, the shift from a positive appraisal of Muslim/Mughal historical contribution to an elision thereof in Marathi manuals is most jarring. Whereas the Class 4 Marathi textbook of 1982 incorporated a lesson on Id Mubarak, described as an occasion for celebrating friendship and amity, its successor no longer makes any mention of any Muslim festival whatsoever. This stands in deafening contrast with the new and overabundant references to Hindu festivals. In the same manual, even the sites of distinct Muslim heritage have been elided in implicit attempts at highlighting and reclaiming the pre-Muslim history of the region. For instance, the only mention of Aurangabad district sets the scene for a visit to the fort of Daulatabad, designated in the lesson under its pre-Islamic name of Devgiri and indicated as such on the corresponding map. Thus, the implicit notion of a historical Hindu continuity wherein Islamic presence is but a minor accident is reinforced. It is as if all the good work of preaching unity (*ekatmata*) and living together with people "with other costumes and *dharma*" (Chapter 1) had been gradually relegated to the background, when not bluntly thwarted.

Obviously varying according to institution, teacher, and caste is how the teaching of this subtly Hinduized curriculum is made explicit and negotiated, especially in the presence of Muslim students. These account for 6 percent to 10 percent of the student population in the majority of privately run schools, including the outwardly *Hindutwadi* Varsity Marathi School.[8] Here, some methodological and theoretical clarification is in order. Much as it has long been the Faustian fantasy—and even less realistically, the claim—of many an anthropologist, reaching an understanding of any social actor's inner thoughts and feelings is, of course, impossible. Even the expression of these thoughts and feelings runs the risk of overinterpretation: anthropologists may ascribe extra meaning to any anodyne incident for the sole reason of its occurring within a social group that occupies a sensitive position within society (on the dangers of overinterpretation, see Lahire 1996; Lenclud 1996; Olivier de Sardan 1996; especially Paul Veyne 1996). In other words, the very constitution of social and cultural facts on the basis of supposedly objective "indices, signs and traces" (Ginzburg 1989) is itself an arbitrary process always susceptible to subjective and distorted construction. However, neither historians nor anthropologists have found any better method. Consequently, by tracking down the minute details that appear salient to *them*, anthropologists and historians can eventually draw a plausible—even if always impressionistic—picture of the experiences, feelings, and understandings of individuals and their constitutive interaction within and among social groups. Clues for such paintings are arguably not exclusively located in exceptional or cyclical events; rather, they are best found in the daily workings of school life, where most of them either largely go unnoticed or appear unproblematic, possibly because of their frequent occurrence.

The labeling of "indices, signs and traces" is particularly apposite here. In Maharashtra and Kolhapur in particular, overt and explicit manifestations of attitudes or expressions of thoughts and feelings against Muslims were rare. Both Muslims and non-Muslims of all castes and classes were usually prompt to praise the good work achieved at the turn of the twentieth century by the local ruler Shahu Maharaj toward promoting social and economic welfare as well as harmony among the diverse sections of the population. These achievements were often discursively linked to the history of social reform movements that targeted Brahmins in the area in the late nineteenth century (Kavlekar 1979), and in which the local raja participated (Copland 1973; Benei 1999). Such a discourse in principle negates the possibility of communal violence comparable to that prevailing in northern India, or even in Mumbai. This local history has become the distinctive feature of Kolhapur, whether to insiders or outsiders, also operating as a check against public pronouncements of overly ethnic, social, political, or religious antagonism. In the privacy of homes, however, ordinary social actors are more likely—either inadvertently or deliberately—to shed their reserve on the issue of Muslims. Often, this issue came up in a discussion of regional history and of the Maratha nation's accomplishments enabled by Shivaji. Thus, one cold evening in December 2000 as I was sitting on the stone floor of Baba Pankat's main room together with all the family members (the family introduced in Chapter 2), the conversation veered toward the "Muslim issue" for the first time in the several years that I had known them. Perhaps because I was cognizant of their past experience of social stigmatization as Bhangis (Untouchables, scavenger caste), their father's past affiliation with Marxism and his late conversion to Buddhism, and their overall tolerance—including of minorities and foreigners—I was rather ill prepared for the exchange that followed. Earlier that evening we had been talking about Shivaji and the popularity of historical films about him, especially those of filmmaker Bhalji Pendharkar. As Mohand, the middle son, had just expressed professional, personal, and political distrust of Muslims, I prompted him further. His younger brother, Ramesh, stepped in:

> "You see, had it not been for Shivaji Maharaj, tonight, we would not be sitting and chatting together."
>
> I, surprised: "How so?"
>
> Mohand, with aplomb: "First of all, we would not even be speaking Marathi, but Urdu. And then you see, had the Muslims [*sic*] continued ruling us, had Shivaji not vanquished them and established our swaraj, tonight you would be sitting over there [*pointing to the kitchen*], with all the women [*all of whom were presently sitting in the main room*], and we would not even be able to see each other as we talk: there would be a curtain [*pardah*] between here and there; between you and us [*referring to the custom of* pardah, *the veiling of Muslim women*]. So, suppose we wanted to chat together; well, this would not be possible. Well, thanks to Shivaji Maharaj, this is not so, and we are free to talk all together tonight."

own rule

In this and other narratives surfaces a deep sense of otherness in relation to "Muslim customs and practices." Muslims in these accounts emerge as the unspoken other: always ever present in the shadow of public stages and at the back of non-Muslim Maharashtrians' minds, archetypically antagonistic but rarely acknowledged as such in ordinary dealings, save on the platforms of Hindu right-wing politicians. Even the phrase "non-Muslim Maharashtrian" sounds somewhat like a pleonasm. As if, on either side of the divide, Muslims could never truly be Maharashtrians, and conversely, "true Maharashtrians" could never be Muslims.[9] Therefore, at the risk of overinterpreting, even the slightest wink of an eye in public has to at least be recorded. It is the price to be paid for reaching a more sensitive and nuanced account of intercommunal relations and in order to illuminate the institutionalized production of difference occurring within schooling.

Examples of daily production and explication of difference abound at school. They often involve a lot left unsaid but whose undertones are quite perceptible. Consider, for instance, the small, apparently meaningless incident that occurred in December 1998 when the headmistress of Varsity Marathi School, Kirari Bai, took me on a tour of all the classrooms. According to the routine during such a tour, at each stop she would test the students after briefly introducing me. The occasion was always a somewhat solemn one for the pupils, who would dutifully welcome the unexpected official guests with formal greetings. Yet the atmosphere in such circumstances was rather cheerful. As we stopped in one

Class 2, Kirari Bai asked a benign question on the plural form in Marathi. Its purpose was to emphasize the difference between oral (*boli bhasha*) and written language (*pramanit bhasha*). Judging by the lack of response the question elicited, it had clearly failed. Only one alert-looking pupil attempted an answer. The headmistress then asked him:

> "What do you speak at home?"
>
> [*The child instantly began to show signs of nervousness.*]
>
> Kirari Bai rephrased her question thus: "What does Mummy speak at home?"
>
> A shadow darkened the little boy's face as he pleadingly answered: "Now, now I speak Marathi."

It turned out that this boy was Muslim and that the language spoken at home was "Hindi." I was never able to find out this child's particular history of schooling. It is possible that he had already been confronted about his "Muslimness" in school, having gone through kindergarten and Class 1, and this may have influenced his response to the headmistress. Whether it was part of a willingness to integrate, to not be singled out from his classmates as "other" is probable (James 1993). The fact is that during the conversation, a perceptible sense of uneasiness gradually pervaded the room as pupils and teachers watched the scene unfold. The atmosphere had become unusually tense. Clearly, this had to do with more than a mere encounter with archetypal representatives of school authority. Moreover, the very fact that the headmistress felt a need at the end of the exchange to reassure the child by saying, "You can speak your language at home, there is no problem, nothing will happen," precisely suggested otherwise, especially in public spaces in this part of Maharashtra. For, apart from large cosmopolitan cities such as Mumbai—and Pune to a lesser extent—to speak Hindi in public spaces marks one as "not belonging." "True" Maharashtrians do not speak Hindi publicly unless they address "strangers." Furthermore, in the present case it was understood that the Hindi spoken was, rather than the official language of India, a hybridized form derogatorily dubbed "Mussalmani."

This exchange must also be envisaged in relation to larger notions of morality, justice, and rectitude associated with learning to become a good citizen. As we saw in Chapter 2, the correct mastery of the Marathi language is fundamental to the training of proper and fit social and political persons. This is particularly evidenced in the emphasis laid by teachers upon the notion of *pramanit bhasha* in opposition to *boli bhasha*, or "the correct, authoritative lan-

authoritative langy

guage" versus the unruly "oral language" spoken at home or more generally in everyday life. From this perspective, it is particularly significant that the headmistress should have selected these contrasting notions for testing the pupils in the classroom. Indeed, implicit in the project of schooling is the understanding that school is the very space where students should internalize *pramanit bhasha*. This also applies to students of lower-caste or non-Hindu backgrounds, whose spoken idioms are the most likely to be further removed from the version acknowledged as "proper and standard" Marathi. In these confrontations and attempts at "disciplining difference" (Pandey 2001: 152), the stigmatization teachers operate is nowhere more evident than in the discursive shaming of home, especially through the mother trope. It is in this light that the Muslim pupil's reaction of acute embarrassment to the question of the language spoken at home through the formulation of "What does Mummy speak at home?" should be envisaged. Such a phrasing encapsulates both the above notions associated with the authoritative version of the Marathi language and the stigma attached to difference from it. Explicit acknowledgment that the mother spoke something "other" was a more general admission of otherness. As we saw in Chapter 3, Marathi schools cultivated a deeply anchored equation of the virtues of motherhood with Hinduness and Indianness. Hence, in attracting attention to linguistic difference, the shaming of the mother operated as the single most crystallizer of otherness, further illustrating the fact that "[u]ltimately," as Michael Herzfeld wrote, "the language of national or ethnic identity is indeed a language of morality" (1997: 43).

Furthermore, experiences of otherness were not uncommon among Muslim children studying in Marathi schools, as I later discovered. Unfortunately, I never dared broach the topic so explicitly with them lest I further reinforce a perceived sense of discomfort at being singled out as members of a largely antagonized minority community. The data I was able to collect in this respect predominantly came from my own observations of school life and from conversations with adult Muslims. Many of those educated in Marathi across several generations emphasized the distorted and biased character of the narratives commonly told in Marathi institutions. These, they claimed, were exploited by Hindu right-wing parties such as the Shiv Sena. No less important, many Marathi-educated Muslims nonetheless reasserted the official secularist version of Maharashtrian regional history reappropriating for themselves the ecumenical notion of *Hindavi swaraj* associated with Shivaji. As seen in the previous chapter, today the term is contentiously and frequently translated as "self-rule of the Hindus" instead of "those living in Hind," which is to say "India" (from the Persian, designating the part of India above the Indus River). Marathi-educated Muslims would often point to the all-encompassing dimension of social, cultural, and religious toler-ance entailed in the phrase, which is in contrast to an oft-encountered version in Marathi schools today. Thus, Shaheen Hussain, former corporator of the slum adjacent to Sachar Bazar and Marathi educated, insisted:[10]

> Shivaji has been recuperated by the Shiv Sena, but this does not mean that Shivaji belongs to Hindu people only, since he created Hindavi swaraj; Shivaji Maharaj did; therefore, he was against Mughals, and there were more Hindus on the whole territory of Bharat and Pakistan. But Shivaji's swarajya included all religions [*sarva dharma*]: Hindu, Muslim, etc. Even his bodyguard was a Muslim.

The easiness with which Marathi-educated Muslim adults spoke about those matters contrasted greatly with the blatant avoidance displayed by Urdu-educated teachers. Even those who, because of a lack of Urdu educational fa-cilities in their villages, had had to study in primary Marathi schools prior to joining Urdu higher educational institutions were rather reluctant to discuss official regional history. Whenever I attempted to broach the subject in the later course of research, they promptly put an end to the conversation. The pupils themselves sometimes claimed they did not like Shivaji's history because it was "written in small prints." In the end, their experiences, together with the imag-inings of exclusively Urdu-educated ones, combined into irrefragable rejection of official regional history. So the Class 4 teacher at Urdu Corporation School contented himself upon our very first encounter with merely asking the names of Shivaji's close kin from his pupils. This was already more than what they ought to know.

Building Competing Narratives, Reconstructing Pan-regional Bonds

That Urdu-educated Muslims rejected the official version does not mean they did not have their own version of regional history. However, rather than delim-ited by regional boundaries, this history is interregional and follows the lines of demarcation of former Indo-Muslim kingdoms. This became apparent as I went with the Urdu Corporation School's teachers and students on their annual outing in March 2000. That year, they decided to go to Bijapur in the neighbor-ing state of Karnataka. The town was founded in the eleventh century by the

Chalukya dynasty and became the capital of the reputed Indo-Muslim dynasty of the Adil Shahi in 1489. The Adil Shahi presided over one of the sultanates in the Deccan region and are renowned for their artistic refinement and sophistication (Eaton 1978). As we shall see, this trip represented a key moment feeding into the teachers' self-constructions as Muslims, especially through a reconnection with an architectural past symbolizing former Muslim grandeur. Commenting upon this kind of symbolization in an essay entitled "The Muslim Malaise in India," Akbar S. Ahmed remarked:

> [B]y the end of the Mughal period, in the last century, the Muslims had tumbled down from the top. Their political role was terminated, their language rejected and their very identity threatened. The trauma of this downfall lies at the heart of the Muslim problem in India today. The Muslim monuments . . . appear to mock the Indian Muslims. Their present impotence and lowly status are exaggerated by the splendour and scale of the buildings. (1988: 85)

Contrary to what Ahmed further argued, however, "clinging to the past" and the "fantasy provided by it" (86) do not necessarily elicit "emotional anorexia" among Muslims. Rather, the process of reconnecting with this architectural heritage through the outing to Bijapur allowed the participants to actively render it as their own. It also enabled them to reinscribe this past within a larger national narrative, duly reinstating the glorious contribution of Muslim rulers to the Indian nation. Arguably, this one-day trip offered an occasion for teachers and children to relate to, and celebrate, a rather different kind of history from the Maharashtrian official version imposed on them. Here was a history dominated by victorious Muslims and ornate mosques wherein visions and imaginings of former glory and political power blended with ones of architectural and religious achievements. Throughout the day, students and teachers appropriated this heritage by various means, ranging from elaborate speeches and lively discussions to good-hearted comments and photograph-taking sessions; the most dedicated had brought notebooks and jotted down notes and impressions about the greatness of Indo-Muslim rule. Let us accompany them on that trip.

The outing begins early in the morning around 7:30 a.m. After a few hours of driving punctuated by a flat tire, we halt at our first site, the Mulup Maidan Top. This fort takes its name from the cannon (*top*) that made it famous. Next the group goes to see another nearby fort before having lunch in the gardens of the mausoleum of Muhammad Adil Shah (ruled 1627–56), famous for its echo chamber inside. Legend has it that the ruler wanted to build a mausoleum comparable to that of his father, Ibrahim Adil Shah II. Because his father's monument, known as Ibrahim Rauza, was considered exceptional in composition and decoration, the only means of avoiding direct competition was through size. The Gol Gumbaz (literally, "round dome"), is one of the largest single-chambered structures in the world, covering an area of 18,225 square feet (1,693 square meters). This monument is clearly among the favorite sites visited that day. After lunch, teachers and children alike merrily fill the mausoleum's imposing structure. In an attempt at verifying what they have just heard from one of the local guides, they proceed to testing the echoing quality inside. The round building was erected with such architectural skills, so the story goes, that anybody whispering at one point of the upstairs gallery can be heard all around. The students nudge each other in excitement as the sound circles the walls. The relaxed and cheerful atmosphere starkly contrasts with that following soon after reaching the Jamma Masjid, the main mosque in Bijapur. This is the only site in the course of the outing where the mood suddenly changes into one of concentrated seriousness. It is also the only moment when the teachers explicitly ask me to take a picture of the pupils sitting in prayer. The visit is followed with a halt at another attraction, the Taj Bawdi, a sort of square pond where women can be seen washing clothes. Next is the mausoleum of Ibrahim Rauza. The architectural site is renowned for its delicately carved windowsills and wooden shutters, as well as the floral motifs and Quranic inscriptions decorating its painted walls and doors. We rest there for a while. Two of the teachers, as they have repeatedly done since our arrival into Bijapur that morning, comment on the beauty and refinement of some details, again calling my attention to them. Arabic, Persian, and Quranic inscriptions are also among the motifs invariably evoking delighted wonderment. Finally, just before taking the road back to Kolhapur, we stop by two Muslim shrines (*dargah*), where the (male) teachers disappear to pay homage. By then, everybody is tired, and all sit listlessly in wait as the day's exhilaration wanes.

We saw in Chapter 4 how schooling in Maharashtra has furthered a sense of history among members of a literate public. At the smaller and more specific scale of communities and family narratives, such a sense of history often blithely combines scholarly authentication with fantasized processes of reconnection. The same observation obtains with respect to Urdu schooling among Muslim students and teachers. Throughout the annual outing to Bijapur, teachers and students appropriated the history associated with these monuments for themselves, even at the risk of some factual inaccuracies. For instance, at the

Mulup Maidan Top, the most senior teacher explained in a scholarly way that Adil Shah had made the fort and the cannon. This was soon disputed by an improvised local guide, the postcard seller who diligently enlightened us about the weapon's place of origin and maker.[11] Arguably, these factual inaccuracies were part of the identification that teachers and students effected with this past. Questions of who had made the cannon might have been relevant to historiographers, but to these pilgrims of one day, they did not contain any intrinsic historical value. They were only meaningful inasmuch as they served the purpose of celebrating the greatness of Muslim ancestors from Turkey, Arabia, Persia, and so on. In the process, these objectively factual inaccuracies operated as so many historical strands of Islamic political rule woven into a tapestry of Muslim past grandeur. Thus, through this appropriation, pupils and teachers alike did at the same time construct a relationship to the Muslim world at large. The fact that they marveled at inscriptions in Persian and in Arabic, drawing their traveling companions' attention to them, suggested an act of (re)connection with origins long lost sight of in a now hostile environment. This was also in keeping with the fact, noted earlier, that a sizable number of children and adults (including the headmaster) in the *mohalla* had recently begun to take evening Arabic

On the way to the "top" during the outing to Bijapur with Urdu Corporation School, Kolhapur, March 2000.

classes. It is, of course, doubtful whether anybody in the school had any known family ancestry dating back to Arabia, Turkey, or Persia. Indeed, in Maharashtra as in the rest of South Asia, the majority of Muslims were not of immigrant stock, coming over the centuries as invaders or to serve existing Muslim-ruled states (Taylor 1983: 182). A conversion process associated with the growth of agricultural communities began in the fourteenth century through to the Mughal period (1526–1858), by the end of which converted Indian Muslims had become a "majority community" in the eastern and western wings of the subcontinent (Eaton 2000: 36). Consequently, most of the Muslim residents in Maharashtra today come from autochthonous converted families. Yet these extraneous locations associated with Muslim rule functioned as topoi for creating links comparable to that of the religious Islamic community of believers (*umma*), even though the latter notion was not necessarily explicitly mentioned.

That this heritage was to be particularly cherished was made further manifest in the weeks that followed the outing. The next morning, the new headmaster who had succeeded the previously encountered headmistress upon her retirement, had set up a big polystyrene board with eight of the postcards bought in Bijapur corresponding to the sites visited. His intention, as he later explained that morning, was to allow even those students (the younger ones in particular) who had not been able to go to benefit from the school trip. The headmaster started the day with one of his inordinately long lectures, this one lasting even longer. In the weeks to come, pupils would be asked to draw and write about what they had seen and to deliver small speeches in turn in their classrooms. One teacher had taken photographs, and these, together with my photographs, were neatly arranged on a large poster decorated with children's drawings and texts. The poster still occupied pride of place in the head's office when I last visited the school in the summer of 2003.

The site of Bijapur did not have significance only for Urdu-educated Muslims. It also held a central position in the respective and competing imaginings of Muslims and Hindus, as further testified soon after the outing. Teachers of other schools often asked where I had been if they did not see me for more than a couple of days. Upon returning from Bijapur, I made no mystery to Marathi schoolteachers of my recent whereabouts. In some institutions, I thought I could detect a slight sense of dejection from the faces pulled by some teachers, although no one made explicit comments. Some said somewhat stuffily: "Oh yes, there are Muslim forts and all over there, yes, Adil Shah, that was his place." At times, I perceived a sly, even if fleeting smile on the same faces. Seemingly compounding their discomfort at the thought of my deserting Maratha history were the pains I took to pronounce the place's name in Hindi, as per the Urdu teachers' ways. Each time, the Marathi teachers would correct me, emphasizing the Marathi pronunciation of "*Vijapur.*" In so doing, Marathi speakers also gave prominence to the city's pre-Muslim past.[12] At the same time, they established a phonetic connection with the neighboring kingdom of Vijayanagar across the Krishna River from the Bahmani kingdom of the Adil Shah, thus significantly reinstating the preeminence of what has come to be seen as a "Hindu past" today. All this despite the fact that, as Eaton has cogently argued, the issue was never one of Muslim or Hindu rule when the southern Bahmani and Vijayanagar kingdoms united in their fight against northern Delhi ruler Muhammad bin Tughluq (2000: 152–53). Both states emerged as revolutionary regimes evolved out of armed resistance to common, northern, imperial power alien to Deccan culture (160). Distinctions then were predicated upon regional linguistic features rather than on religious ones. Today, regional linguistic and religious traits have become inextricably interwoven with one another, crystallizing polarization of Maratha Hindus and non-Maharashtrian Muslims. The result is that, while national history has been rewritten in communalist terms by Hindu right-wing academics occupying positions of power in the BJP-led coalition central governments of the last decade until May 2004, Muslims in southern India are also reappropriating this regional history as part of a Muslim rather than a southern Indian one.

Reinscribing National Narratives, Visceral Nationalism, and the Irony of Display

It is difficult to assess the place that such pan-regional connections to a wider Muslim history and culture assumed in the imaginations and psyches of Urdu students and teachers. Obviously, this varied from person to person. Zamadar Sir, for instance, was the eldest teacher in the school. He was at the time among the most assiduous in performing his prayer (*namaz*) throughout the day,[13] preparing himself for the pilgrimage to Mecca. His own representation and understanding of these pan-regional connections may have differed from those of Kashid Sir, the headmaster, who tended to be slightly "forgetful" of *namaz* and at times leaned toward downright self-indulgency to the point of having coffee during the day at the time of *Ramzan*.[14] Kashid Sir was also an active member of the local Congress Party branch, suggesting a stronger political involvement in regional matters than his colleague's. More generally, then, it is difficult to compare this reconstruction of a wider Muslim world with the investment some of the teachers constantly displayed in the Indian nation. For beyond their respective idiosyncrasies, they had in common a favorite topic for discussion, whether with me or in their morning lectures to the students: national matters. Indeed, reconnecting with lost Muslim political power, as well as with a sense of belonging to an Islamic community of believers transcending the mere regional or national frontiers of (southern) India,[15] *only partially* accounts for the processes entailed by the regenerative trip to the site of past political and religious Muslim splendor.

In effect, Urdu teachers and students were concomitantly staking a claim in the grand narrative of the Indian nation, willfully demanding participation in its making. What some of them—for instance, the headmaster more than others—did was not only to reappropriate "Muslim history" but also to reinscribe its valuable contribution into the larger story of Indian accomplishment, from which it has increasingly become excluded: the so-called Muslim period tends to be glossed over in textbooks (see previous discussion); so, too, is the role of Muslim leaders in the struggle for independence. The Hindu/Muslim competing emphases on the mere pronunciation of *Bijapur* thus represent a minuscule tip in the iceberg of the many processes of rewriting history at play since independence. Already in British times, the history of India had been carved into a succession of three watertight sections: the "Hindu," "Muslim," and "colonial" periods (Chatterjee and Ghosh 2002; Thapar 2004). James Mill, in his *History of British India* published in the early nineteenth century, was the first to promote a notion of antagonism between the first two periods, maintaining that Muslims were alien to the subcontinent. To a large extent, the postindependence sectioning of history is but a continuation of this colonial trend. More recent, however, are attempts at deleting purely and simply all so-called Muslim history from the Indian past, as described previously and as has been copiously documented with reference to secondary education in the course of the latest controversies over textbook revision in the past few years (Raychaudhuri 2000; Sahmat 2002; Deb 2003; staff correspondent, *The Hindu* 2003). Although these attempts were particularly perceptible until the elections of May 2004, which saw the defeat of the central *Hindutva*-led coalition, some of them are still ongoing due to the permanency of *Hindutva*-appointed officials and scholars in top educational positions. As a consequence, there remains a long way to go before redressing and correcting both recent distortions in the national curriculum and attempts at erasing all the contributions of Muslim freedom fighters in the struggle for independence. These obliterating attempts amount to a denial of Muslim citizens' right to actively share in the nation's past (Mohammad-Arif 2005), thus undermining the legitimacy of their status as fully fledged Indians.

In such a political context, it is easy to understand how the declaration quoted at the opening of this chapter had special resonance for the school's headmaster, who liked referring to the great Muslim leader Abul Kalam Azad in so many of his speeches.[16] To him, the answer to the question of whether a Muslim can be an Indian (Pandey 2001: 154) was a resounding "yes." Azad's quoted declaration indeed reinstated the worthy historical and cultural contribution of an increasingly marginalized "community." To the headmaster, it was crucial to raise this community's self-esteem and self-confidence through the promotion of education. For this reason, he often peppered his morning speeches with copious references to some of the great Muslim leaders of independent India, including the third president, Dr. Zakir Husain, and the current one, the nuclear physicist and "father of the Indian atomic bomb," Dr. A. P. J. Abdul Kalam (see later discussion). All these examples were meant to serve as role models for children to look up to and emulate.

Arguably, the Urdu school functioned as a special performative space where teachers and children further constructed both their religious and linguistic identity and their national identification. Perhaps because the latter, in their case—unlike in Marathi schools—was not mediated by any notion of tightly circumscribed regional identification but stood at odds with any attachment other than pan-Islamic, teachers were well aware of the apparent contradiction that most Maharashtrians might see in such a dual identification. Urdu also happens to be the national language in archrival Pakistan. So students and teachers constantly made explicit their love of the Indian nation and their dedication to impart their love to the younger generations. This love was manifested through the morning rituals (singing the national anthem, reciting the pledge and the *dua*, the Urdu morning prayer, all the rituals being a Muslim equivalent to the Hindu practice in Marathi schools with Hindu *shlok*s). It also assumed the form of elaborate and intensive preparations for national celebrations, especially of Independence Day and Republic Day. On these occasions, the students would rehearse parades and military drills and prepare patriotic songs. They also recited paeans to the nation (never conceived of as Mother-India, unlike in Marathi schools) and speeches on national leaders' birthdays.[17]

It should also be noted that Urdu schools are not the exclusive agents of potentially threatening otherness in Maharashtra. More generally, all minority

communities of non-Marathi speakers are deemed in greater need of ingraining of national devotion. This idea is suggestively expressed in the usage of
what Gananath Obeyesekere (1981) has called "psychogenetic symbols." Here,
these include nursery rhymes and other poems and recitations that have public, cultural meaning for members of the Hindu Maratha majority in Maharashtra. Consider, for example, the state-produced Marathi textbook for Class 5
children whose native tongue and primary medium of instruction is not the
regional language. These students begin their study of Marathi in Class 5. Scat-
tered throughout the book are injunctions serving as constant reminders to the
pupils. Thus, a popular Marathi nursery rhyme entitled "We Are Soldiers, Brave
and Cunning Heroes and Warriors" (Sainik amhi shur hushar) is reproduced
in lesson 14. The song teaches numbers and is interspersed with admonitions to
show respect for the country, protect the national flag, and so on. It ends with
"Embrace the religion of devotion to the nation" (Chapter 1).[18]

   To return to the case of Urdu instruction, the issue of national allegiance is
obviously further compounded by the fact that it is today the official language
of Pakistan. Non-Urdu and non-Muslim Indians—Maharashtrians in particular—have increasingly tended to conflate linguistic and religious identification
with national identification. This was particularly perceptible in the events of
the late 1990s. The nurturing of a sense of loyalty to the Indian nation among
Urdu-educated Muslims occurred within a political climate of heightened tensions. As discussed in the Introduction, in May 1998, India proceeded to nuclear tests in Pokhran thanks to Dr. A. P. J. Abdul Kalam. This was a welcome
event for the Urdu teachers on two counts: it was a matter of great rejoicing
and pride that "one of them" had done such service to the country by producing nuclear missiles for India. It also promoted a positive image of Muslims as
scientifically minded, progressive, and educated patriots. A few months later,
Pakistan, in turn, proceeded to nuclear tests. In the years that followed, the
tension mounted between the two nation-states over the issue of Kashmir. As
the conflict climaxed in a war in the summer of 1999, the pressure on Muslims
to make public displays of allegiance in the media became more and more
perceptible.

   It is unclear to what extent the Muslim residents of Sachar Bazar felt a similar pressure in their daily lives. Even in ordinary times, comments were frequent
about Indian Muslims accused of supporting the Pakistani cricket team against
their national one. Whatever the case may be, the Urdu teachers always took
great pains to emphasize both to me and to the students how they should fur-

ther advance their community (*Muslim samaj*) through education and service
to their country.[19] It is important to emphasize that these displays of patriotism
must not be read as ostentatious ones whose purpose was to convince outside
observers (municipal corporation officials, the anthropologist, and so on) of
the teachers' and students' devotion to India. Arguably, they were also meant
for themselves and especially for the benefit of the community, with the passing
anthropologist possibly acting as an interface mirror: reenacting their attachment to the Indian nation in my presence and interacting with me on these topics provided them an outside—and possibly more neutral—background upon
which to perform their national devotion. As important, school provided an
intermediary location at the crossroads of various spaces ranging from domestic and familial to religious (the mosque just adjacent to the school), to regional
and national. School was a site where negotiation of state injunctions took place
and where social actors were thus able to give shape to a newly defined sense
of community, one premised on religious and linguistic notions, but one that
could also reconcile unconditional allegiance to the Indian nation. In other
words, school operated as a space that made a new kind of fully fledged Urdu
Muslim Indian citizen possible. At the same time, it further reinforced dichotomies in the very definitions of communities.

Given the constant pressure on Muslims to demonstrate unconditional allegiance, it is particularly ironic that Mr. Kashid's deep-seated sense of belonging
to the Indian nation came out most forcefully on the issue of Kashmir. More
than any other, this one brought out how visceral his anchoring to India was.
Both he and his colleagues often insisted that Kashmir should remain a part
of India. Such a profound conviction was most poignantly expressed one day
in January 2000 over lunch, as we shared a *biryani* in the school office-turned-
canteen. As we were discussing the recent developments in Kashmir, the headmaster vehemently asserted that "they" should not part with it. I asked why. He
swiftly grabbed the miniature plastic map of India that lay on his desk. Holding
the educational aid in full view, he began pedagogically:

> "Look, this is India, isn't it?"
> "Yes."
> "You see, up there, this is Kashmir." [*He pointed to the top of the map.*]
> "Yes, this is Kashmir."
> "Well, this is like a head [*sar*]."
> "???"

"Yes, Kashmir, you see; it is on top, on top of India, India's body [*sharir*]. Well, Kashmir is a part of India, it is a part of our country, it is its head." [Kashmir Bharat ka ek bhag hai, hamare desh ka ek bhag hai, uska sar hai.]

"I see."

"Now," the headmaster gravely said, "what do you think will happen if we cut the person's head?" [*At this point, he successively imitated the gesture of chopping off the plastic map's upper tip and, lest I had not understood, repeated the same movement upon his own throat*]. "Well, you see, the person will die. Well, like this, India will become lifeless." [Baijan ho jaega.] "This is why we cannot part with Kashmir. Kashmir is ours; we cannot give it." [Ham de nahi sakte.]

This was probably the most solemn moment I ever experienced in the company of the Urdu teachers. The other two staff present shared it with acute intensity, forcefully nodding in approval of the masterly demonstration. Clearly, such a visceral nationalism was as profound as that nurtured through the idiom of the region in Marathi schools. Interestingly, it was also expressed in not too dissimilar an idiom. Although Urdu Muslims unequivocally rejected the idiom of the mother figure incarnating the notion of Bharat Mata so common in Marathi schools and in wider Maharashtrian society, they nevertheless embraced the idea of India as fused in the convergence of (here, a masculine) body and map. Such an organic kind of national identification was unexpected. It also suggests that the dominant cultural forms of Indianness today had been incorporated among Muslims, too, possibly because most of the Urdu teachers did study in the Marathi language at some point.[20] In a contrapuntal version to the brand of regional nationalism produced in Marathi schools, the sensory configuration developed in Urdu schools was one that daily connected Urdu—as the language of Muslims but also a close associate to the national language, Hindi—with Islam (the dua was a staple of the morning liturgy) in the construction of the body of schoolchildren and India. The sense of nationalist belonging thus produced and reproduced on a quotidian basis was as visceral as its Marathi counterpoint, if only differently anchored in regional and national identifications.

Furthermore, such nationalism did not make any allowances for "fellow Muslims" on the other side of the Indo-Pakistani border. That the headmaster, like most of his colleagues, hailed from southern India (southern Maharashtra and northern Karnataka, Belgaum district) and had no personal or familial intimate experience of the exodus and the violence that erupted in the north following the Partition in 1947 made him more uncompromising in his position toward Pakistan: no sense of common Muslim brotherhood forged in ripped-apart flesh and spilled blood could ever unite them beyond nation-state allegiances. Clearly, the "shadow lines" that were being laboriously created in 1947 and that Amitav Ghosh has so brilliantly evoked in an eponymous novel have now become integral to the contemporary histories of rival nation building. They have succeeded in leaving their imprint in the imaginaries and self-representations of Muslims (Hasan 2000), including in this part of India. Consequently, if a sense of unity to a common *umma* was possible among Urdu schoolteachers, it was not so much predicated upon a hypothetical fraternity with Muslims on the other side of the modern nation-state's border as on collected and reconstructed past genealogies of Islamic imperial splendor.

This sense of *umma* did not affect the intensity of Urdu Muslim teachers' visceral loyalty toward the Indian nation-state. Seen in this light, it seems ever so ironic that Indian Muslims should have been called upon to demonstrate their allegiance, as they have been since the Partition (Pandey 2001: 152–74). This, of course, was never fully or explicitly acknowledged by any of the Urdu-speaking residents of Sachar Bazar, nor, for that matter, by any other Muslim Indian with whom I interacted. The issue was far too sensitive and shameful to talk about openly. Yet in an infinity of ways, the eagerness with which elder students and teachers would get involved in the performance of the morning liturgy and in national celebratory preparations suggested a converse amount of pain and suffering at having their patriotism questioned. In the end, Urdu Muslims in Sachar Bazar asserted and turned their difference into a template for minority community identity while striving for recognition into the national fold. In the process, they distanced themselves from any dominant regional bond, further crystallizing polarization of perceived differences on either side. Yet such a polarization obfuscated the long-standing social and cultural proximity existing between Muslims and Marathas in Maharashtra.

(Urdu) Muslim Others, (Hindu) Maratha Brothers: Of Archetypal Myths, Social Agency, and Economic Constraints

Studies of nationalism and communal violence have highlighted how the construction of nationalism and a sense of belonging to a national community are predicated upon an exclusivist principle: the definition of an elected group of members at the exclusion of unworthy "others," whether fabricated or real

(Eriksen 1993; Kakar 1996). Nationalist discourses, then, proffer narratives of difference as a dominant motif. Difference may be spelled positively within the group thus defined. Conversely, it may become a justification for stigmatizing and excluding outsiders on the grounds that "they are so different; they are not like us, in customs, practices, beliefs, and so on." In the process, the sense of belonging to the community gets reaffirmed among participant members. As we saw earlier, the image of Muslims in this part of India has long served the purpose of further tightening together the larger dominant community of Marathas and allied castes: despite assertions of communal harmony, whether in urban or rural areas, Muslims in Maharashtra have increasingly been presented as the radically different other. Yet this imagined, "hystericized" difference (Balibar 1991) largely runs contrary to empirical evidence and confirms the theory that cultivation of heightened difference is often achieved through targeting an internal enemy very close to oneself (Eriksen 1993; Hayden 2002). Indeed, in the present case, the mutual enemies share in common an even greater number of features with one another than with members of social groups ordinarily deemed in a relation of greater social and cultural proximity. In western Maharashtra, the group Muslims are closest to in social and cultural practices are Marathas. As noted previously, most Muslims in Maharashtra, as in Bengal, do not have origins in locations outside India. Rather, they descend from local families who converted to Islam. Therefore, a number of common traits exist between them despite repeated claims to the contrary.

In the 1990s, during my first fieldwork in urban Pune and rural areas of the same district, I found that although the small Muslim community in the village of Keraone where I lived was relatively well integrated, many villagers regularly referred to Muslims' different mores and customs (Chapter 4). Jains and Hindus, including families with known nonvegetarian members, mentioned dietary practices as the epitome of difference. In these families, however, women often claimed they did not eat meat, unlike in Muslim ones. Marriage practices came second in an enumeration of reasons for difference. On closer inspection, the marriage practices extant among Muslim communities in this part of Maharashtra had much more in common with the non-Brahmin Hindu ones than would generally be conceded. In particular, Muslims and non-Brahmin Hindu communities, especially Maratha and so-called allied castes, shared the preferential marriage between brother's daughter and sister's son, the warrior ritual ideology, and lexical usages pertaining to some marriage rituals and transactions (Benei 1996; Chapter 6). Such findings are by no means exceptional and seriously puncture two oft-encountered myths: that which Hindu right-wing extremists have been promoting for many years of a fold common to Hindu, Brahmin, and Jain beliefs and practices; and of utmost political importance, that of radical difference between Muslims and the dominant Hindu community living in a given region (Marathas in this part of India).

Returning to Stuart Hall's distinction between "being" and "becoming," I hope to have provided a sense of what "learning to be (Urdu) Muslim in western India" has entailed over the past years for Urdu-educated residents in Sachar Bazar. Muslims have increasingly sought to reinscribe their existence within the larger narrative of national history, attending to the social suffering experienced when their emotional attachment to the nation is questioned and challenged. Today, this is compounded by—and potentially competing with—a mounting awareness of belonging to a stigmatized international community, which may also further strengthen a radicalization of representations. As shown by the incident that opened this chapter, social actors are increasingly polarizing themselves in their self-perceptions as communities defined by language and history. The communities thus conceived are steeped in immutable caricaturing: on the one hand, an aggressive Marathi community celebrating their martial past; on the other, a subdued Muslim one shunning their victors' history and keeping aloof from wider Maharashtrian society. A significant number of Urdu-speaking families definitely isolated themselves from their regional surroundings by opting for an all-Urdu-medium education for their children. Women and girls, in particular, tended to be confined to homes where Urdu/Hindi is spoken. Remarkably, literate young mothers had become the targets of religious Quranic education meant to ensure proper transmission of the features of Islamic community, and were as vocal as men in their assertion of an Urdu-mediated religious-linguistic identity. Some may find a certain measure of irony in that Urdu in northern India was a mark of the literary elite. In Maharashtra today, it has become a key identification marker, linguistic and religious, for a majority of newly literate Muslims who have turned it into a community symbol.

This is only a partial account of what it means to be Muslim in this region of India today. For in Sachar Bazar alone, Muslims did not represent a homogeneous group, whether in educational choices or in religious affiliations. In some ways, such defined communities stand at either end of a continuum ranging from sheer aloofness to full integration into dominant Maharashtrian society. If not overly frequent, examples are common enough of Marathi-educated

Muslim social activists and educationists (including the founder of a recent Marathi primary school) that claimed a full integration into regional society. Furthermore, in between these two extremes lies a proportion of Marathi- and English-educated Muslims. Some (often better-off) families made choices motivated by economic opportunities, whereas others followed ideological criteria. Others attempted to reconcile the tensions resulting from either option by not sending their children to the same schools. Within many families living in Sachar Bazar, siblings would be sent to different institutions depending on the family's socioeconomic position and the views prevailing on gender expectations. So there would often be at least one male Marathi speaker in the family. This might at times have been accompanied with perceptible tensions, especially in the case of joint families making differing choices.

This was the case in Mobina Behari's family, who lived with her father, his six brothers, and their respective wives and children. Mobina's father had a small *paan* shop around the corner, while all the other brothers practiced their caste's calling of being butchers. Out of the fifteen boys and the sixteen girls, only two boys attended Marathi school, the semiprivate one in the vicinity. All the other children went to the Urdu Corporation School. Even though some of the wives had themselves been educated in Marathi (whether in Kolhapur or in the surrounding areas), they were all vocal about the necessity of sending their children to Urdu instruction. To be sure, the decision may also have been determined by financial constraint, as it would clearly have been impossible for all the children to be sent to the same Marathi semiprivate school. However, this was not the only choice available: across the road was another corporation institution, a Marathi school where one of the wives had herself studied. But as Mobina's mother and Meena, the wife of the fourth brother, forcefully explained in the course of that conversation in late October 2000: "The Urdu school is good; it is very good; Urdu is the language of Muslims." As the only two Marathi-educated boys in the family walked into the house, Meena raised her voice, pointing an accusing finger at them and reproachfully proclaiming: "We, Muslims, should all study in Urdu medium." As the two boys walked past, attempting to look unconcerned, she gathered momentum and added: "This is Muslims' strength." Turning toward me, she firmly concluded: "Yes, we, Muslims, we are strong." Here was clearly evidenced a connection between not just a community's strength and the practice of a language as identity marker; the reference to Urdu functioned as a symbol of past political power endowed with potential for future generations, in which official education was to play a constitutive part.

Such a suggestive combination of language, political icon, and educational potential was not necessarily shared by all Muslim residents, especially the followers of the Tablighi Jama'at, an Islamic missionary and revival movement that originated in the South Asian subcontinent in the late 1920s (see Metcalf 1996). Although the Tablighi had played an influential part in Urdu increasingly becoming one of the defining elements of "Muslim identity" all over India (Talib 1998), there was nevertheless a perceived line of fracture in Sachar Bazar between what the headmaster called "progressist Muslims," who allowed their girls to be educated, and "these obscurantist followers" opposed to all formal education, regardless of gender or medium of instruction. Whether among other Muslims or non-Muslims, such a view of followers of Tablighi Jama'at was rather widespread in the neighborhood, where they accounted for 80 percent of the Muslim population.[21] Whether this view was fully substantiated or not, in its most covert aspect the perceived opposition between so-called progressist and obscurantist factions was manifested by the suspicious glances that some devotees regularly cast from across the mosque gate. The opposition sometimes led to open clashes between the headmaster and some influential members of the *mohalla*.

All the above examples show the range of differential representations and implications of Urdu schooling in Sachar Bazar: from the pure version of "Muslim language" to be nurtured at all costs, to an obstacle to regional integration and socioeconomic mobility. The common thread, however, was the notion that Urdu increasingly stood as a marker of cultural and religious distinctiveness for Muslims, however families combined and negotiated it. This, as we have seen, was not always the case, whether in Maharashtra, where most Muslims spoke Mussalmani, or in northern India, where Urdu was also spoken by Hindu speakers.

Language, "Community," and Politics:
Schooling Effects and Impossible Citizens

In more ways than one, becoming an Urdu-educated Muslim in this part of India today signifies developing a heightened awareness of one's condition as a member of an ostracized social group increasingly defined as *a minority community*. The three words count here: the *a* homogenizes extremely varied perceptions of what it means to be an Indian Muslim, especially a common awareness of stigmatization. *Minority* refers not only to demographics but also conveys a sense of belittlement perceptible in many arenas of quotidian life at regional and national levels, and which the events in Gujarat certainly reinforced. This sense of belittlement also obtained among Muslims in Kolhapur, who dealt with it in various ways: from a mother's claims of being strong in opposition to the sense of weakness or inferiority connoted by the word *kam* sometimes used for "minority," to the headmaster's constant invocation of the need for the community to go forward and educate themselves, members of the Muslim community would either overtly fight social stigma or harness it into educational projects. Finally and congruently, the notion of "community" has further defined Indian Muslims as a collective social, cultural, and *political* agent, which they never really were. To be sure, even in the case of relatively well-defined groups, there is no homogeneity of sentiments of belonging. Social actors may invest their senses of belonging with various meanings. By the same token, they may also make this social identification relevant in some contexts and not in others. For instance, the same Urdu school headmaster who was so vocal in the building of a "strong Urdu Muslim community" would at times play the "Marathi-speaking card" in his political dealings with the local National Congress Party. Conversely, even the ecumenical Marathi school founder and director, Zamadar Sir, had lately begun strategizing marriage alliances with predominantly Urdu-educated families.

It is to be feared, however, that a radicalized perception has further fed on the genocidal events that occurred in the spring of 2002 in the neighboring state of Gujarat. There is little doubt that these events were discussed at length both within school and homes at the time and that the tensions generated by the state-orchestrated killings of Muslims in retaliation for a massacre of Hindu right-wing activists (*kar sevaks*) will have been felt in Kolhapur. The Urdu teachers at the corporation school, for instance, were acutely aware of the RSS's existence and activities. In the spring of 2000, they were already anxiously discussing the dangers posed by Gujarat's sudden move to authorize government employees to join the RSS. To be sure, they often added that such risks were lower in this part of Maharashtra thanks to the social reformist work accomplished in the times of Shahu Maharaj. Nevertheless, when I went back to Kolhapur in the summer of 2003 a few days before the national celebrations of Independence Day, I found Urdu teachers more than ever feverishly absorbed in ostentatious displays of national allegiance.

Furthermore, if language may be used to affirm or reaffirm hierarchies of power (Heath 1972; O'Barr and O'Barr 1976; Eickelman and Piscatori 1996; Rahman 1996), it may also serve to subvert them. By using Urdu as a primary marker of ethnic identity (encompassing language and religion), Muslims in this part of India are also accomplishing two cathartic processes. First, they are subverting the contemporary hierarchies of power partly resulting from their ancestors' displacement from a position of significant political power to one of merely tolerated minorities.[22] Second, by embracing a language earlier associated with an elite group whose members could make a claim—however fictive—to a foreign origin, who appreciated Persian culture, owned land, and had a tradition of service to the government in responsible positions (Taylor 1983), Muslims in Kolhapur and more generally in Maharashtra today are appropriating for themselves a glorious past in the building of a positive self-image. In addition, they may be reclaiming a due denied them over half a century ago: that of "their" linguistic contribution to the production of the Indian nation. For when debates took place over the issue of a national language soon after independence, the qualification of Urdu as a national idiom jointly with Hindi was a matter of contention. Finally, in the highly charged political atmosphere of those times and despite Jawaharlal Nehru's efforts, Urdu was rejected as a national language (Hasan 1997: 156–60).

These recent developments may signal a new direction in the evolution of what it means to be Muslim in India today. They also point to more general trends elsewhere, congruently with the objectification that spread to all parts of the "Muslim world" by the late 1980s:[23] basic questions about the meaning of being Muslim came to the fore in the consciousness of large numbers of believers. To be sure, the notion of objectification as applied to South Asia is not new. Bernard Cohn (1987a) in one of his famous essays had already suggested that the various modes of representing and categorizing knowledge developed by the British in collaboration with Indians forced the latter to pose questions about things and people in ways that they perhaps would not have otherwise done. What may be more recent, however, is the area and scope of applicability of the notion. Arguably, today a more systematic process of objectification has been enabled by mass education. In India, the official learning facilities provided for Muslim Urdu speakers have contributed to the production of a sense of belonging to a newly linguistically defined community. It is possible that the effects of mass education are now being felt more strongly among Muslims across the world, after the initial phase of a decade ago (Eickelman and Piscatori 1996: 39).

At this point it may be useful to ponder again the kinds of effects produced by schooling. As we saw in the preceding chapters, school operates as an idealized locus of, and for, the nation (and the region) that seeks to transubstantiate a

make nationalism ōberja .

heterogeneity of class, caste, and so on into a homogeneity of patriotic devotion. Yet at the same time that the space of school generates normative performances, it crystallizes identifications and polarizations. Moreover, such a production of crystallized identifications must be understood in dialectical relation to a wide array of cultural and ideological structures of feeling and practices extant within society at large. Schools, as should by now have become clear, are not state machineries crushing poor passive subjects to reassemble and manufacture them into dutiful citizens at will. Rather, they are spaces shaped by the social and cultural agency of various actors, ranging from teachers, parents, and pupils, to educational officials, inspectors, and so on. Here, then, schooling effects partly stem from negotiated reconstructions of language and history mediating senses of belonging. These effects have a rather paradoxical potential. On the one hand, they can induce further polarization and isolation of a community.[24] On the other hand, these effects also bear transformative potential for the elaboration of ideal citizens. Ideal, yet historically impossible. This requires elaboration.

Arguably, there exists a parallel between the situation of Urdu-educated Muslims in twentieth- and twenty-first-century Maharashtra and that of Jews in nineteenth- and twentieth-century Germany and France. In his book about French and German citizenship and residence issues, *Droit de cité*, Étienne Balibar elaborated on the historical conditions of nineteenth-century Germany and France wherein assimilated Jews were alien to regional belonging and rooting (*étrangers à l'appartenance régionale, à l'enracinement* [1998: 51–52]). Ironically, this very fact made Jews *national* citizens par excellence. Because they were devoid of any regionalist and particularistic anchoring, Balibar argues, Jews were the archetypal figure of the citizen of a new modern nation-state in which attachments of all kinds were to be transcended in favor of that to the nation. This point is, of course, debatable. It can be argued, following Michel Callon, Pierre Lascoumes, and Yannick Barthe (2001) and against idealized conceptions of citizenship à la Arendt, Habermas, or Rawls, that such a citizen is precisely impossible. Citizenship *needs* to be anchored in specificities, local, ethnic, religious, or other. But it may also be argued that Jews in Germany were anchored in a kind of urban cosmopolitanism that furthered a sense of common belonging to a "Jewish community," however the latter was defined.[25] Therein lies the parallel with the case of Urdu-speaking Muslims in Maharashtra today. They may be Indian citizens par excellence, inasmuch as they are grounded in a wider regional history that transcends a more immediately localized sense of regional and national belonging. Furthermore, they occupy a potentially privileged linguistic position in view of their proximity with Hindi (only the script differs), often improperly dubbed "the national language." Yet Muslims' status has increasingly become one of second-class citizens, turning this tremendous potential into impossible citizenship. Here, the call of history beckons to us. Perhaps more than ever before, civil vigilance has become crucial. The genocidal history of twentieth-century Europe and the xenophobic policies toward Jews that progressively stripped them of their full status as citizens even before the outbreak of World War II and the Holocaust resonate portentously with the deep-seated antagonism directed against Muslims in Maharashtra and more generally in India today. Recent events in Gujarat and institutional attempts elsewhere cannot but alarm us to an ever-unfathomable potential for human violence. Especially so that the concomitant development of an *umma*-like sense of brotherhood among Urdu Muslims may be fueled by ongoing international events related to what is increasingly being felt as, more than a war on terrorism, a war on Muslims.

Playing, Dreaming, Musing, Longing

Anita, six years old: "War, war, war, that's all you boys know!"

Oh, and why should we keep on playing this silly game, anyway? bellows Anita, her shrill voice resonating in the narrow street where she lives, near Potala Chowk in the heart of town. I am quite fed up with it. War, war, war, that's all you boys know! For once Ashok and Kumar let us play with them; they are bothering us, shooting on us, phat-phat-phat, phat-phat-phat, phat-phat-phat. And they won't even let us play the Indians! Always the Pakistanis, we are. Anyway, Pakistanis, Indians, I have had enough; I don't want to play war anymore. Oh well, at least not now, no. Yes, we did have a lot of fun the other day with Shivaji and our little fort; we took our fort for a ride across the gallis. And the drumming and the music we played for fun. Just as they did at Shivaji Potala that day. But this wasn't really war. Well, maybe it was, Suresh says. He knows; he is in Class 4. He's learned it all, our Shivaji Maharaj, our beloved Shivaji and how he fights all the Muslims, just like he did at Panhala. That was great fun, too, that Sunday when we all went with Ai and Appa, Suresh and little brother Amol. It is so beautiful there. And there is a playground with lots of games for children. This is all ours, Ai says, not the Muslims'. But my friend Malika, she is my friend. And she is Muslim, she says. And her elder brother, Hussain, he is so good to us. He always protects us when we play, even against Ashok and Kumar. Oh, I don't know. Some grown-up thing.

Usman, seven years old:
"If I could fly"

I wish I could fly. I wish I could fly high above the ground, high above the mohalla, beyond Sachar Bazar, beyond this gaon. I wish I could see all these things from above. I could see all the houses and the buildings and the temples and the mosques. Our mosque. Not that I really care about it; I don't really like having to go there too often. I don't really like going to school either. This new teacher, he really works us so hard. When I know it doesn't really do anything. I know, Dawood says so. He went to Marathi school. He says even though he now drives a rickshaw, having gone to school hasn't done anything for him. And my elder brother, he knows everything. He knows even more than Bappa, who never went to school. I love Bappa, though, and I don't mind the smell of meat on his clothes when he comes back from the butcher shop. Not sure I want to become a butcher like him, too, though. What else can you do? If I could fly, I could visit all these places, the Taj Mahal, the Delhi Durbar, the Red Fort in Agra. I could even go back to Bijapur like we went last year with the [Urdu]

Drawing of a mosque, a fort, or Mecca? Urdu Corporation School, Kolhapur, February 2000.

school. The Gol Gumbaz, that was a lot of fun. So maybe I will continue going to school for a while.

Bismilla, eleven years old:
"Even our monuments are closed"

I wonder why Kishor was so upset last night. Is it what I said? Well, I thought he was my friend, even though we don't go to school together. But we've played together for so long, as long as I can remember. But maybe Minoddin is right, after all, maybe you can never be friends with a Hindu, let alone a Maratha. I thought Kishor and I were friends, though. I used to invite him for Urs, and he would sneak in at Ramzan in the evenings to share our food, and we used to stuff ourselves with his mother's puranpoli at Ganesh Jayanti. And we played Shivaji's wars, too, he and I on the same side, even when his other friends didn't want us to. All I know about Shivaji, Kishor has taught me, because here at Urdu school, no one will say anything. But I know he was a good guy, because he had Muslim generals in his army, too. Kishor and I have played this. We even played the drums with his friends, on this Shivaji Jayanti thing and at other times. Come to think of it, Minoddin was never too happy about it, although as my father's younger brother he kept quiet. But maybe he was right. You cannot trust them. He knows, because he has been with them. And he works with them, too. Cannot be trusted. But who can I talk to, if I can't talk to Kishor? If it weren't for him, there'd be no fun in this mohalla. No dreams, either. Stay in the community, they say. But what's in this community for me? Where else can I look? Even our monuments are closed.

Madina, eleven years old:
"When I grow up"

When I grow up, I want to be a doctor. I hope Ma and Baba will allow me to study. Ma doesn't seem too keen; she says what's the good of it if I am to be married anyway? Better go to Quranic school in the evening. But Baba says if the girl wants to study, let her. I think he is proud of me. Proud of his eldest daughter. He says I am the cleverest of his children. That is why he wanted to send me to Marathi school. But Ma said no, what is the use, we should stick to our own; besides, her brothers went to Urdu, so why send her to that Marathi school? It won't do anything for her. I hate it when Ma is like this. But I know why she's so concerned. I wouldn't want to do her wrong, anyway. But I know what's on her mind. My cousin Hasina, Ma's sister's daughter, she went to Marathi school,

Drawing of the Gol Gumbaz of Bijapur, Karnataka. Urdu Corporation School, Kolhapur, February 2000.

she too wanted to become a doctor. And then she ran away with this Hindu boy. The havoc in the community! Well, I am not going to be like this. I will do my parents proud. But I so wish they allowed me to go on to higher school. Baba said I would, if I topped my class. So I am working so hard every night, even after helping Ma with everything. I so want to help and cure people, not just in our own society, but all my Indian brothers and sisters; like the Sheikhs, they live close by, he is a chemist, she a physician, and all their three children went to that Christian English school a little further. I don't know them well, but Mrs. Sheikh I know better, because she is the one that visited us when little brother Mohamed was ill last winter. I also went to pick up the medicine from her house. So I got to know her a bit, and I really like her. She is so calm, unlike Ma. Mrs. Sheikh is always so quiet, and her house so beautiful, with hard tiled floor and all. Not this phalshi that we have to plaster every so often with dung. When I grow up, I want to be a doctor and be calm and live in a neat house, like Mrs. Sheikh.

6 Constructing New Citizens in Military Schools

Gender, Hybridity, and Modernity in Maharashtra

Soldiers and the people are one family.

Mao Tse-tung, *The Little Red Book*

Genders can be neither true nor false but are only produced as the truth effects of a discourse of primary and stable identity.

Judith Butler, *Gender Trouble*

AS YOU ARE HEADING TOWARD the industrial town, gigantic chimneys seem to spring up from the earth, black clouds billowing around them. These are not made of alloy residue belching out of metallurgic furnaces but of smoke generated by sugarcane factories (*sakhar karkhana*). In this part of India, known as the "sugar belt area," the recent industrial, economic, and agricultural history is intricately linked to sugarcane production. You are now approaching the town precincts. All around you, the air is charged with wreaths of light soot impregnating your clothes. Large, wide, rectilinear, tree-lined avenues with flower beds are filled with endless regular alignments of square concrete buildings. Neat and clean streets methodically branch off these avenues. Everywhere, well-kept pavements meet the eye; even the traffic lights seem to be working and heeded by careful drivers, irrespective of their diverse vehicles: cars, scooters, bicycles, bullock carts, coaches, buses, as well as tractors, vans, and trucks. This is the city of order, neatness, and progress, the southernmost city of a Nehruvian dream made reality in Maharashtra. Welcome to Pratinagar, the model industrial town of Kolhapur district, Tashil Panhala. Situated twenty kilometers from Kolhapur, Pratinagar is the brainchild of Tattyasaheb Kore, a Maratha by caste. In 1957, Tattya Kore anchored a rural cooperative movement in what was then a land devoted to market gardening. Today, the founder's imposing statue stands at the main crossroads leading to the supermarket, almost overshadowing that of the icon of hegemonic Maharashtrian identity, Shivaji Maharaj.

According to the local narrative, Tattya Kore was hardly educated ("not even matriculate") but a very experienced man deft at seizing political and economic opportunities. When the Co-operative Act of Maharashtra was passed in the mid-1950s, Tattya Kore set up the Pratinagar experiment. The sugarcane plant was among the first to see the light of day in the region. Pratinagar soon became the headquarters of a cluster of seventy villages of rural southwestern Maharashtra straddling the districts of Kolhapur and Sangli. Today, most of the sugarcane production of the two districts is processed at the Pratinagar Cooperative Society's huge factory towering over the town. Several other plants and economic and financial outlets have followed suit. They include a paper factory, the biggest high-tech dairy in the district, a poultry farm, a *papad* and a chocolate factory, a supermarket, and a bank. In the late 1990s, Pratinagar and its village cluster attracted the national newspaper headlines by constituting the first information technology (IT) network in rural areas in India.[1] Other similar IT development projects have since emulated it across the country.

Pratinagar's present success story also owes a great deal to its carefully crafted social and educational achievements. These spanned several decades, during which proper training was provided in various fields to further agro-economic development and increase productivity and profits. Some of the profits were channeled back into the creation of educational institutions. Thus were started an engineering and technology college, an agricultural college, primary and secondary schools, an arts and commerce college, followed by an IT college, and various student hostels.[2] All of these institutions exist under the aegis of Pratinagar Shikshan Mandal, an "educational society" headed by Tattya Kore's grandson, A. Vinay Kore, and run by a secretary, Mr. Chapekar. These socioeconomic and educational developments are coupled with a concern for the general betterment of the local population, which also entails health management: health facilities include a hospital named after the Mahatma Gandhi.

Although the Pratinagar project is largely remembered in local social memory as the realization of one man, it is undeniably a collective one. Its cooperative and democratic ideals reflect in its overall conceptions of trade: in Pratinagar, even the chamber of commerce's architecture replicates that of the Indian Parliament. Today, the town has become a model of socioeconomic, agro-industrial, political, and educational achievement as well as an object of reverence and admiration in the area. Schoolchildren from the nearby industrial megalopolis of Kolhapur are sometimes taken to Pratinagar on a visit to acquaint themselves with this successful exemplar of Indian modernity. In this chapter, however, I shall not take you on such a visit with dozens of screaming, excited pupils and enthusiastic teachers. Rather, I want to introduce you to an altogether different, highly disciplined setting: that of the ultimate addition to the cooperative complex, namely, the Tattyasaheb Kore Military Academy. The "Pratinagar Sainik School," as it is also known, is the educational society's latest creation. Founded in 1998, it became officially acknowledged in 1999 as *the* military (boarding) school for the entire district of Kolhapur. The students enter at Class 5 and graduate at Class 12. In the academic year 2000–2001, at the time of my last visit, the school housed 189 male pupils aged ten to thirteen studying in Classes 5 to 8. The aim was to open one new class each year, up to Class 12.

In taking you to this military school, I wish to unravel further the skein of Maharashtrian- and Indian-schooled "modernity," more specifically, the procedures of its gendered production and sustenance. How does the Pratinagar military academy envisage and realize the advent of an alternative, modern citizen in the postcolonial context of the twenty-first century? While exploring the modalities of the military school's production of future generations of elite citizens and leaders, I shall discuss the "hybrid" quality of its political project building upon contradictory visions of national progress. These visions articulate conceptions of the self predicated on negotiated notions of pedagogy, prophylaxis, and diet, together with political and industrial development. Furthermore, such a political project assumes particular significance in regard to regional and national identifications and their localized shapes.[3] This makes military schools ideal sites for observing the crystallization of values and ideals shared by large sections of Maharashtrian society.

This chapter also continues the discussion of gender production started in earlier chapters. Although situated within the opening field of studies of gender in South Asia—especially the prominently emergent one of "masculinities" (Chopra, Osella, and Osella 2004; Srivastava 2004)—the analysis also seeks to go beyond usual gender dichotomies still prevalent in most of this body of work by exploring further the potential of the pedagogical conceptions (and implementations) at the root of the military school's apparent gendered project. We saw in Chapters 3 and 4 how schools are privileged sites for the gendered production of social persons in a modern nation-state. In keeping with the ideology usually underlying military projects, one might expect a "heavily gendered organizational culture" (Connell 2000: 23) to prevail at the Pratinagar military school. Indeed, some Euro-American and Indian gendered conceptions of modernity are imbricated in today's postcolonial world (dis)order: these conceptions are shot through with a hegemonic version of masculinity largely associated with various forms of violence. Such an association is especially visible in the aggressive militarism that characterizes late twentieth-century imperialism and capitalism (Connell 1993). Surprisingly, the present study of a most extreme form of same-sex institution reveals processes of gender construction to be much more complex compared with the many localized versions and narratives of modernity obtaining in other parts of India and elsewhere.[4] Examining these processes in turn illuminates some of the most intriguing aspects of this "hybrid" political project aimed at creating a new kind of modern person and citizen. It also forces us to consider the heuristic potential of "queer theory." But first, it is necessary to outline the meaning of the notion of "hybridity" running through this chapter.

Hybridity, Scientific Temper, and Modernity in Maharashtra

"Hybridity" is an important concept for illuminating the various layers of combined values and ideals at stake in the Maharashtrian military school project. Yet my use of the term differs significantly from Bhabha's (1984) or even Srivastava's (1998). Hybridity here intersects with notions of political modernity, science, and scientific outlook as well as bodily, prophylactic, pedagogic, and gender conceptions. Rather than indicating mimicry or negotiated adoption, the concept denotes the combination of sometimes contradictory—although not necessarily exclusive—ideologies and discourses.[5] It is of course debatable whether hybridity in this sense is specific to the modernity under discussion. In some ways, it might well be argued that all historic moments, whether qualifying as modern or not, are to some extent marked by hybridity. Yet the use of this term in the present context has the advantage of stressing the lack of internal consistency of many political projects often presented as too beautifully coherent, whether by ideologues or scholars. This is so especially of *Hindutva* ideology, whose various features are the products of negotiated encounters (colonial and other) but tend to be envisaged as definite markers of "pure" *Hindutva* political projects. By contrast, the example of the Pratinagar military school complicates this view and highlights the bricolage quality inherent in its project.

The Pratinagar military school is a particular type of hybrid on several counts. First, it is so by virtue of its location—both spatial and ideological. In addition to largely espousing a British model, the school is part of a wider educational project that feeds on the particular vision of modernity developed in Pratinagar. Built in the Nehruvian period, the town owes its very existence to a combination of industrialist, agricultural, economic, and political principles reminiscent of the national leader's thought. It is true that Jawaharlal Nehru has often been portrayed as a champion of industrialization at all costs. However, in his reflective and programmatic *Discovery of India*, his alternative conception of industry is intricately connected with agriculture (1998: 301). This conception was largely inspired by the Chinese example providing "a democratic basis to small industry, and develop[ing] the co-operative habit" (406). Clearly, the Pratinagar project in its entirety accomplishes this merging of political, industrial, and agricultural aspirations. It offers a human-scale model of industrial development eliminating the "psychological and biological dangers of loss of contact with the soil [resulting] from life in great industrial cities" feared by the staunch advocate of industrialization himself (406).

Nehru's vision of total "development" undergirded by a "scientific temper" (409) is further reflected in the town's exhaustive educational setup, especially at the Pratinagar Sainik School. Its underlying conception espoused the national leader's concern for constituting the necessary military resource to ensure the construction as well as the preservation of the nation. As he remarked even before independence when Congress governments dominated in the provinces, "[M]any of them were eager to encourage some form of military training in the universities and colleges" (444). In this respect, it should be noted that even if delineated in different terms, such a military project is convergent with that put forth by the proponent of *Hindutva*, the recently much glorified Vinayak D. Savarkar. To the Maharashtrian ideologue, militarization (in his conception, of the "Hindu race" alone) was a vital necessity. It should therefore come as no surprise that a Nehruvian-inspired educational complex put forward a proposal for setting up one such school, nor should the fact that such proposals were invited and provision made for their creation in Maharashtra by a Hindu right-wing government. Both ideologies converged in the desirability of military training combined with a scientific temper of sorts.

The Pratinagar Sainik School was geared toward developing a scientific temper among its students. It had set itself the objectives to provide them with a good preparation in sciences and to enable them to complete the national administration's examinations. Armed with such training, the educational society's secretary believed, students would know how to run a district and perform various administrative duties, such as those of district collectors.[6] Consequently, a strong emphasis lay on scientific preparation, including physics, chemistry, and biology, as well as computer training at state-of-the-art IT facilities. Later, we shall see that this scientific disposition also pervaded the military institution's larger pedagogical dispensation. For the moment, let me situate the school's project within popular conceptions of education and nationalism in Maharashtra.

The Idea of Military Schools in Maharashtra: Regional Mediation, Love of Nation, and Personal Discipline

Many nationalist movements have used military education as a resource for promoting their ideals and visions. Although such association has also obtained in India, its history largely remains to be researched in the entire subcontinent (Cohen 2002). Nation building and, more crucially, the *protection* of the nation have been obvious incentives for the creation of military schools. In India, central military schools were started across the whole of the Union territory around 1962 at the time of the Sino-Indian war. Two of these schools were located in Maharashtra, in Satara and Nashik. Until 1996, no regional state had made any provision for the creation of more military schools. The BJP–Shiv Sena government gave new impetus to such a project in Maharashtra (Benei 2001b). The new government announced its intention to create military schools in each district soon after it came into power. The government issued authorization in 1996, and in 1997 thirteen schools for boys and one for girls were founded across the regional state. The Pratinagar military school was one of them, thanks to the educational society's will to expand its activities and possession of the necessary assets (i.e., financial means, staff, and space). In the secretary's words, the society was among the first to "take up the 'challenge'" and put forward a proposal. The school began soon after being authorized and succeeded in attracting a viable number of students from its inception. The main difference in syllabus between the central government military schools and the new ones in Maharashtra is that the former follow the Central Board of Secondary Education's English curriculum, whereas the latter abide by the ordinary curriculum of the Maharashtra state, using a combination of English and vernaculars (Hindi and mostly Marathi).

Despite their obvious *Hindutva* original taint, it would be incorrect to see in these new military schools the brainchild of an exclusive, rabid, sons-of-the-soil coalition government. To be sure, the Shiv Sena Party cadres are well known for their self-professed image of ardent defenders of the mother-nation—whether defined in national or regional terms. Yet it is crucial to understand that the idea of military schools in Maharashtra is attractive to all members of the political spectrum. Most politicians agreed on the desirability of setting up such schools, and some of them even sent their children to these institutions.[7] By the same token, the various district educational societies that applied for government permission to start one such institution had varied politics. The selection process was sanctioned by the coalition government on the basis of each educational society's reliability—both financial and institutional—rather than according to political orientation.[8] Even today, military schools are officially supported and encouraged by the regional secondary education boards, whose representatives are always invited as special guests on various ceremonial occasions. Furthermore, the idea of *sainik* academies does not only enjoy wide currency among politicians but also meets with popular support.

The idea of military schools is appealing in southern Maharashtra on two counts: it both encapsulates a historical relation to the locality and the region and mediates that to the nation at large. Many social actors in this part of India explained the attractiveness of these schools through identification with the Maratha warrior past (Chapter 4). Such historical identification is effected through symbolically and spatially reenacting a relation to regional (western Maharashtra in particular) and local (Kolhapur district) places. "Place" here has a specific meaning, as we have seen: it is the historical product of the relationship ordinary people in Maharashtra are expected to entertain with a hegemonic Maratha past, the latter which is mostly emblematized by the character of Shivaji, the founder of the "Maratha nation." The secretary of the educational society appositely summarized this intricate set of relations when referring to the long-standing tradition of fighting and war (*ladai ani yuddha*) in the local area as "particularly visible in places like Panhala, Jyotiba, and the like." These famous sites in the vicinity of Kolhapur are closely connected with the history of Shivaji, whose heritage also pervades all ordinary schools. Pupils learn about the sites both through the official narratives of Shivaji's military exploits as related in the same, unchanging textbook manuals since the creation of the regional state in 1960, and through the pilgrimages—secular or religious—they make with their families on various occasions throughout the year. Interestingly, as we shall see, celebrating regional heritage by way of hero glorification is almost absent at Pratinagar, unlike in ordinary schools.

Although spelled in regional terms, the idea of military schools also explicitly articulates with a national ideal. As explained in Chapter 4, the hegemonic conception among Maharashtrians is that of a martial historical heritage that has bearing upon the Indian nation. The construction of the Maratha nation is deemed prototypical for its modern counterpart. Consequently, the Maratha/

Maharashtrian heritage ought to serve and benefit the Indian nation at large. One way of putting this heritage at its service is to produce future members of the military through such schools. As the secretary clarified, the Pratinagar Sainik School was set up "for the 'nation' [*sic*]."[9] This echoed the opening statement made by Tattyasaheb Kore's grandson in a meeting of all Maharashtrian *sainik* schools' directors a few days before: "love of country" (*desh prem*), he asserted, was the basis of the school, which, in case of war, would provide well-trained people able to fight and serve as role models for the rest of the country. This claim to national recognition was also espoused by the teachers at Pratinagar Sainik School, who opined that military schools provided an avenue for Maharashtrians to regain the place that ought to be theirs in the national military war effort.[10] This was a place from which they had been demoted in the nineteenth century in spite (or because) of their belonging to the "martial races" of India. This reference to the colonial category surfaced in the course of discussions with various members of the public. That the British largely constructed such a category, even though it varied according to the needs and political alliances of the time, is not at issue here. What is at issue is the historical and emotional resonance that being finally declassified from this category has had for Maharashtrians: after the events of 1857, the men from Oudh (close to Maratha territories and seen as allied to them) were deemed unsuitable and replaced by the Punjabis, who then formed a new "martial race."[11] This, together with the final surrender of the Marathas to the British a few decades earlier (1818), has to this day borne its mark on Maratha social memory (Chapter 4). The resulting sense of loss and injustice goaded some nationalist fighters into action at the turn of the twentieth century. It also made the idea of regional military schools even more attractive for fulfilling national purposes a century later.

From a sociological perspective, the attraction exerted by military schools in this part of Maharashtra cuts across occupation, caste, class, age, political affiliation, religion, and gender. It is not confined to teachers or educational officers, or even prominent Maharashtrians; other families in Kolhapur often made favorable judgments, regardless of their educational strategies. Nor are such favorable voices the preserve of Hindus, whether Brahmins, Marathas, or allied castes; ex-Untouchables and Muslims, too—even those bent on nurturing a distinct non-Maharashtrian Muslim identity—upheld the creation of military institutions in the name of the Indian nation. The staff at the Urdu school in the Sachar Bazar slum (Chapter 5), among others, was vocally supportive of the Maharashtra government's project at the time of its announcement. It was actually in that school that I first heard of the project in March 1999. The teachers had just received a poster from the educational board and attached it to the main office wall. At the time, I interpreted this move as strategic compliance with government instructions, especially so in light of their delicate relationship with the corporation officials. Yet, as became clear later on, the teachers possessed genuine concern for the defense of the nation. Thus, during a discussion on a morning break over a year and a half later in December 2000, Shakeel, the otherwise nonchalant Class 3 teacher then in his midthirties, firmly propounded: "Yes, [military schools] should be set up, they should be made compulsory, we need them to defend the nation" (Han, hona cahiye, compulsory [sic] hona cahiye). Ibrahim, the rural soft-hearted Class 1 teacher in his early fifties, further opined: "This is good, it is necessary, this way children get disciplined and their health becomes strong" [straightening his torso, arms, and fists in a gesture conveying physical strength], "and it also begets love of nation" (acchi hai, cahiye, bacchon ko discipline [sic] ati hai, aur tabiyat strong [sic] ban hoti hai, aur rashtrapar prem hota hai).

These arguments were strikingly resonant with those encountered among parents whose sons studied at the Pratinagar Sainik School. The necessity of protecting the country was a particularly prominent and recurrent motif in some parents' expressions of their military aspirations for their offspring. The usual annual gathering was a special site for ostentatious display of such aspirations. During the yearly celebrations in March 2000, one father concluded his rather lengthy speech by advocating the need to train boys to prepare for war in case of events similar to those in Kargil in northwestern India. This speech took place at a time when the lingering war trauma was still acutely perceptible, in Maharashtra as elsewhere in India. It was further compounded by the Taliban hijacking of a plane a few weeks later, in which Pakistan was suspected to have played a major part. Some weeks before the school's annual function, Kesharbai, mother of Pramod, then in his second year at the military academy, had similarly explained to me: "Here in India, we need [military schools] because of China and Pakistan. China is very close by, and we do not get on well with them; Pakistan, because they are our enemies since the beginning." After a pause, she added: "We go to such a school, we train pupils from a very young age; all this is for fighting against Pakistan, it is the objective [dhyey]. This is why love of nation [rasthra prem], love of country [desh prem], and protection of nation [rashtra suraksha] need to be developed and nurtured."[12]

Obviously, there is much more to the diversity of representations about military schools in Maharashtra. While sharing in the concerns and ideas presented above, other voices may give prominence to other considerations. Consider, for instance, Pankat Baba, whom we met in previous chapters. Pankat Baba is the patriarch of a Bhangi (scavenger) family who successfully embraced the production of mechanical spare parts in Kolhapur. Baba acknowledged that military schools were needed to cultivate national love as well as to ingrain discipline (*shista*) at a tender age. As you will no doubt recall, Baba himself came from an underprivileged background: he had had to start in life doing his caste's calling and had achieved socioeconomic success through hard work and perseverance. To him, such a project importantly entailed educational and socioeconomic benefits. Because it was based on merit (forty students were selected through the State "Class 4 scholarship exams" followed by an interview), he opined, it had potential for bettering the living conditions of those categories of people usually left out by the nation-state's promise; the uneducated, low class, low caste. Baba, however, was also keenly aware of the financial elitism prevailing in the new military school. He knew that only members of relatively "wealthy" (*shrimanta*) classes could afford to send their sons. Even though the regional state and the Pratinagar educational society took care of teachers' salaries and infrastructure, respectively, parents had to pay substantial additional fees (thirteen thousand rupees per child per year, plus a further twelve thousand for miscellaneous costs, meetings, travels, and outings). To most parents, these fees involved financial sacrifices. The school counted among the parents celebrities, such as the Marathi film star Usha Naik, and a few upper-middle-class urban families of the deputy inspector of police, judge, lawyers, doctors, Tahshildars, members of the (State) Legislative Assembly (MLAs), and bank managers, but the remainder were more "modestly" well-to-do farmers (even though they possessed their own land and dwellings as well as modern conveniences, often including a car).

There was another, pragmatic and ideological, reason for the popularity of these schools. In addition to having national and socioeconomic ideals in common, most parents shared a fascination with other members of the public, regardless of their caste background.[13] This was a fascination for discipline, which military schools alone appeared successful in actualizing.[14] Dating such a fascination is not easy; it may well be a negotiated product of local conceptions of power and colonial encounters. In the present context, it is also noteworthy that the notion of discipline was part of Mao Tse-tung's revolutionary project, which so inspired Nehru. As reminisced a Mr. Zhang, Chinese immigrant in the United States, during his high school years in the 1960s he was made to recite quotes from the *Little Red Book* that promoted discipline together with work and study.[15] The valuing of discipline by the end of the twentieth century cut across all backgrounds in western Maharashtra. The prevalent "common sense" was that ordinary schools were notoriously unsuccessful in producing discipline, despite their constant discursive and performative emphasis thereon. And as many parents saw it (confirming the teachers' views), discipline was itself a prerequisite for better education and the making of good, docile people. Even my landlady, an elderly retired Brahmin headmistress, asserted that "these military schools [were] really doing a good job of disciplining children." As a matter of fact, her eldest son was at the time contemplating this option for his own elder son. As for parents at the Pratinagar school, they, too, often lay great stress on discipline and military schools' other associated benefits, such as healthy development through the practice of sports and other physical activities. As Kesharbai elaborated, in no other educational institution could so many activities be found, whether in larger cities or in Kolhapur. Being a teacher in a secondary school, she was familiar with the overcrowded classrooms and the teachers' inability to give proper attention to all students that plagued even some of the most favored privately run schools.[16] She had vetoed sending her children to any of these schools. Against her husband's and in-laws' will, and supported in her endeavor by her own parents—both of whom were village teachers—Kesharbai had aimed for "something better" for her son. It is this articulation of personal situations and family narratives with values and ideals cutting across large sections of society that makes the Pratinagar Sainik School such an important site for exploring the construction of this Maharashtrian hybrid kind of modernity.

Discipline, Routine, and Order at the Pratinagar Sainik School

Shista is a buzzword in Maharashtra, but its practical translation is most uniquely pervasive at the military school. At Pratinagar, it is buttressed by the establishment of a strict daily routine aimed at training local boys into regional and national elites while retaining western Maharashtrian specificities. To this end, the principal and the society's secretary adapted the routine from their own observations of the famous Doon School in Dehra Dun and the central military schools in Satara (Maharashtra) and Bijapur (Karnataka). The resulting routine, however, shares much in common with those obtaining elsewhere in the military: just as in any U.S. or British basic training camp (Hockey 1986; Lovell and Hicks Stiehm 1989: 176), the daily schedule is demanding. It must be learned and enacted with clockwork precision regulating every trivial aspect of daily life, including the proper way of folding one's clothes and making one's bed. What is at stake here is clearly the production of a disciplined, orderly collective body of individuals (see also Gill 1997 on Bolivia). It may be that very few of the students at Pratinagar will eventually become military officers. Yet following a tight schedule every hour of the day together with almost two hundred other people was likely to be part of the memory that pupils would retain from this collective experience (MacDougall 1999, 2005). To get an idea of what this involves at Pratinagar, let us accompany Pramod Keshar, already introduced by his assertive mother, on one of the last days of November 2000. It was his second year at the Pratinagar Sainik School. Pramod then was eleven years old and studying in Class 6.

A Day in the Life of Pramod Keshar at the Pratinagar Sainik School

5.15 a.m. The bell has just tolled its long, lingering sound. Outside in the dormitory's corridors can be heard a muffled, almost sleepy hubbub as some pupils are already getting up. Their peers will gradually follow suit. The noise increases steadily as the late risers have finally come to terms with the idea of yet another day at the military school. Pramod reluctantly extirpates himself out of the bed's warmth and drags himself down to the lavatory at the corridor's end.

6:00 a.m. Downstairs in the main hall, Pramod has joined his own division, one of four where his fellow pupils have assembled. They are all wearing their tracksuits, as the principal is. Only the military instructor (*shikshan nideshak*) and the "commander" (each day a different pupil from Class 8) are sporting khaki green pants and shirts and a black military cap bedecked with a red plume. The instructor blows his strident whistle. All the children sit down on the floor, cross-legged. The commander now takes the rolls from each class *pramukh* (literally, "chief," "leader"; here the one pupil who came out first in the previous term's examinations). The instructor then starts bellowing orders. These, as well as the ones following throughout the day, are in Hindi. Pramod and his fellow students begin chanting the "Omkar," consisting of the sacred syllable *Aum*. They repeat it ten times with eyes closed, uttering "Shanti" (peace, quiet) at the end and rubbing their eyes with their hands before opening them again. This, together with the chanting of the "Pasaydan" at the end of the day, will be the only form of prayer and commonplace religious ritual performed in the space of the Pratinagar Military School, unlike in some ordinary school classrooms where explicit acts of Hindu worship (*puja* being among the most common) may be performed at the beginning of class.

Next, each "house" gets up and walks to the parade ground outside, a few hundred yards away.[17] They stop by the entrance, standing in columns as the commander hoists the school flag. Each division *pramukh*, in turn, trots up to the instructor to inform him of the class numbers, which information the instructor relays to the principal. All this is conducted in military fashion, with much stern saluting and raising right hand to temple, clicking heels—swift, jerky movements—and sharp pivoting before trotting back to one's division. As Pramod watches this sullenly and noncommittally, the instructor orders the boys to sing the daily prayer, "Om Nama Shivay." This was the town's founder's favorite *shlok*, which he liked to chant upon rising every morning. After the chanting, some privileged pupils—those with running difficulties—are allowed to walk to the stadium. Meanwhile, Pramod regretfully starts running to the nearby ground with his companions.

6.25 a.m. It is still dark as we reach the running ground. From a distance, one can see the opaque black smoke belching out of the *sakhar karkhana*. The latter never stops, working twenty-four hours a day. Already the early risers in town can be seen from afar, walking briskly along the wide, flowered, tree-lined central avenue. At the stadium, the boys are made to run five to six laps of four hundred meters each, at increasing speed and finishing with a sprint. The sun has now risen. The pupils assemble for warm-up exercises: the drills are highly varied and energetic and carried out efficiently and speedily; much more so than in most ordinary schools.

6.45 a.m. While Pramod and most other pupils start sprinting again, the few overweight boys are given two more laps to run. After more running and sprinting, everybody ends the morning exercises with physical training (PT) movements, akin to the calisthenics performed in ordinary schools (Benei 2001b). In addition, one of the instructors teaches the pupils *yogasan* every morning. Although this is supposed to be part of the new government curriculum, the Pratinagar Sainik School is the only place where this is as effectively and thoroughly done.

7.05 a.m. The pupils are about to leave the stadium for the main hall. During their running and exercising, the heavy, foul smell of molasses has penetrated the atmosphere. The nauseating vapor is reminiscent of a distillery's, but stronger. Throughout the day, Pramod, like all other pupils, teachers, and other

Pratinagar inhabitants will undergo an unconscious adaptation to the smell of industrial progress in this part of Maharashtra. No one seems perturbed by the fact that, like many other forms of industrial development, this one stands in stark opposition to the healthy diet and way of life de rigueur in Pratinagar. But perhaps this is after all congruent with the hybrid modernity so characteristic of the late twentieth and early twenty-first centuries, whether in India or elsewhere.

7.10 to 7.45 a.m. It is bath time, with cold water. Pramod has by now become used to it, although each time he comes back from one of the annual holidays, it is days before he stops longing for the comforting home feel of warm water. Bath time is also when, in rotation, the pupils clean their collective rooms, sweep and wipe the corridors clean, and arrange their belongings in their respective cupboards. Today, Pramod luckily escapes all the collective chores. Unlike his friend Anil, who does not really mind either way, he frankly hates those extra duties. It is already quite enough for him to attend to his own belongings daily. The principal checks the state of each dorm room every morning, always at a different time. And he expects all the beds to be well made and the cupboards to be in order. The most disorderly among the students, like Pramod in his early days at the school, are gratified with a daily inspection; the cupboards lacking order and tidiness are immediately brought to their owners' attention. Such a procedure is highly reminiscent of that existing in basic training camps all over the world (see Woodward 2003 for an account of British ones), although without the harshness and sadistic cruelty usually obtaining, perhaps because the recruits here are children rather than young adults. That day, I accompany the principal again in his daily inspection as I did on my very first visit to the school, eight months earlier. Then as now, the opening of any cupboard door at random reveals neatly folded linen, squarely piled-up notebooks and other properly stacked items, congruent with disconcertingly impeccable beds, with shoes systematically aligned beneath.

7.45 to 8.15 a.m. It is now breakfast time, before which the military instructor has checked the appearance of each pupil lined up for inspection. That day, breakfast consists of bread and jam, a banana, and a glass of unsweetened hot milk.

8.15 a.m. Pramod, together with his friends, runs out of the hostel carrying his satchel on his back, heading toward the teaching hall a few hundred yards away. The hall's entrance walls are decorated with posters of national leaders (from Jyotiba Phule to Indira Gandhi) in English, Hindi, and Marathi. Once there, our friend walks straight to his classroom. All of them have been partitioned with plywood. Unlike in ordinary schools, all rooms have proper benches and desks, although hardly any wall decoration. On the board, the roll number is written within the colored chalk drawing of an Indian flag. The first short period is devoted to revision (*pathantar*): while the pupils are rehearsing English words, translating and spelling them, the English teacher, Mr. Khare, checks the home-work. According to him, the technique used is the same one "as in the ashram when they would learn things by heart" (*path karayce*). The *pathantar* is done, Mr. Khare further explains, so that students get familiar with the "totally foreign [English] language." Spelling, he insists, is very important; otherwise, the pupils could not write. Here, traditional Hindu pedagogy is used as a resource to cultivate what in the elite national school of Dehra Dun pertained to polishing a new, modern, "cured" self in colonial times (Srivastava 1998: 203).

8.30 a.m. It is time for the "morning liturgy." Pramod and his fellow students march out of the classroom to assemble outside on the front ground. The roll is taken again, in similar fashion as at dawn. Then the "secular" prayer (*prarthana*) begins: "Khara to ekachi dharma." The principal himself chose it for its ecumenical character. It was written by Maharashtrian freedom fighter and educationist Sane Guruji and is also sung in some ordinary Marathi schools (Chapter 1). At Pratinagar, too, pupils sing it with hands joined and eyes closed, as done for any Hindu prayer. Next is the pledge of national allegiance, performed in English. Unlike in most schools in Kolhapur, the recitation ends with the shouting of "Jay Hind, Jay Maharashtra," with right hands raised. Then follows the singing of the national anthem, punctuated at the end by three shouts of "Bharat Mata ki Jay," rather similarly to ordinary schools' routine. This part of the morning liturgy is over. The rest will follow in the classrooms, where Pramod and the other students return marching.

8.45 to 9.05 a.m. Moral education (*naitik shikshan*) takes place. It consists of Marathi, Hindi, and English news and some general knowledge, plus one story read from Sane Guruji's *Shyamci ai* volume (Chapters 1 and 3). The students finally sing the "Gayatri mantra" (in Sanskrit). Out of these practices, the only mandatory ones are singing the national anthem, volunteering a thought for the day, the *pathantar*, and a moral story (*samskar katha*); the rest is performed depending on the amount of time remaining every day. As can be seen, the moral education enforced is one that blends secular and religious elements in a way not dissimilar to the procedures carried out in some ordinary schools. If anything, it appears less Hindu and Marathi centered.

9:05 a.m. to 12:30 p.m. The students attend six other teaching periods of twenty-five to thirty minutes each, starting with English and followed by math classes (two periods), history, science, and geography, interspersed with two recesses of fifteen to twenty minutes each, during which they will be served a glass of hot unsweetened milk. When the subject is doubled (i.e., two periods in a row), the second period is devoted to practising exercises. This is the only school where I can see students working through full periods without any interruptions caused by a teacher being called out of the classroom for various reasons. Meanwhile, particles of soot and flakes of sugarcane waste are billowing around into the classroom, leaving their smear upon us. I cannot help pondering the climate's insalubrity. What worth can tuberculous schoolboys possibly be for serving the nation?! Yet, on the whole, Pramod and his fellow pupils look rather healthy, alert, and articulate, displaying a high amount of responsive and attentive participation. Judging by the pedagogy used, there is a real concern for students' understanding here. Whenever a difficulty arises, the teacher switches back into Marathi.

12.30 p.m. Morning classes have ended; it's time for lunch. The boys leave the building for the hostel in groups of eight, led by each division *pramukh* after he has counted the roll. They are all marching back to the building, at whose entrance the guard (also a pupil) counts each entering student; he will later report the total number to the principal. The guard will stand by the iron grid, controlling access into and out of the building while the pupils are in the dormitory.

1.05 p.m. The bell rings. The commander has tasted the food and eaten his lunch. The other children can now follow suit. The staff are eating among them. No *shlok* is chanted before or after eating. The reality of the outside world somehow manages to creep in that day in the guise of failed punctuality: lunch is served especially late because one of the two chapati makers is missing. Lunch will nevertheless be followed by the usual full rest hour.

3:00 p.m. Except on Wednesdays, the remaining part of the afternoon is devoted to supervision of studies, followed with additional lessons in computers and drawing, with a ten-minute break in-between. Every Wednesday and Saturday afternoon is what Pramod, unlike some of his friends, dreads most: laundry. Each pupil must wash his own clothes using soap and cold water.

4.30 to 5:00 p.m. Snacks (*nashta*) are served, consisting of biscuits and fruit, bakery items, and samosas, alternatively. That day, it is an apple. But first the pupils assemble in the hall, standing in columns according to their divisions, arms alongside their bodies and eyes closed. Each division *pramukh* reports the unruly students to the PT teacher, who scolds them in Hindi. This seems to calm everybody down after the last ten to fifteen minutes of free time, marked by muffled sounds of stampede and suppressed shouts in the corridors. Each division then goes marching toward the hall for their *nashta*. Afterward, the pupils get ready for sports.

5:00 to 6:00 p.m. They perform various sports activities in teams in the stadium. These range from some of Pramod's favorite ones, such as football, running, and hockey, to Marathi games like *lejhim* (Chapter 4), *dandapatta* and *kabbadi*, long and high jump, discus, *thali* (similar to, but bigger than, an average discus), to military training and physical education, alternatively.

6:00 p.m. The commander takes down the flag. This marks the end of the school day and the return to domestic activities: the next forty-five minutes are devoted to room sweeping and cleaning on rotation, followed by another cold bath.

7:00 p.m. Pramod and his fellow students are allowed to sit in the dormitory hall downstairs to watch the fifteen-minute Marathi news bulletin on TV. Supervised homework follows for the next hour.

8.30 to 9.15 p.m. This is much-awaited dinnertime.

9.15 p.m. Pramod and his friends prepare their beds for the night and go to brush their teeth.[18] Then the children sit cross-legged on the floor in the corridors for the "Pasaydan," the famous extract from the "Dnyaneshwari" composed by regional poet Dnyaneshwar in the thirteenth century (Chapter 1 in particular). The "Pasaydan" is traditionally sung in ordinary schools at the close of day. Of late, however, it has increasingly been replaced with the controversial Hindu-inflected "Vande Mataram" (Benei 2002a; Chapter 3), although the latter is not regularly sung here.

9.30 p.m. The lights go off. Soot particles have penetrated into the buildings, depositing onto furniture and beds. All day long, the gigantic chimney has belched out its polluted black smoke. Now ends an ordinary day in the life of Pramod at the Pratinagar military school.

"Etiquette," "Sense of Time," and Languages:
The Making of Civil(ized) Citizens

In the first ever sociological study of an operational army unit in the United Kingdom, John Hockey remarked that the formal structure of the army is predicated upon the Weberian model of bureaucracy: bureaucratic qualities such as reliability, impersonality, precision, routine and predictability, respect for traditions, and obedience to authority permeate the organization (1986: 2). At the Pratinagar Sainik School, these qualities are subsumed under the notion of "etiquette and a proper sense of time [*sic*]." Having these qualities, in the educational secretary's opinion, is conducive to good national management. "This is one of India's biggest problems: the lack of commitment to a strict schedule, so people are always late. A proper sense of time must be instilled in children from an early age onwards. Good manners must be acquired right from the beginning."[19] This statement is strikingly reminiscent of British educational inspectors' discourses in the nineteenth century in the Bombay presidency who regularly bemoaned the indigenous population's lack of sense of time and manners. Whether defined in colonial or postcolonial terms, the implication of such projects is that mastering the rules of "etiquette" is the distinguishing factor between those who are indeed "civilized" and those who are not (Elias 1982). In India as elsewhere (see Mamdani 1996 on Africa), "civilization" was in the colonial era deemed a prerequisite for the possible emergence of citizens. In postcolonial times, it has come to be seen as a concomitant process.

At Pratinagar, etiquette is closely militarized and accompanies the children down to the minutest details of their school life. In such militarization, the body acts as a crucial mediation to the various daily regimentation processes.[20] Although military training was minimal and physical punishment surprisingly absent from both the pedagogical conceptions and pragmatics of the school, discipline was taught and learned in an explicitly physical way. In addition, the pupils' bodies were submitted to a regimentation process through various painless if tediously repetitive bodily techniques meant for developing a "proper sense of time." All activities were strictly carried out according to a precise timetable and involved sports and hygienic and domestic practices (daily bath and washing of clothes, cleaning of rooms, arranging of cupboards). Class teaching was also an occasion when students were taught particular behavioral practices (marching instead of walking to the teacher's desk, sitting stiffly upright while focusing one's attention on the teacher's words, raising one's hand before being allowed to speak, and so on). Moreover, all of this was accomplished while the pupils wore military uniforms. The fact that all the clothes involved in this disciplining of bodies are strictly uniforms adds to the fabrication of a collective negating individuality. The various outfits that pupils learned to wear according to the activities performed throughout the day also served to mark a sense of the quotidian passage of time. If Pramod and his fellow students learned anything at Pratinagar, it was that there is a time for everything and that there are *clothes* for everything and every moment. Registering itself into the pupils' minds and bodies, this sartorial timing thus marked the entire day wherein all in all, the schoolboys changed six times on an average.

Arguably, because the performativity described here is enshrined in a daily repetition of bodily and other techniques, the extent to which pupils at Pratinagar had internalized discipline and order was unique. Indeed, their overall orderly and eager behavior contrasted greatly with the proper unruliness characterizing ordinary schools as soon as the morning liturgies were over, despite teachers' obstinate attempts at impressing a military-like atmosphere (Chapter 2). By contrast, the muzzling and bridling of youth at the *sainik* academy was both impressive and frightening. Whether or not such a second nature was a lasting one does not matter; it may well be that most children took to their original behavior again once they were back in their family homes. Some of them may even have developed strategies to thwart the institution's pedagogical designs; sleep, for one, was a costless medium for resisting the duties of assiduous study (Benei 2005b). It was certainly one of Pramod's favorite ones. Yet this schooling experiment also spoke of human behavioral and situational plasticity, as well as of the powerfulness of disciplinary projects.

This particular disciplinary project was also buttressed by a pedagogy aimed at making a complete person in Maharashtra, according to the concept of *samskar*. As argued in Chapter 1, such a conception cuts across political and religious inclinations. But the richness of the notion comes to better light in the Sainik School. There, *samskar* clearly refers to completeness, to the making of a well-rounded social person, one whose high academic and sports achievements are matched with a fully fledged moral personality reflected in his behavior. The successful making of such a complete person is sanctioned by the prize for "best student of the year" awarded at the time of the annual gathering (*sammelan*). The winner must meet an exhaustive set of requirements, including academic results, sports (cross-country, volleyball, cricket, basketball, football, swimming, horse riding, shooting), military training (both practical and written), extracurricular activities (essay writing, handwriting, drama reading, singing, general knowledge, folk song, folk dance, and so on), dormitory discipline, room and cupboard cleanliness, as well as demonstration of self-confidence and "mental ability" [*sic*] through group discussion and a personal interview. It may be that such actualization of *samskar* is in reality a rather elitist one; it would indeed be impossible to achieve in any ordinary school. Yet the Pratinagar project plays on a different kind of elitism from that prevalent in other institutions such as the Doon School (Srivastava 1998).

In comparable institutions, access to modernity and citizenship is reserved for a minority of international English-educated elite who will become alienated from the ordinary, vernacular masses. By contrast, these new military schools in Maharashtra give full treatment to the complex issue of multilingual instruction. The Pratinagar Sainik School theoretically allows any Maharashtrian from a rural area to become one of these elite citizens. In addition, the latter are envisaged as an interface between the local population and national and international levels of governance. To this end, their linguistic polyvalent competence is developed from the time of their admission, congruently with Sainik School's directors' strong preference for instruction in English. The latter was evidenced in the clear consensus emerging in the board's discussion of November 2000. Favoring English as a medium of instruction was nevertheless not considered to be at the expense of vernacular languages. The argument was that if Marathi was truly part of "our culture," it was not necessarily jeopardized by a shift to English; rather, it could also be preserved through it. Consequently, none of the usual tensions between Marathi as an irredeemable part of Maharashtrian identity and the opportunities offered by the command over English seemed so crucially at play at the Sainik School (Benei 2005c; Chapter 2). The aim, and the result, was that pupils at Pratinagar spoke noticeably good and fluent English. There was another implication, too, this one emotional. Because of the boarding school structure, emotional nourishment was integral to every moment of life at school and might be expressed in any of the three languages spoken.[21] Rather than being uprooted from their vernacular education and background, the pupils were therefore given access to, and encouraged to, nurture the worlds of the vernacular (national and regional) along with the English one.

Science, Reason, and Prophylaxis: Constructing Healthy Citizens' Bodies

Militarization of young recruits at Pratinagar, then, appears fairly resonant with a standard process common to all nation-states. Yet it also shows specific signs of Maharashtrian hybridity in its underlying pedagogical conceptions (and their implementation). These are intricately associated with a prophylactic and dietary vision of nation building, itself a negotiated product of colonial scientificity, Western and indigenous therapeutics, and local notions of bodily and environmental strength and purity. The latter notions are part of a "humoral" system encompassing physical well-being, social and ecological harmony together with an ethical mode of governance characteristic of "old patriotisms" in India (Bayly 1998: 17; Chapters 1 and 2). They are also attuned to Gandhi's pedagogy of personal development, in which inner purity is conducive to national (re)generation (Srivastava 1998: 200–202; Alter 2000: 55–112). Such a conceptual hybridity contributes to the shaping of the Pratinagar Sainik School as specifically Indian and Maharashtrian at the turn of the twenty-first century, as will now be exemplified.

Gymnastics and sports have been central to many nationalist projects from the nineteenth century to this day, in Europe and elsewhere (see Klein 1999 on Israel). In Maharashtra, whether at Pratinagar or in other schools, the making of fit bodies was also crucial to the project of nation building. Unlike in ordinary schools, however, at Pratinagar this entailed constructing healthy bodies through various activities practiced both indoors and outdoors. As we saw, the sports practiced were a successful combination of Western gymnastics—reappropriated through scouts' movements that saw the light of day at the beginning of the twentieth century concomitantly in India and Britain (van der Veer 2001)—with the handling of regional instruments and yoga poses. *Yogasan* played a special part in the formation of a good body and character (*apna man ka samtol*). In addition to the ten poses practiced regularly, the most fundamental one of "salute to the sun" (*surya namaskar*) was often performed while facing the rising sun at the stadium in the morning. Incidentally, this pose has been a topic of media coverage, as shown by numerous photographs of RSS morning PT assemblies. It is perhaps no coincidence that the sports instructor studied at the PT school in Pune. Like some other teachers' training colleges in Maharashtra, the Pune one is famous for its RSS sympathizers. Yet this *Hindutva* heritage is not the sole legacy feeding into the practice of yoga at Pratinagar. Interestingly, *surya namaskar* was also developed by the raja of Aundh in the first half of the twentieth century: the raja deemed it conducive to the development of self-discipline leading to "a kind of democratic regimen" implemented in mass drill performances in village schools (Alter 2000: 100). Moreover, congruently with his biopolitical and pedagogical experiment aimed at turning his loyal subjects into good citizens, the monarch had a preoccupation for cleanliness, good health, and inner purity. Such a preoccupation also transpired through the daily routine implemented at Pratinagar.

Bodily cleanliness (entailing two daily cold baths plus one midday wash) was not only a prerequisite to good health. It also stood in a dialectical relationship with the mind, in keeping with earlier colonial pedagogical projects in this part of India (Benei 2002b). Such conceptions of a harmonious and well-rounded mind-body relationship premised on inner purity were reflected in the choice of lecture topics during the school's annual camp: every day for an entire week an outside guest would give the pupils two-hour lectures on various topics.[22] Moreover, these conceptions invoked a close connection with the immediate natural environment. Thus, the students were expected to thoroughly perform the morning prayer, "Om Nama Shivay" for five minutes, with a purpose to cleanse themselves of pollution, help their concentration (*ekagrata*), and expel carbon dioxide. Similarly, their bathing in cold water was meant to maintain them "in tune with the 'environment' [*sic*], and to freshen the body" in keeping with the prophylaxis advocated by German nature-cure doctors of the late nineteenth century. These, as is well known, were influential in the reshaping of yoga and aesthetic practices—including Gandhi's—in India (Alter 2000; Chapter 3). Cold baths were also advocated for their sexually restraining effects (discussed later). Furthermore, the Mahatma's own emphasis on the importance of natural material (1951) also obtained at Pratinagar, where all clothes were made of cotton and viscose. Obviously, such Gandhian borrowing did not really go well with the contradictory, almost antithetical industrial setting of a military school. The Mahatma was famously averse to use of physical force and aggression as well as to industrial development and its resulting pollution. Yet the evident paradox between different ideological borrowings need not be seen as producing irreconcilable tensions and inconsistencies. What dominated at Pratinagar was the cultural logic of preserving one's *inner* environment (however this may be collectively defined), regardless of the *outside* environment. As in other spaces, the former clearly superseded the latter in importance (Kaviraj 1997). The immediate, tangible environment, one that could be worked upon, was what mattered. Thus, if nothing was (or could be) done about the soot and sugarcane residues permanently polluting the atmosphere, by contrast, ample and bright classrooms matched airy and exceptionally spacious dorm rooms (compared with many university hostel rooms in India). Every room contained four metal beds as well as a metal closet for each student, and all beds were fitted with mosquito nets to help prevent malaria.

All these prophylactic measures worked toward the formation of a modern citizen whose body and mind would be reconciled and developed in a harmonious relationship with his immediate environment. Such an objective also entailed a normative construction involving careful and regular bodily quantification: each month, measurements were taken of the pupils' weight and height. In addition, the general observance of dietary rules gave rise to minute scientific calculations for *all* students.[23] Diet at the Pratinagar military school was integral to the scientific and rational making of future proper and healthy citizens. Such a project was similarly undergirded by a combination of seemingly contradictory values. On the one hand, it shared Gandhi's dietary scientific outlook (Alter 2000: 20). On the other, it ran contrary to the Gandhian ideal of nonviolence and stood much closer to "traditional" Maratha and other Indian martial values and practices, as well as to colonial ones: diet could be either vegetarian or nonvegetarian, depending on the child's background and personal choice. A "nonveg" Maharashtrian preference was nonetheless strongly encouraged.[24] By the same token, table manners followed "the Indian way," eating with fingers from a *thali*.

Furthermore, the dietary science of cooking and eating practices was thoroughly supervised. A special menu was ascribed to each day of the week for all three meals; it entailed a careful balance of dairy products, fruit, grain, pulses, eggs (plus meat on Sundays), and measured servings. Pupils were expected to eat everything and show an impeccably empty *thali* to a staff member before being allowed to wash their dishes. Such dietary observances sometimes verged on the extreme, into an almost irrational belief in an all-achieving scientific regimen supposedly conducive to ideal personal and collective development. Thus, food rations were very carefully measured and prepared to a specific daily total (fourteen hundred calories). A big chart occupied pride of place in the mess hall. The principal had proudly pointed it out on one of my first visits to the school: it was a diet board showing all recommended servings of each item for each daily meal, the quantities in grams per pupil per day, from pulses to vegetables and grain. Conscientiously going through every item, the principal repeatedly insisted on the necessity of such careful measurements to achieve a good dietary balance. Another sheet pasted in the canteen showed the daily intake per pupil of calories, protein, and other nutrients and vitamins. The principal's devoted attention to this information further reflected his ever-pervasive belief in the scientific virtue of rationing. Despite his acknowledged ignorance of some of the items in the chart, he had calculated the daily amount of fat, protein, and calories for the pupils' ingestion.[25]

In such a conjunctive training of students' bodies and minds, the entire person was tentatively appropriated and molded by the institution. This training was congruent with nineteenth-century British educational ideals and can in part be seen as a legacy of the system put in place in the Bombay presidency at the time (Benei 2002b). But it is also more than this. In some ways, such emphasis on science and reason is a direct product of earlier Indian national-ists' repeated attempts at creating a national prophylaxis in the context of the distinctive governmentalization of the colonial state (Prakash 1999). Thus set-ting the background for the cultural imagination of the modern nation, this prophylaxis sought to act on a body produced by the knowledge and prac-tices of colonial government while incorporating indigenous forms of self-subjection. The resources of the Indian past mobilized in this endeavor both assimilated and exceeded the discipline of Western medicine.[26] Furthermore, the emphasis on science and reason in the Pratinagar project is highly char-acteristic of late twentieth- to early twenty-first-century modernity, in which various social actors played different, sometimes conflicting parts, whether of Gandhian, Nehruvian, or Hindu nationalist and/or Maharashtrian inspira-tion. Such hybridity unexpectedly reflects in the treatment of gender at the military school.

Gender and Family at Pratinagar Military School: Punctuating the Usual Divide

Congruently with the observation of Cornwall and Lindisfarne that "virile male bodies are often seen to be at one with the body politic" (1994: 21), one might see in the pedagogical and political project at Pratinagar a concern with im-planting masculinity in the students' bodies (to hijack Robert Connell's [1995a] formulation). Indeed, at first glance it could be argued that the Pratinagar mili-tary school plays the classic role of a site where young boys are initiated into the predominant constraints and expectations of hegemonic masculinity. At the Sainik School, however, the body politic under construction contained more or less hidden the seeds of another potentiality, a potentiality most apparent when envisaging masculinity—and gender—in the plural. Rather than an individual possession, masculinity is indeed a fluid and relational concept framed in terms of institutional practices located in structures of power.[27] Such a conception leaves theoretical and pragmatic space for perspectives other than hegemonic.[28] As will be seen, the process whereby "male" persons are constituted at Pratina-gar is a lengthy one that also involves cultivating "femaleness"—as culturally defined in Maharashtra and India.

The military school may at first appear as an ideal locus for the construction of masculinity. It is concretely gender ordered, underpinned by a hierarchical principle in which male-to-male relationships are cultivated at the expense of male-female ones. Such valuing is particularly salient on special occasions, including the school's annual gathering. During the celebrations of March 2000, for instance, the ritual and rhetorical space was prominently male. The women and children were seated together—though in two separate groups—crouching or sitting cross-legged on a plastic sheet spread out on the ground. Although children were placed in the main central space, women were relegated to the periphery. Meanwhile, the men occupied the rest of the center, seated on chairs behind the children. Every single moment further suggested celebration of maleness, from the *puja* to the Sainik School's founders (the Kore male family line), to the students' garlanding the VIPs—all males but one—the principal's opening speech, the pupils' welcome song (*swagatam*), and the military instructor praising the virtues of military education before swiftly distributing sports prizes. Occupying pride of place in these celebratory displays were father-son relationships, surrogate and real. Thus, among the guest speakers, the director of Kolhapur District Secondary Education Board welcomed and supported the creation of the Sainik School, and the army major wished to see all of the boys become army men. Both public characters projected themselves as substitute father figures in their respective speeches. The rhetorical blending of fatherhood and national fulfillment extended with the succession of male parents' speeches. A boy's father next appeared on the stage and marveled at length on the school's achievements, extolling the excellent and "necessary national preparation" provided by the institution in the case of another war against Pakistan (his speech was loudly applauded in those times of perceived insecurity heightened by the then unfolding diplomatic crisis between the two countries). The emphasis on the father-son relationship was also most visible in the children's skits that followed. Besides a song honoring the country, the only other one interpreted was "My Daddy" (Mere Pappa) from the Hindi movie *Pappa the Great* (2000). The song, in praise of fathers, tallied a list of their almost godlike qualities.

All of these public performances—including the sports prize distribution ceremony—seemed to principally serve the purpose of both stripping off any feminine dimension from the boys and negating mothers' supposed power over their sons. Such emphasis on men and father-son relationships stood in stark contrast with the constant rhetoric of love for the mother and the motherland embedded in the *deshbhakti* that places mothers on a patriotic pedestal in ordinary schools (Chapter 3). At Pratinagar, no grace was rendered to them for producing and giving up their sons for the nation. Women's discursive and performative absence was particularly noticeable throughout the ceremony, especially given that they constituted a good two-thirds of the parental audience. Yet the conspicuous absence of the mother trope was in keeping with the daily life of the Sainik School. It may be that such absence owes to the "insufficiency" of the nation as mother to "ensure masculine ideas . . . within the armed forces," as Sunindyo (1998: 14) suggested in the case of military training in Indonesia, with the *sainik* school providing a new military modern acculturation—to be "men in the modern way." Yet in India, the mother trope is definitely a powerful one in gendered conceptualizations of national and filial duty, especially in relation to sons and men, as we saw in Chapter 3. It may be argued, then, that the motherly trope was *unnecessary* at Pratinagar by virtue of the reconstruction of a filial genealogy through fathers (see also McClintock 1993 on nationalist genealogies). Indeed, the obvious emphasis laid on fathers expressed an acknowledgment of habitual gender relations in this part of India, and as important, it signified the recognition of fathers as embodiments of the family, as will now become clear.

Shifting Allegiances: School, Family, and Nurturance

At the military school more than anywhere else, turning young boys into proper patriots entailed fortifying a dedication overriding all other possible sources of allegiance. In particular, it involved a shift from family-oriented to nation-oriented allegiance. In ordinary primary schools, such a shift assumes the form of a daily movement of back and forth along a continuum of spheres.[29] Here, by contrast, the school space mediates the nation *as well as* the family. Consequently, links with individual families were made as rare as possible, and the schoolboys were expected to shed their attachments to parents and siblings. Parents' visits were no longer encouraged after November 2000. From an earlier average of one per month, visits were simply banned outside the time of the annual gathering, the holidays (three weeks at Diwali and one and a half months in the summer), and exceptional circumstances. This new measure was taken in order to "prevent disruption in the routine" from taking its toll upon the children. Thus, the principal explained, when these monthly visits used to take place, three days before, "only the children's bodies [*sharir*] were there, but their minds [*man*] would already be over there, at home." Upon returning to school, the children would be sick for the following two days, complaining of "cold, heat, tummy ache, and so on."[30] Interestingly, the principal's explanation was radically—and perhaps deliberately—down to earth: "Their mother, their father, or maybe an aunt, et cetera, will have given them too many sweets." The disruption was always attributed to the inadequacy of the "other world" of the familial space that must be rendered alien, rather than to military school life and the difficult emotional implications of severing ties from the natal surroundings.

Even during the holidays, the memory of military school life did not easily fade away but was kept vibrant in the pupils' minds and bodies. From teachers' recommendations of a strict daily schedule—getting up at 5:00 a.m., taking cold baths, cleaning one's clothes and the house, finishing up one's food, and so on—to set homework and assigned "projects," all acted as a constant link to, and reminder of, the school in the child's family life. Of course, teachers were well aware of the possibility for their distant orders not to be obeyed once the pupils were back in the comfort of home. Parents themselves were often reluctant to submit their offspring to the rigors of the military regimen. They tended to indulge their children, thus unwittingly thwarting the very pedagogy that had initially motivated their choice of a military school. It was precisely around such a structural divide between school and home life—characterized, respectively, by coldness, strict prophylaxis, diet, and household chores on the one hand and warmth, domestic leniency, and dietary sweetness on the other—that the school's pedagogical project was conceptualized. Furthermore, congruently with its claim upon pupils as an overriding space for the construction of personhood and citizenship, the school sought to appropriate some of these home-ascribed features and re-create a family atmosphere within the *sainik* academy's environment.

Although home was deliberately kept at a distance, a "home atmosphere" was tentatively re-created in the school through a network of ties formed with other schoolchildren (pseudo-siblings) as well as with teachers (pseudo-parents and adult relatives). The principal played a prominent part in this reconstruction, together with his wife, who in the process drew upon the children's past experiences and recollections of home and family. Thus, aided by three or four other women, she would bake *puranpolya* (sweet wheaten pancake traditionally stuffed with raw sugarcane) for the pupils on particular occasions. In Maharashtra, *puranpoli* is a sweet treat popular with children. It is also associated with many festivals (evoking Ganapati in particular) and special occasions (guests, school success, and so on) when it is prepared at home. Its connection with familial festive life and rejoicing is very powerful, and its choice here best suggests the intention of re-creating a family atmosphere at the military school.

The principal had also instituted another "familial" ritual whereby each pupil's birthday was celebrated, if only rather perfunctorily (it was merely announced by the respective *pramukh* in the evening, after which the birthday boy would stand up and be given an ovation by his fellow pupils).

Furthermore, the principal incarnated the figure of the benevolent yet strict parental substitute. During evening study time, he would often be in his office surrounded by children showing him their notebooks, poems, and so on. To him, this was evidence of the trust-based relationship that he had developed with the pupils. This relationship included consoling and comforting. For instance, during a horse-riding session at the summer camp, a boy fell off his horse. The skin on his back was scraped, and he was subsequently upset and frightened about the incident; the principal promptly sat him under the shade of a nearby tree and massaged his back gently. Such a behavior on the part of the main authority figure in the school stands at obvious variance with that found in military training camps, where emphasis is ordinarily put on the denial of physical pain and fright (see Woodward 1998: 293–94 for a U.K. example). The close interaction between pupils and teachers did not, however, sacrifice hierarchy; on the contrary, it enabled the building of a strong sense of respect for superiors premised on that shown to fathers. But such a fatherly image is more complexly gendered than an ordinary recourse to Freudian or Lacanian psychoanalysis would suggest. Indeed, the principal's imago was one blending authority with nurturance, the latter value being more often associated with femininity or femaleness, whether in India or elsewhere. My observations of incidents such as the horse-riding one were supplemented by the principal's own self-aware projection as this nurturing figure. In his view, the sensitivity he combined with nurturance enabled him to deal most efficiently with children's emotional needs.

The principal offered further evidence of his nurturing ability through his recollections, some of which resonated with those of the pupils involved. Thus, he explained how Atul, the best student in the entire school, "used to cry every night in his first year because he missed his mother so much." The principal slept next to him once, and since then the boy had settled in. Atul incidentally confirmed this to me one day, although laying emphasis on his having made many friends as the successful reason for his integration. If the principal's were all unconditional success stories, their varying confirmation by other pupils centered more on the lengthy process of integration within the school's internal network of relationships and the complexity of adjusting to new surroundings. The young narrators made a point of appearing brave and settled in their schooling environment, while often acknowledging the entanglements and anxieties generated by juggling the two irreconcilable worlds of military school and family. Upon their return to school, there were always "two or three days" when they missed their families very much, as noted by Kishor—the first boy enrolled in the military school in 1997—before things settled in again. (In many cases, these "two or three days" tended to extend into weeks.)

Even the principal's favorite narratives of his handling of particular students' families lend themselves to a reading differing from their intended official interpretation. In some of them emerges the poignant difficulty for children as well as families in accepting the discipline involved in having a child sent to a military boarding school. In particular, these accounts point to the disturbing experience of children living through prolonged separation from their familiar surroundings at a young age, and the ensuing negotiation on both sides. They also indicate acute parental emotional investment both in the child and his education, highlighting the tension between despair at the consequent "loss" of the child and resolve to sever the connection for the purpose of its education and the fulfillment of family and/or national ideals. Certainly the most illustrative story is that of one father who lived relatively close to the school. Every evening, he would ride his motorbike past the dormitory on his way home. Each time he saw his son watching from a distance, both of them would cry. This went on for several days. Then one evening, the boy was standing on the front ground; as he saw his father ride by, he escaped through a hole in the fence and ran home after him. The principal was alerted; he immediately left for the boy's house. There, the child's mother and grandmother held on tightly to him. Nobody would let him go back to the school; he was an only child. At last, the father agreed to have him sent back. The principal carried the boy back with him, holding him close. He recommended that the father should henceforth make a six-kilometer detour to go home, for both his son's psychological benefit and his own. The father agreed. At the time of my visit three years after the incident, the boy was still at the military school.

These narratives also confirm the metonymic relation between the father trope and that of the family: the relationship between families and sons was predominantly mediated through fathers. In this dispensation, mothers were conspicuously absent or powerless; the relationship nurtured in the intimacy of family—in which women play a central role—was projected onto a masculine public sphere that left women as invisible traces of the child's earlier life. This is so partly because "[w]ithin the South Asian context, . . . the Father-Son relationship is the key paradigm that encodes forms of hierarchy between men" (Chopra, Osella, and Osella 2004: 31), a seemingly appropriate paradigm for military schooling and its predicate of discipline and respect for hierarchy. Furthermore, these emotional displays and discursive constructions of powerful relationships between father and son were valued as a *worthier* indication of the "sacrifice" and devotion agreed to by the families giving up their sons for the nation. That a mother should be depicted as devastated by the "loss" of her male progeny might seem too predictable; by contrast, that men should be portrayed as soft and tender with their sons suggested the value, and accrued praiseworthiness, of their sacrifice.[31] Emotions between fathers and sons were publicly expressed both in the name of the larger family bond and as a personal testimony of masculine recognition, making them the central pillars of the child's present and future life. The military school, then, apparently offers a very pronounced example of male socialization comparable with the many instances documented in other parts of the world, whether pertaining to the military (Hockey 1986; Collier 1998; Woodward 1998, 2000, 2003) or to more "traditional" rituals (see, e.g., Godelier 1986). However, it is also a much subtler example. What follows is an attempt at further exploring the complexity and its potential for constructing yet a newer type of modern citizen.

Roles and Experiences of "Femininity": Toward a "Queering" of Gender

Cultivation of masculinity may be a definite part of the pedagogical process at the military school. Yet several aspects of this process suggest that the production of masculinity and the shedding of "female" elements are not done as systematically as might be expected from the literature on male socialization and initiation rituals across the globe (Read 1952; Herdt 1982; Herzfeld 1985; Bloch 1986; Godelier 1986; Hockey 1986; Economou n.d.). Rather, an apparent tension operates between traditionally ascribed gender roles. On the one hand, young boys were encouraged to develop their physical and masculine abilities through physical exercise and sports. On the other hand, they were also invited to share in some kind of femininity through performance of female-ascribed roles usually not found among boys their age. For instance, the students were expected to perform the daily chores usually reserved to women and young girls. These, as we have seen, included washing one's own personal items of clothing, polishing one's shoes, clearing cupboards, cleaning and sweeping rooms and corridors, washing up plates, and so on. To be sure, such a "feminization" of domesticity is also extant in other military schools across the world. In all the cases documented, however (Hockey 1986; Barrett 1996; Klein 1999; Woodward 2003), this feminization stands devalued in relation to a masculine sphere of military activity constructed as superior and radically antagonistic. In some ways, it may be part of being an "independent male." What seems to suggest otherwise, or at least, more, is that boys in the present case were not only made to embrace the domestic chores usually reserved to girls and women; in addition, they were encouraged to master a recreational activity usually the latter's preserve: that of *rangoli* drawing. The term *rangoli* refers to the colored powders used for drawing motifs on floors and in front of houses, either daily or on special occasions. It is an activity in which young girls often revel. Most important, it pertains to the social, cultural, and aesthetic apparatus every woman should master as part of her domestic skills. At the military school, boys not only learned *rangoli* drawing but also were even seriously encouraged to pursue it. The activity was held in such importance that it led to the organizing of a competition judged by outside guests and sanctioned by prizes. Arguably, these elements contributed not so much to blurring a usually sharp gender differentiation as to enabling what in the first place may be termed "appropriation" of the feminine.

Whether such appropriation was total and systematic is obviously open to question. To be sure, neither masculinity nor femininity can be ascribed a static "place" in the structure of gender relations because they are "active social constructions." Moreover, socialization does not imply dealing with passive learners. Rather, it is constituted through the boys' active engagement with masculinity (Connell 2000: 23) or more largely, gender, testifying to the fact that rather than a *given* in a social group, gender is always a *process* constructed in various ways, even in a military school. Many pupils at Pratinagar had seemingly "adjusted" to the school's project of overtly nurturing traditionally female-ascribed qualities within them. Some of them even seemed to derive pride from being lauded for their *rangoli* drawings. Yet a significant number appeared rather impervious to what they perceived as subaltern "female roles" and had developed various strategies for shirking the daily "female duties." The washing of clothes, in particular, was one sphere of activity where, away from the teachers' gaze, the most reluctant among them could find a way out by conveniently forgetting to use soap, contenting themselves with a perfunctory soak of garments.[32] The boys' diverse negotiations of gender further illustrate the limitations of Erving

Goffman's (1976) notion of "total institution" as extended to schooling: total institutions though they may be, schools are not isolated, watertight sites independent of the wider society (Srivastava 1998). Rather, they are loci of social and cultural refraction and negotiation. Given the enduring predominance of a hierarchical male orientation in Indian and Maharashtrian society—including among parents—the dominant reluctance found among pupils to unproblematically embrace feminine qualities is not surprising.

It may be that as the school expands and the boys become older, such appropriation of what is culturally constructed as the feminine in this part of India will be lessened. Pondering it at this moment in history allows one to reflect further on the meaning of gender-role construction in relation to discourses of modernity and the nation-state. At the time of observation the military school operated as a site where prolonged male socialization and ritual initiation occurred. It was also a site where the males constructed in the process were given an opportunity to perform "traditionally" feminine-ascribed roles *at the same time*. As I have argued elsewhere (Benei 2005b), such a gender project stands in stark contrast with those known to have occupied prominent places in the Indian public sphere over the past two centuries. In these projects, even the attributes of Indian femaleness and maleness deployed toward a common goal were dichotomized in terms of ideals of disciplined masculinity versus virtuous femininity (Gupta 2001). In contradistinction to such dichotomous constructions—including those prevalent in Maharashtrian society[33]—the Pratinagar military academy project ultimately offered a synthesis of the two habitually gendered qualities of discipline and virtue. The synthesis thus tentatively effected is one of a fuller, more complete social person than is usually allowed by institutions within Maharashtrian, Indian, and most other societies.[34] There is, however, more to the project than the formulation of "synthesis" may at first suggest. Indeed, the story so far told is one "that constructs a discrete gender identity and discursive location which remains relatively fixed" (Butler 1989: 329). But the Pratinagar military school is also much more. It is arguably the site of a modern utopia where gender values may also eventually be reconciled, transcended even, into the production of an archetypal new, modern, expansive citizen. This bears some elaboration.

The military school remarkably operated as a site where an ideal of service to the nation was transmitted in a fuller and less bellicose way than in ordinary schools. This was so mainly for two reasons. First, even the notion of discipline, which lay at the heart of the school founders' as well as the parents' conceptions of good and proper schooling, was here enacted in a rather unexpected fashion. Discipline was produced through the observance of a heavily ritualized structure of activities *as well as* the reproduction of relations of authority and respect between pupils and teachers predicated upon familial models of father-son relationships that included fondness and closeness. Congruently, the usual combination of discipline with pain—whether physical or psychological—extant in ordinary military schools was not part of the pedagogical apparatus at Pratinagar. As a consequence, the discourse of masculinity produced was at variance with common "models of military masculinity" whose supreme incarnation lies in the iconic figure of the hardened hero-warrior (Woodward 2000: 644). Here, by contrast, and despite perfunctory reverence to Shivaji's history, neither were regional, historical, martial referents given prominence nor a form of aggressivity encouraged among the boys, apart from academic (and sports) competition.[35] The reason is arguably that the political/regional inclination of the boys was not nurtured toward the region alone but encompassed a wider ambit linked to national and international spheres of power and knowledge. In addition, such an unexpected lack of adherence to hegemonic norms of masculinity owes to the relevance of other forms of masculinity ordinarily "marginalized and subordinated" that may "stress restraint and responsibility rather than violence" (Connell 1995a: 127–28). In the Indian case, Gandhi stands as the most obvious example. The Mahatma's influence at Pratinagar is reflected in the attempted production of a specific body: one similarly disciplined and raised on careful prophylactic, physical, and dietary practices, including daily consumption of milk at repeated intervals and bathing in cold water—famously known to "cool" the senses—yoga and breathing practices, physical exercise, and environmental concerns. All these measures and activities were geared toward fulfilling an ideal of internal disciplining of the mind, soul, and body guided by an overarching rule of self-restraint.[36]

This self-restraint, together with the special dietary and hygienic regimen imposed upon the boys, suggests a project congruent with the ideal of male celibacy promoted by Gandhi and discussed by Joe Alter in his thesis on nationalism. Alter's argument is worth considering at some length here, for it offers a refreshing insight into discussions of nationalism. In an earlier work, Alter (1993) had explored how physical fitness and nationalism were incarnated in the heroically masculine physique of the Indian wrestler. This physique was an embodied statement of masculinity aimed at countering British colonial and postcolonial projections of Indian effeteness. In a subsequent work focusing on the ideal of celibacy (*brahmacharya*) usually associated with wrestling, Alter (1994) claimed that it had become reendowed at a later period with a particular value: that of counter-Westernization. The *brahmacharya* stands as *the* political alternative to the "postcolonial libertine" for whom masculinity is an ideology of domination, self-gratification, and control of others. Contrary to this "almost pathologically individualistic" ideology (58) emphasizing waste of bodily fluids, the *brahmacharya* offers a model in which "gender identity derives from a regimen of self-control, balance, integration of self with natural truth." Such a model stands as a "persuasive form of embodied opposition to the legacy of colonial sexuality" (58). Arguably, the military school at Pratinagar encapsulates this *brahmacharya* model.

To be sure, this model is not exclusive and also stands in competition with other visions of postcolonial citizenship embedded in the production of future elite regional and national citizens. Among such visions, as we have seen, are military and martial ideals espoused by a great majority of Maharashtrians coming from all walks of life, whether close to the RSS or not. These ideals may stand in various degrees of tension with the secularist and modernist Nehruvian socio-politico-industrial project as well as with various religious inclinations in Maharashtra. In this respect, the heavily ritualized structure of activities at the Pratinagar military school paradoxically shows a considerably more nuanced case of *Hindutva* appetence than commonly exists in ordinary schools, thereby further calling into question the validity of the categories of "religious" and "secular" in reflections about the politics of identity (Chapter 1).

Furthermore, Gandhi's project was never hegemonic. In addition, it was disparagingly qualified as "effeminate," or "feminine," by the ardent promoters of aggressive Hindu masculinity (Osella et al. 2004: 19). Yet this should not foreclose the emergence of a new regime of masculinity building on a Gandhian nonviolent conception of the self, especially because the Mahatma articulated his version of nonviolence not just with celibacy but also with the spiritual elevation of *androgynous* forms of being (Caplan 1987, cited in Bharucha 1985). Gandhi had at least two counter models to Western notions of gender, one of which was characterized by equality of "manliness and womanliness . . . , but the ability to transcend the man-woman dichotomy is superior to both."[37]

It is here that queer theory has heuristic potential for understanding the implications of the Pratinagar military school project. Queer theory delimits "another discursive horizon, another way of thinking the sexual . . . that debunks the stability of identity categories by focusing on the historical, social, and cultural constructions of desire and sexuality intersecting with other identity markers, such as race, class, and gender" (de Lauretis, cited in Yep, Lovaas, and Elia 2003: 2). In its best versions, then, queer theory describes a horizon of possibilities. Rather than making any claim to a rigid and fixed theoretical model, its interest lies in its openness. Such openness particularly reflects in the emphasis on categories of "indeterminacy," "shifting," "unstable," and "volatile" operating in explorations of meanings of gender and positions of identity (Jagose 1996; Pinar 1998; Kirsch 2000). To be sure, when referred to the Pratinagar experiment, the treatment of desire is rather problematically eclipsed.[38] Consequently, this precludes the project from qualifying as "queer," and the citizen thus constructed from being labeled such. Even so, queer theory is useful here for the conceptual possibilities it has to offer.

In a pioneering book entitled *Gender Trouble*, Judith Butler (1990) argued that gender operates as a regulatory construct privileging heterosexuality. At the military school, as we saw, gender is in the first place "refigured as cultural fiction, a performative effect of reiterative acts." It is "the repeated stylisation of the body, a set of repeated acts within a highly rigid regulatory frame that congeal over time to produce the appearance of substance, of a natural sort of being" (33). Butler here does not acknowledge the potential for change and subversion inherent *in the very process* of "congealing": inasmuch as this artificial naturalness is itself historically and culturally situated, it is also unstable and subject to change. As the Pratinagar experiment suggests, ultimately the entire project is also shot through with multiple tensions and inconsistencies, the combination of which generates new potentialities. The *rangoli* drawing performance, for instance, subverts the original heterosexually inflected gender production (*rangoli* as characteristic of "feminine tasks"), thereby potentially fruitfully disrupting a gender-based order, thus allowing for a new, genderless citizen to emerge. In this respect, it should be stressed that neither in the secretary's nor in the principal's rhetoric was pride of place ever given to masculinity and the forging thereof, unlike in most same-sex military-type institutions (Addelston and Stirratt 1996). Rather, prominent in both their discourses was the making of a *citizen*. To be sure, this citizen was implicitly gendered. Yet emphasis was laid more on dutiful responsibility to the nation than on the *gendered* production of a person, subject, or citizen.

Hybridity, Modernity, and Universalist Citizenship: An Impossible Expansiveness?

Returning to the second quotation opening this chapter, I contend that the Pratinagar military school project bears potential for transcending the category of gender. The ideal citizen here no longer appears as implicitly gendered (masculine) but as a genderless, at last truly "universal." Whether such a project is a conscious one is difficult to say and even irrelevant. As noted by Chun in his study of a Taiwanese middle school, "bodily ontologies and socialising routines of institutional and cultural life" are as much the product of "conscious" political ideologies as of "unconscious" socializing forces (2005: 59–60). In the end, that all of the project's implications may not be fully articulated by its designers does not preclude their attempt at constructing something new, more attuned with the negotiated understandings of cultural, historical, social, and political experiences—though fragmented, uneven, and inconsistent as they may be.

This has wider implications for the (re)production of Maharashtrian—and possibly Indian—society at large. Only in the Pratinagar Sainik School, and *not* in ordinary schools, was gender—at least notionally—transcended. Moreover, despite a strong ideological agenda framed in terms of martial service to the nation, the atmosphere was far less bellicose than in ordinary schools. Military training was even superseded by well-rounded physical education and preparation for exams to higher civil and administrative positions. Arguably, rather than trying to produce aggressive soldiers or army officers, the Pratinagar military school strove toward producing peaceful, gender-reconciled citizens. An obvious caveat is in order. If (rather ironically) the rainbow flag was adopted by the school for symbolizing unity beyond the pupils' different backgrounds, such a seemingly homogeneous view of Indian society is misleading, even at Pratinagar. For the type of Maharashtrian and national society envisaged is also clearly predominantly Hindu. It is so despite the Sainik School directors' political allegiances cutting across the political spectrum and the lack of any explicit agenda of Hinduism in the school ethos. Even the praise of Indian/Hindu culture common in the ordinary Marathi schools was unheard. Greater interest was remarkably shown in the outside world (although the comparison would in the final instance, and in all patriotic fairness, favor India). Nevertheless, the society thus conceived was implicitly and primarily Hindu, made of Maratha, allied, and Brahmin backgrounds. Testifying to this is the fact that only two Muslim pupils and one Christian were registered out of a total 189.[39] As noted by "caste-conscious" Pankat Baba, it is precisely the "Pawars" and Marathas and upper castes to whom admission was given to the military schools, *not* the "Kambles" and other Mahars (Untouchables). If we bear this caveat in mind, the Pratinagar military school might still be understood as a locus for the possible emergence of a new form of citizenship, a genderless one in which the Hindu male search for postcolonial recuperation would no longer necessarily strengthen aggressive and masculine Hindu right-wing militantism (Hansen 1996, 1999). To be sure, the example of the Pratinagar military academy is a specific and possibly unique one when compared with the other *sainik* schools started at around the same time. Yet its potential for developing an alternative vision of modernity in which the particularistic ties of bellicose, gendered nationalism would be transcended must be acknowledged. The military is sometimes viewed as a forceful institution in constructing images of masculinity in society at large (Klein 1999: 47), in molding male citizens, and instilling civic consciousness in them; in short, it is envisaged as effecting a kind of "gendered process of moral regulation" (Gill 1997: 533). Could it be, rather unexpectedly and contradictorily, an original site of emergence for such a genderless citizenship to find its way within society at large?

Of Inspirations and Aspirations

Writing between the Lines

How did the pupils cope with being away from home at the military school? What kind of free space was left them for self-expression? What did Pramod and his friends tell their parents? What did they write to them? When did they write? Here again, these issues were rather formalized. Every week, pupils sent a letter to their parents, alternating languages: one week would be in English, another one in Marathi, and yet another in Hindi. It is easy to imagine the kind of widening gap to which this may contribute when the parents are not conversant with English, or when they are not very literate. But it is more difficult to tell what goes on in the students' minds as they are made to write these letters using one of the pro formas given to them by each language teacher at the beginning of the year. Indeed, they know that the teacher corresponding with the language of the week will check on the letters before these are actually sent. Here is an example of an English letter written by a Class 8 boy, Nirmal. The parentheses, punctuation, and italics are kept as in the original:

> (My) Dear father and mother, I received your letter. I am (very) fine here with my friends and teachers. I am studying well. I am taking my food and exercises regularly. Pay my namaskar to *either* all madams *or* grandfather, grandmother and uncle. Leave (for) Nirmal.

It is possible that, as French writer and novelist Nathalie Sarraute recounts in her *Enfance*, some of the pupils similarly found a way to negotiate the interstices between extreme constraints of surveillance in setting up a "secret code" whereby the most seemingly innocuous wording, transformed through brackets and italics, indicated more accurately how they felt. Nirmal's letter may be read in this way, although I must add that (unsurprisingly) none of the pupils ever confided in me about any subversive letter-writing technique. Some other students may also have been exercising passive resistance through the making of deliberate mistakes. Thus, another student, failing to sign his card, wrote in almost surrealistic prose:

> studing well I am taking. My food and exercises regularly to grandfather and grandmother. and the uncle have for rail. I am ~~student in~~ very fine. My class and [*illegible*] class is the very fine.

It is also possible that in some cases, the amount of negotiation was minimal, and whether they contained errors or not, the letters were not intended to mean anything more than what they indicated. In yet other instances, there appeared to be clear congruence between what was expected of the pupil and his displayed inclination. Thus, in one letter, a boy had drawn a soldier with helmet and rifle in hand. The measure of spontaneity involved in the latter instance obviously remains at issue, given the military surroundings.

Interestingly, some of the letters written by the parents seemed as stereotyped as those of their progeny. Thus, on the same day when the principal showed me all the letters about to be sent out, some twenty others were delivered to the school later that morning. All were in Marathi, save one in English. It read thus:

> Pillu you are very lucky boy. Keep your study and don't waste time. Don't think about me. Keep your [inspiration]* from NDA, this will be enough for me. You are superior in all activities.

Building a Career, or Building the Nation?

The fact that I became acquainted with the school through a parent rather than through institutional channels obviously made a difference in the students' eyes. They did not take me for an inspector of sorts invested with a mission to spy on them; the first contact had been rather friendly and direct and had also given me an opportunity for making clear the purpose of my presence among them. Yet the introductive parent was a strict teacher and a hard mother, who had imposed military schooling on her son against the will of the boy's father. This was unusual enough to be known to many children. Moreover, my often being

---

* The word for "inspiration," *prerna*, was the only Marathi one in the letter and written in Devanagari.

escorted by a teacher—purportedly for explaining things to me—hindered the building of any deep relationship of trust or confidence. I therefore had limited interaction with the boys, apart from my interviews with them. I need to clarify, however, that these interviews were conducted in the presence of nobody else but the interviewee and myself. The discussions revealed a wider diversity of aims, ambitions, hopes, and desires, as well as vigorous refusals, than might have been expected. The ambitions and hopes reflected were not only those of the boys' families who had sent them to the military school in the first place, nor those of the teachers and other adults who visited them regularly, lecturing them on inspiring topics of various sorts. They also testified to pupils' active appropriation, choosing, or not, to live up to others' expectations.

Remember Arun, in Class 8, who had sung "Mere Pappa" at the time of the camp's celebrations (Chapter 6)? A few months later, as he handed me the song's words written to the best of his recollection, Arun told me he wanted to become a "soldier." In his parlance, this did not mean any ordinary soldier, but an army officer: it involved taking the NDA examination. I then asked him whether this was also the wish of his parents, which he conceded. In an attempt at opening a conversational space for possible dissent, I asked whether he actually liked the idea. His bodily gesture was as eloquent as his spoken reply: "Yes!" he said firmly as his body stiffened assertively, a large smile illuminating his shining eyes. Then, releasing his tension, he added in a more even voice: "For the country. Something has to be done for the country, hasn't it?" This was the voice of obviousness, although I thought I could detect a ring of resignation to it.

In a more modulated vein, Kishor, also in Class 8, wanted to take the NDA exams after Class 12 but had already made plans "in case he failed": he would become an aeronautics engineer. He reckoned that out of his whole class, only five out of forty-five pupils wanted to take the NDA exams (against ten, as per the official estimate). As for the others, he gathered, they mainly wanted to become doctors and engineers. Interestingly, none of the administrative professions mentioned by either the secretary or the principal appeared in Kishor's enumeration. By contrast, Anil, in the same class, said he would like to become either a doctor or a district collector. He had no interest in NDA either, although he claimed that a good 75 percent in his class wanted to take the examination. Such a discrepancy in the students' perceptions and replies ultimately bears witness to the various (and often unpredictable) ways in which they negotiate socialization processes.

Rangoli drawing. Pratinagar Sainik School, Pratinagar, January 2000.

Conclusion

Desire arising through pain or pleasure, hatred or love,
is greater in proportion as the emotion is greater.

Spinoza, *Ethics*

IT HAS BEEN THE ARGUMENT of this book that the educational processes occurring right from the beginning of socialization and as early as kindergarten and primary school are crucial to the production of local, regional, and national attachments. Parents, teachers, and educational officials play an influential part in these processes, as they negotiate and shape state injunctions, relating them to ongoing political events, both within and outside the country. All these negotiated productions may crucially contribute to the social and political construction of persons and citizens, feeding on structures of feeling extant within society. Conversely, the (re)production of these structures of feeling is also relayed and drawn upon, even crucially informed and reshaped by state institutions. Schooling plays a particular role in this dispensation, especially given the recent access to public instruction for a majority of people in Maharashtra. When earlier generations of Maharashtrians did have but a modicum of education at best, schooling played only a marginal role in the everyday forging of symbolic bonds and imaginings of identity—ethnic, religious, or linguistic. By contrast, in the past twenty years of generalized literacy, the site of school has come to acquire greater visibility and prominence in ordinary people's lives, operating as another site of identity crystallization.

In contrast to occasional eruptions of violence heretofore the subject of most studies of nationalism, documenting these sites of early bonding has shed light both on the tenuous distinction between religious nationalism, secularism, and patriotism (Chapter 1), and on the constitution of senses of belonging in the everyday banality of the nation—and of the region—(Chapters 2–5). It is noteworthy that although gender and kinship are clearly embedded within the production of emotions and senses of belonging, inasmuch as most of the devotional daily production revolves around the gendered figures of mothers and sons as emblematic of the nurturing nation, which in turn needs the protection of the nurtured (Chapter 3), some kinds of emotions are nevertheless similarly cultivated among both boys and girls. The bellicose emotion attached to the defense of the soil, especially in this part of western India, has particularly dominated the writing, reshaping, and transmitting of regional history over almost two centuries. More recently (in the last four decades), this patriotic affect has been relayed, reproduced, and encouraged by the modern state institution of schooling (Chapters 4 and 5). Yet, arguably, such institutionalized bellicosity is not specific to India. Rather, it has become characteristic of the "late modernity" of nation-states (Epilogue). In this respect, it stands in stark and unexpected contrast with the example of the military school of Pratinagar recently started at the time of research, where a sense of reconciled peaceful and genderless patriotism seemed pervasive (Chapter 6). Whether this paradox is the quintessence of post- or late modernity is obviously open to question. What will become of the military school remains to be seen.

To return to the senses of belonging nurtured in ordinary Marathi schools, the fact that they are incorporated as sensory and linguistic repertoires (Chapter 2) drawing upon the intimacy of home and family (Chapter 3) also makes them potentially powerful resources to be activated in times of heightened conflict. Although schooling draws upon existing structures of feeling and material constitutive of ordinary social actors' repertoires of public culture and popular knowledge, it also operates a crystallization of these repertoires while reshaping them in tune with dominant narratives and more immediate concerns about contemporary events occurring within wider society. Thus, while concomitantly reappropriated by social actors, these crystallized bodies of knowledge harnessed in the production of regional and national allegiance become naturalized, authentic, and legitimate. This has implications for the ways in which notions of modernity, sensory perceptions, and nationalism intersect.

Nationalism, Modernity, and Sensory
Perceptions: Producing Visceral Citizens

*C'est ça la modernité. C'est: aujourd'hui. On commence. Tout ce qui a été fait
avant n'est pas important. . . . À chaque fois, c'est toujours: nous commençons une
nouvelle époque. Et dire que nous commençons, c'est dire un rapport au temps qui
est celui d'une promesse de futur.*

Jean-François Lyotard, Interview, 1997

It is not the purpose here to conduct a full reflection on the concept and experience of "modernity."[1] It is a well-known fact among historians that modernity is a largely fuzzy concept, difficult to situate both in its theoretical and temporal dimensions. Even scholars laying greater emphasis on the role of state formation in the advent of a so-called modern period continue to significantly disagree upon its dating: when, let alone where, does the state begin is still a moot point. The situation appears somewhat easier for those scholars privileging other factors of modernity, such as the decline of religion and the rise of secularism. Regardless of this definitional predicament, however, it is now an accepted fact that the concept of "modernity" is not the sole prerogative of the West. Recent work has shown that in many other societies and cultures, and at other points in time than those European ones arbitrarily universalized, there have been major moments of rupture that ushered in new modes—whether social, artistic, literary, or political—of operating, producing, understanding, and categorizing knowledge (Eisenstadt 2000).[2]

These new modes have often been linked to transformations occurring in sensory apparatuses, dispositions, and environments. Although these sensory apparatuses are often more implicitly assumed than explicitly discussed, they have nevertheless had considerable purchase on current epistemologies—anthropological ones in particular—with implications for the validity and definition of a notion of "Indian modernity." Let me explain. A sensorium is varyingly defined according to time, space, and culture. What sense (or senses) becomes predominant and privileged over others is a matter of cultural, social, historical, and of course, political circumstances. With respect to the Euro-American and South Asian contexts, the notion of sight seems of particular relevance.

As discussed earlier (Introduction), sight has acquired predominance in many appraisals of modernity. In fact, sight—and the change in perspective it accompanied—has been envisaged as the one sense that came to overshadow all others with the advent of modernity in Europe (Latour 1986). In the colonial context, however, this point has only been made in ways more implicit than not.

Walter Ong (1991), for instance, referred to the variegated ways in which sensory perceptions are privileged from one culture to another. Earlier, Paul Stoller (1989, 1997) had developed a critique of Western epistemology by attacking its major premise of visual and spatial cognition over any other, the auditory one in particular. Similarly, Ian Ritchie in his work on African sensorium (2000) suggestively argued that European cultures gradually came to privilege sight over any other sense in the nineteenth century, both "at home" and "overseas."

This colonial sensory redeployment had bearing on the politics of British representation to the "natives" in which displays of imperial grandeur primarily involved the sense of sight—both in Africa and in India.[3] Such an emphasis on sight also had repercussions on colonial as well as anthropological epistemes. Binary sets of categories, though the object of much discussion and dispute, largely informed modes of understanding "otherness," from what resembled most closely Euro-American societies to what stood furthest away. The point has repeatedly been made that what was being constructed by means of such dichotomous typologies was a ranking of "other" societies according to their degree of commonality with European societies. Of particular interest here is the association of the notion of "societies without writing" with a Weberian notion of stateless, more particularistic, irrational, and emotional political mode of governance. Its logical extension is that societies tending toward a more "oral/aural" and "auditory" mode have been implicitly deemed more irrational and emotional, and hence politically more unstable. Even today, the analysis of "ethnic conflict" and political violence (especially in African societies) is often tainted with such an assumption (see Taylor 2002 for a counter position). Yet sight does not exhaust the constitution and lived experience of a "modern" sensorium. Following Paul Stoller's invitations (1989, 1997), an anthropological perspective needs to acknowledge the importance and meaningfulness of other senses in a given modern social, cultural, and political context.

The question is obviously complicated in the present case, given the importance of the notion of sight prevalent in Indian society today. Derived from the Sanskrit root *drsh*, "to see," the term *darshan* is often translated as either "sight" (in the sense of an instance of seeing something or somebody) or the act of "seeing." The term may also refer to a "vision," "apparition," or even a "glimpse." One may ask whether the emphasis placed upon the term in Indian/Hindu culture today—both by popular common sense and by academics—might be a negotiated outcome of the colonial encounter standing as the closest equivalent to the sensory aspect central to a European conception of modernity (Pinney

2003). Vindicating such a hypothesis is the comparative lack of understanding and tolerance that the British demonstrated in their fight against what they considered an assault on other senses, especially the auditory one (as suggested by Michael Roberts [1990] in his work on noise as a cultural struggle in Sri Lanka in the 1880s–1930s). Even the fact that one of the most common usages of *darshan* is a religious one today may fit with such a hypothesis. The term often refers to "visions of the divine," of a god, a holy person, or even an artifact (Eck 1998). One can have *darshan* of a deity in a temple or experience an inward awareness. Whether in popular Indian postindependence or Indianist anthropological conventional wisdom, the term's religious connotation is most salient. Given the Orientalist vicissitudes, misunderstandings, and deceptive reappropriations that other concepts (such as caste, see Dirks 2001) and religious matters have known in India, however, one may rightly wonder whether the contemporary religious emphasis is a relatively recent phenomenon stimulated by the colonial encounter. In other words, while simultaneously erecting *darshan* as the predominating sensory perception in the modern Indian reconfiguration of the senses—similar to a Euro-American conception—a spiritual and religious dimension may have been stressed in accordance with an Orientalist mode of understanding "the East," *in fine* providing a sensory illustration of the "but not quite" of Bhabhaian mimicry.

Nevertheless, it should be emphasized that the production of emotions and sensorium occurs jointly and *is not* specific to particular cognitive structures. Neither does a written/oral distinction nor a preliteral/literal one successfully capture the pervasiveness and universality of the processes taking place right from infancy. Finally, as has been demonstrated, the role of the state, especially through schooling, is crucial in the production and reshaping of emotions and sensorium. Indeed, national projects of self-formation largely rely upon the constitution of a "national primary sensorium" and, as in the present case of the state of Maharashtra, that of a regional one. Characterizing the regional state of Maharashtra today is its preemptive take on the population's sensory world, a take putting at its service the sensorium developed from a recomposed musical tradition fusing devotional *abhanga*s, prayers, yoga, and physical education drills as well as martial rhythms. Such a recomposed tradition predicated upon existing sensory structures of feeling conversely both emblematizes and undergirds the regional state. It also articulates with the sensory transformations brought about by new technologies and industrialization in various forms, from the sounds and fumes of trucks and tractors; to the music belching out from loudspeakers outside temples, houses, theaters, and polling stations; to the visual redeployments of local patriotism and nationalism (flagged at the time of the war against Pakistan in Kargil). It is the recomposition of this sensorium that the state attempts to capture and that makes it so modern. Thus, through songs glorifying the Marathas, the independence struggle from the British, as well as other nationalist and postcolonial songs, the notion and lived experience of love for the mother-nation and its people is (re)produced at school; not just on the occasion of annual gatherings and school competitions effecting an acute conflation and telescoping of different historical moments (redefined in the process as foundational ones) but also in the daily conflation of different layers of sensory stimulations in the production of regional, national, and familial allegiance in ordinary school life.

The notion of sensorium elaborated here has further heuristic potential for understanding the political and ethical implications borne by the emotional and linguistic structures of feeling (re)produced in everyday life and the naturalization of senses of belonging effected in the process. Indeed, working with the notion helps bring to light the illusory character of the "public/private" dichotomy and the untenability of a distinction between the construction of social persons and that of interiorized selves.[4] Political modernity is often characterized by a sharp contrast between a public, democratic space and another, private one, the true realm of the authentic self. Contrary to such a perspective, the notion of sensorium (as well as that of embodiment) helps us think precisely through the all-pervasive nature of all political and socialization processes. As a consequence, the risk of fascism threatening most citizenries today, against which Étienne Balibar cautioned in his writings about the vicissitudes of identity as a gaze (identité comme regard)—a gaze through which the other becomes the demonized impossible coresident (1998: 114–20)—is "only" a matter of amplitude rather than kind. Arguably, the nature of political democracy today is such that the three distinct levels at which identification is supposed to take place, namely, the family; the professional, confessional, and other institutions in which we might include schools; and the "hegemonic" community, or nation, are not flattened out in the case of fascism only. Rather, the three levels tend to coalesce in most projects of political modernity, whether frankly fascistic or not. In Maharashtra, as we saw, school, belonging to the second level of social organization, has become a very special locus both mediating and conflating the spaces of family and nation (that is, of the first and third levels). Rather than demonstrating that the state of Maharashtra is verging on fascism, this suggests the ideological perils inherent in any institutional, and especially educational, modern nation-state project today. Furthermore, if the mark of "ultimate modernity" lies in the regional state's pursuit of a distinctive postcolonial project that seeks to both capture and harness citizens' sensorium into the making of Indian (Hindu) nationals, the increasingly marked Hinduness of such a project requires elaboration.

Toward a Hinduization of Structures of Feeling?

> *The energy that actually shapes the world springs from emotions—racial pride, leader worship, religious belief, love of war—which liberal intellectuals mechanically write off as anachronisms, and which they have usually destroyed so completely in themselves as to have lost all power of action.*
> **George Orwell, "Wells, Hitler and the World State"**

When in 1961 Raymond Williams expanded on his notion of "structures of feeling" (originally proposed in *Culture and Society* [1958]), he was attempting to capture the complexity of accounting for and recounting the specificity of social and cultural processes occurring within given temporal and spatial locations, what the French call *l'air du temps* of a particular period. In *The Long Revolution* (1961), Williams carried further his perceptive discussion of the difficulties of documenting what is in its very essence undefinable: a culture snapshot at a suspended moment in time. Drawing on Williams's insights I now want to explore further the apparent Hinduization of "structures of feeling" in western India, especially in the regional state of Maharashtra.

Elsewhere (Benei, 2004) I touched on the shift in sensibilities that apparently occurred in relation to Maharashtrian sons-of-the-soil patriotism over the past decades. Using the example of filmmaker Bhalji Pendharkar's historical cinema of the emblematic figure of Shivaji (Chapter 4), I showed in particular the differential ways in which generations related emotionally to this cinema. The point I want to make here is a larger one. It is that whatever shifts in sensibilities have been occurring, they have been more gradual and subtle, taking place over a longer period of time than is usually allowed for in contemporary analyses of *Hindutva* movements. The (Hindu) nationalist atmosphere dominating public culture in most parts of India, and certainly in western Maharashtra today, may partly owe to the power of a recently more vocal nationalist discourse, or even to the weakness of a counter-discourse in the face of increasing external pressures to "globalize" and the attendant anxieties generated by such pressures. Yet, as we are reminded by Chetan Bhatt (2001: 209), the relatively recent lineage of the *Hindutva* movement does not preclude the tremendous purchase that both "Hindu" and Hindu nationalist political and ideological formations have had since the nineteenth century.

The extent of Hinduization of the curriculum and the bearing thereof upon the production of Maharashtrian/Indian citizens is difficult to evaluate for two reasons. First, a wide consensus seems prevalent in Maharashtra today with respect to a Hindu cultural and social environment. Even the most secular-minded teachers—whether neo-Buddhist, Muslim, Maratha, or Brahmin—did not clearly object to some of these distinctly Hindu songs and prayers being sung in the space of school. Rather, they envisaged them as part of the dominant culture, "Indian culture" (*Bhartiya sanskruti*). More "simply," just as in a predominantly Christian nation-state the majority culture is informed by Christian ethics, rituals, and rhetoric—regardless of all multiculturalist assertions, policies, or even lip service conveniently paid to these conceptions of citizenship—in India, the dominant cultural idiom is that of Hinduism, regardless of the definitional issues involved. In this respect, it is significant that even the increasing performance of the alternative song "Vande Mataram" at the end of the school day was rarely commented upon by social actors in Kolhapur. Although the song had been a staple of school gatherings since 1964 and a number of teachers and parents in Kolhapur claimed to have sung it regularly as schoolchildren, it only recently began to replace the long popular regional "Dnyaneshwari" in Marathi schools (Chapter 1). By the end of 1999, it had spread widely throughout the schooling network and was performed in many other (private as well as corporation) schools, either during collective assemblies or separately in each classroom. By the same token, some songs (such as "Guru Brahma Guru Vishnu") were sung in Kolhapur for the past fifteen to twenty years only in some Marathi schools (the most Hindu-sympathetic) but more recently in others. This definitely marked Hinduization is very likely a product of recent schooling and especially refresher courses systematically organized for primary schoolteachers throughout Maharashtra in the mid- to late 1990s under the BJP–Shiv Sena coalition government.

Second, and nevertheless, the changes that occurred under the BJP–Shiv Sena coalition government were not the exclusively distinctive mark of Hindu right-wing ideology. Rather, they were in keeping with an already tense ideological atmosphere in this part of Maharashtra, including within educational circles. That "SMART PT" training sessions were organized in each and every state district for several years for all primary education teachers and often run by overzealous officers—at times clearly former RSS recruits—is only part of the story. The other part is that wider ideological transformations occurring in the region were reflected in an increasingly Hinduized curriculum that was not entirely under Hindu right-wing government control. Despite the autonomy of the textbook bureau in charge of preparing primary school manuals in the state of Maharashtra, the new syllabus was markedly more Hindu in content (see Chapter 1, note 31 on textbook preparation). Although not blatantly distorting history as in the averred case of secondary manuals prepared at the national level of the NCERT at that time, the primary curriculum in the regional state more subtly elided positive Muslim and non-mainstream Hindu presence from public view (Chapter 5).[5]

Where these recent transformations were potentially harmful was, of course, in the sense of reassurance they provided for some more Hindu-inclined teachers to celebrate an Indian heritage as distinctly and exclusively Hindu, thus playing into Hindu right-wing ideology and denying the status of fully fledged members of the national community to other non-Hindus. This suggests that the dangers of limited negotiation inherent in the kinds of identities thus produced are similar in fascistic regimes *and* in most democratic ones today. A note of hope should, however, be sounded on two counts. First, it is important to bear in mind that teachers were not the passive recipients of a state-imposed project but active social agents. Indeed, they exercised much more autonomy than might have been expected, even in the performance of the *moral education* sessions prescribed by the new program.[6] Second, social actors' understandings and representations are always negotiated products of processes occurring within a range of locales, from home and domestic space to school and other "public" spaces, and any negotiation of these processes is always fragmentary: they do not form part of any coherent whole of a social unit of analysis, be it that of the state, the so-called public sphere, or elsewhere. Granted, they may be articulated at various levels encompassing structures of the locality, the region, and the nation-state, as well as transnational flows and formations. Yet their apparent encompassing and neat Russian-doll articulation is but a *vue de l'esprit*, only just a way of seeing, what is more, from above. Regardless of what goes on at the pyramidal level of the state, to the social actor on the ground, nation-state or even regional or local realities do not necessarily form part of a coherent experience. What most social actors do experience and negotiate is the ever incompleteness of such projects of self-formation—local and regional as much as national—by nature always fragmentary and labile while paradoxically grounded in a historical, cultural, and phenomenological web of structures of feeling. By the same token, social actors' senses of belonging are of a *fragmentary* and protean nature even in their dialogical construction with the nation-state's institutions, the mass media, and other forms of public culture. Incorporation of senses of belonging is neither an exhaustive nor a final process even though it may have long-standing consequences in projects of self-formation. Various moments of incorporation may be called upon in an infinity of situations and circumstances, and it is also this changing and fleeting character that makes any project of nationalism or self-formation ever so unpredictable in its developments on the ground. Because of this constant tension and incompleteness, because of the "measure of openness onto heterogeneous realities of every ideological structure, however absolutist" (Massumi 2002: 263), or more simply what Thomas Hansen has called "the impossibility of identities" (1996: 60–65), even the most "efficient" state schooling cannot preclude the eruption of the unpredictable in daily routine, let alone in extraordinary circumstances. By the same token, it is also this fragmentary and unpredictable dimension that makes it impossible to paint a picture of 99 percent of Hindu Indians as *Hindutva* sympathetic, even in averred cases of sharing values with those commonly proffered by right-wing exclusivist organizations. The latter's proponents, as is well known, have precisely succeeded in capturing and appropriating for themselves the semiotics of Hinduism by transposing them onto a visible "public" sphere. In the end, even carefully crafted state projects attempting to capture citizens' sensory and phenomenological experiences of lived social, cultural, and political realities cannot tame the unpredictable, contingent nature of social action.

Epilogue

But if nationalism with a human face is not realized, we might once more abandon the world to oppression and war.

George Mosse, *Masses and Man*

BECAUSE OF THE NECESSITIES of narrative exposition, the comparative perspective advocated at the beginning of this book has largely remained in the background. It is time to finally foreground this dimension and its heuristic potential for understanding further the formation of popular and political affects relayed by educational state projects. To this end, I concentrate on how a war culture has become increasingly integral to our more recent understanding of "late modernity."

War Culture and Nationalist Ideologies

In some ways, I have attempted in this book to document the everyday production of violence: violence of the pedagogical process, of the formation of exclusivist sentiments, and more generally of any socialization process. As important, this account has revealed how the production of violence within cultural parameters may also naturalize and legitimize its extraordinary eruption in times of war or communal riots. Here I want to conjure the figure of a German-born historian who from the 1960s onward devoted all his intellectual energies toward studying the rise of fascism: George L. Mosse. Until Mosse's pioneering work, right-wing nationalism in Europe had been studied as an intellectual movement with major thinkers such as Hegel, Gobineau, and Nietzsche enrolled as its potential precursors. Mosse envisaged this approach as fundamentally flawed: fascism had less to do with high theories and philosophies, and more with popular culture, from racist graffiti to pietist legacy to grand architectural realizations. In many unsuspected ways, fascism was a cultural project with roots in Christian religious movements and an attendant quest for proper, normalized sexual behavior predicated on a rigorous gender-role division. However, rather than leading to a civilizing process *à la Elias* where senses of bodily comportment and civility are seen as the product of courtly and bourgeois ideas of dignity and distinction, and cruelty and violence a historical accident in the civilizing process, Mosse argued that fascism had given rise to a "brutalization of the masses" whereby the experience and brutality of war became legitimized and banalized in order to be rendered livable. Mosse's insights have opened up wide intellectual horizons, calling for more work on the cultural anchorage of nationalist movements in Europe and elsewhere. In particular, reflection has been stimulated on systems of popular representations—on the battlefields and at the rear—in the two so-called world wars. The Great War (WWI) has since received a fair amount of academic attention, renewing perspectives heretofore sunk into the murky sands of uninspiring military history. Jay Winter in the United States, Jean-Jacques Becker in France, and many others after them have been inspired by the notion of "war culture." Although specifically concerned with Europe, these works have emphasized how a war culture as the "field of all the representations of the war entertained by its contemporaries" (Audoin-Rouzeau and Becker 2002a: 252) was crucial in the banalization and inscription of the tropes of war and violence *at the heart of daily life.* It is obviously not my intention here to trivialize the specifics of either the European or the Indian experiences of violence and war in the past century. The two world wars, the 1947 violence of the Partition, and the subsequent wars of 1962 (with China), 1965 (with Pakistan), and 1971 (in support of the creation of Bangladesh) obviously possess very different histories and bearing upon those who have had a direct experience of them, as well as on the social and collective memories they have fed and shaped. The point of such an excursion into the tribulations of nation building and war in Europe is to highlight potentially fruitful similarities in both contexts. In a curious round of history, the end of the twentieth century is somehow resonant with its beginning, as nations are once again perceived as ethnic, even biological entities (Audoin-Rouzeau and Becker 2002a: 251). Even if the war culture described throughout this book may be of a less brutal kind than that extant in the European interwar period of 1919–39, the one that became exacerbated in the late 1990s in the immediate aftermath of the Kargil war is of the same kind, if only "latent." This war culture entails gendered, religious, and almost biological notions of the "nation under attack" and in need of protection, as well as glorification of heroes drawing upon both recent histories and earlier regional structures of feeling.

The parallel realities referred to by notions of war culture in Europe and India are important for at least three reasons. First, in addition to confirming Mosse's thesis of mass brutalization, they support the argument propounded by Zygmunt Bauman of rational violence, bureaucracy, and scientificity being at the heart of political projects characteristic of late modernity, that is, of the late twentieth and early twenty-first centuries. Bauman (2000) argued that far from being a historical accident and a throwback to a "premodern" state of "savagery" and "barbarism," genocidal programs such as the Holocaust were very much products of modernity. Through the rise of the nation-state characteristic of Western modernity, power and means of force became centralized under state control. In this socially engineered quest for equality and attempted production of homogeneous citizens, race and ethnicity became new ways of differentiating human beings. The new hierarchy of "human" and "not fully human" was further implemented by means of impersonal bureaucracies, thus substituting technical proficiency for moral responsibility. Bauman uses the metaphor of the gardener weeding out undesirable plants to illustrate the social-engineering goal of genocide, that is, the creation of a "better and different world" by rationalized means, in which order and homogeneity reign supreme. Thus, the Eliasian thesis of an overall nonviolent modern civilization ultimately appears unfounded, an "illusion": it is an "integral part of its self-apology and self-apotheosis, in short, its legitimising myth." Such legitimizing myth is also pervasive in Maharashtrian schooling today. This is, of course, not to say that primary schooling in the state of Maharashtra has deliberately been reformed toward a genocidal end. Maharashtra is *not* Gujarat, and one should not confuse one with the other: the state-orchestrated anti-Muslim pogroms and rioting that have taken place in the state laboratory of *Hindutva* violence since 2002 have not yet occurred on a comparable scale in Maharashtra. Nor is the state's ideology openly Hindu dominated any longer. Yet the many subtle and nuanced Hindu-inflected transformations that characterize the "new" curriculum—so far left unchanged under the current non-*Hindutva* government—suggest wider and deeper changes occurring within society at large, whereby the space left for those citizens not conforming to the dominant ethnic, religious (and in the regional state of Maharashtra, linguistic) idiom of citizenship are increasingly considered as "not belonging."

Second, these parallel experiences and notions of war culture point to the fact that legitimacy of the nation as the product of a popular will is most forcefully achieved through war. As Mosse (1990) so suggestively demonstrated in the case of Europe, the "myth of war" constructed in between the two world wars played a powerful role in promoting the notion of war's sacredness and sanctity in a Christian context where "fallen soldiers" were no longer mercenaries but "sons of the national soil."[1] A similar argument holds with regard to many modern nation-states—whether dominated by a Christian ideology or not—where armies consist of national sons of the soil whose deaths in battle are conceived as sacrifices for the nation's preservation and regeneration. This sacredness makes war a potent trope, even in times of peace. Arguably, it is a sacredness of this sort, although here a Hindu one (however defined), that operated in the post-Kargil events with renewed vigor, daily cultivated in schools and reenacted through performative displays of male virility and iterations of allegiance to the divine motherland.

Third, however, these parallel histories also shed new light on discussions of violence and cultural specificity. Anthropologists (recent examples include Daniel 1996; Hinton 2002; Scheper-Hughes 2002; Taylor 2002) have disproved the oft-encountered assumption of a correlation between violence and culture, and these cases also forcefully bring home that if the modalities of violence are culturally variable, its production itself is not the prerogative of any given culture. This is important on two counts: that of schooling's effects and that of the conditions of possibility for the eruption of violence in modern nation-states. I want to reiterate once more: schooling alone does *not* produce jingoism so the supposedly "logical inference" from what I have presented in this book that unschooled people would be less jingoistic or less predisposed to violence is an unfounded one (as Pandey's work published in 1990 amply suggests). One reason is that what takes place in the space of school may be conducive to both integration, tolerance, and other much-needed virtues in times of world jingoism, *and* unprecedented crystallization and polarization of the same "impossible identities" already referenced. These latter processes are not necessarily part of any overt or even conscious agenda but more often than not pertain to the "unintended consequences" of institutionalized schooling (Willis 1977) as both a cultural *and* social and economic process. A second reason is that as in the friend/enemy distinction *even within* the nation as theorized by Carl Schmitt, what matters is the *possibility* of conflict:[2] as emphasized by Balakrishnan (2000), this potentiality of violent action is always enough for the distinction to be actuated with real consequences.

Furthermore, Maharashtrian—and Indian—modernity is more than a product of the state's attempts, whether at capturing and utilizing its citizens' sensoriums, or at producing bellicose identities. Social actors, whether teachers, parents, or children, are also complicit in these projects, as evidenced by the unabated war culture that remained in Maharashtra long after celebration of war veterans had dwindled and become almost nonexistent in 2003. As we saw throughout this book, very little of the war culture daily produced in its most banalized forms was actually commissioned by the state.

What space is left for those citizens who do not recognize the dominant cultural definition of a nation is a poignant and ever so disturbing question. That Muslims, to name the most targeted and visible of India's non-Hindu minorities, should regularly be called upon to demonstrate their allegiance to the nation is proof enough of the potent and deleterious character of modern political projects of sensory and embodied nationalism. To those citizens whose historical and cultural contribution to the nation has been erased from public view and recognition, a paradox seems to apply: in contrast to the deliberate glossing over of their positive contribution to the formation of the nation, they are given visibility as members of an undesirable community whose distinct features are further strengthened in the process. As a consequence, it has become extremely difficult for a Muslim not to be identified and marked as "a Muslim" in India today, even when he or she is not speaking in that name or from that location. Conversely, it has become impossible to speak openly about Islamic faith or claim any identity other than that of a secular Muslim. By the same token, the secularist view of any markedly Hindu action is de facto a condemnatory one: a teacher conducting daily *puja* in her classroom at the beginning of the school day (Chapter 3) cannot be but a staunch defender of *Hindutva*. Thus, the slightest display of *Hindu* cultural features in public rituals and performances is interpreted as the ultimate proof of the demonic stamp of Hindu right-wing ideology.

What bearing the present political developments have on children-citizens of the twenty-first century as they grow up remains to be seen. Of course, we are more than the total sum of our national backgrounds. These can hardly exhaust the fabulous wealth of material of which we as persons are made. Yet to a large extent, the answer to this question will depend on how children incorporate, make meaning of, and reconstruct existing structures of feeling and senses of belonging, a large part of which will have been reproduced and relayed by various institutions. In a word, the answer lies in the disposition of these citizens-in-the-making for schooling passion.

Referen

Notes

Prologue

1. The formulation is Michael Billig's (1995), echoing Hannah Arendt's reflection on the "banality of evil" (1963).

2. This is so despite the phrase being primarily coined with respect to Western European and North American nations (Billig 1995).

3. The army is another potent source of national integration and stability, as Hobsbawm (1992) pointed out.

4. Conceptual clarification is in order here. In using the term "Hindu," I am aware of the risk of reproducing the categories right-wing nationalists have so actively been promoting in their construction of a Hindu nation, calling into its fold many varied religious traditions. (Ironically, these same categories were reinforced, even if not constructed, in colonial times.) If the category "Hindu" cannot operate as an analytical one, its empirical usages must be must reckoned with, given the wide currency it has gained among ordinary actors.

5. In a pioneering volume published over thirty years ago, Clifford Geertz (1973) discussed the future of postcolonial democracies and analyzed the politics of the post-colonial world in terms of two opposing forces: "primordial attachments" and "civil sentiments." Primordial attachments were based on "blood, race, language, locality, religion, or tradition." Whereas these were understood as disruptive, civil ties were considered a virtuous prerequisite to a harmonious society premised on Western principles of good governance. Thus, irrational imperatives of blood and belonging, ethnicity, language, and race were opposed to the attractions of a sober and rational modernity. Decades later, Geertz maintained that independence was more than a mere transfer of power from colonial structures to "native" ones; it carried with it potential for deeper transformations, those usually associated with democracy, civil

society, public sphere, and citizenship. Essentially it entailed "a metamorphosis of subjects into citizens" (Geertz 2000: chap. 11). However, as noted by Jonathan Spencer, the insistence Geertz and others following him lay on primordial ties as both a focus of analysis and a cause of concern has obscured the factitiousness and contingency of that other, contrapuntal category of "civil ties" (1997: 7). Furthermore, the protracted use of the categories of "civil" and "primordial" amounts to endorsing their historical trajectories as universal(ist) ones—a position against which postmodernists, post-Enlightenmentists, postcolonialists, and other "postists" have been rightly fighting for some time now.

6. See Mabel Berezin (1997, 1999) for an exception documenting political emotions during the Fascist regime.

7. See also Turner (2000) and Fox (2002) for a similar point.

8. Boyer and Lomnitz (2005) discuss the role of intellectuals in the praxis of nationalism.

Introduction

1. This is reminiscent of women's involvement and participation in flag processions during the civil disobedience movement in the 1920s; see Virmani (1999) for an account of the tribulations of the Indian flag and its nationalization of signs of the empire.

2. One of them, a young teacher living in an extended family, even chose nationalist clothes for her kin's offspring. To her sister-in-law, who returned to the maternal home for her first child's delivery in November 2000, she gave an infant's outfit similar to those found in Western countries and increasingly common among the urban middle classes of India. The pattern on this particular outfit consisted of a multitude of little Indian flags and colored balloons.

3. The voices of dissent were few and far between, mostly concentrated in the English press.

4. Interestingly, however, children's pictorial production showed a conflation of both events in their interpretations ("Drawing Gender, Drawing War").

5. There is obviously a difficulty with the term "region," and it is not my intention here to dwell on its wide range of meanings (Cohn 1987b). I am aware of the possible confusion arising from using this term with respect to Maharashtra, since the homonymous state is itself made of what might be called "regions." Nevertheless, I use the term throughout to refer to Maharashtra, especially its western part.

6. Kantorowicz (1981) also discusses a similar process occurring over several centuries in Europe.

7. The names of all schools and people have been changed to ensure confidentiality in accordance with current codes of ethical conduct.

8. There is a larger argument to be made regarding a full embrace of "modern"

spheres, such as the state apparatus or the industrial world—despite earlier projects such as those carried out at Manchester—as worthy objects of study. See Gupta (1995); Herzfeld (1997); Fuller and Benei (2001); Hansen and Stepputat (2001); and Parry on the Bhilai steel plant (e.g., 1999). Moreover, the initial neglect of formal education by anthropologists working in the Indian subcontinent may appear especially surprising given the long tradition of schooling. Formal education there has deep and steep roots in indigenous systems of knowledge predating the British encounter, as well as in colonial negotiated practices, as historians have shown (Basu 1982; Viswanathan 1989; Kumar 1991; Crook 1996).

9. Two educational reports (Kothari, 1964–66, 1986) on which NCERT recommendations were subsequently based were published after independence. The Kothari report is considered to have marked a significant step in the history of education in post-1947 India. The 1986 report was mostly a follow-up, with greater emphasis laid on scientific and vocational education and a concern for universal literacy. A slightly modified version of this report appeared in 1992.

10. In addition to setting national goals, the same schooling pattern should be adopted throughout India. Familiarly known as "10+2+3," it dates from the National Policy of 1966 and is in force in most states today. Students are expected to enter school at the age of six, and after ten years of schooling (presently, five in the primary section and five in the lower secondary), they may take their Secondary School Certificate (SSC). This can be followed by two years of junior college leading to a Higher Secondary Certificate (HSC), after which they may aim for a Bachelor of Arts or Bachelor of Science, to be completed in three more years. In most states, there are no provisions for kindergartens.

11. Attempts made by the coalition to take back power in the state have failed. At the level of local Maharashtra elections, however, the BJP–Shiv Sena coalition has been oscillating between regular comebacks and subsequent defeats. After suffering serious reverses in all the assembly by-elections in 2005 and 2006, the coalition achieved electoral victory in the Brihanmumbai municipal corporation elections in February 2007.

12. The textbook bureau was created in 1967 following the Kothari report of 1966. Aimed at homogenizing primary and lower-secondary education throughout the state, this autonomous body is in charge of preparing textbooks for Classes 1 to 8 in all subjects.

13. Raymond Williams defined the notion of "structure of feeling" in *Culture and Society* (1958) and expanded on it in *The Long Revolution* (1961) thus: "[I]t is as firm and definite as 'structure' suggests, yet it operates in the most delicate and least tangible parts of our activity. In one sense, this structure of feeling is the culture of a period: it is the particular living result of all the elements in the general organization" (1984: 64).

14. Csordas (1999) reviews some of the founding texts on the topic.

15. See, for instance, Classen (1993) on the importance of other senses across

history and cultures. See also Stoller (1989), and, in a somewhat different vein (1997), his suggestive plea for academic sensuousness. Alain Corbin documented the transformations occurring with regard to the other senses in the course of industrialization and technological modernization in the "long 19th century" in France. From a study of the sense of smell and the social construction and imagination of odor (1986), he later analyzed the shifts in the nineteenth-century experiences of auditory landscape and sensory culture (1998); see Sima Godfrey (2002) for a nuanced overview of Corbin's work. The thrust of such a phenomenological history of sensibility was not specifically political. Yet the retracing and documenting of affects together with sensory perceptions opened a suggestive avenue of inquiry. See Christophe Prochasson's plea for a social history of political emotions envisaging symbolic and affective aspects in addition to a cognitive dimension (2002: 431–32); Craig Calhoun's (2001) advocating the articulation of a sociology of emotions (also acknowledging their bodily dimension) with a politics of identity. See also Sophie Wahnich (2002, 2004) for a perceptive argument about the shift in aesthetic sensibilities associated with the period of *La Terreur* during the French Revolution.

16. As I was putting the finishing touches on this manuscript, Prachi Deshpande's beautiful work on historical memory and identity in western India, 1700–1960, was published (2007). My regret is for it not to have been available earlier; my hope is that of possible future conversations between our two books.

17. Pierre Bourdieu and Jean-Claude Passeron (1977) discuss schooling as reproducing and legitimizing the established social order. See also Paul Willis's classic ethnography of schooling among British working-class children (1977); Tim Scrase's study of schooling and social inequalities in India (1993); Aurolyn Luykx's account of limited subversion of, and resistance to, the nation-state pedagogy among Aymara normal school students in Bolivia (1999); Gillian Evans's work on school failure among white working-class children in Britain (2006); and Sam Kaplan's work (2006) on the post-1980s challenges of the Turkish "pedagogical state."

18. So does the tuition paid for after-class tutoring to which many well-off urban middle-class families are increasingly resorting. As for the sociological complexities of the contemporary relationship of Marathi to English as a medium of instruction, I have partly addressed them in Chapter 2 and in Benei (2005c).

19. I consider political socialization to be integral to socialization, and concomitant to early processes thereof, rather than subdued or subsequent to them (Percheron 1974). Conversely, I do not envisage political socialization as a determinant of all processes of socialization.

20. On ethnography as fiction, see Moore (1994).

21. See Dipesh Chakrabarty (2004) for an insightful discussion.

22. This has become a recurrent trope in what is now a diluvian literature on anthropological writing (see the landmark works by Clifford and Marcus 1986; Behar

and Gordon 1995). Considering there is hardly any way out of this predicament for anthropologists, ethnography continues to be the main starting point for base material. The point, however, is that even when "the ethnography is rich," as may be commented, it remains secondary to the researcher's imagination and skills at conveying such richness.

23. The town numbered around 800,000 inhabitants in greater Kolhapur at the time of research, spread over the period 1998–2003.

24. Pune Pandits were notoriously engaged in colonial philological endeavors in the mid-nineteenth century that were instrumental in legitimizing their own version of Marathi as the standard (see Chapter 2).

25. The grandparent generation was generally illiterate, whereas the parents' education was highly gendered: male small farmers and laborers had often been schooled for the first four years of primary education (in the older system), with the wealthiest among them educated up to the first three years of lower secondary schooling (then Classes 5 to 7). The women were either illiterate or had received a modicum of instruction, and more rarely so for the entire period of primary schooling.

26. See Chapters 4 and 5. However, more recent works (Kooiman 2002; Copland 2005) have since shed light on my observations.

Chapter 1

1. See Lelyveld (1995) on musical developments in India, especially the novelty of the harmonium as a European import and its effect on a new harmonic scaling. Bakhle (2005) provides an account of the nationalization of Indian music into "classical music" in the late nineteenth and early twentieth centuries as well as the importance of *bhajan* devotional forms for Hindu proselytizing by "*bhakti* nationalists" (6).

2. Anthony Smith (1999) thoroughly discusses the modalities and typologies of nations through the ages; and Benedict Anderson (1983), their cultural dimensions.

3. For good measure, so, too, did Mussolini much later in his endeavors at securing a Fascist Italian nation (Berezin 1997, 1999).

4. Mosse (e.g., 1975). Since the early nineteenth century, singing and songs have played a central part in Germany in developing and spreading national culture and language among children and, indirectly, within the larger population. Ludwig J. Arnim's collection of "folklore," *Des Knaben Wunderhorn* (*The Child's Wonderhorn*), compiled with Clemens Brentano, defined "German singing stock" (*deutsches Liedgut*) and became part of a tradition salvaged for the purpose of creating German national unity (Thiesse 1999: 63).

5. Abidazeh (2005) discusses Fichte's famous text and its subsequent reception as an icon of German nationalism in the twentieth century.

6. These songs refer to the Germanic saga of Siegfried, the plot of which is also found in the Icelandic *Edda* and the Scandinavian *Völsunga saga*. Although the saga

was written in the early thirteenth century in Austria, Johann J. Bodmer popularized it anew by publishing parts of it in 1757. Richard Wagner partially drew upon it for his well-known *Tetralogie*.

7. Some of these were explicitly anti-Muslim *powada*s celebrating the heroic deeds of Shivaji against Afzal Khan and other representatives of Mughal and Deccan sultanate rules. For a discussion and up-to-date bibliography, see Laine (2003).

8. In many ways, it can be said that the Indian conception of *mantra* is a precursor to contemporary Western theories of performativity (Austin 1962).

9. See Bloch (1975) and Brenneis and Myers (1984) for a discussion relating to other parts of the world.

10. It may seem ironic that the song was officially adopted as India's national anthem (two days before the republic was declared) in 1950, when the British government held it in high regard, rather than "Vande Mataram," the singing of which brought forth accusations of sedition at the time (see Chapter 3 for discussion on a gradual reintroduction of the song in ordinary schools in Maharashtra).

11. Brunner (1963 1:xxxv–xxxvi), quoted in Reiniche and L'Hernault (1999: 38).

12. This standard version originates from Pune. The "lesser quality" (roughness) of Kolhapuri Marathi is even acknowledged by Kolhapuri Brahmins, although somewhat reluctantly. In Kolhapur, teachers of all castes tacitly recognize that Brahmins' claims to better pronunciation are justified. Although such a privilege may be disputed by other castes—including Marathas and former Untouchables—it is still part of a wider symbolic and ideological "common knowledge" (Chapter 2).

13. Reiniche and L'Hernault (1999: 36, emphasis added). In some ways, the enumeration of regions and landscapes in the national anthem is an illustration of the discursive resolution of "rival 'national' identities in the subcontinent . . . through and on the mother's body" (Ramaswamy 1998: 88).

14. By contrast, the songs do not pertain to the repertoire written by Tilak. This bypassing of the Pune Brahmin's contribution may be specific to Kolhapur.

15. "The obligation alone, functioning as an injunction, of performing strictly and in the prescribed order what must be done seems to be governing the daily ritual and ensures its efficiency" (Reiniche and L'Hernault 1999: 36).

16. On Agamic institutionalized learning, see Fuller (2003).

17. Thanks are due to Radhika Singha for pointing this out to me.

18. Rocking to and fro is not specific to this context; rather, it is a pedagogical technique commonly used for memorization in India.

19. On the importance of mapping as pedagogical practice, and especially the body of India, see Ramaswamy (2001, 2004).

20. In many ways, the singing of the nation into existence also amounts to "speaking the national public into existence," thus creating a space for the discursive imagining of the nation (Warner 2002).

21. This occurred even though Tamil non-Brahman Dravidian nationalism was anti-Congress and tended to be pro-British, with the understanding that *swaraj* would amount to *Brahman raj*.

22. The notion of *bhakti* was closely associated with that of language in many ways. Long before any lexicographic endeavor on the part of English and Scottish missionaries in the nineteenth century, Maharashtrian saints played an essential role in forging a flexible, popular language, Marathi, from regional vernacular languages (*prakrits*) (Bayly 1998: 23).

23. Jayant Lele (1981) discusses *bhakti* movements, especially the influential Warkari sect of Pandharpur in Maharashtra.

24. Ramdas is usually associated with *deshbhakti* in the times of Shivaji and, consequently, has also been reappropriated by Hindu militant organizations in Maharashtra for purposes of rallying ordinary devotees to the cause of *Hindutva*.

25. Save for a line later removed concerning the good treatment of animals, the pledge is the exact version of the text proposed for national "emotional integration" in 1961 (*Report of the Committee on Emotional Integration*; Chapter 2).

26. Lorenzen (1996) distinguishes between *saguni* and *nirguni bhakti*—i.e., "with" or "without qualities"—and claims its ideological relevance. According to Hawley (cited in Prentiss 1999: 21–22), however, the distinction *saguni/nirguni* seems predicated on the very localized tradition of sectarian anthologies of *bhakti* poetry in Hindi that were produced in northern India in the sixteenth and seventeenth centuries. In Maharashtra, this distinction seems irrelevant.

27. The songs people aged fifty and over were made to sing as schoolchildren in the 1950s were exclusively in Marathi. Although they were familiar with the Hindi songs as they heard them blasting out from loudspeakers in public spaces or on special occasions, these were not taught as part of a common repertoire in Maharashtra.

28. For an in-depth presentation of *dharma*, see P. V. Kane's magnum opus, *History of Dharmashastra* (1975).

29. Whether the implications in terms of caste ranking associated with the notion are applicable in the schooling context—especially in the use that some Brahmin teachers make of the notion—is unclear. Even fiercely socially aware Dalit teachers shared the notion of *dharma* in its moral meaning and often discriminated between that meaning and the constraining hierarchical implication inherent in the Brahminic interpretation.

30. On the definitional issue of the term "Hinduism," see von Stietencron (1997).

31. Other illustrations pepper the Marathi textbooks, such as Class 3, lesson 2, which presents a poem/song titled "Little Brothers and Sisters" (Chotese bahinbhau). The song replicates the pledge of allegiance while praising the values of amity. It also emphasizes sharing a happy life between sexes, *desh* (here, can refer to country as well as province or region), languages, and costumes (*vesh*). The figure in the school

manual shows a boy and a girl holding hands, among one other girl and three other boys, one of whom is wearing a Muslim cap. The implication—confirmed by some teachers—is that children at this age cannot understand the concept of *jat* or *dharma* but can work on the premise of dress difference. Needless to say, such a premise and its pictorial consequence crystallize representations of otherness, allowing for much more confusion in imaginaries, if only because textbook depictions are often at odds with regional realities. For instance, contrary to textbook representations, married Muslim women did not wear a *salwar-kameez*, whether in Kolhapur or in the rest of Maharashtra. Rather, they wore saris, as other married women did (Chapters 3 and 4, and "Moments of Suspension").

32. Kabir was a fifteenth-century Sufi saint, born to a Hindu widow and raised by Muslim weavers. His poems are revered by Sikhs, Hindus, and Muslims alike.

33. Pers. comm., June 2007.

Chapter 2

1. The word *jat* can refer to both castes and faiths (Chapter 4).

2. Steven Feld (1990 [1982]) is an early exception who paid attention to the physiological aspects of the work of emotions.

3. See also Lyon and Barbalet (1994); Boellstorff and Lindquist (2004); Good (2004); Wilce (2004). Craig Calhoun (2001: 47) also advocated the integration of a reflection on emotions into sociological theory.

4. See Leavitt (1996) for a similar position. What we identify as emotion involves experiences of feeling as much as of meaning, of body as much as of mind. For this reason, these experiences transcend the divisions still operating in theoretical thought (516).

5. Butler (1989: 334–35). See also Csordas (1999) for an excellent review of some of the founding texts on the topic.

6. Margaret Lyon (1995) has also noticed this in her assessment of the anthropology of emotions calling for the end of unproductive dichotomizations.

7. The centrality of the body thus conceptualized has theoretical potential extending beyond anthropological considerations, as can be seen from recent work on emotion in the neuroscience and cognitive sciences. These disciplines share interesting parallels in their theoretical trajectories. Despite the precursory works of Charles Darwin, William James, and Sigmund Freud on different aspects of emotion, neuroscience in the twentieth century until the 1990s tenaciously overlooked the seriousness of emotion as a topic of rational enquiry (Damasio 1999: 38). As in the social sciences, the notion of emotion predominantly stood at the opposite end of reason. Since the mid- to late 1990s, if anthropology has helped thinking about the ways in which emotion is socially constructed, neuroscience and cognitive science have demonstrated the inseparability of consciousness and emotion (16). Bridging a gap between psychobiol-

ogy and social science, Damasio demonstrated how emotion, feeling, and consciousness share the body as an "essence" whose representations they depend upon for their execution (284). But the view that thought processing and rational decision making are necessarily undergirded by emotion does not imply a "bypassing of the subject" in an attempt to get at "what really goes on." Not only does it forcefully reinscribe the notion of emotion at the heart of discourses of rationality but it also leaves room for the work of culture and society in the building of second-order representations "necessary for core consciousness, [and] representations of relationship between organism and object [i.e., emotion]" (280). It is this work of culture and society operating in socialization processes that interests me in the project of emotional incorporation of the nation.

8. This song was written by the iconic Marathi poet and playwright Kusumagraj (1912–99). Kusumagraj, alias Vishnu Waman Shirwadkar, was a man of letters, a political observer, and actor of his times. He took a lead role in the *satyagraha* movement launched by Dr. Ambedkar for allowing Dalits into the Kalaram temple in Nashik in 1932 and was also associated with the linguistic Marathi movement of the 1940s and 1950s. The Samyukta Maharashtra Samiti was instrumental in the creation of the state of Maharashtra in 1960.

9. The quote is worth citing at length, as it explicitly links bodily practices of regimentation with other types of institutions (1990: 167): "If most organizations—the Church, the army, political parties, industrial concerns, etc.—give such a big place to bodily disciplines, this is to a great extent because obedience is belief and belief is what the body grants even when the mind says no (one could, on the basis of this logic, reflect on the notion of discipline)" (1990: 167).

10. This is not the place to recapitulate the history of linguistics and the linguistic turn of the 1960s on either side of the Atlantic. Suffice it to mention two main theoretical strands. One, drawing in part on a long-forgotten article by Pierre Bourdieu (1975) in which he took a stand against the then-prevailing theories of Saussure, Chomsky, Jakobson, and Bloomfield, has in the last ten to fifteen years in the United States sought to reinstate language as a social praxis shot through with ideological configurations of power (Heath 1983). The other has played on Peircian notions of iconicity and indexicality to develop the notion of language meta-pragmatics and examine implicit and explicit commentaries on language and its uses (Michael Silverstein's work in particular).

11. Silverstein (2000) suggestively argues that the erasure of linguistic variation within Anderson's "imagination" is itself an exemplification of a nationalist ideology, rather than its analysis.

12. McDonald (1968a, 1968b). This is not to say that ideas and values were not broadly shared before (Chapter 1). But, as David Washbrook has insisted, "their transmission owed little to uniformities of language" (1991: 180). See Talbot (1995), however, for a refined reevaluation of this claim in the case of Andhra Pradesh.

13. In contrast with other parts of India (Tamilnadu for instance; Ramaswamy 1997), Maharashtra presents an interesting case of accommodation of Hindi as national language, concomitantly with the development of Marathi as a regional *and* national idiom. Today, both idioms serve as powerful vectors of nationalist ideology and knowledge within the regional state. In Kolhapur schools, orders pertaining to the singing of national songs and recitation of the pledge were given in Hindi, whereas the performance was for the most part carried out in Marathi. Similarly, children learned many Hindi national songs, and some teachers taught them compositions of their own for purposes of national celebration (for instance, for Republic Day, January 26). In this dispensation, however, Hindi was made largely subservient to, and encompassed by, Marathi in regional conceptualizations.

14. On the reconfiguration of *desh* in nineteenth-century India, see Goswami (2004). The triadic conceptualization was further deployed in the Marathi Samyukta movement of the 1940s and 1950s; it also bears important similarities to that around the Hindi language ideology in northern India, encapsulated in the famous motto "Hindi! Hindu! Hindusthan!" in the second half of the nineteenth century (Kumar 1992). See also Lelyveld (1993) on the fate of Hindustani in the project of a national language.

15. For instance, it may encompass various situations such as "Let's go and have tea together" (Apan chaha piuya) to "We left early this morning" (Amhi sakali lavkar nighalo) narrated to a third party, to "Our family/country is like this" either to a third party (Amca kutumb/desh asa ahe) or meant inclusively (Apla kutumb/desh asa ahe).

16. In fact, the emotional resonance of the notion of "mother tongue" is such that even scholars writing on the topic (Skutnabb-Kangas and Phillipson 1989) may find themselves beholden to it in a rather "unscholarly" fashion.

17. See Daniel (1984) for a Peircian approach of language and substance in the Tamil case.

18. This understanding of "naturalness" is not confined to ordinary levels of discussion; it also pervades debates between educationists on the respective benefits of learning in one's mother tongue and English (Kumar 1994).

19. Literature on digestion in Hindu thought abounds. See in particular, Malamoud (1975); Parry (1985); Wadley and Derr (1990). Furthermore, if such semantic extension of the notion of digestion is also common in European languages, and here may have come from an English influence, as argued by linguist Ashok Kelkar (pers. comm., December 1998), its redeployment in the Marathi language ideology is nevertheless meaningful.

20. Tariq Rahman (2004) appraises the debates over instruction in English and vernacular in Pakistan. On the colonial period, see also Viswanathan (1989); Kumar (1991); Crook (1996); Zastoupil and Moir (1999); and Kumar (2000), among others. On

the issue of authenticity and language politics in contemporary India, see Rashmi Sadana (2007).

21. The verb *watne* is not a mere overlay but crucially involved in emotional experience itself. In everyday speech, it is used in reference both to emotions and to bodily sensations. The same phenomenon obtains in many other languages, including English (Leavitt 1996: 517). In Marathi, it may also be used for thought, as in "Mala watte, sat varshe jhali astil" (I think this must have [occurred] seven years ago). In addition, the verb can convey a moral judgment, as in "He mala barobar nahi watet" (I do not think this is correct [right]), and also describe emotional, moral, or bodily strangeness or discomfort: "Mala kasa tari watte" (It feels strange/bizarre/uncomfortable to me).

22. Furthermore, if discourses of emotion equally possess a performative dimension whereby to verbally express an emotion may also have an auto-persuasive impact on the speakers themselves (Prochasson 2002: 437), this is arguably the particular case of discourses of embodied language ideologies.

23. Such a project shares much with its historical antecedent, the codification and standardization of the Marathi language (see previous discussion, and Benei 1998 on morality and standardization).

24. Such unruliness is *not* characteristic of members of particular classes or castes: neither class nor caste structures determine students' behaviors and idiosyncrasies, even though bodily hexis (deportment, speech, etc.) may develop and play out differently among children as they grow up. All the students, regardless of class and caste backgrounds, participated in the bedlam. Rather than being clear evidence of differential classes and/or castes requiring different kinds of nationalist embodiments, or of the unruly students acting out an ideal of the nation consisting of the production of class-differentiated subjects through the process of schooling, this instance illustrates human plasticity and resilience to disciplinary projects. Such unruliness, contrary to that documented by Willis (1977) among working-class "lads," is unchanneled, although it is integral to the sense of citizenship that young pupils developed. Where the argument of differentiation in the production of citizens is useful, however, is in the analysis of the negotiation of unruliness: the kind of interpretation teachers construct of unruliness often are themselves indicators of the (re)production of social hierarchies within the space of school.

25. That is, if the concept of "self" still has any meaning distinct from that of "person," as Michelle Rosaldo (1984) has also wondered.

Chapter 3

1. Mehboob Khan's 1957 film *Mother India* offers a remarkably suggestive illustration of this deployment in an era of transition from agrarian to industrial society.

2. One of the most time-consuming chores of women's daily lives in urban India even today is cooking. Despite the increasing availability of ready-made products,

most middle- and lower-middle-class women in Kolhapur spent an average of five hours per day cooking, preparing chapatis, various vegetables, rice, chutney, etc., much of which requires a significant number of stages.

3. See Banerjee and Miller (2003) on various usages of the sari throughout India.

4. Dress code here functions as a field of "symbolization." I should emphasize that all of what I am discussing here pertains to Marathi-speaking schools only. English-speaking primary schools exist in very limited numbers in Kolhapur and cater to a tiny minority of schoolchildren, often from more cosmopolitan backgrounds. The female teachers working there prided themselves on being freer in their dress code. Most of them wore Punjabi suits, regardless of their marital status.

5. Later, we shall see how such a conflation also operates in conceptualizations of the nation, in the association of mother with country. For the moment, the reader may want to remember the encounter with the highly symbolic dimension of the "flag sari" (see Introduction) that women and teachers were seen wearing in Kolhapur and other parts of Maharashtra in 1999 and 2000. Arguably, the symbolism of the flag sari and its functioning as corporeal envelope accrues the production of meaning for a national primary sensorium.

6. However, see Julius Lipner's reconsideration of this issue (2003) in an introduction to his new English translation of Chatterji's magnum opus.

7. Ramaswamy (2006) also documents the complex relationship of the map to the mother in politics of nationalist presentation in the twentieth century.

8. The elderly instructor claimed he had learned the latter in 1970. The date interestingly precedes the war India waged against Pakistan in support of what was to become Bangladesh in 1971.

9. Harlekar (1983: 15). A more common translation is "Victory to Mother-India," but it does not include the vernacular discursive interaction between teachers and children (discussed later).

10. This exchange seems to have been common for at least the last fifteen years in some schools and was acknowledged practice at the official level of the DIET College.

11. See *The Trauma of Birth* (1924).

12. Mitchell describes Klein's work, especially of the later period, as a "fascinating instance of the repression of siblings from observation and theory" (2003: 114). Certainly the sectarian violence between Hindus and Muslims that has shaken the very foundations of the postcolonial Indian nation can be read in terms of competing desires of/for the nation, even though many Muslims objectively reject the figure of Mother-India.

13. In such instances, the teacher's role played an important part in my interaction with the children. I am also aware that my presence and questions may have contributed to heightening awareness of national feelings. Yet the clarification Sonyabai volunteered illuminates ramifications and associations that would otherwise remain unverbalized in most everyday situations.

14. On the relation of Marathi speakers to the Hindi language and slogans in particular, see Chapter 2 and Benei (2001b). Although pupils in the state of Maharashtra do not start learning Hindi until Class 5 (age ten and older), they have numerous occasions to hear the "official language" thanks to the popularity of Hindi movies regularly shown on TV and played in town year-round. Urban middle-class families are great consumers of these movies, whether at home (on TV or, increasingly, video) or in cinemas, with the effect of increasing children's exposure to the Hindi language.

15. "Pahila Namaskar" (literally, "First Salutation") is remarkably congruent with *Hindutva* ideology for its phenomenological incorporation of love of god, family, teacher, and land of birth combined. I heard it sung only in the privately run schools whose educational societies were originally founded by Brahmins. There, it was daily performed in the morning by all pupils from Classes 1 to 4, whether at the time of collective moral education or immediately afterward, in the classroom. "Pahila Namaskar" consists of five strophes, each devoted in turn to God, mother, father, teacher, and motherland, or more precisely, "birthland" (*janmabhumi*). No one was able to confirm its authorship in the schools where it was chanted. According to a college teacher, the composition, syntax, and lexicon (higher number of Marathi words than Sanskrit ones) signaled it as "recent," possibly written fifty or sixty years ago. Although the fourth strophe points to the poem's purpose of being sung in schools, Mr. Patil—now in his midfifties—never had to sing it as a schoolboy. These are the five lines:

Pahila namaskar karito devala	The first salutation I do to God
Ghatle janmala jyane maj-jyane maj (1)	The one who gave me life
Dusra namaskar aila nemane	The second salutation regularly to mother
Vadhavile jine preme maj preme maj (2)	The one who brought me up with love
Tisra namaskar pitayace payi	The third salutation at my father's feet
Theuniya doi karin mi, karin mi (3)	I shall touch his feet with my head
Chautha namaskar guruji tumhala	The fourth salutation to you my teacher/ guru
Shikavita majala avadine, avadine (4)	Who teaches me with liking/fondness/ interest
Pacava namaskar janmabhumi tujala	The fifth salutation to you land of my birth
Vahin dehala tujhya payi. (5)	I will sacrifice my body at your feet.

16. This was most conspicuous in the case of the class held by the elderly instructor presented earlier. As he narrated and sang, most of the listening trainees' body language was reminiscent of enraptured children's, with sparkly eyes, tense muscles, and straightened postures, smiles and head nods being among the most common features. Such moments seem to trigger a process of "reaching out to one's inner child" (to borrow psychologist Erik Erikson's phrase) while drawing on the ritualized productions of infancy.

17. See Ramaswamy (2003) on imaginaries revolving around India's geobody.

18. For instance, cleanliness was high on the teachers' checklist upon the pupils' arrival at school. They would not hesitate to send the children back home, in an endeavor to "teach the parents" a lesson at the same time. In these and other instances, the child was an obvious recipient as well as transmitter of pedagogical-cum-national messages.

19. Chodorow (1994) draws attention to the implicit assumption of homogeneous models of femininity and masculinity that misleadingly reinstate notions of norm and deviance. If anything, these categories are arbitrary and relative (Foucault 1973).

20. As has been argued by feminist theorists, this repertoire of categories was organized around the hetero-/homo- divide that included public/private, masculine/feminine, secrecy/disclosure, ignorance/knowledge, and innocence/initiation (Sedgwick 1990, quoted in Epstein and Johnson 1998: 92).

21. See Tanika Sarkar (2002) in the case of North India, Radha Kumar (1993) for an illustrative overview, and Charu Gupta (2001) for an account of the gendering and communalizing of spaces and its polarizing effect on Hindu and Muslim "communities." Sudipta Kaviraj (2001), too, emphasized the blurring, and at times, overlapping of private and public spaces.

22. Nita Kumar (2005) makes a similar point with reference to the gendering of the history and discourse of education in South Asia.

Chapter 4

1. Thus, the name Shivaji Chhatrapati ("he who is worthy of a ceremonial umbrella," used for kings and rulers) under the Hindu right-wing BJP–Shiv Sena coalition government was officially conferred in 1995 upon the international and domestic airports in Mumbai as well as on the main train station (the latter previously called "Victoria Station," affectionately "V.T.," even today). Hansen (2001) and Jasper (2002) discuss instances of renaming, and their political implications.

2. Prachi Deshpande (2006) also points to the ways in which the Maharashtrian perspective—and its notable lack of opposition toward national discourse throughout the colonial period—brings to bear a more nuanced discussion of the region-nation relationship.

3. Similarly, the state attempts to reach out to parents through their children, and in this sense the family/school relation may also be conceptually reversed, as we shall see further.

4. On instances of textbook analyses with regard to communalism and to class and social inequalities, respectively, see Mohammad-Arif (2005) and Scrase (1993).

5. Since then, the maharaj has been gratified with a *third* date for his birthday celebrations, as a result of further dissensions. Thanks are due to Lee Schlesinger for drawing my attention to this.

6. The other two are the privately run progressive All India Marathi School and an Urdu corporation school; see Chapter 5.

7. It also presented the work of Savitri Bai Phule aimed toward educating girls in the late nineteenth century, which arguably sheds light on the quasi-automatic litany of names that many people of all walks of life would often volunteer when discussing *deivat* and other important people in Maharashtra and India: "Shivaji Maharaj, Gandhiji, Nehru Chacha, Shahu Maharaj, Savitribai Phule, Senapati Bapat, Dr. Babasaheb Ambedkar."

8. See http://www.hillstationsinindia.com/west-india-hill-stations/panhala.html. The use of the term "redolent" makes for an interesting sensory formulation worth pursuing.

9. Although she and her husband were Brahmins originating from the Konkan, they were proud of their Kolhapuri ties of several generations and, with an outsider like myself, often played on both registers of "Konkanicity" (thus justifying their consumption of fish as part of their "coastal background" and "Kolhapuriness," taking great pride in the local—inordinately spicy—cuisine.

10. The fort subsequently came under the control of the Yadava dynasty, then of the Bahamanis of Bidar in the fifteenth century before being absorbed into the kingdom of Bijapur at the start of the sixteenth. Long after Shivaji's rule, Panhala fell to Aurangzeb before the Marathas recaptured the fort and made it their state capital until 1782. In 1844, the British took it over.

11. Lesson 9 (1996: 38–42). Unless otherwise stated, the page numbers are those of the English version, which closely follows the numbering of the original Marathi edition.

12. God Jyotiba is the brother of Kolhapur's goddess Mahalakshmi; her husband is god Tirupati in Andhra Pradesh. Sunday is the day of worship for Jyotiba, and from dawn to about 4 p.m. devotees flock in from the environs to get the *darshan* of the deity. On any given Sunday, the road to Jyotiba is packed with cars, numerous scooters, motorbikes, and municipal buses. On the way back to Kolhapur, passengers without a large smear of purple as *tikka* mark on their foreheads, a sign of one's visit to the temple, are few and far between.

13. Of course, an ethnographic study focusing on the manuals' production would probably reveal the intricacies of power configurations at play.

14. See Benei (2004) on how influential and yet inconspicuous the "Shivaji cinema" of Bhalji Pendharkar has been in promoting particular versions and portrayals of Shivaji. It was in fact sitting through history lessons in Kolhapur primary schools that first made me aware of the importance of Bhalji Pendharkar's "Shivaji cinema." While depicting or clarifying a particular episode, teachers in their forties and fifties would at times refer to "Bhalji Pendharkarance chitrapat" in an attempt to elicit reminiscing of a particular scene among pupils. Yet, interestingly, imaginaries appeared

so powerfully informed by these films that their usage as a mnemonic resource went unnoticed, in the textbooks as well as in classrooms, where the same teachers did not hold Shivaji films influential in their teaching.

15. Pers. comm., Mumbai, summer 2003.

16. The several controversies generated by attempts at revising the textbook in the subsequent decades are in themselves interesting enough to warrant separate treatment. Suffice it to say that the most recent of these controversies occurred in the 1990s; the barely revised textbook raised such a hue and cry that its publication was finally canceled.

17. For ethical reasons, these critics' names will not be mentioned.

18. By the same token, while taking the oath to construct *swaraj*, before meeting with Afzal Khan or before his coronation, Shivaji is portrayed performing pious deeds toward Hindu gods and goddesses, namely, Shambhu Mahadeo and Bhavani (1996: 34–35).

19. See www.atributetohinduism.com/Glimpses_VIII.htm. What secularist critics seem to be ignoring, however, is the symbolic dimension of these narratives of warfare in the phantasmic economy of Shivaji and the Maharashtrian nation. As Laine (1995) points out, the narrative of Shivaji entails the spilling of blood as a form of sacrifice. This is worth pondering because sacrifice of blood is one of the main founding acts of Hindu dynasties (Fuller 1991). Here, not only the enemy's blood is spilled throughout so many textbook pages but also that, sanctifying, of Shivaji's most faithful followers, as some of the lessons reiterate at length (lessons 13 and 17).

20. "Phituranna tyanni kadak shiksha kelya. Mag to apla aso kinwa parka aso." *Parka* refers to "other, foreign, not among one's own," in opposition to *apla* (see discussion in Chapter 2 on the importance of the exclusive pronoun *apla* in a linguistic economy of Marathi belonging).

21. "Tyancya armardalatil adhikari daulatkhan siddi misari, tasec tyanca vakil kajhi haidar he musalman hote. Pan he sare swarajyace nishtavant paik hote" (*Marathi* 1996: 72).

22. According to local scholars, although the nineteenth-century Mali gardener and eager social reformer has become an icon of progress, his version of Shivaji as the defender of the downtrodden has had little currency within the population at large, whether in urban or in rural areas.

23. For that matter, this masculinity is closer to that embodied by Shivaji's impersonator on the movie screen (Chandrakant Mandare), notably in Bhalji Pendharkar's films.

24. The Marathi original is more succinct, emphasizing the theatricality of rank and stature through bodily positionings. Furthermore, in contrast with the indirect style used in the English translation, the Marathi text presents the scene as a first-person reflection by Shivaji, thus in a more direct and engaging form: "We are the king

of Maharashtra; we should be made to *sit* in the *first* row. But the emperor is making us *stand* in the *back* row; what is this supposed to mean?" (emphasis added; Apan Maharashtrace raje, apla man pahilya ranget basnyaca. Pan Badshahane aplyala magil ranget ubhe karave mhanje kay?).

25. "Swoosh" seeks to render the adverb *khaskan*, an onomatopoeic imitation of the sound imagined to indicate a sudden, strategic blow. The entire passage in Marathi reads thus: "Atyant chapalaine [Shivajinni] bichwa khaskan Khanachya potat khupasla. Khanaci atadi baher padali. Khan kosalla" (36).

26. The expression *poti jagne* (literally, "to be born in the belly of") also means "to spring from," *whether* the female parent *or* the male.

27. Conversion (here, to Islam) has often been interpreted as loss of Hindu manhood in the history of the subcontinent; Menon (2002) discusses attendant anxieties following Partition and during the program of recovery of abducted women.

28. The passage on the ruler's large-heartedness and religious tolerance is itself ambiguous even in its English rendering: "Shivaji showed respect for all religions. He never hated Muslims simply because they were Muslims" (73).

29. The tradition is by no means recent: it harks back to the shift in the late nineteenth century from debates between cultural nationalists and social reformists about age of consent and other issues to assertion of the centrality of the mother-son relationship, both in family life and as a model and source of patriotic devotion to the motherland (Kumar 1993; Sarkar 1995, 2001; Setalvad 1995; Goswami 2004), whose reconstruction was intricately interwoven with that of a Muslim other (see Gupta 2001 for a suggestive account).

30. Indiscernibility may exist only in cases of dominant, majoritarian identities being coproduced. At the level of the region, the dominant hegemonic Maharashtrian identity is primarily constructed as a Hindu one and is therefore in accordance with the larger national one whose iconic representation has become the "Hindu Mother-India Goddess." By contrast, for Muslim children (Chapter 5), mainstream schooling itself produces a distinct, "othered" identity that may generate a desire for majoritarian adherence or, more simply, a "hegemonic subject," as in the case of Aymara (older) students in Bolivia documented by Aurolyn Luykx (1999). The phrase accounts for the fact that "the subject positions being created [by the students] are not under students' control and are also ideologically naturalized rather than being made vulnerable to critique" (304). But this "othered" identity may also further strengthen a sense of alienation from the national or the regional community.

31. See Benei (1996); Appadurai (1996) on the imbrication of scales at *any* given level; Tambiah (1997) on the dynamics of riots articulating local and national issues; Brass (1997) and Varshney (2002) for contrasted discussions of economic competition as a crucial dimension of communal riots.

32. On the notion of memoryscape, see Jennifer Cole (2001).

33. Lesson 18 (70). By contrast, one of his lieutenants, strong and valiant Tanaji, who loses his life in battle, is referred to as "father" of the Mawlas. Significant here is that Shivaji does not die in combat, therefore not "living the death" of great hero-warriors befitting "real fathers" in this sociocosmic order. Interestingly, Shivaji's androgynous quality resurfaces in an analogy between him and his beloved subjects, "a mother who loves her children" (70). Rather than insist on a potential fatherly figure, the narrative resorts to a motherly bond to define the type of relationship Shivaji entertained with his subjects. This—if only analogical—androgyny goes against the grain of *Hindutva* masculine recuperations of the Maratha hero and certainly calls for further exploration.

34. See introduction in Centlivres, Fabre, and Zonabend (1999).

Chapter 5

1. All Urdu institutions are attended only by Muslims, although the converse is not true. Moreover, Urdu speakers in India number almost 44 million (*Census of India* 1991). The largest numbers reside in the state of Uttar Pradesh, followed by Bihar, Andhra Pradesh, Maharashtra, and Karnataka, accounting for 85 percent of the national Urdu-speaking population. Accurate figures for Muslim children according to school type and medium of instruction were hard to obtain in Kolhapur since the collection of this information is not mandatory.

2. See Dhooleka Raj (2003) for a discussion of the notion of "community" in the case of the South Asia diaspora.

3. Muslims represent 13.4 percent of the total Indian population (per the 2001 census), 10.6 percent in Maharashtra, and approximately 6 or 7 percent in Kolhapur.

4. Whereas some historians have focused on the unity inherent in diverse Islamic reform movements (Metcalf 1982), and the political and literary activities of the Urdu-educated elite in northern India in the nineteenth and twentieth centuries (Ahmad 1967; Ahmad and Grunebaum 1970), others have paid closer attention to the interaction with British colonial power and the role of a new educational system in the transformation of a sense of "Muslimness" from the mid-nineteenth century onward (Lelyveld 1978). Yet others have highlighted the homogeneous perceptions and attendant polarizations resulting from colonial encounters (Hasan 1985; Robinson 1985; Pandey 1990). Much of the discussion in the subcontinent nevertheless tends to center on imaginary and invented notions of Muslim cultural homogeneity and continuity (Jalal 1997). Even within the Muslim Urdu-speaking intelligentsia, the entailments of being Muslim were hotly debated. It may be, as Marshall Hodgson argued, that wherever Islam has spread, there has been a continual pressure to persuade all Muslims to adopt the same standards and ways of living, accompanied by a keen consciousness of the world Muslim community and a sense of a common cultural heritage. But, as Robinson remarks (1985: 345), "this is a far cry from saying that these fundamental ideas . . . bore the same meaning for all Muslims."

5. The latest institution was created in 1993 by a locally influential Islamic society, the Sunnat Jamaat. This society rents out the building for the Urdu school in Sachar Bazar.

6. In most rural areas of southern Maharashtra, Urdu educational facilities were not available.

7. See later discussion. Hindi is considered the official language in India and is dubbed "national" across the northern part of the peninsula (Chapter 2). Although Hindi and Urdu differ mainly in written form (see Lelyveld 1993), Maharashtrians largely view them as two radically different languages, two ethnic religious and national markers.

8. The school sometimes employs temporary non-Hindu teachers. In the academic year 1998–99, for instance, there was one young Muslim teacher out of twenty staff.

9. See Chapter 4 on the anxieties surfacing in a number of accounts of failed or reprehensible conversion to Islam on the part of Shivaji's lieutenants.

10. A corporator is a member of a neighborhood who is elected by its residents to represent them at the level of the municipal corporation.

11. It was in fact cast by a Turkish officer in the regiment of the king of Ahmadnagar (en route to Aurangabad) and moved to and refitted in Bijapur after being won as a war trophy. Material prowess was also a topic of the guide's marveling: the gun could fire five 40 kg bullets at a distance of twelve kilometers, hence its name "Lord-of-the-plains" (*Malik-e-maidan*). It still retains its character today, with fine casting and artwork bearing inscriptions in Arabic and Persian.

12. Named Vijayapura (literally "city of victory") during the Chalukya dynasty (sixth–ninth centuries), it was the capital of the Yadava dynasty in the twelfth and thirteenth centuries before falling into the hands of the sultan of Delhi, Alaa ud-Diin Khaljii. It was taken over by the rising Bahmani kings of Bidar in 1347. A century and a half later, it became the capital of the Indo-Muslim dynasty of the Adil Shahi.

13. In this way, school life was punctuated by the rhythm of daily religious life, with each muezzin call to prayer coming from the adjacent mosque.

14. *Ramzan* (*Id-Ul-Fitr*), celebrated by Muslims all over India, refers to breaking of the fast of the holy month of Ramadan; alternatively, the term is used to refer to the fasting period of Ramadan.

15. Some Muslim intellectuals had done the same in the late nineteenth and early twentieth centuries with the Khilafat movement (Ahmad 1967).

16. Abul Kalam Azad was even averse to the label "Muslim" because this category took no account of his distinct position and obfuscated the fundamental differences he had with other Muslim organizations (e.g., the Muslim League, or the Jamaat-e Islami; Hasan 1992: 5).

17. Among them, Shahu Maharaj and "Chacha Nehru" were clear favorites. More than the promoter of education for all, Shahu represented to children the king with animal trophies in his palace. Nehru was favored because of the founding role he

had played in the building of a secular, socialist, and progressive India. Also, he was known to get along well with children, so he was more approachable than the daunting, bespectacled Dr. Ambedkar, however much revered the awe-inspiring "writer of the Constitution" and Untouchable leader was.

18. Such warnings targeting non-Marathi speakers was in keeping with the rhetoric dominant among educational officials, whether in Pune or Kolhapur.

19. The headmaster also made sure that the national news would be read to the students every morning, in conformity with official instructions and as also observed in most Marathi schools.

20. They, too, made references to the trope of the mother and, although less explicitly establishing a connection between mothers, teachers, and the nation, accompanied with performance of calisthenics—more than ever scrupulously followed since the new headmaster's arrival—thereby created the means for an incorporation of the nation.

21. Furthermore, according to Shaheen Hussain, former corporator in the adjacent neighborhood and social worker, the twenty-one mosques existing in Kolhapur had links with the Tablighi Jama'at in the late 1990s (pers. interview, February 23, 1999). Some of the families interviewed openly acknowledged their links with the Tablighi Jama'at, adding that almost every Muslim family in the neighborhood were followers. Evidence of this, in their views, lay in the large number of local residents attending the international gatherings in Kolhapur in late 1997 and mid-1998 with followers from France and the United States, and from Yemen and Thailand, respectively.

22. They do so regardless of how historically inaccurate or methodologically problematic the notion of "their ancestors" is.

23. The phrase "Muslim world" is borrowed from Eickelman and Piscatori (1996: 37–38), although they do not specify whether it defines a project or a reality.

24. There is a real risk of ghettoization inherent to Urdu-medium schooling in Maharashtra. For this reason, Marathi-educated Muslim social activists and educationists tend to favor the creation of Urdu classes *within* Marathi schools. In this respect, it is no coincidence that permission was given to open 350 more Urdu schools throughout the state under the BJP–Shiv Sena coalition in power at the regional state level from 1995 to 1999.

25. Stephan Feuchtwang (pers. comm., July 29, 2004).

Chapter 6

1. Its aim was to serve farmers' information needs on different cultivation practices of major crops, pest and disease control, marketing information, and dairy and sugarcane processing. *The Times of India*, June 1, 2002; *Manage Bulletin*, April–May 1999, www.manage.gov.in/managelib/bulletin/Current/aprmay99.htm.

2. An orchestra, created in 1970, searches for members among children from all of the above-mentioned institutions. It has already traveled to many places outside India.

3. It is understood that the local is not a given but a contested field of historical imaginings and affective reappropriations, as shown in Chapters 4 and 5.

4. See, for instance, Gill (1997) on Bolivia; Addelston and Stirratt (1996) on the United States.

5. At issue are not oppositional structures of a binary kind: the hybridity I am referring to is *not* a cross of *two* species only, as the use of the term might suggest in the natural sciences. It is an embrace of *several* ideologies, regardless of their definition at a given moment; such a conception obviously acknowledges the transient and unstable nature of these ideologies.

6. According to the principal, the students who do not pass the National Defense Academy (NDA) prepare for the Indian Service Union Public Service Commission and the Maharashtra Public Service Commission. The former is meant for aspiring Indian Administrative Service (IAS) officers, the latter for Tahsildars.

7. In the roll for the year 2000–2001 at the Pratinagar Sainik School, the fathers of two boys were MLAs, one from the Shiv Sena, the other from the Shetkari Kamagar Paksha (Farmers' and Workers' Party), independent from both the Shiv Sena and the Congress.

8. I interviewed most of the new military school directors at the time of a meeting held at Pratinagar in December 2000; their political sympathies appeared to range from *Hindutva* to former Congress in equal proportions. Moreover, the schools were allowed to continue after the next new Congress government came into power in 1999, although, granted, under strenuous financial circumstances hotly discussed in the course of the above meeting.

9. When, in response to his question, I explained to the chairman that such military schools existed in "my country" only for students aged seventeen and older, he opined that it was too late then: "It has to be developed, the right thing, from an early age: starting right after Class 4 is a good thing" he went on, because the time is ripe; it is when they "start to think" and "will develop affection [*sic*] toward the entire nation."

10. No member of staff was trained in a military school, either as a child or later in secondary studies. The common denominator to most of them was the education they received in one or several of Pratinagar's institutions.

11. See Enloe (1980: 36–37); Cohen (2002).

12. A discrepancy, however, gradually surfaced between general parental display of loyalty to the nation and families' revised positions as national and international events unfolded and the media reported human losses in Kargil. Over the period 1999–2001, even the most ardent patriots among parents felt increasingly disinclined to see their sons embrace a military career (only 25 percent remained in favor of the idea).

13. About 74 percent of the student body was composed of members of the Maratha or allied castes in 2000–2001. The rest belonged to the following groups: Mahars,

Mangs, and Chambhars (15 percent); Jains (less than 6 percent); Brahmins (less than 3 percent); Muslims (less than 1.6 percent); and only one Christian.

14. Such a conception of the military as a site where discipline is learned and taught effectively is not specific to Maharashtrians, or Indians, for that matter. At the time when I grew up in France, the virtues of discipline were also largely associated with military pedagogy, and it was not uncommon to hear parents threatening their sons (more rarely their daughters) with the prospect of sending them to a military school "to teach them discipline." This view was similarly shared in the United States in the 1980s, even among mothers who saw the military as a last resort for their sons' betterment (Forcey 1987: esp. chap. 7).

15. http://www.princeton.edu/~ferguson/adw/mao.shtml.

16. By contrast, at Pratinagar, each class had an average of forty-five pupils, and there were eight teachers: one for math and science; another one for math (the only female teacher); one for English; one for Hindi; one for drawing, history, and geography; one for computer studies; and two for PT (including the military instructor, *sainya*).

17. Four houses are allocated, so that each one has an approximately equal number of Class 5, 6, 7, and 8 students (one-fourth of each class). Every house is assigned a different color (blue, red, yellow, green) to be worn by its respective members. All sports competitions take place between the houses. Both horizontal (between peers in each classroom) and vertical (across divisions) solidarity and competition are thus encouraged by the formal organization of relations in the school.

18. This is rather unusual: dental hygiene in Maharashtra is more often a morning-only duty marking the beginning of day.

19. On how representations of time pertain to multiple temporal and social orders, and the extent to which they are negotiable within specific institutional contexts, see Greenhouse (1996).

20. The gendered body becomes "performative," according to the notion Judith Butler developed in her pioneering essay reconceptualizing gender. Performativity refers to "acts, gestures, and desire produc[ing] the effect of an internal core or substance, but produc[ing] this on the surface of the body. . . . Such acts, gestures, enactments, generally construed, are performative in the sense that the essence of identity that they otherwise purport to express becomes a *fabrication* manufactured and sustained through corporeal signs and other discursive means" (1989: 337). This formulation of "surface" performativity adequately qualifies the stages of daily production of bodies at the Pratinagar Sainik School, following the "deep" embodiment of the first four years of primary schooling.

21. Unlike what occurs in most all-English-language institutions, there was no ban on speaking a vernacular language outside the classroom, and teachers encouraged the use of all three idioms.

22. In the school year 1998–99, these included *yogasan*, superstition (*anddha-*

shradha), students' health (*arogya*), the importance of military instruction, sports, road rules for traffic, valley crossing and trekking, martial arts, moral edification through stories exemplifying good filial and institutional conduct (*goshtirupatun samskar*), the importance of healthy teeth, child psychology (*bal manashastra*), and body building.

23. The measurement of weight determined the pupils' division into three groups (overweight, normal, and underweight), with special exercises and personalized diets for members of the first and third groups, respectively.

24. At Pratinagar, the pupils were not forced to engage with "Western food," unlike in the elite schools and the military, whether in colonial or postcolonial times (Cohen 2002; for a suggestive rendering of the extreme physical reaction experienced by eating the "traditional British eggs and bacon," see Ghosh 2000).

25. To give an example of how minute the calculations were, considering that two chapatis weighed 57 grams, out of which there are 5 grams of protein, 5.5 of fat, and 193 calories, the principal had figured out that on Mondays children should absorb 39.435 grams of fat, 50.969 grams of protein, and 1,585.88 calories.

26. Such a project of self-formation also emphasized the concept of *brahmacharya*, both as a referent to sexual abstinence and spiritual self-discipline reconfiguring the body in order to serve the nation (to be discussed later).

27. Connell (1993, 1995a, 1995b); Gill (1997); Collier (1998). On the variegated constructions of masculinity within different sectors of the U.S. Army, see also Barrett (1996).

28. This is especially important in the case of Indian masculinity: as Rustom Bharucha observed, "men in India—cutting across class, community, and ideology—have yet to dismantle the constructions of their own gender and sexuality" (1995: 1613).

29. As we saw, *women* play a prominent and visible part in those daily spheres, contrary to the all-male invested one of the military school (Benei 2002b; Chapter 3).

30. The siege of harm was the stomach, which in Marathi is the seat of emotions and much more (Chapter 4). It is often used metaphorically to refer to a traumatic event, e.g., the national shame incurred by the loss of a battle that goes "undigested" (*apacavleli*). Furthermore, it is a primary site mediating children's various pains, whether purely physiological, organic, or psychosomatic (anxiety, fear, and so on).

31. This dispensation of gender roles contrasts greatly with the "division of labor" at play in other contexts. In Nicaragua, for instance, it is the women who publicly "cry, and plead, and moan at the prospect of military service," thereby supplying what Lancaster calls "the antidote to men's machismo about these matters" (and apparently also to men's own appreciation; 1992: 196–97).

32. The shirking stood along a continuum ranging from sheer compliance to passive resistance. Such a range of actions and strategies has been observed in other military settings (Hockey 1986). Yet it is also characteristic of many other social and power

relations. Here, it is strikingly similar to that deployed by married women in adjusting to their new marital homes and functions (Benei 2005b).

33. It is significant that even apparently "genderless" discussions of discipline among social actors in Kolhapur were nevertheless gendered: parents always evoked military schools and the possibility of sending their children there in relation to boys alone, despite the existence of one military school for girls.

34. See Gilmore (1990) for a general account, although with the caveat of his positivist stance: for him, as rightly noted by Cornwall and Lindisfarne (1994: 27), "both masculinity and men are 'real,' 'out there' and amenable to 'scientific' study."

35. Furthermore, inflicting pain was not part of the pedagogy. Its emergence was avoided and its occurrence resolved, rather than cultivated.

36. Whether this rule was systematically observed is, of course, difficult to assess. Yet the students' respectful behavior toward the women rarely around them was remarkable. It certainly appeared far removed from the mutual nudging and casting of concupiscent glances toward any representative of the other sex common among ordinary schoolboys that age.

37. Nandy (1988), cited in Bharucha (1995). Nandy's categories may be essentialized ones, "operating at the level of principles rather than historical difference" (1614). But as Bharucha acknowledges, "[T]hey offer a grid for possible contentions and speculations on alternative masculinities" (1614).

38. This is so for obvious reasons of fieldwork constraints.

39. It is far from the average 6 percent in ordinary schools in Kolhapur. Furthermore, Adivasis in the directors' rhetoric were also excluded from the vision of progress proffered by these new *sainik* schools. Throughout the board's meeting, reference to Adivasis as an embodiment of "pampered minorities" operated as a contrapuntal leitmotif.

Conclusion

1. Granted, such a reflection would entail questioning the relevance of this concept for anthropologists, who at first blush appeared the best equipped to comment upon the relative and strategic value of the concept of "modern." More often than not, however, they have enthusiastically embraced the notion. Yet, as Spencer pointed out (1996), the latter suggests rather untenable absolutism in its apprehension of social change in any given society.

2. All of these new modes might be termed "modern" by contrast to what preceded in the local *longue durée*. The difficulty, of course, is to ensure that the historical lens adopted to envision the *longue durée* is of a long enough scope. The colonial encounter, along with the advent of colonial modernity in South Asia, is a case in point. On the one hand, one may see in the colonial encounter a radical break from existing structures of social and political governance. The kind of state effects described by

Foucault with reference to Europe have also been at play since the nineteenth century in India, albeit in a less totalizing form for historical reasons related to the limited expanse of the British Raj, a fact often left in oblivion in discussions of matters colonial in India, as historian Ian Copland (1990) has insisted. On the other hand, some schemas, especially linguistic and cultural, appear to have been redeployed through to the present day in postcolonial India, contributing to the shaping of contemporary political forms of modernity.

3. See Andrew Apter (2002) on imperial assemblages as colonial state spectacles producing new epistemologies of knowledge (or at least, new redeployments in visual practices) in Africa; Mary Ann Steggles (1997) on the Bombay presidency in the nineteenth century; Chris Pinney (2003), among others. That sight became the primary mode of acquiring and producing knowledge during colonial times is evidenced in both colonials' and the indigenous population's promoting—at times competing, at other times colluding—"performative displays" as well as "visions," "images," and "visual practices" that progressively (re)shaped a general episteme. Even newspapers bear direct relation to this process, not only because of Ben Anderson's so-oft discussed argument of print capitalism (whereby a community of readers would imagine itself as a community of nationals), but also because of publishing being part of a process of making things *visible* in order to make them understandable. On another level, mapping and charting of all kinds, as Anderson and others (Cohn 1987a in particular) have noted, were also integral to cognitive operations of "making visible."

4. Jonas Frykman (1996) makes a similar point in his account of gymnastics as everyday lived production and sensory experience of modernity in Sweden in the 1930s.

5. Teachers never commented upon this, whether at school or privately. This is not to say that their silence was always deliberate. What stood out most in their accounts of the SMART PT training they had undergone was the value of the new pedagogical approach placing the child at the center of educational attention and promoting interactive learning. This, however, was matched with an equal measure of resignation in the face of such an impractical task in overcrowded classrooms.

6. After the initial few weeks of conscientious application, some schools and teachers would promptly revert to the old routine; whereas in others, they added a few elements from the new program. In other institutions, most of the changes took place in teachers' classrooms alone, whereas the bulk of the morning liturgies remained unchanged.

Epilogue

1. Kantorowicz (1981) discusses the Christic aspects of the notion of *patria*.

2. To be sure, the question arises of the conditions that might give rise to a generalization of friend/enemy distinctions. Here, economic and political conditions certainly play a crucial part. Yet they do not exhaust the total field of possibilities.

Glossary

This selective glossary is exclusively devoted to Marathi words, although some of these are common to other languages (e.g., Hindi, Urdu, Sanskrit). The glossary only supplies meanings strictly relevant to this book. It also excludes names and terms occurring only once or twice in the text. For the transliteration system, please see "Note on Transliteration"; listed in parentheses are words whose common spelling is used when diacritics are removed.

āī (*ai*): mother

alaṅkāra (*alankara*): decoration ritual performed during *puja*, involving the re-creation of a goddess (*devi*)

āmce, -ā, -ī: our, our own (exclusive)

āmhī: we (exclusive)

āpaṇ: we (inclusive)

āple, -ā, -ī: our, our own (inclusive)

aswābhāvik: unnatural, alien, improper, contrived

bālawādī: kindergarten

barobar: right, correct, just, good

bhajana: hymn, adoration, singing in praise of a deity

bhakti: deep devotion, worship, attitude of loving devotion to deity; refers to stream of Hinduism emphasizing such devotion; cf. *deśbhakti*

Bhārat (Bharat): India

Bhārat Mātā (Bharat Mata): term used to refer to India as a mother-goddess or
    "Mother-India"

bhāṣā (*bhasha*): language; cf. *bolī bhāṣā, mātṛ bhāṣā, prāmāṇit bhāṣā, swabhāṣā*

bhāū: brother

bhāūbaṇḍ (*bhauband*): kinsman, brotherhood

bolī bhāṣā: oral speech, dialect, spoken language

cāngale (*cangle*), -*ā*, -*ī*: good, proper

cukṇe: to make a mistake, to err (also, to miss)

darśana (*darshan*): sight, vision (of a deity)

deivat: god, deity, object of idolizing, pet, darling; also used affectionately for
    Shivaji Maharaj; cf. Śivājī

deś (*desh*): land, country, nation, region; also smaller unit of territorial
    belonging, homeland, *patria*; cf. *deśbhakti, swadeś*

deśbhakti (*deshbhakti*): devotion to the land, loyalty to the homeland,
    patriotism

dharma: way of life, ethics, religion; cf. *swadharma, Hindū dharma*

gāō: village; but also, and by extension, district, region, country

ghar: house, home

gīta (*git*): song; cf. *rāṣṭragīta*

Gyāneśwar (Dnyaneshwar): thirteenth-century *bhakti* saint and poet of
    Maharashtra

Gyāneśwarī (Dnyaneshwari): epic poem, Marathi commentary on the
    Bhagavad Gita, written by Gyāneśwar; it is considered one of the great
    foundational texts of Marathi language and literature

Hindavī swarājya (*Hindavi swaraj*): own rule or dominion of "those who are
    from the Hind"

Hindū dharma (*Hindu dharma*): Hindu ethics, way of life, religion

Hindutva (*Hindutva*): "Hinduness," Hindu nationalism

jāt (*jat*): caste, group, kind, species, class, tribe; but also faith, in the Marathi
    school context

jawān (*jawan*): soldier

jay: conquest, victory, triumph; also used as exclamation in praise of a god, a hero, etc., as in "Bharat Mata ki Jay" (Victory to Mother India); cf. *jayjaykar karṇe*

jayjaykar karṇe: to celebrate the praises of, to extol with acclamations and shouts

kīrtana (*kirtan*): celebration of the praises of a god with music and singing

mantra: ritual formula, chant

mātṛ bhāṣā (*matru bhasha*): mother tongue

nāgarik (*nagarik*): citizen

naitik śikṣaṇ (*naitik shikshan*): moral, ethical education

namaskār: salute, salutation

paripāṭha (*paripath*): habitual action, custom; at school, the routine performed during morning assembly

pāṭhāñtara (*pathantar*): recitation, something learned by heart; at school, it usually includes basic notions learned so far in the year, and it is performed following the *paripāṭha*, once in the classroom

pavitra: holy, sacred

prāmāṇit bhāṣā (*pramanit bhasha*): standard, authoritative language

prārthanā (*prarthana*): prayer

pratigyā (*pratidnya*): pledge, promise; at school, the pledge of allegiance to the Indian nation; it may be recited in English, Hindi (official language), or Marathi (regional language)

pūjā (*puja*): worship

rāṣṭra (*rashtra*): nation; cf. *rāṣṭragīta*

rāṣṭragīta (*rashtragit*): national anthem

śāḷā (*shala*): school

saṃskār (*samskar*): rite, but also and more commonly purification, improvement, refinement; also designates a state of being cultured, well reared, and of refined taste, accomplished

sanātana dharma: eternal religion, term for Hinduism among modern reformist Hindus

saṃskṛti (*sanskruti*): civilization, culture: *Bhārtīya saṃskṛti* (*Bhartiya samskruti*): Indian culture

sāwadhān (*sawdhan*): "Attention!"; call to attention marking the beginning of both military and nationalist school drills, as well as ending the first ritual in wedding ceremonies in Maharashtra

śikṣaṇ (*shikshan*): education, instruction, teaching; cf. *naitik śikṣaṇ*

śista (*shista*): discipline, focus; as adjective, "proper"

Śivājī (Shivaji): seventeenth-century Maratha king, considered the founder of the Maratha nation

śloka (*shlok*): strophe, stanza

suvicār (*suvichar*): good thought, proverb

swabhāṣā (*swabhasha*): one's own language; one of three notions central to the definition of senses of belonging in Maharashtra; see also *swadeś* and *swadharma*

swābhāvik (*swabhavik*): natural, native, proper, simply, spontaneously; cf. *aswābhāvik*

swadeś (*swadesh*): one's own country; one of three notions central to the definition of senses of belonging in Maharashtra; see also *swabhāṣā* and *swadharma*

swadharma: one's own religion, ethics, way of life; one of three notions central to the definition of senses of belonging in Maharashtra; see also *swadeś* and *swabhāṣā*

swarājya (*swaraj*): own rule or dominion; cf. *Hiṇdavī swarājya*

trās (*tras*); *trās yeṇe*, *trās deṇe*, *trās hoṇe*: trouble, harm (can be psychological, emotional, as well as physical); to come to harm, to inflict harm, for harm to happen

uccār: pronunciation

vīr (*vir*): hero, warrior, intrepid fighter

wāīṭ (*wait*): bad, wrong, evil, foul, filthy, dirty, objectionable

yātrā (*yatra*): pilgrimage, procession; by extension, trip

Bibliography

Abélès, Marc. 2005 [1990]. *Anthropologie de l'État*. Paris: Payot.

———. 2006. *Politique de la survie*. Paris: Flammarion.

Abizadeh, Arash. 2005. "Was Fichte an Ethnic Nationalist? On Cultural Nationalism and Its Double." *History of Political Thought* 26 (2): 334–59.

Abu-Lughod, Lila. 1986. *Veiled Sentiments: Honor and Poetry in a Bedouin Society*. Berkeley: University of California Press.

———. 1990. "Shifting Politics in Bedouin Love Poetry." In *Language and the Politics of Emotion*, edited by Lila Abu-Lughod and Catherine Lutz, 24–45. Cambridge: Cambridge University Press.

Abu-Lughod, Lila, and Catherine Lutz, eds. 1990. *Language and the Politics of Emotion*. Cambridge: Cambridge University Press.

Addelston, Judi, and Michael Stirratt. 1996. "The Last Bastion of Masculinity: Gender Politics at the Citadel." In *Masculinities in Organizations*, edited by Cliff Cheng, 54–76. London: Sage Publications.

Ahmad, Aziz. 1967. *Islamic Modernism in India and Pakistan, 1857–1964*. London: Oxford University Press.

———. 1999 [1964]. *Studies in Islamic Culture in the Indian Environment*. Delhi: Oxford University Press.

Ahmad, Aziz, and G. E. von Grunebaum, eds. 1970. *Muslim Self-Statement in India and Pakistan 1857–1968*. Wiesbaden, Germany: Otto Harrassowitz.

Ahmed, Akbar S. 1988. *Discovering Islam: Making Sense of Muslim History and Society*. London: Routledge and Kegan Paul.

———. 1992. *Postmodernism and Islam. Predicament and Promise*. London: Routledge.

Alter, Joseph. 1993. "The Body of One Color: Indian Wrestling, the Indian State and Utopian Somatics." *Cultural Anthropology* 8 (1): 49–72.

———. 1994. "Celibacy, Sexuality, and the Transformation of Gender into Nationalism in North India." *Modern Asian Studies* 53:45–66.

———. 2000. *Gandhi's Body. Sex, Diet and the Politics of Nationalism*. Philadelphia: University of Pennsylvania Press.

Amalvi, Christian. 1988. *De l'art et la manière d'accommoder les héros de l'histoire de France: essai de mythologie nationale*. Paris: Albin Michel.

Amin, Shahid. 1995. *Event, Metaphor, Memory: Chauri Chaura, 1922–1992*. Berkeley: University of California Press.

———. 2005. "Representing the Musalman: Then and Now, Now and Then." In *Muslims, Dalits, and the Fabrications of History*, edited by Shail Mayaram, M. S. S. Pandian, and Ajay Skaria, 1–35. New Delhi: Permanent Black.

Anderson, Benedict. 1991 [1983]. *Imagined Communities. Reflections on the Origin and Spread of Nationalism*. London: Verso.

Anzieu, Didier. 1989. *The Skin Ego*. New Haven, Conn.: Yale University Press. (Orig. pub. 1985.)

Appadurai, Arjun. 1996. *Modernity at Large: Cultural Dimensions of Globalization*. Minneapolis: University of Minnesota Press.

Apter, Andrew. 2002. "On Imperial Spectacle: The Dialectics of Seeing in Colonial Nigeria." *Comparative Studies in Society and History* 44 (3): 564–96.

Arendt, Hannah. 1963. *Eichmann in Jerusalem: A Report on the Banality of Evil*. New York: Viking Press.

Arfuch, Leonor. 2002. *El espacio biográfico. Dilemas de la subjetividad contemporánea*. Buenos Aires: Fondo de Cultura Económica.

Ariès, Philippe. 1965. *Centuries of Childhood: A Social History of Family Life*. New York: Vintage Books. (Orig. pub. 1960.)

Asad, Talal. 1993. *Genealogies of Religion: Discipline and Reasons of Power in Christianity and Islam*. Baltimore: Johns Hopkins University Press.

Assayag, Jackie. 1997. "Le corps de l'Inde. La carte, la vache, la nation." *Gradhiva* 22:14–29.

———. 2001. *L'Inde. Désir de nation*. Paris: Odile Jacob.

Audoin-Rouzeau, Stéphane. 1993. *La guerre des enfants 1914–1918*. Paris: Armand Colin.

Audoin-Rouzeau, Stéphane, and Annette Becker. 2002a. *1914–1918. Understanding the Great War*. London: Profile Books. (Orig. pub. 2000.)

———. 2002b. "Violence et consentement: la 'culture de guerre' du premier conflit mondial." In *La politique et la guerre. Pour comprendre le XXè siècle contemporain*, edited by Stéphane Audouin-Rouzeau, Annette Becker et al., 251–71. Paris: Agnès Viénot-Noesis.

Austin, John L. 1962. *How to Do Things with Words: The William James Lectures Delivered at Harvard University in 1955*. Oxford: Clarendon Press.

Bagwe, Anjali. 1995. *Of Woman Caste: The Experience of Gender in Rural India*. London: Zed Books.

Bakhle, Janaki. 2005. *Two Men and Music: Nationalism in the Making of an Indian Classical Tradition*. Oxford: Oxford University Press.

Balakrishnan, Gopal. 2000. *The Enemy: An Intellectual Portrait of Carl Schmitt*. New York: Verso.

Balibar, Étienne. 1991. *Race, Nation, Class: Ambiguous Identities* (Étienne Balibar and Immanuel Wallerstein, orig. pub. 1988). London/New York: Verso.

———. 1998. *Droit de cité*. La Tour d'Aigues: L'Aube.

———. 2003. *L'Europe, l'Amérique, la guerre: réflexions sur la médiation européenne*. Paris: La Découverte.

———. 2004. *We, the People of Europe? Reflections on Transnational Citizenship*. Princeton: Princeton University Press. (Orig. pub. 2001.)

———. 2005. "Educating Towards a European Citizenship: To Discipline or to Emancipate? Reflections from France." In *Manufacturing Citizenship: Education and Nationalism in Europe, South Asia, China*, edited by Véronique Benei, 37–56. London: Routledge.

Banerjee, Mukulika, and Daniel Miller. 2003. *The Sari*. Oxford: Berg.

Barrett, Frank J. 1996. "The Organizational Construction of Hegemonic Masculinity: The Case of the US Navy." *Gender, Work and Organization* 3 (3): 129–42.

Basu, Aparna. 1982. *Essays in the History of Indian Education*. New Delhi: Concept.

Bauman, Zygmunt. 2000 [1989]. *Modernity and the Holocaust*. Ithaca, N.Y.: Cornell University Press.

Bayly, C. A. 1998. *Origins of Nationality in South Asia: Patriotism and Ethical Government in the Making of Modern India*. Delhi: Oxford University Press.

Bear, Laura. 2005. "School Stories and Internal Frontiers: Tracing the Domestic Life of Anglo-Indian Citizens." In *Manufacturing Citizenship: Education and Nationalism in Europe, South Asia, and China*, edited by Véronique Benei, 236–261. London: Routledge.

———. 2007. *Lines of the Nation: Indian Railway Workers, Bureaucracy, and the Intimate Historical Self*. New York: Columbia University Press.

Beatty, Andrew. 2005. "Emotions in the Field: What Are We Talking About?" *Journal of the Royal Anthropological Institute* 11:17–37.

Becker, Annette. 1994. *La guerre et la foi. De la mort à la mémoire 1914–1930*. Paris: Armand Colin.

Behar, Ruth, and Deborah A. Gordon, eds. 1995. *Women Writing Culture*. Berkeley: University of California Press.

Benei, Véronique. 1996. *La dot en Inde: un fléau social? Socio-anthropologie du mariage au Maharashtra*. Paris: Karthala; Pondicherry: French Institute.

———. 1997. "Education, Industrialization and Socio-economic Development: Some Reflections for Further Sociological Research in Western India." In *Industrial Decentralization and Urban Development*, edited by Véronique Benei and Loraine Kennedy, 101–8. Pondy Papers in Social Sciences 23. Pondicherry: French Institute.

——. 1999. "Reappropriating Colonial Documents in Kolhapur (Maharashtra): Variations on a Nationalist Theme." *Modern Asian Studies* 33 (4): 913–50.

——. 2001a. "A Passion for Order: Vernacular Languages, Morality and Race in the Mid-19th Century Bombay Presidency." Paper presented at South Asian Studies Programme, Asian Studies Centre, St. Antony's College, Oxford, January 23.

——. 2001b. "Teaching Nationalism in Maharashtrian Schools." In *The Everyday State and Society in Modern India*, edited by C. J. Fuller and V. Benei, 194–221. London: Hurst. (Orig. pub. Delhi: Social Science Press, 2000.)

——. 2002a. "Teaching of History and Nation Building." *Economic and Political Weekly* 37 (47): 4697–98.

——. 2002b. "Missing Indigenous Bodies: Educational Enterprise and Victorian Morality in the Mid-nineteenth Century Bombay Presidency." *Economic and Political Weekly* 37 (17): 1647–54.

——. 2004. "Public Culture, Private Technology and Hindu Regionalism/Nationalism: 'Shivaji Films' in Maharashtra." Paper presented at workshop, An Anthropological Study of Regionalism, Nationalism and Globalisation in India, London School of Economics, Department of Anthropology, April 23.

——. 2005a. "Introduction." In *Manufacturing Citizenship: Education and Nationalism in Europe, South Asia, China*, edited by Véronique Benei, 1–34. London: Routledge.

——. 2005b. "Serving the Nation: Gender and Family Values in Military Schools." In *Educational Regimes in Contemporary India*, edited by Patricia Jeffery and Radhika Chopra, 141–60. New Delhi: Sage Publications.

——. 2005c. "Of Languages, Passions and Interests: Education, Regionalism and Globalization in Maharashtra, 1800–2000." In *Globalizing India: Locality, Nation and the World*, edited by Jackie Assayag and Chris Fuller, 141–62. London: Anthem.

Benjamin, Walter. 1968 [1936]. "The Work of Art in the Age of Mechanical Reproduction." In *Illuminations*, by Walter Benjamin, edited by Hannah Arendt. New York: Schocken Books.

——. 1999. *The Arcades Project*. (Prepared after the German volume edited by Rolf Tiedemann.) Cambridge, Mass: Belknap Press.

Berezin, Mabel. 1997. *Making the Fascist Self. The Political Culture of Interwar Italy*. Ithaca, N.Y.: Cornell University Press.

——. 1999. "Emotion, Nation, Identity in Fascist Italy." In *State/Culture: The State-Formation after the Cultural Turn*, edited by George Steinmetz, 355–77. Durham, N.C.: Duke University Press.

Besnier, Niko. 1990. "Language and Affect." *Annual Review of Anthropology* 19:419–51.

Bhabha, Homi K. 1984. "Of Mimicry and Man: The Ambivalence of Colonial Discourse." *October* 28:125–53.

Bharucha, Rustom. 1995. "Dismantling Men. Crisis of Male Identity in 'Father, Son and Holy War.'" *Economic and Political Weekly*, July 1, 1610–16.

Bhatt, Chetan. 2001. *Hindu Nationalism. Origins, Ideologies and Modern Myths.* Oxford: Berg.

Billig, Michael. 1995. *Banal Nationalism.* London: Sage Publications.

Bloch, Maurice, ed. 1975. *Political Language and Oratory in Traditional Society.* London: Academic Press.

——. 1986. *From Blessing to Violence: History and Ideology in the Circumcision Ritual of the Merina of Madagascar.* Cambridge: Cambridge University Press.

Boellstorff, Tom, and Johan Lindquist. 2004. "Bodies of Emotion: Rethinking Culture and Emotion through Southeast Asia." *Ethnos* 69 (4): 437–44.

Borneman, John, ed. 2004. *Death of the Father: An Anthropology of the End in Political Authority.* New York: Berghahn Books.

Bose, Sugata, and Ayesha Jalal, eds. 1997. *Nationalism, Democracy and Development: State and Politics in India.* Delhi: Oxford University Press.

Bourdieu, Pierre. 1975. "Le fétichisme de la langue." *Actes de la Recherche en Sciences Sociales* 4:2–32.

——. 1990. *In Other Words. Essays towards a Reflexive Sociology.* Stanford: Stanford University Press.

——. 1999. "Rethinking the State: Genesis and Structure of the Bureaucratic Field." In *State/Culture: The State-Formation after the Cultural Turn,* edited by George Steinmetz, 53–75. Durham, N.C.: Duke University Press.

Bourdieu, Pierre, and Jean-Claude Passeron. 1977. *Reproduction in Education, Society and Culture.* London: Sage Publications. (Orig. pub. 1970.)

Boyer, Dominic, and Claudio Lomnitz. 2005. "Intellectuals and Nationalism: Anthropological Engagements." *Annual Review of Anthropology* 34:105–20.

Brass, Paul R. 1997. *Theft of an Idol: Text and Context in the Representation of Collective Violence.* Princeton: Princeton University Press.

Brenneis, Donald L., and Fred H. Myers, eds. 1984. *Dangerous Words: Language and Politics in the Pacific.* New York: Columbia University Press.

Burghart, Richard. 1996. *The Conditions of Listening: Essays on Religion, History and Politics in South Asia.* Edited by C. J. Fuller and Jonathan Spencer. Delhi: Oxford University Press.

Butalia, Urvashi. 2004. "Gender and Nation: Some Reflections from India." In *From Gender to Nation,* edited by Rada Ivekovic and Julie Mostov, 99–112. New Delhi: Zubaan.

Butler, Judith. 1989. "Gender Trouble, Feminist Theory, and Psychoanalytic Discourse." In *Feminism/Postmodernism,* edited by Linda J. Nicholson, 324–40. New York: Routledge.

——. 1990. *Gender Trouble. Feminism and the Subversion of Identity.* New York: Routledge.

Calhoun, Craig, ed. 1997 [1992]. *Habermas and the Public Sphere.* Cambridge, Mass.: MIT Press.

———. 2001. "Putting Emotions in Their Place." In *Passionate Politics: Emotions and Social Movements*, edited by Jeff Goodwin, James M. Jasper, and Francesca Polletta, 45–57. Chicago: University of Chicago Press.

Callon, Michel, Pierre Lascoumes, and Yannick Barthe. 2001. *Agir dans un monde incertain. Essai sur la démocratie technique*. Paris: Seuil.

Cashman, Richard I. 1975. *The Myth of the Lokamanya: Tilak and Mass Politics in Maharashtra*. Berkeley: University of California Press.

Centlivres, Pierre, Daniel Fabre, and Françoise Zonabend, eds. 1999. *La fabrique des héros*. Paris: Mission du Patrimoine Ethnologique, Collection Ethnologie de la France, Cahier 12.

Chakrabarty, Dipesh. 2002. *Habitations of Modernity: Essays in the Wake of Subaltern Studies*. Chicago: University of Chicago Press.

———. 2004. "History and Historicality." *Postcolonial Studies* 7 (1): 125–30.

Chatterjee, Partha. 1993. *The Nation and Its Fragments: Colonial and Postcolonial Histories*. Princeton: Princeton University Press.

Chatterjee, Partha, and Anjan Ghosh, eds. 2002. *History and the Present*. New Delhi: Permanent Black.

Chodorow, Nancy. 1978. *The Reproduction of Mothering: Psychoanalysis and the Sociology of Gender*. Berkeley: University of California Press.

———. 1994. *Femininities, Masculinities, Sexualities: Freud and Beyond*. London: Free Association Books.

———. 1999. *The Power of Feelings*. New Haven, Conn.: Yale University Press.

Chopra, Radhika, Caroline Osella, and Filippo Osella, eds. 2004. *South Asian Masculinities: Context of Change, Sites of Continuity*. New Delhi: Kali for Women and Women Unlimited.

Chun, Allen. 2005. "The Moral Cultivation of Citizenship in a Taiwan Middle School, c. 1990." In *Manufacturing Citizenship: Education and Nationalism in Europe, South Asia, China*, edited by Véronique Benei, 57–75. London: Routledge.

Classen, Constance. 1993. *Worlds of Sense: Exploring the Senses in History and across Cultures*. London: Routledge.

Clifford, James, and George E. Marcus, eds. 1986. *Writing Culture*. Berkeley: University of California Press.

Cohen, Stephen P. 2002 [1990]. *The Indian Army. Its Contribution to the Development of a Nation*. New Delhi: Oxford University Press.

Cohn, Bernard S. 1985. "The Command of Language and the Language of Command." In *Subaltern Studies IV—Writings on South Asian History and Society*, edited by R. Guha, 275–329. Delhi: Oxford University Press.

———. 1987a. "The Census and Objectification in South Asia." In *An Anthropologist among the Historians and Other Essays*, 224–54. Delhi: Oxford University Press. (Orig. pub. 1967.)

———. 1987b. "Regions Subjective and Objective: Their Relation to the Study of Modern Indian History and Society." In *An Anthropologist among the Historians and Other Essays*, 100–35. Delhi: Oxford University Press.

———. 1996. *Colonialism and Its Forms of Knowledge: The British in India*. Princeton: Princeton University Press.

Cole, Jennifer. 2001. *Forget Colonialism? Sacrifice and the Art of Memory in Madagascar*. Berkeley: University of California Press.

Coles, Robert. 1986. *The Political Life of Children*. New York: Atlantic Monthly Press.

Collier, Richard. 1998. *Masculinities, Crime and Criminology. Men, Heterosexuality and the Criminal(ised) Other*. London: Sage Publications.

Connell, Robert W. 1975 [1971]. *The Child's Construction of Politics*. Melbourne: Melbourne University Press.

———. 1993. "The Big Picture: Masculinities in Recent World History." *Theory and Society* 22:597–623.

———. 1995a. "Masculinity, Violence, and War." In *Men's Lives*, edited by Michael S. Kimmel and Michael A. Messner, 125–30. New York: Macmillan.

———. 1995b. *Masculinities*. Cambridge: Polity.

———. 2000. "Arms and the Man: Using the New Research on Masculinity to Understand Violence and Promote Peace in the Contemporary World." In *Male Roles, Masculinities and Violence. A Culture of Peace Perspective*, edited by I. Breines, R. W. Connell, and I. Eide, 21–34. Paris: UNESCO.

Coomaraswamy, Ananda. 1939. "Ornament." *The Art Bulletin* 21 (4): 375–82.

Copland, Ian. 1973. "The Maharaja of Kolhapur and the Non-Brahmin Movement 1902–1910." *Modern Asian Studies* 7 (2): 209–25.

———. 1990. *The Burden of Empire: Perspectives on Imperialism and Colonialism*. Oxford: Oxford University Press.

———. 2005. *State, Community and Neighbourhood in Princely North India, c. 1900–1950*. New York: Palgrave Macmillan.

Corbin, Alain. 1986. *The Foul and the Fragrant: Odor and the French Social Imagination*. Cambridge, Mass.: Harvard University Press. (Orig. pub. 1982.)

———. 1998. *Village Bells: Sound and Meaning in the Nineteenth-Century French Countryside*. New York: Columbia University Press. (Orig. pub. 1994.)

Cornwall, Andrea, and Nancy Lindisfarne. 1994. "Dislocating Masculinity: Gender, Power and Anthropology." In *Dislocating Masculinity: Comparative Ethnographies*, edited by Andrea Cornwall and Nancy Lindisfarne, 11–47. London: Routledge.

Crook, Nigel, ed. 1996. *The Transmission of Knowledge in South Asia: Essays in Education, Religion, History and Politics*. Delhi: Oxford University Press.

Csordas, Thomas J. 1994. *The Sacred Self: A Cultural Phenomenology of Charismatic Healing*. Berkeley: University of California Press.

———. 1999. "The Body's Career in Anthropology." In *Anthropological Theory Today*, edited by Henrietta L. Moore, 172–205. London: Polity.

Damasio, Antonio. 1999. *The Feeling of What Happens: Body and Emotion in the Making of Consciousness*. New York: Harcourt Brace.

Daniel, Valentine. 1984. *Fluid Signs: Being a Person the Tamil Way*. Berkeley: University of California Press.

———. 1996. *Charred Lullabies: Chapters in an Anthropography of Violence*. Princeton: Princeton University Press.

Davis, Richard. 1991. *Ritual in an Oscillating Universe. Worshipping Shiva in Medieval India*. Princeton: Princeton University Press.

Deb, Siddhartha. 2003. "Textbook Troubles: India's Hindu Nationalists Rewrite Their Country's Past Conveniently." *The Boston Globe*, June 1.

Deshpande, Prachi. 2006. "Writing Regional Consciousness: Maratha History and Regional Identity in Modern Maharashtra." In *Region, Culture and Politics in India*, edited by Rajendra Vora and Anne Feldhaus, 83–118. New Delhi: Manohar.

———. 2007. *Creative Pasts: Historical Memory and Identity in Western India, 1700–1960*. New York: Columbia University Press; New Delhi: Permanent Black.

Dighe, V. G. 1961. "Modern Historical Writing in Marathi." In *Historians of India, Pakistan and Ceylon*, edited by C. H. Philips, 473–80. London: Oxford University Press.

Dirks, Nicholas B. 2001. *Castes of Mind: Colonialism and the Making of Modern India*. Princeton: Princeton University Press.

Divekar, V. D. 1990. "Rashtreeya Kirtankars in Maharashtra—Their Role in the Indian National Movement." In *Regional Roots of Indian Nationalism—Gujarat, Maharashtra and Rajasthan*, edited by M. Mehta, 214–32. New Delhi: Criterion Publications.

Doniger, Wendy O. 1980. *Women, Androgynes and Other Mythical Beasts*. Chicago: University of Chicago Press.

Donzelot. Jacques. 1980. *The Policing of Families*. London: Hutchinson. (Orig. pub. 1977.)

Eaton, Richard M. 1978. *Sufis of Bijapur, 1300–1700: Social Roles of Sufis in Medieval India*. Princeton: Princeton University Press.

———. 2000. *Essays on Islam and Indian History*. New Delhi: Oxford University Press.

Eck, Diana. 1998. *Darshan: Seeing the Divine Image in India*. New York: Columbia University Press.

Eckert, Julia M. 2003. *The Charisma of Direct Action: Power, Politics, and the Shiv Sena*. New Delhi: Oxford University Press.

Economou, Leonidas. n.d. "Basic Training: Induction into the Greek Army." Unpublished paper, Athens, Panteion University.

Eickelman, Dale F., and James Piscatori. 1996. *Muslim Politics*. Princeton: Princeton University Press.

Eiland, Howard. 2005. "Reception in Distraction." In *Walter Benjamin and Art*, edited by Andrew Benjamin, 3–13. London and New York: Continuum.

Eisenstadt, Shmuel N. 2000. *Daedalus*. Special issue, *Multiple Modernities* 129 (1): 1–29.

Elias, Norbert. 1982. *History of Manners*. New York: Pantheon Books.

Enloe, Cynthia H. 1980. *Ethnic Soldiers: State Security in Divided Societies*. Harmondsworth, U.K.: Penguin.

Epstein, Debbie, and Richard Johnson. 1998. *Schooling Sexualities*. Buckingham, U.K.: Open University Press.

Eriksen, Thomas H. 1993. *Ethnicity and Nationalism: Anthropological Perspectives*. London: Pluto Press.

Erikson, Erik H. 1963. *Childhood and Society*. New York: Norton.

———. 2002 [1979]. "Report to Vikram: Further Perspectives on the Life Cycle." In *Identity and Adulthood*, edited by Sudhir Kakar, 13–34. New Delhi: Oxford India Paperbacks.

Errington, J. Joseph. 1998a. "Indonesian('s) Development: On the State of a Language of State." In *Language Ideologies: Practice and Theory*, edited by Bambi B. Schieffelin, Kathryn A. Woolard, and Paul V. Kroskrity, 271–84. New York: Oxford University Press.

———. 1998b. *Shifting Languages. Interaction and Identity in Javanese Indonesia*. Cambridge: Cambridge University Press.

Evans, Gillian. 2006. *Educational Failure and Working Class White Children in Britain*. London: Palgrave.

Feld, Steven. 1990 [1982]. *Sound and Sentiment: Birds, Weeping, Poetics, and Song in Kaluli Expression*. Philadelphia: University of Pennsylvania Press.

Feldhaus, Anne. 2003. *Connected Places: Region, Pilgrimage, and Geographical Imagination in India*. New York: Palgrave Macmillan.

Feldman, Allen. 1991. *Formations of Violence: The Narrative of the Body and Political Terror in Northern Ireland*. Chicago: University of Chicago Press.

———. 1994. "From Desert Storm to Rodney King via Ex-Yugoslavia: On Cultural Anaesthesia." In *The Senses Still*, edited by Nadia Seremetakis, 87–108. Boulder, Colo.: Westview Press.

Firth, Raymond. 1973. *Symbols Public and Private*. London: Allen and Unwin.

Forcey, Linda R. 1987. *Mothers of Sons. Towards an Understanding of Responsibility*. New York: Praeger.

Foucault, Michel. 1973. *The Birth of the Clinic: An Archaeology of Medical Perception*. New York: Pantheon Books.

———. 1979. *Discipline and Punish*. London: Harmondsworth. (Orig. pub. 1975.)

———. 1981. *The History of Sexuality*. Vol. 1, *An Introduction*. London: Harmondsworth. (Orig. pub. 1976.)

Fox, Richard G. 2002. "East of Said." In *The Anthropology of Politics: A Reader in Ethnography, Theory and Critique*, edited by Joan Vincent, 143–52. Oxford: Blackwell.

Frykman, Jonas. 1994. "On the Move: The Struggle for the Body in Sweden in the 1930s." In *The Senses Still*, edited by Nadia Seremetakis, 63–85. Boulder, Colo.: Westview Press.

Fuller, Chris (with Adrian Mayer and Norbert Peabody). 1991. "Hinduism and Hierarchy." *Man* 26:549–55.

Fuller, C. J. 1984. *Servants of the Goddess: The Priests of a South Indian Temple*. Cambridge: Cambridge University Press.

———. 2003. *The Renewal of the Priesthood: Modernity and Traditionalism in a South Indian Temple*. Princeton: Princeton University Press; Delhi: Oxford University Press.

Fuller, C. J., and Véronique Benei, eds. 2001. *The Everyday State and Society in Modern India*. London: Hurst. (Orig. pub. Delhi: Social Science Press, 2000.)

Gal, Susan. 2002. "A Semiotics of the Public/Private Distinction." *Differences: A Journal of Feminist Cultural Studies* 13 (1): 77–95.

Gandhi, Mohandas K. 1951. *Basic Education*. Ahmedabad: Navjivan Publishing House.

———. 1997. *Hind Swaraj and Other Writings*. Edited by A. Parel. New Delhi: Foundation Books; Cambridge: Cambridge University Press.

Garrett, Paul B., and Patricia Baquedano-Lopez. 2002. "Language Socialization: Reproduction and Continuity, Transformation and Change." *Annual Review of Anthropology* 31:339–61.

Geertz, Clifford. 1973. "The Integrative Revolution: Primordial Sentiments and Civil Politics in the New States." In *The Interpretation of Cultures*, 255–79. New York: Basic Books.

———. 2000. *Available Light: Anthropological Reflections on Philosophical Topics*. Princeton: Princeton University Press.

Geertz, Hildred. 1974 [1959]. "The Vocabulary of Emotion: A Study of Socialization Processes." In *Culture and Personality*, edited by R. A. Levine, 249–64. Chicago: Aldine.

Gellner, Ernest. 1983. *Nations and Nationalism*. Ithaca, N.Y.: Cornell University Press.

———. 1991. "An Interview with Ernest Gellner." By John Davis. *Current Anthropology* 32 (1): 63–72.

Ghosh, Amitav. 2000. *The Glass Palace: A Novel*. London: HarperCollins; New York: Random House.

Ghosh, Suresh C. 1995. *The History of Education in Modern India, 1757–1986*. New Delhi: Orient Longman.

Gill, Lesley. 1997. "Creating Citizens, Making Men: The Military and Masculinity in Bolivia." *Cultural Anthropology* 12 (4): 527–50.

Gilmore, David D. 1990. *Manhood in the Making: Cultural Concepts of Masculinity*. New Haven, Conn.: Yale University Press.

Ginzburg, Carlo. 1989. *Clues, Myth and the Historical Method*. Baltimore: Johns Hopkins University Press. (Orig. pub. 1986.)

Godelier, Maurice. 1986. *The Making of Great Men: Male Domination and Power among the New Guinea Baruya*. Cambridge: Cambridge University Press.

Godfrey, Sima. 2002. "Alain Corbin: Making Sense of French History." *French Historical Studies* 25 (2): 381–98.

Goffmann, Erving. 1976 [1961]. *Asylums*. Chicago: Aldine.

Gokhale, J. B. 1975. "The 'Mahratta' and Nationalism in Maharashtra." *The Indian Political Science Review* 1:1–26.

Gold, Ann Grodzins. 1988. *Fruitful Journeys: The Ways of Rajasthani Pilgrims*. Berkeley: University of California Press.

Gold, Ann Grodzins, and Gloria Goodwin Raheja. 1994. *Listen to the Heron's Words: Reimagining Gender and Kinship in North India*. Berkeley: University of California Press.

Good, Byron. 2004. "Rethinking 'Emotions' in Southeast Asia." *Ethnos* 69 (4): 529–33.

Goodwin Raheja, Gloria, ed. 2003. *Songs, Stories, Lives: Gendered Dialogues and Cultural Critique*. New Delhi: Kali for Women.

Gore, M. S. 1989. *Non-Brahman Movement in Maharashtra*. New Delhi: Segment Book Distributors.

Goswami, Manu. 2004. *Producing India. From Colonial Economy to National Space*. Chicago: University of Chicago Press.

Greenhouse, Carol J. 1996. *A Moment's Notice: Time Politics across Cultures*. Ithaca, N.Y.: Cornell University Press.

Guha, Ranajit. 2002. *History at the Limit of World-History*. New York: Columbia University Press.

Gupta, Akhil. 1995. "Blurred Boundaries: The Discourse of Corruption, the Culture of Politics and the Imagined State." *American Ethnologist* 22:375–402.

Gupta, Charu. 2001. *Sexuality, Obscenity, Community: Women, Muslims and the Hindu Public in Colonial India*. Delhi: Permanent Black.

Gutmann, Matthew C. 1996. *The Meanings of Macho. Being a Man in Mexico City*. Berkeley: University of California Press.

Habermas, Jürgen. 1989. *The Structural Transformation of the Public Sphere: An Inquiry into a Category of Bourgeois Society*. Cambridge, Mass.: MIT Press.

Habib, Irfan, Suvira Jaiswal, and Aditya Mukherjee. 2003. *History in the New NCERT Textbooks: A Report and Index of Errors*. Kolkata: Indian History Congress.

Hall, Kathleen. 2002. *Lives in Translation: Sikh Youth as British Citizens*. Philadelphia: University of Pennsylvania Press.

Hall, Stuart. 1996. "Who Needs Identity?" In *Questions of Cultural Identity*, edited by Stuart Hall and Paul du Gay, 1–17. London: Sage Publications.

Hansen, Thomas Blom. 1996. "Recuperating Masculinity: Hindu Nationalism, Violence and the Exorcism of the Muslim Other." *Critique of Anthropology* 16 (2): 137–72.

———. 1999. *The Saffron Wave: Democracy and Hindu Nationalism in Modern India*. Princeton: Princeton University Press.

———. 2001. *Wages of Violence: Naming and Identity in Postcolonial Bombay*. Princeton: Princeton University Press.

Hansen, Thomas Blom, and Finn Stepputat, eds. 2001. *States of Imagination: Ethnographic Explorations of the Postcolonial State*. Durham, N.C.: Duke University Press.

Hasan, Mushirul, ed. 1985. *Communal and Pan-Islamic Trends in Colonial India*. Delhi: Manohar.

———, ed. 1992. *Islam and Indian Nationalism. Reflections on Abul Kalam Azad*. Delhi: Manohar.

———. 1997. *Legacy of a Divided Nation. India's Muslims since Independence*. London: Hurst.

———, ed. 1998. *Islam, Communities and the Nation: Muslim Identities in South Asia and Beyond*. Delhi: Manohar.

———, ed. 2000. *Inventing Boundaries. Gender, Politics and the Partition of India*. New Delhi: Oxford University Press.

Hasan, Zoya, ed. 1994. *Forging Identities: Gender, Communities and the State in India*. New Delhi: Kali for Women.

Hastings, Adrian. 1997. *The Construction of Nationhood: Ethnicity, Religion and Nationalism*. Cambridge: Cambridge University Press.

Haugen, Einar. 1991. "The 'Mother Tongue.'" In *The Influence of Language on Culture and Thought. Essays in Honor of Joshua A. Fishman's Sixty-fifth Birthday*, edited by Robert L. Cooper and Spolsky Bernard, 75–84. Berlin: Mouton de Gruyter.

Hayden, Robert H. 2002. "Imagined Communities and Real Victims: Self-Determination and Ethnic Cleansing in Yugoslavia." In *Genocide: An Anthropological Reader*, edited by A. L. Hinton, 231–53. Oxford: Blackwell.

Heath, Shirley Brice. 1972. *Telling Tongues. Language Policy in Mexico. Colony to Nation*. New York: Teachers College Press; London: Columbia University Press.

———. 1983. *Ways with Words. Language, Life, and Work in Communities and Classrooms*. Cambridge: Cambridge University Press.

Herdt, Gilbert H., ed. 1982. *Rituals of Manhood: Male Initiation in Papua New Guinea*. Berkeley: University of California Press.

Herzfeld, Michael. 1985. *Poetics of Manhood: Contest and Identity in a Cretan Mountain Village*. Princeton: Princeton University Press.

———. 1997. *Cultural Intimacy*. New York: Routledge.

Hinton, Alexander L. 2002. "The Dark Side of Modernity: Toward an Anthropology of Genocide." In *Annihilating Difference: The Anthropology of Genocide*, edited by Alexander L. Hinton, 1–40. Berkeley: University of California Press.

Hobsbawm, Eric J. 1992. *Nations and Nationalism since 1780: Programme, Myth, Reality*. 2d ed. Cambridge: Cambridge University Press.

Hockey, John. 1986. *Squaddies: Portrait of a Subculture*. Exeter, U.K.: Exeter University Publications.

Howes, David. 1991. "To Summon All the Senses." In *The Varieties of Sensory Experience: A Sourcebook in the Anthropology of the Senses*, edited by David Howes, 3–21. Toronto: University of Toronto Press.

Irvine, Judith T. 1990. "Registering Affect: Heteroglossia in the Linguistic Expression of Emotion." In *Language and the Politics of Emotion*, edited by Catherine A. Lutz and Lila Abu-Lughod, 69–91. Cambridge: Cambridge University Press.

Irvine, Judith, and Susan Gal. 2000. "Language Ideology and Linguistic Differentiation." In *Regimes of Language: Ideologies, Polities, and Identities*, edited by Paul V. Kroskrity, 35–83. Santa Fe, N.M.: School of American Research Press, SAR Advanced Seminar Series; Oxford: James Currey.

Jagose, Annamarie. 1996. *Queer Theory. An Introduction*. New York: New York University Press.

Jalal, Ayesha. 1997. "Exploding Communalism: The Politics of Muslim Identity in South Asia." In *Nationalism, Democracy and Development*, edited by Sugata Bose and Ayesha Jalal, 76–103. Delhi: Oxford University Press.

James, Allison. 1993. *Childhood Identities*. Cambridge: Cambridge University Press.

James, William. 1884. "What Is an Emotion?" *Mind* 9 (34): 188–205.

Janov, Arthur. 1970. *The Primal Scream: Primal Therapy—the Cure for Neurosis*. New York: Putnam.

Jasper, Daniel. 2002. "Commemorating Shivaji: Regional and Religious Identities in Maharashtra, India." Ph.D. diss., New School, New York.

Jeffery, Patricia, and Roger Jeffery. 1996. "What's the Benefit of Being Educated? Girls' Schooling, Women's Autonomy and Fertility Outcomes in Bijnor." In *Girls' Schooling, Women's Autonomy and Fertility Change in South Asia*, edited by Roger Jeffery and Alaka Basu, 150–83. New Delhi: Sage Publications.

Jeffery, Roger, and Alaka Basu, eds. 1996. *Girls' Schooling, Women's Autonomy and Fertility Change in South Asia*. New Delhi: Sage Publications.

Kakar, Sudhir. 1996. *The Colors of Violence: Cultural Identities, Religion, and Conflict*. Chicago: University of Chicago Press.

———. 1999 [1978]. *The Inner World. A Psycho-analytic Study of Childhood and Society in India*. Delhi: Oxford University Press.

———, ed. 2002 [1979]. *Identity and Adulthood*. New Delhi: Oxford University Press.

Kane, Pandurang Vaman. 1975 [1968]. Vols. 1.1, 1.2. *History of Dharmashastra: Ancient and Mediaeval, Religious and Civil Law*. Pune: Bhandarkar Oriental Research Institute.

Kantorowicz, Ernst H. 1981 [1957]. "Pro patria mori." In *The King's Two Bodies: A Study in Mediaeval Political Theology*, 232–72. Princeton: Princeton University Press.

Kaplan, Samuel. 2006. *The Pedagogical State: Education and the Politics of National Culture in Post-1980 Turkey*. Stanford: Stanford University Press.

Kapur, Ratna, and Brenda Cossman. 1996. *Subversive Sites: Feminist Engagements with Law in India*. New Delhi: Sage Publications.

Kaur, Raminder. 2004. "At the Ragged Edges of Time: The Legend of Tilak and the Normalization of Historical Narratives." *South Asia Research* 24 (2): 185–202.

——. 2005. *Performative Politics and the Cultures of Hinduism: Public Uses of Religion in Western India*. London: Anthem.

Kaviraj, Sudipta. 1992. "Writing, Speaking, Being: Language and the Historical Formation of Identities in India." In *Nationalstaat und Sprachkonflikte in Süd- und Südostasien*, edited by D. Hellman-Rajanayagam, and D. Rothermund, 28–65. Stuttgart: Franz Steiner.

——. 1995. *The Unhappy Consciousness: Bankimchandra Chattopadhyay and the Formation of Nationalist Discourse in India*. Delhi: Oxford University Press.

——. 1997. "Filth and the Public Sphere: Concepts and Practices about Space in Calcutta." *Public Culture* 10 (1): 83–113.

——. 2001. "In Search of Civil Society." In *Civil Society. History and Possibilities*, edited by Sudipta Kaviraj and Sunil Khilnani, 287–323. Cambridge: Cambridge University Press.

Kaviraj, Sudipta, and Sunil Khilnani, eds. 2001. *Civil Society. History and Possibilities*. Cambridge: Cambridge University Press.

Kavlekar, K. 1979. *Non-Brahmin Movement in Southern India 1873–1949*. Kolhapur: Shivaji University Press.

Kesari, V. 1998. "RSS Wants Sanskrit, Yoga in All Schools." *The Asian Age* (Mumbai), April 28.

Kimmel, Michael, and Michael Messner, eds. 1989. *Men's Lives*. New York: Macmillan.

King, Christopher R. 1996. *One Language, Two Scripts. The Hindi Movement in 19th C. North India*. Bombay: Oxford University Press.

King, Robert D. 1998 [1997]. *Nehru and the Language Politics of India*. New Delhi: Oxford University Press.

Kirsch, Max H. 2000. *Queer Theory and Social Change*. London: Routledge.

Klein, Melanie. 1964. "Love, Guilt and Reparation." In *Love, Hate and Reparation*, edited by Joan Riviere and Melanie Klein, 57–119. New York: Norton.

Klein, Uta. 1999. "'Our Best Boys'—the Gendered Nature of Civil-Military Relations in Israel." *Men and Masculinities* 2 (1): 47–65.

Kooiman, Dick. 2002. *Communalism and Indian Princely States. Travancore, Baroda and Hyderabad in the 1930s*. New Delhi: Manohar.

Koonz, Claudia. 1987. *Mothers in the Fatherland: Women, the Family, and Nazi Politics*. New York: St. Martin's Press.

Kroskrity, Paul V., ed. 2000. *Regimes of Language: Ideologies, Polities, and Identities*. Santa Fe, N.M.: School of American Research Press, SAR Advanced Seminar Series; Oxford: James Currey.

Kulkarni, A. R., and N. K. Wagle. 1999. *Region, Nationality, and Religion*. Mumbai: Popular Prakashan.

Kumar, Krishna. 1989. "Secularism: Its Politics and Pedagogy." *Economic and Political Weekly* 24 (44–45): 2473–76.

———. 1991. *Political Agenda of Education. A Study of Colonialist and Nationalist Ideas.* New Delhi: Sage Publications.

———. 1992. "Hindu Revivalism and Education in North-Central India." In *Fundamentalisms and Society,* edited by Martin Marty and Scott Appleby, 536–57. Chicago: University of Chicago Press.

———. 1994. *Learning from Conflict.* Delhi: Orient Longman.

———. 2001. *Prejudice and Pride. School Histories of the Freedom Struggle in India and Pakistan.* New Delhi: Viking.

Kumar, Nita. 2000. *Lessons from Schools. The History of Education in Banaras.* New Delhi: Sage Publications.

———. 2002. "Why Do Hindus and Muslims Fight? Children and History in India." In *Everyday Life in South Asia,* edited by Diane P. Mines and Sarah Lamb, 337–56. Bloomington: Indiana University Press.

———. 2005. "Mothers and Non-mothers: Gendering the Discourse of Education in South Asia." *Gender and History* 17 (1): 154–82.

Kumar, Radha. 1993. *The History of Doing: An Illustrated Account of Movements for Women's Rights and Feminism in India, 1800–1990.* New Delhi: Kali for Women; London: Verso.

Kumar, Ravinder. 1968. *Western India in the Nineteenth Century: A Study in the Social History of Maharashtra.* London: Routledge and Kegan Paul; Toronto: University of Toronto Press.

Kymlicka, Will. 1995. *Multicultural Citizenship: A Liberal Theory of Minority Rights.* Oxford: Clarendon Press.

Lahire, Bernard. 1996. "Risquer l'interprétation: pertinences interprétatives et surinterprétations en sciences sociales." *Enquête.* Special issue, *Interpréter-Surinterpréter* 3:61–87.

Laine, James W. 1995. "Shivaji as Epic Hero." In *Folk Culture, Folk Religion and Oral Traditions as a Component of Maharashtrian Culture,* edited by Gunther Dietz Sontheimer. Delhi: Manohar.

———. 2003. *Shivaji: Hindu King in Islamic India.* Oxford: Oxford University Press.

Lancaster, Roger N. 1992. *Life Is Hard. Machismo, Danger, and the Intimacy of Power in Nicaragua.* Berkeley: University of California Press.

Latour, Bruno. 1986. "Visualization and Cognition: Thinking with Eyes and Hands." *Knowledge and Society: Studies in the Sociology of Culture, Past and Present* 6:1–40.

Leavitt, John. 1996. "Meaning and Feeling in the Anthropology of Emotions." *American Ethnologist* 23 (3): 514–39.

Lele, Jayant, ed. 1981. *Tradition and Modernity in Bhakti Movements.* Leiden, The Netherlands: E. J. Brill.

Lelyveld, David. 1978. *Aligarh's First Generation: Muslim Solidarity in British India.* Princeton: Princeton University Press.

———. 1993. "The Fate of Hindustani. Colonial Knowledge and the Project of a National Language." In *Orientalism and the Postcolonial Predicament: Perspectives on South Asia,* edited by Carol Breckenridge and Peter van der Veer. Philadelphia: University of Pennsylvania Press, 189–214.

———. 1995. "Upon the Subdominant: Administering Music on All-India Radio." In *Consuming Modernity: Public Culture in a South Asian World,* edited by Carol A. Breckenridge, 49–65. Minneapolis: University of Minnesota Press.

Lenclud, Gérard. 1996. "La mesure de l' excès: Remarques sur l'idée même de surinterprétation." *Enquête.* Special issue, *Interpréter, Surinterpréter* 3:11–30.

Levinson, Bradley A., Douglas E. Foley, and Dorothy C. Holland, eds. 1996. *The Cultural Production of the Educated Person: Critical Ethnographies of Schooling and Local Practice.* Albany: State University of New York Press.

Lipner, Julius J. 2003. "Re-translating Bankim Chatterji's *Ananda Math.*" *India International Centre Quarterly* 30 (1): 59–71.

Lloyd, Justine. 2002. "Departing Sovereignty." *borderlands e-journal* 1 (2). www.borderlandsejournal.adelaide.edu.au/vol1no2_2002/lloyd_departing.html.

Lorenzen, David, ed. 1996. *Bhakti Religion in North India: Community Identity and Political Action.* New Delhi: Manohar.

Lovell, John P., and Judith Hicks Stiehm. 1989. "Military Service and Political Socialization." In *Political Learning in Adulthood,* edited by Roberta S. Sigel, 172–202. Chicago: University of Chicago Press.

Lutz, Catherine A. 1988. *Unnatural Emotions: Everyday Sentiments on a Micronesian Atoll and Their Challenge to Western Theory.* Chicago: University of Chicago Press.

Lutz, Catherine A., and Lila Abu-Lughod, eds. 1990. *Language and the Politics of Emotion.* Cambridge: Cambridge University Press.

Lutz, Catherine A., and G. M. White. 1986. "The Anthropology of Emotions." *Annual Review of Anthropology* 15:405–36.

Luykx, Aurolyn. 1999. *The Citizen Factory: Schooling and Cultural Production in Bolivia.* New York: State University of New York Press.

Lynch, Owen M., ed. 1990. *Divine Passions: The Social Construction of Emotion in India.* Berkeley: University of California Press.

Lyon, Margot L. 1995. "Missing Emotion: The Limitations of Cultural Constructionism in the Study of Emotion." *Cultural Anthropology* 10 (2): 244–63.

Lyon, Margot L., and J. M. Barbalet. 1994. "Society's Body: Emotion and the 'Somatization' of Social Theory." In *Embodiment and Experience: The Existential Ground of Culture and Self,* edited by Thomas J. Csordas, 48–66. Cambridge: Cambridge University Press.

Lyotard, Jean-François. 1984. *The Postmodern Condition: A Report on Knowledge*. Minneapolis: University of Minnesota Press. (Orig. pub. 1979.)

———. 1993 [1982]. "Answering the Question: What Is Postmodernism?" In *Postmodernism: A Reader*, edited by Thomas Docherty, 35–46. New York: Harvester Wheatsheaf.

MacDougall, David. 1999. "Social Aesthetics and the Doon School." *Visual Anthropology Review* 15 (1): 3–20.

———. 2005. "Doon School Aesthetics." In *Values and Education*, edited by Patricia Jeffery and Radhika Chopra, 121–40. New Delhi: Sage Publications.

Malamoud, Charles. 1975. "Cuire le monde." *Purushartha. Recherches de Sciences Sociales sur l'Asie du Sud* 1:91–135.

Mamdani, Mahmood. 1996. *Citizen and Subject: Contemporary Africa and the Legacy of Late Colonialism*. Princeton: Princeton University Press.

Massumi, Brian. 2002. *Parables for the Virtual: Movement, Affect, Sensation*. Durham, N.C.: Duke University Press.

Mauss, Marcel. 1950. *Sociologie et anthropologie*. Paris: Quadrige-Presses Universitaires de France.

McClintock, Ann. 1993. "Family Feuds: Gender, Nationalism and the Family." *Feminist Review* 44:61–80.

McDonald, E. E. 1968a. "The Growth of Regional Consciousness in Maharashtra." *Indian Economic and Social History Review* 5 (3): 223–43.

———. 1968b. "The Modernizing of Communication: Vernacular Publishing in 19th C. Maharashtra." *Asian Survey* 8 (7): 589–606.

McKean, Lise. 1996. *Divine Enterprise: Gurus and the Hindu Nationalist Movement*. Chicago: University of Chicago Press.

McLaren, Peter. 1993 [1986]. *Schooling as a Ritual Performance: Towards a Political Economy of Educational Symbols and Gestures*. London: Routledge.

Menon, Parvathi, and K. Rajalakshmi. 1998. "Doctoring Textbooks." *Frontline*, Nov. 20, 14–18.

Menon, Ritu. 2004. "Do Women Have a Country?" In *From Gender to Nation*, edited by Rada Ivekovic and Julie Mostov, 43–62. New Delhi: Zubaan.

Merleau-Ponty, Maurice. 1989. *Phenomenology of Perception*. Basingstoke, U.K.: Macmillan. (Orig. pub. 1945.)

Metcalf, Barbara D. 1982. *Islamic Revival in British India. Deoband, 1860–1900*. New Delhi: Oxford University Press.

———. 1996. "Meandering Madrasas: Knowledge and Short-Term Itinerancy in the Tablighi Jama'at." In *The Transmission of Knowledge in South Asia: Essays on Education, Religion, History, and Politics*, edited by Nigel Crook, 49–61. Delhi: Oxford University Press.

Mills, C. Wright. 1940. "Situated Actions and Vocabularies of Motive." *American Socio-logical Review* 5 (6): 904–13.

Mitchell, Juliet. 2003. *Siblings. Sex and Violence*. Cambridge: Polity.

Mohammad-Arif, Aminah. 2005. "Textbooks, Nationalism and History Writing in India and Pakistan." In *Manufacturing Citizenship: Education and Nationalism in Europe, South Asia, China*, edited by Véronique Benei, 143–69. London: Routledge.

Moore, Henrietta. 1994. *A Passion for Difference: Essays in Anthropology and Gender*. Bloomington: Indiana University Press.

Mosse, George L. 1975. *The Nationalization of the Masses. Political Symbolism and Mass Movements in Germany from the Napoleonic Wars through the Third Reich*. New York: Howard Fertig.

———. 1980. *Masses and Man. Nationalist and Fascist Perceptions of Reality*. New York: Howard Fertig.

———. 1990. *Fallen Soldiers. Reshaping the Memory of the World Wars*. New York: Oxford University Press.

———. 1996. *The Image of Man: The Creation of Modern Masculinity*. New York: Oxford University Press.

Mudaliar, Chandra. 1978. "The Kolhapur Movement." *Indian Economic and History Review* 15 (1): 1–19.

Muralidharan, S., and S. K. Pande. 1998. "Taking Hindutva to School." *Frontline*, Nov. 20, 4–10.

———. 2000. "Past and Prejudice." *Frontline*, Mar. 4, 30– 31.

Naik, J. P., and S. Nurullah. 1995 [1945]. *A Students' History of Education in India, 1800–1973*. New Delhi: Macmillan India.

Nambissan, Geetha B. 2003. *Educational Deprivation and Primary School Provision: A Study of Providers in the City of Calcutta*. Brighton, U.K.: University of Sussex, Institute of Development Studies.

Nandy, Ashis. 1990. "The Politics of Secularism and the Recovery of Religious Tolerance." In *Mirrors of Violence: Communities, Riots, and Survivors in South Asia*, edited by Veena Das, 69–93. New Delhi: Oxford University Press.

Naregal, Veena. 2002 [2001]. *Language Politics, Elites, and the Public Sphere: Western India under Colonialism*. London: Anthem; New Delhi: Permanent Black.

Nehru, Jawaharlal. 1998 [1946]. *The Discovery of India*. New Delhi: Oxford University Press.

Nemade, Bhalchandra. 1990. *The Influence of English on Marathi. A Sociolinguistic Study*. Kolhapur: Rajhans.

Neveu, Catherine, ed. 2007. *Cultures et pratiques participatives: perspectives comparatives*. Paris: L'Harmattan, Coll. Logiques Politiques.

Noiriel, Gérard. 1991. *La tyrannie du national. Le droit d'asile en Europe 1793–1993*. Paris: Calmann-Lévy.

———, ed. 2001. "Enseigner la nation." *Genèses—Sciences sociales et histoire*. Special issue, *Enseigner la nation* 44:2–75.

O'Barr, William M., and Jean F. O'Barr, eds. 1976. *Language and Politics*. The Hague: Mouton.

Obeyesekere, Gananath. 1981. *Medusa's Hair: An Essay on Personal Symbols and Religious Experience*. Chicago: University of Chicago Press.

———. 1990. *The Work of Culture: Symbolic Transformation in Psychoanalysis and Anthropology*. Chicago: University of Chicago Press.

Ochs, Elinor, and Bambi Schieffelin. 1989. "Language Has a Heart." *Text* 9:7–25.

O'Hanlon, Rosalind. 1985. *Caste, Conflict, and Ideology: Mahatma Jotirao Phule and Low Caste Protest in Nineteenth-Century Western India*. Cambridge: Cambridge University Press.

Olivier de Sardan, Jean-Pierre. 1996. "La violence faite aux données. De quelques figures de la surinterprétation en anthropologie." *Enquête*. Special issue, *Interpréter-Surinterpréter* 3:31–59.

Omvedt, Gail. 1976. *Cultural Revolt in a Colonial Society: The Non-Brahman Movement in Western India, 1873–1930*. Bombay: Scientific Socialist Education Trust.

Ong, Walter J. 1991. "Shifting Sensorium." In *The Varieties of Sensory Experience: A Sourcebook in the Anthropology of the Senses*, edited by David Howes, 25–30. Toronto: University of Toronto Press.

Ortner, Sherry. 1995. "Resistance and the Problem of Ethnographic Refusal." *Comparative Studies in Society and History* 37 (1): 173–93.

———. 1996. *Making Gender: The Politics and Erotics of Gender*. Boston: Beacon Press.

Ozouf, Mona. 1988. *Festivals and the French Revolution*. Cambridge, Mass.: Harvard University Press. (Orig. pub. 1976.)

Pandey, Gyanendra. 1990. *The Construction of Communalism in Colonial North India*. Delhi: Oxford University Press.

———. 1991. "In Defense of the Fragment: Writing about Hindu-Muslim Riots in India Today." *Economic and Political Weekly*, Annual Number (Mar.): 559–72. (Reproduced in Pandey 2006.)

———. 1994. "The Prose of Otherness." In *Subaltern Studies VIII: Essays in Honour of Ranajit Guha*, edited by David Arnold and David Hardiman, 189–221. New Delhi: Oxford University Press.

———. 2001. *Remembering Partition: Violence, Nationalism, and History in India*. Cambridge: Cambridge University Press.

———. 2006. *Routine Violence: Nations, Fragments, Histories*. Stanford: Stanford University Press.

Pandey, Gyanendra, and Peter Geschiere, eds. 2003. *The Forging of Nationhood*. New Delhi: Manohar.

Parry, Jonathan. 1985. "Death and Digestion: The Symbolism of Food and Eating in North Indian Mortuary Rites." *Man*, n.s., 20 (4): 612–30.

———. 1994. *Death in Banaras*. Cambridge: Cambridge University Press.

———. 1999. "Lords of Labour: Working and Shirking in Bhilai." *Contributions to Indian Sociology* 33:107–40.

Pasqualino, Caterina. 2005. "Ecorchés vif. Pour une anthropologie des affects." *Systèmes de pensée en Afrique noire*. Dominique Casajus, ed. Special issue, *L'excellence de la souffrance* 17:51–69.

Percheron, Annick. 1974. *L'univers politique des enfants*. Paris: Armand Colin and Fondation Nationale des Sciences Politiques.

Phadke, Y. D. 1979. *Politics and Language*. Bombay: Himalaya Publishing House.

Pinar, William F., ed. 1998. *Queer Theory in Education*. London: Lawrence Erlbaum Associates.

Pinney, Chris. 2003. "The Image in Indian Culture." In *The Oxford Companion Encyclopedia of Sociology and Social Anthropology*, edited by Veena Das, 625–53. Delhi: Oxford University Press.

Piscatori, James P., ed. 1983. *Islam in the Political Process*. Cambridge: Cambridge University Press.

———. 1986. *Islam in a World of Nation-States*. Cambridge: Cambridge University Press.

Pollock, Sheldon. 1998. "India in the Vernacular Millennium: Literary Culture and Polity 1000–1500." *Daedalus*. Shmuel Eisenstadt, Wolfgang Schluchter, and Björn Wittrock, eds. Special issue, *Early Modernities* 127 (3): 41–74.

———. 2000. "Cosmopolitan and Vernacular in History." *Public Culture* 12 (3): 591–625.

———. 2006 [2007]. *The Language of the Gods in the World of Men: Sanskrit, Culture, and Power in Premodern India*. Berkeley: University of California Press; Delhi: Permanent Black.

Porqueres i Gené, Enric. 2001. "Le mariage qui dérange: redéfinitions de l'identité nationale basque." *Ethnologie Française* 31 (3): 527–36.

Prakash, Gyan. 1999. *Another Reason: Science and the Imagination of Modern India*. Princeton: Princeton University Press.

Prentiss, Karen. 1999. *The Embodiment of Bhakti*. London: Oxford University Press.

Prochasson, Christophe. 2002. "Émotions et politique: premières approches." In *La politique et la guerre. Pour comprendre le XXè siècle contemporain*, edited by Stéphane Audouin-Rouzeau, Annette Becker et al., 431–49. Paris: Agnès Viénot-Noesis.

Przyblyski, Jeannene M. 1998. "History Is Photography: The Afterimage of Walter Benjamin." *Afterimage* Sept.–Oct. http://findarticles.com/p/articles/mi_m2479/is_n2_v26/ai_21187359.

Rahman, Tariq. 1996. *Language and Politics in Pakistan*. Karachi: Oxford University Press.

———. 2004. *Denizens of Alien Worlds: A Study of Education, Inequality and Polarization in Pakistan*. Karachi: Oxford University Press.

Raj, Dhooleka. 2003. *Where Are You From? Middle-Class Migrants in the Modern World.* Berkeley: University of California Press.

Rajagopal, Arvind. 2001. *Politics after Television: Religious Nationalism and the Reshaping of the Indian Public.* Cambridge: Cambridge University Press.

Rajalakshmi, T. K. 2000. "A Saffron Curriculum?" *Frontline*, Apr. 28, 92–94.

Ramaswamy, Sumathi. 1997. *Passions of the Tongue: Language Devotion in Tamil India, 1891–1970.* Berkeley: University of California Press.

———. 1998. "Body Language: The Somatics of Nationalism in Tamil India." *Gender and History* 10 (1): 78–109.

———. 2001. "Maps and Mother Goddesses in Modern India." *Imago Mundi: A Periodical Review of Early Cartography* 53:97–114.

———. 2003. "Visualizing India's Geo-body: Globes, Maps, Bodyscapes." In *Beyond Appearances? Visual Practices and Ideologies in Modern India*, edited by Sumathi Ramaswamy, 157–95. New Delhi: Sage Publications.

———. 2004. *The Lost Land of Lemuria. Fabulous Geographies, Catastrophic Histories.* Berkeley: University of California Press.

———. 2006. "Enshrining the Map of India: Cartography, Nationalism, and the Politics of Deity in Varanasi." In *Visualizing Space in Banaras. Images, Maps, and the Practice of Representation*, edited by Martin Gaenszle and Jörg Gengnagel, 165–88. Wiesbaden, Germany: Harrassowitz Verlag.

Ranade, Mahadev G. 1900. *The Rise of the Maratha Power.* Bombay: Punalekar.

Rank, Otto. 1957 [1924]. *The Trauma of Birth.* New York: Robert Brunner.

Rao, Velcheru Narayan, David Shulman, and Sanjay Subrahmanyam. 2003. *Textures of Time: Writing History in South India 1600–1800.* New York: Other Press.

Ray, Rajat Kanta. 2003. *The Felt Community: Commonality and Mentality before the Emergence of Indian Nationalism.* New Dehli: Oxford University Press.

Raychaudhuri, Tapan. 2000. "Shadows of the Swastika: Historical Perspectives on the Politics of Hindu Communalism." *Modern Asian Studies* 34 (2): 259–79.

Read, K. 1952. "Nama Cult of the Central Highlands New Guinea." *Oceania* 23 (1): 1–25.

Reddy, William M. 1999. "Emotional Liberty: Politics and History in the Anthropology of Emotions." *Cultural Anthropology* 14 (2): 256–88.

Reiniche, Marie-Louise, and Françoise L'Hernault. 1999. *Tiruvannamalai, un lieu saint çivaïte du Sud de l'Inde.* Vol. 3, *Rites et fêtes.* Paris: EFEO (Presses de l'Ecole Française d'Extrême-Orient).

Renan, Ernest. 1996. "What Is a Nation?" In *Becoming National: A Reader*, edited by Geoff Eley and Ronald Grigor Suny, 41–55. New York: Oxford University Press. (Orig. pub. of this chapter, 1882.)

Ritchie, Ian. 2000 [1993]. "African Theology and Social Change." Ph.D. diss., McGill University, Faculty of Religious Studies. "Chapter 5: The Shifting Sensorium and African

Orality," corrected version available at http://www3.sympatico.ca/ian.ritchie/ATSC.
Chapter5.htm.

Roberts, Michael. 1990. "Noise as Cultural Struggle: Tom-Tom Beating, the British, and
Communal Disturbances in Sri Lanka, 1880's to 1930's." In *Mirrors of Violence: Communities, Riots and Survivors in South Asia*, edited by Veena Das, 240–85. New Delhi:
Oxford University Press.

Robinson, Francis. 1983. "Islam and Muslim Society in South Asia." *Contributions to Indian Sociology* 17 (2): 185–203.

———. 1985. "Islam and Muslim Separatism: A Historiographical Debate." In *Communal
and Pan-Islamic Trends in Colonial India*, edited by Mushirul Hasan, 344–81. Delhi:
Manohar.

Rosaldo, Michelle Z. 1984. "Toward an Anthropology of Self and Feeling." In *Culture
Theory: Essays on Mind, Self, and Emotion*, edited by Richard A. Schweder and
Robert A. Le Vine, 137–57. Cambridge: Cambridge University Press.

Rudolph, Lloyd I., and Susanne H., eds. 1972. *Education and Politics in India: Studies in
Organization, Society, and Policy*. Cambridge, Mass: Harvard University Press.

Sadana, Rashmi. 2007. "A Suitable Text for a Vegetarian Audience. Questions of Authenticity and the Politics of Translation." *Public Culture* 19 (2): 307–28.

Sahmat. 2002. *Saffronised and Substandard: A Critique of the New NCERT Textbooks*.
New Delhi: Sahmat.

Sahmat and Sabrang.com. 2002 [2001]. *Against Communalisation of Education*. New
Delhi: Safdar Hashmi Memorial Trust.

Sangari, Kumkum. 1999. *Politics of the Possible: Essays on Gender, History, Narrative,
Colonial English*. New Delhi: Tulika.

Sangave, Vilas, and B. D. Khane, eds. 1994. *The Vedokta Controversy*. Rajarshi Shahu
Chhatrapati Papers, vol. III. Kolhapur: Shahu Research Centre, Shivaji University.

Sarangapani, Padma M. 2003. *Constructing School Knowledge. An Ethnography of Learning in an Indian Village*. Delhi: Sage Publications.

Sarkar, Sumit. 1997. *Writing Social History*. New York: Oxford University Press.

———. 2002. *Beyond Nationalist Frames: Relocating Postmodernism, Hindutva, History*.
Bloomington: Indiana University Press; Delhi: Permanent Black.

Sarkar, Tanika. 1995. "Heroic Women, Mother Goddesses: Family and Organization in
Hindutva Politics." In *Women and the Hindu Right*, edited by Tanika Sarkar and
Urvashi Butalia, 181–215. New Delhi: Kali for Women.

———. 2001 [2002]. *Hindu Wife, Hindu Nation: Community, Religion and Cultural Nationalism*. New Delhi: Permanent Black; Bloomington: Indiana University Press.

Savarkar, Vinayak D. 1999 [1923]. *Hindutva*. Mumbai: Swatantryaveer Savarkar Rashtriya Smarak.

Scheper-Hughes, Nancy. 2002. "Coming to Our Senses: Anthropology and Genocide."
In *Annihilating Difference: The Anthropology of Genocide*, edited by Alexander L.

Hinton, 348–81. Berkeley: University of California Press.

Schieffelin, Bambi B., Kathryn A. Woolard, and Paul V. Kroskrity, eds. 1998. *Language Ideologies: Practice and Theory*. New York: Oxford University Press.

Schultz, Anna. 2002. "Hindu Nationalism, Music, and Embodiment in Marathi Rashtriya Kirtan." *Ethnomusicology Journal* 46 (2): 307–22.

Scrase, Timothy J. 1993. *Image, Ideology, and Inequality: Cultural Domination, Hegemony, and Schooling in India*. New Delhi: Sage Publications.

Segal, Daniel A. 1996. "Resisting Identities: A Found Theme." *Cultural Anthropology* 11 (4): 431–34.

Seremetakis, C. Nadia, 1994. "The Memory of the Senses, Part I: Marks of the Transitory." In *The Senses Still. Perception and Memory as Material Culture in Modernity*, edited by Nadia C. Seremetakis, 1–18. Boulder, Colo.: Westview Press.

Setalvad, Teesta. 1995. "The Woman Shiv Sainik and Her Sister Swayamsevika." In *Women and Right-Wing Movements*, edited by Tanika Sarkar and Urvashi Butalia, 233–44. London: Zed Books.

Seubold, Günter. 2001. "Some Reflections on Th. W. Adorno's Music Aesthetics." *Canadian Aesthetics Journal / Revue canadienne d'esthétique* 6. http://www.uqtr.ca/AE/Vol_6/articles/seubol.html#_edn7.

Silverstein, Michael. 1998. "The Uses and Utility of Ideology: A Commentary." In *Language Ideologies: Practice and Theory*, edited by Bambi B. Schieffelin, Kathryn A. Woolard, and Paul V. Kroskrity, 123–45. New York: Oxford University Press.

———. 2000. "Whorfianism and the Linguistic Imagination of Nationality." In *Regimes of Language: Ideologies, Polities, and Identities*, edited by Paul V. Kroskrity, 85–138. Santa Fe, N.M.: School of American Research Press.

Skutnabb-Kangas, Tove, and Robert Phillipson. 1989. "'Mother Tongue': The Theoretical and Sociopolitical Construction of a Concept." In *Status and Function of Languages*, edited by Ulrich Ammon, 450–77. Berlin: W. de Gruyter.

Smith, Anthony D. 1999. *Myths and Memories of the Nation*. New York: Oxford University Press.

Spencer, Jonathan. 1996. "Modernism, Modernity and Modernization." In *Encyclopedia of Social and Cultural Anthropology*, edited by Alan Barnard and Jonathan Spencer, 376–79. London: Routledge.

———. 1997. "Postcolonialism and the Political Imagination." *Journal of the Royal Anthropological Institute* 3 (1): 1–19.

Spindler, George D., ed. 1955. *Education and Anthropology*. Stanford: Stanford University Press.

———, ed. 1982. *Doing the Ethnography of Schooling: Educational Anthropology in Action*. New York: Holt, Rinehart and Winston.

———, ed. 1987. *Education and Cultural Process. Anthropological Approaches*. Prospect Heights, Ill.: Waveland Press.

Spindler, George D., and Louise Spindler. 2000. *Fifty Years of Anthropology and Education 1950–2000. A Spindler Anthology.* London: Lawrence Erlbaum Associates.

Spitulnik, Debra. 1998. "Mediating Unity and Diversity: The Production of Language Ideologies in Zambian Broadcasting." In *Language Ideologies: Practice and Theory,* edited by Bambi B. Schieffelin, Kathryn A. Woolard, and Paul V. Kroskrity, 163–88. New York: Oxford University Press.

Srivastava, Sanjay. 1998. *Constructing Post-colonial India: National Character and the Doon School.* London: Routledge.

———, ed. 2004. *Sexual Sites, Seminal Attitudes: Sexualities, Masculinities and Culture in South Asia.* New Delhi: Sage Publications.

Staff Correspondent. 2003. "Historians Plan 'Parallel Textbooks.'" *The Hindu,* Dec. 30 [Mysore, Dec. 29].

Stambach, Amy. 2000. *Lessons from Mount Kilimanjaro: Schooling, Community, and Gender in East Africa.* New York: Routledge.

Staudigl, Michael. 2005. "Toward a Phenomenological Theory of Violence: Reflections following Merleau-Ponty and Schutz." Preliminary version of paper later revised and published online at http://www.springerlink.com/content/b0p857674014w371/.

Steggles, Mary Ann. 1997. "Art and Politics: The Visualization of British Imperialism in the Bombay Presidency, 1800–1927." In *Bombay to Mumbai: Changing Perspectives,* edited by Pauline Rohatgi, Pheroza Godrej, and Rahul Mehrotra, 192–207. Mumbai: Marg Publications.

Steinmetz, George, ed. 1999. *State/Culture: The State-Formation after the Cultural Turn.* Durham, N.C.: Duke University Press.

Stoller, Paul. 1989. *The Taste of Ethnographic Things: The Senses in Anthropology.* Philadelphia: University of Pennsylvania Press.

———. 1997. *Sensuous Scholarship.* Philadelphia: University of Pennsylvania Press.

Strathern, Andrew. 1975. "Why Is Shame on the Skin?" *Ethnology* 14 (4): 347–56.

———. 1993. "Organs and Emotions: The Question of Metaphor." *Canberra Anthropology* 16 (2): 1–16.

Subrahmanian, Ramya, Yusuf Sayed, Sarada Balagopalan, and Crain Soudien, eds. 2003. *Education Inclusion and Exclusion: Indian and South African Perspectives.* Brighton, U.K.: University of Sussex, Institute of Development Studies.

Sunder Rajan, Rajeshwari. 2003. *The Scandal of the State: Women, Law, and Citizenship in Postcolonial India.* Delhi: Permanent Black.

Sunindyo, Saraswati. 1998. "When the Earth Is Female and the Nation Is Mother: Gender, the Armed Forces and Nationalism in Indonesia." *Feminist Review* 58 (Spring): 1–21.

Talbot, Cynthia. 1995. "Inscribing the Other, Inscribing the Self: Hindu-Muslim Identities in Pre-colonial India." *Comparative Studies in Society and History* 37 (4): 692–722.

Talib, Mohammad. 1998. "The *Tablighi*s in the Making of Muslim Identity." In *Islam, Communities and the Nation: Muslim Identities in South Asia and Beyond*, edited by Mushirul Hasan, 307–40. Delhi: Manohar.

Tambiah, Stanley J. 1997. *Leveling Crowds: Ethno-nationalist Conflicts and Collective Violence in South Asia.* Berkeley: University of California Press.

Taussig, Michael. 1993. *Mimesis and Alterity: A Particular History of the Senses.* New York: Routledge.

Taylor, Charles. 1994. *Multiculturalism and the Politics of Recognition.* Edited and introduced by Amy Gutman. Princeton: Princeton University Press.

Taylor, Christopher C. 2002. "The Cultural Face of Terror in the Rwandan Genocide of 1994." In *Annihilating Difference: The Anthropology of Genocide*, edited by Alexander L. Hinton, 137–78. Berkeley: University of California Press.

Taylor, David. 1983. "The Politics of Islam and Islamization in Pakistan." In *Islam in the Political Process*, edited by James P. Piscatori, 181–98. Cambridge: Cambridge University Press.

Thapan, Meenakshi. 1991. *Life at School: An Ethnographic Study.* Delhi: Oxford University Press.

Thapar, Romila. 1985. "Syndicated Moksha." *Seminar* 313 (September): 14–22.

———. 1996. *Time as a Metaphor of History: Early India.* Delhi: Oxford University Press.

———. 2004. "One Nation's Many Pasts." *The Hindustan Times*, Mar. 2.

Thiesse, Anne-Marie. 1999. *La création des identités nationales: Europe XVIIIè–XXè siècle.* Paris: Seuil.

Thompson, Scott J. 2000. "From '*Rausch*' to Rebellion: Walter Benjamin's *On Hashish* & the Aesthetic Dimensions of Prohibitionist Realism." *The Journal of Cognitive Liberties* 2 (1): 21–42. (Also available online at www.wbenjamin.org/rausch.html.)

Trautmann, Thomas R. 1997. *Aryans and British India.* Berkeley: University of California Press.

Trawick, Margaret. 1989. *Notes on Love in a Tamil Family.* Berkeley: University of California Press.

Turner, Bryan S. 2000. "From Orientalism to Global Sociology." In *Orientalism: A Reader*, edited by A. L. Macfie, 369–74. London: Longman.

van der Veer, Peter. 1994. *Religious Nationalism.* Berkeley: University of California Press.

———. 2001. *Imperial Encounters: Religion and Modernity in India and Britain.* Princeton: Princeton University Press.

van der Veer, Peter, and Hartmut Lehmann. 1999. *Nation and Religion: Perspectives on Europe and Asia.* Princeton: Princeton University Press.

Varshney, Ashutosh. 2002. *Ethnic Conflict and Civic Life: Hindus and Muslims in India.* New Haven, Conn.: Yale University Press.

Vasudevan, Ravi S. 2000. "The Politics of Cultural Address in a 'Transitional' Cinema: A Case Study of Indian Popular Cinema." In *Reinventing Film Studies*, edited by

Christine Gledhill and Linda Williams, 132–64. London: Arnold; New York: Oxford University Press.

Veyne, Paul. 1996. "L'interprétation et l'interprète." *Enquête*. Special issue, *Interpréter, Surinterpréter* 3:241–72.

Vincent, Joan. 1990. *Anthropology and Politics: Visions, Traditions and Trends*. Tucson: University of Arizona Press.

Virmani, Arundhati. 1999. "National Symbols under Colonial Domination: The Nationalization of the Indian Flag, March–August 1923." *Past and Present* 164:169–97.

Viswanathan, Gauri. 1989. *Masks of Conquest: Literary Study and British Rule in India*. New York: Columbia University Press.

von Stietencron, Heinrich. 1997 [1989]. "On the Use of a Deceptive Term." In *Hinduism Reconsidered*, edited by Günther Sontheimer and Hermann Kulke, 32–53. New Delhi: Manohar.

Wadley, Susan S., and Bruce W. Derr. 1990. "Eating Sins in Karimpur." In *India through Hindu Categories*, edited by McKim Marriott, 131–48. New Delhi: Sage Publications.

Wahnich, Sophie. 2002. "La terreur comme fondation, de l'économie émotive de la terreur." *Annales, histoire sciences sociales* (July): 889–913.

———. 2004. "Désordre social et émotions publiques pendant la période révolutionnaire." *Raisons pratiques* (Jan.): 227–55.

Warner, Michael. 2002. *Publics and Counterpublics*. New York: Zone Books.

Washbrook, David. 1991. "'To Each a Language of His Own': Language, Culture, and Society in Colonial India." In *Language, History and Class*," edited by Penelope J. Corfield, 179–203. Oxford: Blackwell.

Wilce, James M., Jr. 2004. "Passionate Scholarship: Recent Anthropologies of Emotion." *Reviews in Anthropology* 33:1–17.

Williams, Raymond. 1958. *Culture and Society 1780–1950*. London: Chatto and Windus.

———. 1984 [1961]. *The Long Revolution*. London: Chatto and Windus.

Willis, Paul. 1977 [1981]. *Learning to Labour: How Working Class Kids Get Working Class Jobs*. Farnborough, Hants., U.K.: Saxon House; New York: Columbia University Press.

Wolpert, Stanley A. 1989 [1961]. *Tilak and Gokhale: Revolution and Reform in the Making of Modern India*. Delhi: Oxford University Press.

Woodward, Rachel. 1998. "'It's a Man's Life!' Soldiers, Masculinity and the Countryside." *Gender, Place and Culture* 5 (3): 277–300.

———. 2000. "Warrior Heroes and Little Green Men: Soldiers, Military Training, and the Construction of Rural Masculinities." *Rural Sociology* 65 (4): 640–57.

———. 2003. "Locating Military Masculinities: The Role of Space and Place in the Formation of Gender Identities in the Armed Forces." In *Military Masculinities: Identity and the State*, edited by Paul R. Higate, 43–56. London: Greenwood Press.

Woolard, Kathryn A. 1998. "Introduction. Language Ideology as a Field of Inquiry." In *Language Ideologies: Practice and Theory*, edited by Bambi B. Schieffelin, Kathryn A. Woolard, and Paul V. Kroskrity, 3–47. New York: Oxford University Press.

Yano, Christine R. 1995. "Shaping Tears of a Nation: An Ethnography of Emotion in Japanese Popular Song." Ph.D. diss., University of Hawaii.

Yep, Gust A., Karen E. Lovaas, and John P. Elia, eds. 2003. *Queer Theory and Communication: From Disciplining Queers to Queering the Discipline(s)*. New York: Harrington Park Press.

Zastoupil, Lynn, and Martin Moir, eds. 1999. *The Great Indian Education Debate. Documents Relating to the Orientalist-Anglicist Controversy, 1781–1843*. London: Curzon.

Zelliot, Eleanor. 1970. "Mahar and Non-Brahman Movements in Maharashtra." *Indian Economic and Social History Review* 7 (3): 397–415.

Marathi Sources

Bal Bharati, Itihas, iyatta tisari (History, Class 3). Pune: MRPNASM (MSTB and MSCERT). (Versions in Marathi, English, and Urdu produced by the same bureau.)

Bal Bharati, Marathi, iyatta cauthi (Marathi Language Textbook, Class 4). 1982. Pune: MRPNASM (MSTB and MSCERT).

———. 1998. Pune: MRPNASM (MSTB and MSCERT).

Bal Bharati, Marathi, iyatta dusari (Marathi Language Textbook, Class 2). 1999 [1997]. Pune: MRPNASM (MSTB and MSCERT).

Bal Bharati, Marathi, iyatta pacvi (Marathi as Second Language Textbook, Class 5). 2000. Pune: Maharashtra Rajya Patthyapustak Nirmiti va Abhyaskram Sanshodhan Mandal, MRPNASM (Maharashtra State Textbook Bureau [MSTB], and Maharashtra State Centre for Educational Research and Training [MSCERT]).

Bal Bharati, Marathi, iyatta pahili (Marathi Language Textbook, Class 1). 1998 [1997]. Pune: MRPNASM (MSTB and MSCERT).

Bal Bharati, Marathi, iyatta tisari (Marathi Language Textbook, Class 3). 1982. Pune: MRPNASM (MSTB and MSCERT).

———. 1998. Pune: MRPNASM (MSTB and MSCERT).

Bal Bharati, Shivachhatrapati (Itihas, nagarikshastra ani prashasan), iyatta cauthi (History, Civics, and Administration, Class 4). 1992. Pune: MRPNASM (MSTB and MSCERT). Marathi ed., repr. 1995.

Bal Bharati, Shivachhatrapati (History, Civics, and Administration, Class 4). 1992. Pune: MRPNASM (MSTB and MSCERT). English ed., repr. 1996.

Harlekar, H. 1983. *Marathi gane*. Kolhapur.

Molesworth, J. T. 1982 [1857]. *Molesworth's Marathi-English Dictionary: Corrected Reprint*. Pune: Mehta Publishing House.

Rashtriya Geete (National Songs). 1998 (navin avrutti [new ed.]). Mumbai: Jay Hind Prakashan.

Sangeet ani sharirik shikshan, iyatta chauthi (Singing and Physical Education, Class 4) (navin abhyaskram [new curriculum]). 1998. Vikas series. Mumbai: Navneet Publications.

Other Official Sources

Census of India. 1991. New Delhi: Office of the Registrar General.

———. 2001. New Delhi: Office of the Registrar General.

Education and National Development. 1966. Report of the Education Commission 1964–66. New Delhi: NCERT.

National Policy on Education. 1986. New Delhi: NCERT.

———. 1992. New Delhi: NCERT.

Report of the Committee on Emotional Integration. 1962. Delhi: Ministry of Education, Government of India.

Index